Seven Months
to Oregon

Bringing together several firsthand accounts of a family's overland migration in 1853, Peters vividly recaptures the excitement, the drudgery, the hope, and the heartbreak of ordinary people in extraordinary times.

—John Mack Faragher, Author
Women and Men on the Overland Trails

Not just Oregonians, but all Americans, owe a tremendous debt to the intrepid settlers who secured the Pacific Northwest for the United States. And we are also indebted to Dr. Hal Peters, for publishing these fascinating pioneer accounts for all of us to read. They are a pricelss gift—to America.

—Hon. Mark Hatfield
U.S. Senator for Oregon, 1967-1997
December 2007

At last we have it all. The railroad and stage lines from Upstate New York. The steamboats on the Ohio, Mississippi, and Missouri Rivers. The impatient waiting at the jumping-off places. The long, dangerous covered wagon transit to the Pacific Northwest. All brought to us by the Hines family chroniclers—a thrilling narration of an 1853 adventure to Oregon!

—Gregory M. Franzwa, Author
The Oregon Trail Revisited

Cover illustration adapted from a map of North America (1852) by James Wyld of London, Historical Maps of North America, http://alabamamaps.ua.edu/historicalmaps/northamerica/1851-1900.html; accessed August 6, 2007.

Seven Months to Oregon

1853 Diaries, Letters and Reminiscent Accounts

by

Celinda Elvira Hines
Harvey Kimball Hines
Phoebe Goodell Judson
Gustavus Hines
Joseph Wilkinson Hines
Alta Bryant

Harold J. Peters, Editor

The Patrice Press
Tooele, Utah

Copyright © 2008
Harold J. Peters

Library of Congress Cataloging-in-Publication Data

Dear Librarian:
The CIP Division of the Library of Congress now accepts only electronic requests, and has refused to accept paper submission for this title. We ask you to consult our website, where you will find complete and up-to-date information on all our books. We will no longer be seeking CIP data from the Library of Congress.
http://patricepress.com

Paperback: ISBN 1-880397-65X
Hardcover: ISBN 1-880397-66-8

The paper in this book meets the guidelines for permanence and durability of the Committee on Production Guidelines for Book Longevity of the Council on Library Resources, Inc.

Typographic Conventions
Commentary by the editor is set in 11-point Times New Roman on a 27-pica line. Quotations from the diaries are set in 10-point type, indented to a 25-pica line. The exception to this is in excessively long passages by a diarist or in reminiscent accounts, which are set in 11-point type, indented to a 25-pica line.

The Patrice Press
319 Nottingham Drive
Tooele, Utah 84074
1-435-833-9168
email: books@patricepress.com
http://patricepress.com

Printed in the United States of America

For Bobo, who
got me started in all of this;
and to Ellie, who
helped me finish it

Contents

Maps, Charts, and Illustrations

Foreword

It is no secret that we Oregonians revere the pioneers who came to the Pacific Northwest in the 1840s and 1850s. It took tremendous courage to head west in those years, leaving behind established homes and farms to start anew several thousand miles away.

Those pioneers did more than settle the area. Today they would be surprised to learn of the impact their migration had, but their movement has resonated around the world, even to this day.

They welded the West to the United States, establishing firm continental boundaries to America, from sea to shining sea. This helped lay the groundwork for our nation to become a major player on the world stage, with a form of government that is the envy of the free world. That is the great gift that our pioneers have given to all of us.

Noble as was their quest, their motivation was fundamentally to better themselves. There were others who made that long trek for more selfless reasons—the dozens of Christian missionaries who left their comfortable homes on the Eastern Seaboard to serve their churches. Their goal was only to help the Indian nations cope with the laws and customs of the hordes of whites who were populating their ancestral lands.

Did they succeed? They did not. Marcus and Narcissa Whitman, medical missionaries, had hoped to "Christianize" the Cayuse. Eleven years after their 1836 arrival they were murdered by the same tribe, without gaining a single convert. Jason Lee fared only slightly better at his 1834 mission along the Willamette. But when their mission to the natives failed, they refocused their efforts on building the civic and educational, as well as religious institutions of the new territory and eventual state.

In 1845, with the Indian population decimated and with Jason Lee's successor, George Gary, closing down the Methodist Mission operations, Lee's close associate Gustavus Hines returned to New York to resume his ministerial duties there. But he had not given up on Oregon. He wrote a now classic chronicle of his journey, portraying Oregon as a land of abundant natural resources and unprecedented opportunity. Like a magnet, it

Foreword

drew others with pioneering spirits, and in 1853 Hines himself, along with his brothers and their families, returned to Oregon.

Now, through the dedicated effort of Dr. Harold J. Peters, we have before us the day-by-day diaries and reminiscences of three of those intrepid pioneer missionaries as they traveled to, and settled in, Oregon. Two diarists and their families came overland—a third by sea. Assembled with meticulous care and thoughtfully annotated, Dr. Peters has given us the stories of the travels of those members of his Hines family. He presents those fascinating documents side by side, as the pioneers made their 3,000-mile trek from upstate New York—by rail, by water, and by covered wagon—to our Oregon.

We are all the better for their sacrifice. And we are all the better for Dr. Peters' remarkable presentation of their accounts.

—Hon. Mark Hatfield
U.S. Senator for Oregon, 1967-1997
Salem, Oregon
November 2007

Preface

As I write this in the fall of 2007, I note that it was over a century and a half ago that my Hines relatives were just getting settled in the Willamette Valley of what was then Oregon Territory. They had been part of the massive wave of migration across the continent that according to many historians marked a defining moment in American history. With my modest interest in American history, and for most of my life only an equally modest interest in family genealogy, I have nonetheless been aware since my teenage years of both that great migration and of my relatives' participation. But only dimly aware. My professional career has been centered on science education. My other pastimes have been many and varied, but until about ten years ago, my leisure activities have excluded anything more than trivial involvement in history or genealogy.

Once kindled, however, my interest in genealogy has exploded, engulfing not only my leisure time, but much of my waning time devoted to professional activities as well. Along with the growing involvement in genealogy has come a parallel awakening of an interest in history. As it happens, my Hines relatives have left a massive trail of written material—books, newspaper articles, personal letters—so my genealogical pursuits understandably gravitated toward this document-rich family line. This in turn has channeled most of my study of history toward New York and Oregon in the nineteenth century, and matters pertaining to how Americans migrated from the East to the West.

If the great migration of hundreds of thousands of Americans westward in the mid-nineteenth century was indeed a defining moment in American history, the defining event for the James and Betsey (Round) Hines family of New York was the migration of four out of twelve siblings from New York to Oregon in 1853. I first learned some of the details of that migration through a diary kept by Celinda Hines, daughter of Obadiah, one of the four emigrating siblings. Further details, and a broader perspective arising out of more than seventy-five years of reflection, were added by Phoebe Judson, who along with her husband and young daughter accompanied the Hines party, and who in 1925 wrote a reminiscent account based on her own diary. The accounts of both Celinda and Phoebe have been quoted frequently by trail historians. But writers referencing these two works seem to have been unaware of yet a third account of the same trip—this by Rev. Harvey K. Hines, Celinda's uncle, who also kept a diary. Like Phoebe, he wrote a reminiscent account of the trip, but published it as a serial in 1884-1885, much earlier than hers.

It struck me early on, as I read and reread these three documents, that they ought to be preserved as a unit, both for family interest, and for future trail historians. But as I pieced them together, trying to weave a coherent, self-consistent story of the journey, I kept encountering puzzles. For example, Celinda recorded on May 5, 1853, after they had crossed the Kansas River to start across the plains, *"...at length we were all safely landed in Nebraska at Little St. Louis."* Looking at present-day maps, I could make no sense of this statement whatsoever. Nor did the other two accounts really settle the issue for me. Where did they actually cross the river? Which river did they in fact cross? What led Celinda to write what she did? It took the examination of many other documents and consultations with several trail specialists to sort out these issues. Repeating that process for many such little puzzles has produced a 150,000-word document with hundreds of notes.

The resulting product became, in my opinion as editor, a curious mixture. At times it resembled other historical treatments of western trail journeys; at other times it seemed to be a hodgepodge of so many different types of material from so many different sources that it could be difficult to discern a narrative thread. In short, it looked like what it frankly was: the first effort of a very amateur historian.

Some remarks about editorial choices are in order. My transcriptions of the diary and other documents adhere closely to the originals. Where I have made insertions for the sake of readability, I have enclosed them in brackets, [ ]. Most explanatory additions have been relegated to notes. After much vacillation, I decided to present the different accounts of the journey woven together, so that, for example, different descriptions of the same event would appear close together. To help readers sort out the different voices, I have headed each differently authored contribution with the author's name in boldface type, e.g., **Celinda,** or **Phoebe.** My own editorial commentary within the main body of text has been set in a different type size.

I have a strong personal preference for graphical presentation of information and a love of maps, so I naturally turned to mapping out the

Preface

party's itinerary as I worked out the details of where they apparently were located at different times. For most of the journey, i.e., for New York through Nebraska, I have used maps that were the best 1850-era maps I could find. These are closer to what the travelers themselves would have been using than would be the case with present-day maps, and in some instances include place names, such as Wayne City, Missouri, that were mentioned by our chroniclers, but have since disappeared from our maps today. For the latter part of the journey, through present-day Wyoming, Idaho, and Oregon, I have used topographical relief maps from the U.S. Department of the Interior in order that the roughness of the terrain might be better portrayed.

One further editorial choice should be mentioned. During my research, whenever I found yet another document, whether it be a letter or perhaps a newspaper article with some relevance to the trip, I usually opted to include that full item herein, rather than excerpting just the most obviously relevant parts. For the sake of brevity and a tighter narrative, more excerpting might have been in order, but I opted for completeness.

All the earlier caveats aside, my narrative would not have reached even this stage without the generous help of many friends, relatives and complete strangers. My first thanks must go to Celinda Hines for maintaining a daily diary under what must often have been very difficult conditions; to George Himes of the Oregon Pioneers Association for rescuing and preserving the remains of that diary not already damaged by fire; and to Celinda's great-granddaughter, Cecil Mary Sisk, for her many years of research on the family genealogy together with generously sharing the results, for calling my attention to the diary at an early stage, and especially for her enthusiastic support of my own work on both the Hines genealogy and on this book. No less than to Celinda, I am indebted to her Uncle Harvey and to their traveling companion, Phoebe Goodell Judson, for their respective reminiscent accounts of the trip. The late historian, Kenneth L. Holmes, via his *Covered Wagon Women* series, provided an annotated transcription of the second half of Celinda's diary and gave me my initial introduction to Phoebe's remarkable book. It was another historian, Robert L. Munkres, who informed me of the availability of Holmes's transcription.

Willamette University librarian Ford Schmidt steered me to Robert M. Gatke's *Chronicles of Willamette,* one of my richest sources of information related to Gustavus and Harvey Hines, as well as their friend and hero, Jason Lee. Mr. Schmidt and other Hatfield Library staff were most helpful during our several visits there. The *Chronicles* in turn led me to the *Pacific Christian Advocate* wherein resides so much of Harvey's

Preface

work, including in particular the two serials excerpted for this book. Discovering that the serials appeared in the *Advocate* was one thing; tracking down copies of the actual serials was quite another. All microfilm copies of that newspaper were evidently made from an original that had the second serial neatly clipped out (Someone was sure that it ought to be "saved!"). My rescuer from this frustration was Jocelyne Rubinetti of the Methodist Library at Drew University, who provided nearly complete copies of both serials.

Duncan Funk, an Alta Bryant descendant who was tracked down for me through the unflagging efforts of Vanette Schwartz, social sciences librarian of the Milner Library at Illinois State University, kindly provided the typescripts of Alta's reminiscences prepared by her daughters.

An early contact who has continued to be exceptionally helpful is Stephenie Flora of Oregon, who maintains a cluster of websites containing primary source material regarding early Oregon.[1]

The interlibrary loan departments of both the University of Iowa Libraries and the Iowa City Public Library have responded quickly and efficiently to dozens of requests for microfilm and books which otherwise would have been unavailable to me. The university library's own western history collection is extensive and has been an invaluable resource. The Iowa City branch of the State Historical Society of Iowa library has been of enormous help because of their considerable holdings in history relevant to this project, and in federal census records and other genealogical resources.

Eric Page, curator at the Grinter Place historic site, responded to early questions I posed about the itinerary of the Hines party through the Kansas City area and also pointed me toward two most valuable resources, a book and a research center: Louise Barry's voluminous and richly detailed *The Beginning of the West,* and the National Frontier Trails Center in Independence, Missouri. John Mark Lambertson at that center gave generously of his time and resources during a visit, and has responded to numerous questions arising out of my research. While in the Independence/Kansas City area, we also had the opportunity to meet Brad Woellhof, of the Kansas State Historical Society, who expressed enthusiastic support for my book project, and recommended that I access works by John Mack Faragher, for which I am grateful.

Richard Engeman of the Oregon Historical Society was a gracious host when we visited the OHS archives in 1999, giving us much useful research advice and providing unique source material both during the visit and in later correspondence.

Preface

I am deeply indebted to the late John Hook and Ina Sims, both volunteers at the Methodist Archives in Salem, Oreg., for answering countless questions and providing copies of source materials unavailable elsewhere. It was Ina who in response to one of my early questions in the fall of 1998 sent copies of Hines family research materials deposited in the archives by Cecil Mary Sisk. This was my introduction to Cec.

Michael McKenzie of Keuka College stumbled across my name when he was researching Gustavus Hines material on the Internet, and this has led to a long series of fruitful correspondence, during which he has provided much helpful advice, many source materials, and enthusiastic support for this project, even to the extent of visiting the site of the Snake River crossing, afterward sharing pictures and his own perceptive observations.[2]

Kuri Gill, former curator and education coordinator at the Mission Mill Museum in Salem, Oreg., organized and coordinated a pair of highly successful Methodist Missionary descendants' reunions held in Salem during in 2002 and 2006, which provided those of us attending with numerous new research contacts. Kuri has also kindly responded to the many questions and requests for materials I have directed her way.

My cousin, the late Bill Hines, great-grandson of Joseph Wilkinson Hines, has been a source of considerable inspiration to me, though my stodgy writing pales in light of his own prize-winning style as a long-time journalist of science and technology, the U.S. space program in particular.

Cousins Joe Erwin and Tom Gray, who both are amateur genealogists, are descendants of Celinda's Aunt Malissa. Both have been very supportive of my efforts. Tom is the source of the rare portrait of Malissa included herein. Joe introduced me to his Aunt Alma Ames, who has provided me with continuing encouragement and a wide variety of materials, including many family artifacts. It was through Alma's generous sharing of an 1899 letter from Malissa's son, James Robinson, to his younger brother, Gustavus Hines Robinson, that Joe and I have at last settled a longstanding family debate (shared in by numerous other Gustavus Hines researchers) as to how "Gustavus" was pronounced by the Hines family. (Goo-STAH-vus? GUH-sta-vus? Guh-STAY-vus?) James's letter reveals that Malissa, who named her young son after her own older brother, nicknamed that son "Tave." We leave it to readers to draw their own conclusions.

The late Jean Pixley, another Malissa Hines Robinson descendant and an unusually thorough amateur genealogist, provided me with a great deal of family data early on with regard to the Robinson family, including key obituaries that told of the family's various moves in New York State,

Preface

and from there to Michigan.

Via e-mail I met Margene Goodell, whose husband is a relative of Phoebe's, and this led to the Lynden Pioneer Museum in Lynden, Wash., whose director, Troy Luginbill, has provided the Judson pictures included here.

Holly Carver of the University of Iowa Press and Marianne Keddington-Lang of the Oregon Historical Society Press have both read early drafts of parts of my manuscript and have given encouragement, along with many helpful suggestions.

Steven Semken, of the Ice Cube Press of North Liberty, Iowa, provided just the right calm, good-humored professionalism that enabled me to get out an early version of my manuscript to a handful of family and friends.

Virtually every page of this volume has benefited from the critique of my publisher, Gregory M. Franzwa of The Patrice Press. He has provided innumerable suggestions, minor and major, that have improved both style and content. Errors and infelicities of style that remain are my own failing, not his.

Finally, a special thanks to special people. My mother, the late Mildred Dowling Peters Clark, with her long-running interest in the Hines family, initiated my interest in this project, and her vast store of family history materials helped get my own research off to a running start. Her repeated "This is exciting!" response to my many telephone calls detailing the latest progress served as continually renewed motivation. And her seemingly inexhaustible memory of family members and events was invaluable. My four siblings have given similarly strong support to my genealogy projects, albeit sometimes in the form of "When is that book of yours going to be done?" My wife, Elinore Schmidt Peters, whose indefatigable support has sustained me in all my endeavors, has read countless drafts of the materials making up this volume, offering many corrections and suggestions for increased readability.

[1] See Stephenie's website at http://www.oregonpioneers.com/ortrail.htm

[2] See my fledgling Hines website at http://freepages.genealogy.rootsweb.com/~hinesmemories/ for samples of Mike's observations and photos

1853 Calendar 1853

January	February	March	April
S M Tu W Th F S	S M Tu W Th F S	S M Tu W Th F S	S M Tu W Th F S
1	1 2 3 4 5	1 2 3 4 5	1 2
2 3 4 5 6 7 8	6 7 8 9 10 11 12	6 7 8 9 10 11 12	3 4 5 6 7 8 9
9 10 11 12 13 14 15	13 14 15 16 17 18 19	13 14 15 16 17 18 19	10 11 12 13 14 15 16
16 17 18 19 20 21 22	20 21 22 23 24 25 26	20 21 22 23 24 25 26	17 18 19 20 21 22 23
23 24 25 26 27 28 29	27 28	27 28 29 30 31	24 25 26 27 28 29 30
30 31			

May	June	July	August
S M Tu W Th F S	S M Tu W Th F S	S M Tu W Th F S	S M Tu W Th F S
1 2 3 4 5 6 7	1 2 3 4	1 2	1 2 3 4 5 6
8 9 10 11 12 13 14	5 6 7 8 9 10 11	3 4 5 6 7 8 9	7 8 9 10 11 12 13
15 16 17 18 19 20 21	12 13 14 15 16 17 18	10 11 12 13 14 15 16	14 15 16 17 18 19 20
22 23 24 25 26 27 28	19 20 21 22 23 24 25	17 18 19 20 21 22 23	21 22 23 24 25 26 27
29 30 31	26 27 28 29 30	24 25 26 27 28 29 30	28 29 30 31
		31	

September	October	November	December
S M Tu W Th F S	S M Tu W Th F S	S M Tu W Th F S	S M Tu W Th F S
1 2 3	1	1 2 3 4 5	1 2 3
4 5 6 7 8 9 10	2 3 4 5 6 7 8	6 7 8 9 10 11 12	4 5 6 7 8 9 10
11 12 13 14 15 16 17	9 10 11 12 13 14 15	13 14 15 16 17 18 19	11 12 13 14 15 16 17
18 19 20 21 22 23 24	16 17 18 19 20 21 22	20 21 22 23 24 25 26	18 19 20 21 22 23 24
25 26 27 28 29 30	23 24 25 26 27 28 29	27 28 29 30	25 26 27 28 29 30 31
	30 31		

December 1852: G. Hines & H. K. Hines are transferred to Oregon Conference.

March 8, 1853: G. Hines, H. K. Hines, O. Hines & families depart Buffalo.

March 24: G. Hines, H. K. Hines, O. Hines & families arrive in Kansas City.

May 5: Hines, Judson, & Bryant families start across prairie.

June 20: J. W. Hines & family depart New York harbor for Panama.

June 26: Charles LaBonta Judson is born.

July 4: Hines, Judson, & Bryant families celebrate at Independence Rock.

July 4: J. W. Hines & family celebrate in Panama City.

July 5: J. W. Hines & family depart Panama for San Francisco.

July 25: J. W. Hines & family depart San Francisco for Portland.

August 1: J. W. Hines & family arrive in Portland.

August 26: Obadiah Hines drowns in Snake River.

September 18: J. W. Hines meets brothers & families at Deschutes River.

September 29: Hines, Judson, & Bryant families arrive in Willamette Valley.

October 1: Judson family leaves group to head northward.

October 8: Hines families arrive in Portland.

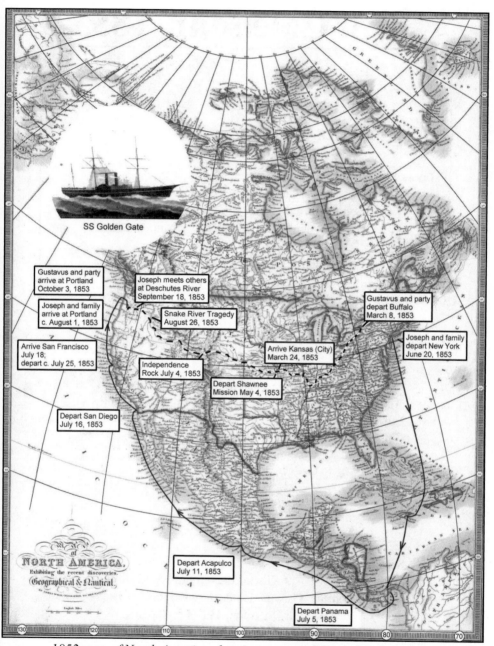

Gustavus and party
arrive at Portland
October 3, 1853

Joseph meets others
at Deschutes River
September 18, 1853

Gustavus and party
depart Buffalo
March 8, 1853

Joseph and family
arrive at Portland
c. August 1, 1853

Snake River Tragedy
August 26, 1853

Arrive San Francisco
July 18;
depart c. July 25, 1853

Joseph and family
depart New York
June 20, 1853

Arrive Kansas (City)
March 24, 1853

Independence
Rock July 4, 1853

Depart San Diego
July 16, 1853

Depart Shawnee
Mission May 4, 1853

SS Golden Gate

Depart Acapulco
July 11, 1853

Depart Panama
July 5, 1853

1852 map of North America showing routes of Hines family members during their 1853 trips

The Travelers

Gustavus Hines Family
Gustavus–Third oldest Hines sibling
Lydia (Bryant) Hines–First wife of Gustavus
Julia Bryant–Younger sister of Lydia; lived with Lydia
and Gustavus
Lucy Anna Maria Lee–Orphaned daughter of Jason Lee

Obadiah Hines Family
Obadiah–Second oldest Hines sibling (Oldest,
Adolphus, stayed in N.Y.)
Eliza (Bennett Roth) Hines–Second wife of Obadiah
Celinda Elvira Hines*–Daughter of Obadiah and first
wife, Lucina Chapin
Gustavus Hines–Son of Eliza(?); adopted(?) by Obadiah

Joseph Wilkinson Hines Family**
Joseph–Tenth of the twelve Hines Siblings
Elizabeth (Meredith) Hines–Wife of Joseph
Melissa E. Hines–Oldest daughter of Joseph and Eliza-
beth
George E. Hines–Oldest son of Joseph and Elizabeth

Harvey Kimball Hines Family
Harvey*–Youngest of the twelve Hines siblings
Elizabeth (Graves) Hines–Second wife of Harvey
(Angeline {Seymor} Hines d. 1851)
Martha Graves–Younger sister of Elizabeth

Reverend Cathard Family
Reverend Cathard–Harvey's alter ego in his *On the
Frontier* serial

Mrs. Cathard–Elizabeth's alter ego in the same serial

Holden Allen Judson Family

Holden–Accompanied Phoebe's parents on 1850-51 trip to Oregon

Phoebe (Goodell) Judson–*Wife of Holden

Annie Judson–Daughter of Holden and Phoebe

Charles La Bonta Judson–Son of Holden and Phoebe; born on trip

Charles Wesley Bryant Family

Charles–Distant cousin of Lydia (Bryant) Hines

Mary (Fay) Bryant–Wife of Charles

Alta–Daughter of Charles and Mary

Lee–Son of Charles and Mary

* Diary or reminiscent account constitutes a major portion of this volume.

**Not members of overland party; traveled by alternate sea route.

Prologue

Fulfilling a Boyhood Dream

> *There is a sublimity in the scenery of the ever-varying and almost boundless prairie, not unlike that presented by the majestic ocean.[1]*
> —Gustavus Hines, June 1853

To the sensibilities of young Harvey Kimball Hines, age 24 when he left his native New York in 1853, the journey to Oregon was awash with emotions—emotions that undulated like the waving prairie grasses in their own mimicry of the ocean. We have a foretaste of Harvey's emotional tendencies already in a reminiscence by him in the late 1890s, when he writes of the departure of his older brother Gustavus on a ship bound for Oregon in 1839:

The departure of these missionaries was a memorable event in the annals of Methodism. To them and to their friends their separation from the civilized world seemed to be utter and final. No one to-day can realize how utter it was. The writer was then a child. An elder brother and his family were among the devoted few that were thus expatriating themselves from home and country. He well remembers how, in that soft October day, when it was understood that these missionaries would sail away for their dark and distant field, he leaned against his mother's side, in the rural home in Oswego County, New York, and listened to her as she softly told of the holy mission on which they were going, and then how his heart throbbed and thrilled as she sung with tears in her eyes but triumph in her heart, Heber's[2] grand missionary hymn:

"Shall we, whose souls are lighted with wisdom from on high.

Shall we to men benighted the lamp of life deny?

Salvation! O Salvation! the joyful sound proclaim.

Till Earth's remotest nation has learned Messiah's name."

Out of that hour, by the voice of that mother in that song, the young heart of the writer felt the first inspiration that, at last, thirteen years after, identified him with the larger work in that same Oregon to which they were destined.[3]

A month earlier this brave mother had written to Gustavus, as he was awaiting departure of his ship from New York,

> i have undergone some very close trials since you left here on account of your arduous undertaking and have felt sometimes as tho i could not have it so. at other times i have felt perfectly resined to the will of God and i feel now while i rite with brim full eyes that it is the will of God that you should go...[4]

Thus it was with the memory of broken family ties, and in the company of a reluctant wife that, in the years that followed 1839, Gustavus Hines spent five as a missionary in Oregon before returning to New York by way of Hawaii, Hong Kong, and South Africa in 1846, and then resuming his ministry in western New York state.[5] Younger brother Harvey in the meantime followed Gustavus into the Methodist ministry, and by 1852 both of them, together with a third brother, Joseph, were stationed in the Genesee Conference of the Methodist Episcopal Church in western New York. The year 1853 found these three brothers, along with a fourth brother, Obadiah, and all their respective families headed to Oregon. This book chronicles that journey.

Essentially the story will be related by the travelers themselves. As Harvey's own introduction indicates, he was coaxed, finally, into committing to paper the stories he had told over the years, resulting in a fifteen-part serial appearing in the *Pacific Christian Advocate* from December 1884 through March 1885, during his tenure as editor. This serial, absent one installment we have been unable to locate, is incorporated herein in its entirety.

Harvey's niece Celinda Hines, daughter of Obadiah, kept a diary during the journey. Although some of this diary was destroyed by fire, what remains provides a rich complement to Harvey's account, and is the only day-by-day chronology available to us covering the events of their trip. Parts of this diary have been published previously, first by the Oregon Pioneer Association in 1918,[6] then as a newspaper serial in 1930,[7] and most recently by Kenneth L. Holmes as a chapter in his *Covered Wagon Women* series.[8] While Holmes' edition is well-researched and annotated, he evidently was unaware of Harvey's account, by which he could have avoided a number of factual errors in his introductory comments and notes.

Our presentation of the diary here builds on Holmes' edition, attempting to address those points and also includes a newly annotated first half of the diary, which Holmes omitted because of his focus on the "covered wagon" segment.

The traveling party included another diarist, Phoebe Goodell Judson, who long after the trip, in 1925, published her reminiscences of the journey as the first part of her story of finding a new home on Puget Sound in present-day Washington.[9] Incorporating Phoebe's account here in parallel with Harvey's reveals her debt to his version, but also provides invaluable insights from her own point of view.

We have no direct documentation of the circumstances leading up to their decisions to emigrate, but Harvey, in a thinly veiled "fictional" narrative of a "Rev. and Mrs. Cathard" provides us with a good approximation of what led to his own decision for Oregon. The first four chapters of that narrative, "On the Frontier," are included in Chapter 2 of the present work. To the extent this narrative mirrors Harvey's own experience, we are led to believe that he and his wife made the decision to emigrate to Oregon independently from the rest of the family. In December 1852 "Rev. Cathard" and his wife read in *The Advocate* a letter from Oregon appealing for more missionaries, decided to apply to the bishop through their presiding elder, and shortly thereafter were notified of their transfer. The *Christian Advocate* of Dec. 16, 1852 records simply,

> Missionaries for Oregon – Rev. Messrs. Hines, of the Genesee Conference – two brothers – have been transferred to the Oregon Conference. Gustavus, the older brother, has been in Oregon as a missionary before.[10]

It appears then that Gustavus must have applied for transfer at a time not very different from Harvey and it is reasonable to assume that there was some family discussion of the respective decisions.

The unnamed younger brother in the above newspaper notice is indeed Harvey; Joseph was not transferred until mid-June.[11] In fact, from their later commentary, it seems that at the time that Gustavus, Harvey, and families departed Buffalo in early March 1853, they assumed they were very likely bidding a final good-bye to Joseph, along with the rest of the extended family. Joseph's transfer was so late in the season that it was judged impractical to begin an overland trip. He went instead by ship from New York to Panama, across the isthmus by rail and by donkey, and up the coast by steamer eventually to Oregon, arriving several weeks ahead of his brothers. Joseph then rode eastward by horseback to meet the others; his own story of their meeting is included in Chapter 16 as an interesting counterpoint to the accounts by Harvey and the others.

Of the four Hines brothers who left for Oregon in 1853, only the oldest, Obadiah, was not a Methodist Episcopal minister. He was nevertheless devout; according to an 1839 narrative by Gustavus, "Spent the following Sabbath with Br. Obadiah, who officiates as an Elder in the Free-will Baptist church in the Town of Smithville, Chenango Co."[12]

But whatever his religious capacity, Obadiah may well have fit his brother Harvey's third category of emigrant, those who "had…a desire to plant the institutions of Christianity in a new field."[13]

Tragically, in by far the most emotional event of the journey, Obadiah drowned while attempting to cross the Snake River.

To complete this prologue, we turn again to the writing of H. K. Hines, in his December 1884 introduction to the serial, "In an Emigrant Wagon."

We have often been solicited, by both "Old Oregonians" and those who have come to this coast in later years, and by more modern means of travel, to write the story of a journey "Across the Plains," when, to "cross the Plains" meant much more than it does at present. We have always felt a desire to gratify our friends and acquaintances in this, but pressing engagements of work and other considerations not necessary to mention have prevented. Now, however, we have decided to do so and as this will be a veritable history, the facts and circumstances drawn from a diary written on the journey, we have chosen to write under our own initials, and when we speak of other persons, we shall speak of them in the same way. The story will be a history, and at the same time it will be a romance to those who have come to the coast in the last decade. It will paint a half year of life, that, to the writer, becomes more and more like a dream as it recedes into the dim past, and yet that has in it a charm of remembrance that haloes no other half year of his existence. We have found it so with all the emigrants of two or three decades ago, and often, when we have had occasion to relate incidents of this journey in the ears of great audiences in New York, Brooklyn, Philadelphia and other great cities of the east we have found they awakened interest akin to that which the story of pioneers and explorers always awakens among an adventurous and resolute people. This is an interest that never seems to flag. The world admires boldness and bravery in any field. The courage that faces danger undaunted; the hardihood that hews out a new path of empire; and the patriotism that lives and dies for country; all awaken deepest admiration in the human soul. There is scarcely a noble element in humanity that did not find its fullest scope and play on "The Plains," in the years that lay between 1834, when the first foot that meant civilization and empire tracked the way from St. Louis to "The continuous wood where rolls the Oregon,"[14] to 1864; thirty years which spanned the kind of emigration to this coast of which we shall speak. Before then an unhistoried barbarism mantled the continent from the Rocky Mountains to the sea. Subsequent to that, modes of transit changed, the rapid locomotive took the place of the ox and the mule, and the palace car of the emigrant cart.

Once, in latter years, as we rode down the valley of the Platte river at the rate of thirty miles an hour, we saw, here and there, an emigrant wagon moving slowly westward up the very road our wheels had marked a quarter of a century before. Returning a month later along the same line of travel, after having spent a week in New York, another in Philadelphia, and made several visits to our relatives, we passed the same emigrants less than 500 miles further west. Some months later, after the cars and stage had brought us to our home in La Grande, the same people met us in the streets of that town. By the rail road we had traveled from sea to sea, attended to much important business, made several visits and reached home again before they had traveled with their emigrant teams two thirds as far as we traveled in the same way in 1853. We speak of this only to show the contrast between now and then. And that contrast was not alone in time, it was in all the conditions of the journey, whether they related to personal comfort, safety, food, or anything that might enter into the fare or fortune of an emigrant. What those contrasts are will appear in the progress of our story, and hence will not be indicated here.

In 1853 the Missouri river bounded the western limit of white settlement north of the state of Missouri. A scattering line of settlements, where adventurous pioneers had pushed the line of advance westward, margined the eastern bank of the river while the western most prairie rolls of Iowa and Missouri had only then and there been upturned by the plow of civilization. Kansas and Nebraska and Colorado and Wyoming and Dakotah and Minnesota were yet unborn commonwealth. The Pawnees and Cheyennes and Omahas and Arapahoes and Sioux and Crows and Shoshones – people whose names we have almost ceased to hear pronounced – were unmolested lords of these plains and mountains. The white man who stood on the eastern bank of the Missouri and looked across its rolling sea up the westward slopes looked over a *terra incognita*, and it required no little resolution to lead wife and children into the shadows of that unknown land from which they might never emerge, the venture that all made who entered that unknown way.

The most of the people who crossed the plains from 1844 to 1864 were from the western or southwestern states. Some were originally from the eastern; restless, adventurous souls, who were born under that star of empire that takes its way westward and had kept following its way, pitching their tents for a time east of the Missouri, and then, their spirit of adventure only kindled deeper by what it had tasted of the bliss of former daring, joined the van of those who broke the trail of empire to the shore of the western seas. They were of a class of people of which the world has ever too few. They were bold, resolute, indomitable. They were strong, and many of them stalwart in frame. Quick of preception [sic] and clear of intention, they saw the results of things before other men understood their beginnings. With a tinge of prodigality in their nature, they had sufficient of moral principle to keep them from criminal looseness, while yet it made them generous and humble. Many of them lacked the culture of the schools, but they had the stronger training of experience, which, if it had not put as shining veneer on the surface of their life, had ingrained a firmer texture to their being. Thus strong, if not beautiful, they were well prepared for the work that came to them and to which they came.

The motives that moved them were not single and simple, but various and complex. Some of them, doubtless, had chiefly ambition for a wider sphere and larger place in life. Others, with the hope of personal advantage desired to deserve well of their country by aiding in the establishment of its rights of empire on the shores of the Pacific. Others yet had even a higher motive than this, a desire to plant the institutions of Christianity in a new field. They had something of the spirit of Paul, which looked for fields afar: "beyond other men's foundations." So, with this diversity of desire and motive, the great caravan of Argonauts searching for the golden fleece lifted their sails to the winds of the prairie-sea and sailed away westward.

Of the incidents of the voyage we are now prepared to write."[15]

---

[1] Writing from the prairie in 1853, Gustavus was also intimately familiar with the ocean, based on his circumnavigation of the globe in 1839-46. *Christian Advocate and Journal,* September 22, 1853, 150.

[2] The English clergyman and poet Reginald Heber (1783-1826) is best known for his hymns, including From "Greenland's Icy Mountains," the third verse of which Harvey quotes here. See, for example, Literary Heritage, West Midlands, U.K., http://www3.shropshirecc.gov.uk/heber.htm; accessed April 7, 2007.

[3] H. K. Hines, *Missionary History of the Pacific Northwest* (Portland, Oreg.: H. K. Hines, 1899) 204-5. In his 1911 memoir, Harvey's brother Joseph describes the same scene, seemingly paraphrasing his younger brother's earlier account. Joseph and Harvey were 15 and 11, respectively, in 1839, and might well both have been at home with their mother on that "soft October day." J. W. Hines, *Touching incidents in the life and labors of a pioneer on the Pacific Coast since 1853,* (San Jose: Eaton & Co., 1911) 34.

[4] Betsey Hines, letter to Gustavus and Lydia Hines (September, 1839), the current editor's transcription of the handwritten original at the Oregon Historical Society.

[5] Gustavus Hines, *A voyage round the world.: with a history of the Oregon mission* (Buffalo: G. H. Derby and Co., 1850).

[6] George H. Himes, Sec'y, *Transactions of the 46th Annual Reunion of the Oregon Pioneer*

Association, (Portland, 1918) 69-125.

[7] Celinda E. Hines, "Diary of a Journey from N.Y. to Oregon in 1853," *Portland Telegram*, March 17-April 18, 1930.

[8] Kenneth L. Holmes, *Covered Wagon Women*, (Lincoln: University of Nebraska Press, 1986) Vol. 6, 77-134.

[9] Phoebe Goodell Judson, *A Pioneer's Search for an Ideal Home*, (Bellingham: Union, 1925).

[10] *Christian Advocate and Journal*, December 16, 1852.

[11] J. W. Hines, *Touching Incidents*, 160.

[12] Gustavus Hines, "Account of last days in the East, 1839," the current editor's transcription of a handwritten manuscript, at the Oregon Historical Society.

[13] H. K. Hines, "In an Emigrant Wagon," *Pacific Christian Advocate*, December 4, 1884, 2.

[14] Harvey quotes frequently from William Cullen Bryant's "Thanatopsis," which can be found in full online at http://www.msu.edu/-cloudsar/thanatop.htm; accessed June 16, 2007. The Columbia River was discovered and named by Capt. Robert Gray in 1792, but the rumored "River of the West" had been called "Oregon" earlier and this latter name persisted as late as 1817, the year of publication of "Thanatopsis." Charles H. Carey, *General History of Oregon*, 3rd ed. (Portland: Binfords & Mort, 1971) 1-15.

[15] H. K. Hines, "In an Emigrant Wagon," *Pacific Christian Advocate*, December 4, 1884, 2. "In an Emigrant Wagon," was a sixteen-installment serial, appearing weekly in the *Pacific Christian Advocate*, from December 4, 1884, through March 26, 1885. Except for the elusive sixth installment, which appeared in the January 15 issue, but has not been located, we include the complete text of all installments in the following chapters, segmented, however, to be interleaved with parallel accounts from the other travelers. Citations will include the abbreviated title, "Emigrant Wagon," and the date of the installment containing the excerpt.

1

1839–1846: The First Hines Trip to Oregon

*Sister Hines almost made me cry; haven't cried in
thirty years.*[1]
—Rev. J. Hemingway, P.E.

The Oregon saga for the Hines family probably began with a call
for missionaries in a church paper in 1839, which we will cite directly. But
first, we need some background. Gustavus Hines, in describing the history
of the Oregon Mission of the Methodist Episcopal Church, wrote in 1850,

> In the year 1832, four Indians, belonging to the Flat Head tribe,
> living west of the Rocky Mountains, performed a wearisome journey on foot
> to St. Louis, in Missouri, for the purpose of inquiring for the Christian's
> Book and the white man's God. Early in 1833, notice of this wonderful event
> was given in the *Christian Advocate and Journal,* published in New York,
> and a general feeling of Christian sympathy was produced in all the churches
> of the land for these interesting heathen, and a proposition was made that the
> Missionary Board of the Methodist Episcopal Church proceed forthwith to
> establish a mission among the Flat Head Indians.[2]

Within two years, the mission was established under the leadership of Rev. Jason Lee, and by 1838 he perceived the prospects for success
among the Indians so great, and his human resources so limited, that he
returned to the eastern states and sought reinforcements. In the March 15,
1839 issue of the *Christian Advocate and Journal*, the following notice
appeared:

A CALL FOR MISSIONARIES AND OTHERS
FOR THE OREGON MISSION.

> Not having yet secured the missionaries which are wanted for this mis-
> sion, by the advice of Bishop Hedding, to whom the appointment of foreign
> missionaries belongs until the next session of the New York conference, it
> has been concluded to call, in this public manner, for volunteers for the Or-

8

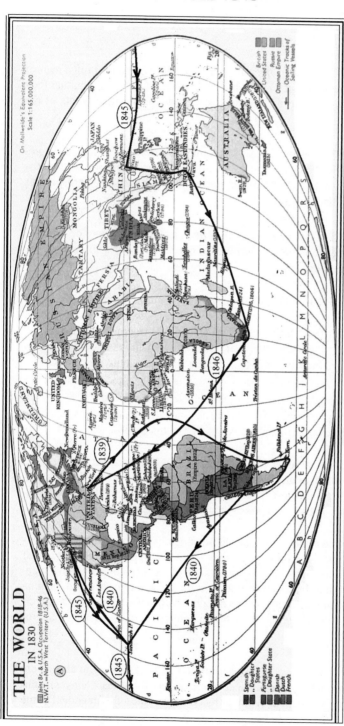

1830 map of the world showing the voyage of Gustavus in 1839-40 from New York to Hawaii and from Hawaii to Oregon. Also shown is his trip from Oregon back to Hawaii and from there to China, South Africa, and finally home to New York.

egon mission. Who will go? He who may say, "Here am I, send me," will please observe the following:—

1. We want *five* missionaries; and we should prefer men of small families, and such as have a knowledge of medicine, that they may administer to the physical as well as the spiritual wants of the people.

2. They must be well recommended by *three elders*, their presiding elder being one, if practicable, for their fitness for such a mission, as to health, piety, talents, and willingness to endure hardships, as good soldiers of Jesus Christ.

3. *They must be clear of debt*, as the board have determined that they will not be responsible for the debts of any who may engage in their employ.

4. Until the 25th day of this month those who may offer their services may direct their letters to *Bishop Hedding*, at Lansingburgh, N.Y. After that, until the 15th of May, direct to him, to my care, 200 Mulberry street; and after that, to *Bishop Waugh*, to whom the care of the foreign missions will then belong. All letters must be post paid.

It is expected that the expedition will sail from the port of New York some time in September next, as we are now negotiating with a gentleman in this city for the charter of a ship, expressly for this purpose.

We do not now advertise for mechanics and farmers, but if any should apply he may direct to me. We have already engaged one farmer, two carpenters and joiners, and, it is expected, a physician also. We still want a blacksmith, a cabinet-maker, a mill wright, and one carpenter and joiner.

Those who apply must be recommended by the preacher of their circuit, and at least three others, members of the church, for their piety, their health, and competency in some one branch of mechanical skill above mentioned, and of their being clear of debt, and their willingness to aid the mission in its spiritual interests, in teaching Sabbath schools, attending prayer-meetings, in teaching the natives, when not otherwise engaged in their appropriate callings.

Men of families are in all cases preferred. And those who engage are expected to continue in the services of the society for at least ten years, unless released by sickness or death, or by consent of the superintendent of the mission.   N. Bangs.[3]

Reflecting in later years on the events that led to his emigration to Oregon in 1839, Gustavus Hines wrote of his response to the above notice.

In answer to a call for missionaries for the Oregon Territory in the Spring of 1839, I addressed the following communication to Bishop Hedding, then in New York.

The letter to Bishop Hedding is dated March 28, 1853.

Rev. and Dear Sir,
It is with extreme diffidence that I take my pen to communicate to you the following. And nothing but a sense of duty would impel me in this way to intrude myself upon you. And such are the sensations of my mind at this time concerning the subject contemplated, that I find myself at a loss in what manner to disclose the matter to you. I would not appear to be presumptuous, nor vain, in this thing. And if my mind had not been led to the deliberate conclusion, that it is my indispensible duty to propose myself to you as a candidate for the missionary work, prudence would dictate that I should reserve my name, and continue cheerfully to move in my present sphere of action.

But impressed as my mind has been for many months, and more especially since the call of Dr. Bangs in behalf of the Oregon Mission, I cannot forbear, without doing violence to my feelings, to throw myself into your hands, to be disposed of [as?] your superior wisdom shall dictate.

For me to say anything with regard to my own qualifications would be superfluous and vain.

Suffice it to say that my family consists of myself and my wife, and a little girl of four years old. The girl is not our own.[4] Her father lives near this. And if you should find us employment in the missionary field, and it should be thought best, she could with perfect convenience be left at home. Not to be misunderstood in this communication, you will regard it as a response to the call of Dr. Bangs through the *Christian Advocate and Journal* of the 15th for five missionaries and others for the Oregon Mission. If you receive this favorably, I should be pleased to be informed of it as soon is convenient. If not, it will not be productive of evil for my respected Father to understand that, attended as the course may be, with deprivations and sufferings, and a premature grave, I long to bear the tidings of Salvation to those that have long sat in darkness and in the region of the Shadow of death.

Submitting this to you for your consideration and praying that the God of Missions may support you amidst your arduous labours, and direct to successful issue the missionary enterprise under contemplation, permit me Rev. and Dear Sir, to subscribe myself.

Your dutiful Son in the Gospel,
Gustavus Hines

Rev. Elijah Hedding
Bishop of the M.E. Church

On Saturday the fourth of day of May I received the following in reply to the above, which was written at Trenton New Jersey, and dated April 26th 1839.

"Dear Brother
You are appointed a Missionary to Oregon, [to] labour under the direction of the Superintendent of that Mission. All necessary information respecting the time of departing from this country you can obtain from Dr. Bangs the Corresponding Secretary. Say to Br. Parish I do not appoint any but Missionaries. The board of missions appoint the Mechanics, his letter will soon be laid before them.

Rev. G. Hines   Yours — Elijah Hedding"[5]

Gustavus's phrase, "…impressed as my mind has been for many months," suggests that he had been aware for some time of the activities of the mission in Oregon. Clearly he was a reader of the *Christian Advocate and Journal*, and in that publication through the latter half of 1838 and early 1839 were included numerous accounts of the activities of Rev. Jason Lee, then superintendent of the Oregon Mission, and actively engaged in promoting it as he traveled through the northeast. Looking back in 1850, Hines writes,

…While these things were transpiring in Oregon, Rev. J. Lee was zealously employed in accomplishing the objects of his visit to the United States. He arrived in the city of New York about the first of November [1838], and on the 14th he was present at a meeting of the Missionary Board, and stated at length the object of his visit. He urged with much earnestness the importance of extending the missionary work in Oregon; and in view of this he plead with great zeal the necessity of sending to that country a large reinforcement. In his opinion it was essential, for the prosperity of the mission, to supply it with the requisite means to furnish itself with food, buildings, etc.; and all the necessary implements for husbandry, and mechanical purposes, should be sent out by the Board. To meet all these demands would require a very heavy outlay, and for this and some other reasons, Mr. Lee met with warm opposition from some of the members of the Board, who sincerely doubted the expediency of the measure; but the superintendent, who had just come from the field of operation, perseveringly and powerfully urged the claims of the mission, and, sustained by Dr. Fisk, Dr. Bangs and others, finally succeeded in obtaining from the Board all, yea more than he demanded;

for in his opinion but two ministers were required, but in the estimation of a majority of the Board, if there were to be as many laymen sent out as Mr. Lee called for, two ministers would not be sufficient. Accordingly, on the 6th of December, 1838, the Board passed a resolution to send to Oregon five additional missionaries, one physician, six mechanics, four farmers, one missionary steward, and four female teachers; making in all thirty-six adult persons. These were all selected and appointed within a few months, the laymen by Dr. Bangs and Mr. Lee, and the missionaries by the Bishop having charge of the Foreign missions. The appointments took place from various parts of the United States, the New England, New York, Troy, Genesee, Illinois, and North Carolina Conferences contributing more or less, to make the numbers of the reinforcement complete. During the summer of 1839, Mr. Lee, attended by Wm. Brooks and Thomas Adams, the two Indian boys whom he brought with him, traveled quite extensively through the New England and Middle States, holding missionary meetings in all the important places, and collecting funds for the Oregon mission. His success was unparalleled, and an interest was excited throughout the land amounting to enthusiasm. Crowds thronged to see and hear the pioneer missionary beyond the Rocky Mountains, and the converted Indians who accompanied him. Liberal collections were taken up for the Oregon mission in almost every place, and these, with the appropriations of the Board for the purchase of goods, amounted to forty thousand dollars. Furnished with all kinds of tools for agricultural and mechanical purposes, and with the necessary articles for the construction of a saw-mill and grist-mill, the great reinforcement, with Mr. Lee at their head, at length found themselves ready for sea.[6]

In October 1839 Hines was part of the group that sailed from New York with Lee, bound for Oregon as the "Great Reinforcement" for the Oregon Mission. Hines and Lee became close associates, and despite some disagreements concerning the management of the mission, evidently remained warm friends. Indeed, it was Rev. and Mrs. Hines who were enlisted by Lee to raise his only surviving child, Lucy Anna Maria Lee.

The voyage to Oregon was chronicled by Hines in his book, *Voyage Round the World*, published in 1850 after his return to New York, and apparently read by many easterners considering emigration to Oregon. Among these, as we shall see later, were the Judsons, who accompanied the Hines families on the 1853 trip. Included here is an excerpt from the book as a modest illustration of the trials in nineteenth century ocean travel, for comparison with those of their no-less-perilous overland journey fourteen years later.

November 1st. [1839] The wind has gradually increased in strength since yesterday, and consequently the sea runs very high. Though I find myself so sick, in consequence of the violent motion of the vessel, that I loathe almost every thing my eyes behold, yet occasionally I draw myself up to the windward by ropes, and, looking over the bulwarks, contemplate the grandeur and sublimity of the mighty ocean, as she proudly and majestically rolls onward her mountain waves. During the night, we were called to encounter a severe gale. For forty-eight hours the wind had been blowing with increasing strength, attended occasionally with rain. But early in the evening the sky became perfectly clear, and the stars glistened with unusual brightness, which gave indication that a still more violent blast awaited us. About midnight, at the loud and well understood call of the second officer, all hands were immediately on deck; for in the midst of a storm, every sailor is converted into a fearless hero. The listening sailors waited for a moment the word of command, when "Clew your main sheet; clew up your main top sail; handle your main top gallant sail; clew your fore tack; close reef your fore top sail;" were heard above the roar of the winds and waves, and met with a prompt obedience. This being done, the captain was called, for the time was considered somewhat perilous. When the captain appeared on deck, the officer said to him, "There is a gale coming, sir, still more heavy than any thing we have had. Shall I not handle the foretop gallant sail, and lay to the gale!" The captain hesitated a moment, when the mate cried out, "The fore top gallant sail must be taken in, sir, or lost in a minute." "Close reef your fore top gallant sail," was heard above the roar of the angry elements, and was obeyed with amazing promptness by the faithful sailors, who had been as quick as thought to every word of command. After the sails had all been taken in, except enough to keep the vessel steady, the man at the wheel was charged to "mind his weather helm." At this moment the whole fury of the blast was upon us. The sea was lashed to foam, and the wind, with fitful gusts, swept angrily across our deck, and howled dismally through our rigging. At every blast of the tempest, the ship creaked in every joint, and, careening to the water's edge, swung her towering masts majestically in the heavens. The huge waves came rolling over our weather bow, and occasionally washed the entire length of our vessel. But the time had now arrived to lay to the wind. "Hard up!" thundered the watchful captain; "Hard up, sir!'"replied the faithful helmsman. The gallant ship turned her face to the wind, and defied the fury of the storm. She lay upon the waves, apparently as light as a feather, and increased the confidence of all in her capacity, by the triumphant manner in which she rode out the gale. At 3 o'clock in the morning the wind slackened, and changing suddenly into the west, brought us again on our course, and at four we were gliding over the billows, at the rate of nine knots an hour.[7]

Beginning with his letter of application to Bishop Hedding, it seems clear from Hines' writings that he went to Oregon with a deeply felt desire to carry Christianity to the Indians there. While his wife may have shared some of that sense of mission, she was acutely aware of the downside. When they were making their farewell tour of western New York in 1839, prior to their departure, they had occasion to address a camp meeting near Smethport. Methodist historian Rev. F. W. Conable attended that meeting.

> The writer recollects that Brother Hines, with his gifted and accomplished wife, attended a camp-meeting near Smethport, at which he preached an impressive sermon on the subject of his mission from Acts xvi, 9, i 10: "And a vision appeared to Paul in the night: There stood a man of Macedonia, and prayed him, saying, Come over into Macedonia, and help us. And after he had seen the vision, immediately we endeavored to go into Macedonia, assuredly gathering that the Lord had called us for to preach the gospel unto them." After the sermon of her husband, Sister Hines stood up in the altar in front of the stand, and in a strong and deeply affecting manner addressed the congregation about her, giving an account of her feelings in view of the sacrifice the great undertaking would cost her and her husband, while the preachers in the stand stood looking down upon the extraordinary scene deeply moved. It was a time to be remembered. Afterward Father Hemingway, the presiding elder, pleasantly remarked, in substance: "Sister Hines almost made me cry; haven't cried in thirty years."[8]

This was not the first time that Lydia Hines had experienced doubts at the prospect of joining in her husband's religious pursuits. Rev. Nelson Rounds, a first cousin of Gustavus, tells of Lydia's initial response to the role of minister's wife.

> In October of this year [1832] her husband received his first license to preach the gospel, and was appointed by his presiding elder to travel the circuit on which they were living; and by this strange providence she [Lydia] very unexpectedly found cast upon her the responsibilities incident to the life of a Methodist itinerant preacher's companion. In all her calculations for the future, she had made no reckoning for this; and for a while it was a source of the severest trial. Itinerating as a Methodist minister's wife, was to her synonymous not only with crushing responsibilities, but with want, destitution, mendicancy. The prospect appalled her, and she recoiled in its contemplation. By a few months, however, of mingling with people, during which she contributed largely to the promotion of an extensive revival, she became convinced that the call of the Church was indeed the call of God: and accordingly yielded the controversy and prepared herself as best she could to become a co-laborer in the gospel field.[9]

By the time the Hines family reached Oregon in 1840, the Indian population had decreased dramatically, and the prospects for converting those that remained to Christianity were considerably dimmed. Illustrative of the disconnect between his missionary efforts and the receptivity of the Indians is the conversation Hines had with a fellow traveler, Margaret Jewett Smith Bailey, as they arrived back in Oregon from a trip to Hawaii in 1844. Mrs. Bailey, a one-time teacher at the Oregon Mission, writes:

> ...Rev. Mr. H____ told me on the passage here that once being requested to preach to the Clackamas Indians, they consented to have him provided he would talk *good* talk, and when he commenced by telling them their hearts were bad, they said they had heard enough, and commenced going out.

Mrs. Bailey continues...

> An Indian woman tells me today that the reason why the Indians will not hear the missionaries is because they have heard that the people of the United States have sent them clothing, and they not having received it, they say their own hearts are as good as the white people's hearts.[10]

Judging from his later statements, such circumstances alone would not have been enough to discourage Gustavus to the point of returning to New York. But his wife apparently found the harsh and lonely wilderness existence an even greater sacrifice than she had anticipated.

Rev. Jason Lee, first superintendent of the Oregon mission, in commenting on dissatisfaction among some of the mission family, made a cryptic but telling remark about the feelings of Lydia Hines: "...there is Bro. Hines and his wife, who never wished to go into the country."[11]

And in a letter to the Missionary Board, dated August 12, 1843, Lee elaborates,

> ...I am informed, that Bro. Hines is determined to leave for the States next year. Perhaps no poor woman was ever more literally dragged into the Missionary Field than Mrs. Hines, and I doubt not, she will succeed in dragging him out.[12]

Lee's opinion was not that of a distant observer; since the death of his second wife, he and his infant daughter boarded with the Hines family.

Gustavus Hines himself was not immune to the sense of loneliness and yearning for home felt by his wife. On a "trip to the interior" of Oregon in 1843, he relates:

I strolled along the banks of the [Columbia] river about one-fourth of a mile, for the purpose of being alone, and coming to a wild apple tree which leaned its trunk over the smooth surface of the waters, I seated myself upon it, and a train of reflections, varying in their influence upon my feelings as they differed in character, passed through my mind. I thought of beloved parents from whom I had not heard for years; of the tears they shed when last I saw them, and received the parting benediction, and of the anxiety they must still feel, if alive, for their wandering son. I thought of all my former associates, of brothers and sisters, and early school mates, and Christian friends, with whom I had taken sweet counsel, and walked to the house of God, and who, if they had not forgotten me, would ask, "Where is he? and what is his employment?" I thought of everything of interest in my native land; of bustling cities, with wheels rattling and hoofs clattering over their pavements; of smiling villages and towns, with their splendid turnpikes and McAdamized roads; of railroad cars and steamboats; of temples erected to the God of heaven; the toll of chiming bells as they informed the waiting thousands that the time of worship had arrived; of crowded assemblies listening to the messengers of Jesus; and of saints rejoicing, and altars thronged with mourning penitents. Continuing these reflections until my mind experienced a kind of abstraction from the objects surrounding me, I fancied myself really amidst the scenes, the contemplation of which had produced this pleasing illusion, and starting up I found myself surrounded with the stillness of death, save the murmuring of the turbid waters of the Columbia that rolled beneath where I sat. Contrasting the land which had passed before my mental vision with that in which I felt myself a voluntary exile, I exclaimed, how changed the scene! This, thought I, is truly a land of darkness. Amidst the solitudes of these forests and plains the gospel is never heard except perchance the missionary of the cross may be passing through the land, and then to but here and there a small group of wretched Indians, who are alternately shivering with ague, and burning with fever, upon the brink of death.[13]

Just a few months later, in fact, toward the end of 1843, Jason Lee and the Hines family set out together for the States. Their plan was frustrated, however, when upon arriving in Hawaii they got the news that the Mission Board had replaced Lee as mission superintendent by Rev. George Gary, who was due to arrive in a few months. In consequence of this, and because of further travel complications, Lee continued on to New York with his plan to address the board, while the Hines family waited in Hawaii for the new superintendent and then returned to Oregon with him.

Rev. Gary refers to this aborted attempt in an extract from his journal, dated July 21, 1845, as the Hines are again contemplating their return (Note that Gary himself is not an altogether happy expatriate.).

Monday 21.—I find it extremely difficult to make myself contented and happy, while famishing for want of news.

Brother Hines and family are in no small difficulty to know what to do, provided they get no news from, or concerning, Rev. J. Lee, they have the charge of Mr. Lee's child.

Brother Hines has for some time been purposing to return to his conference. In the fall of 1843 he started for the States, in company with Mr. Lee, and went as far as Oahu; then returned, but returned with the design of soon going to the States. His family have never felt at home in this territory; and if he leaves, I shall remain another year. I am ready to consent that he may return, provided he so decides; and hope his return will not in any way be prejudicial to his standing with the Board, or in the estimation of any of the friends of the missionary cause. I know the voyage is expensive; yet when a man is satisfied his connection with the work at home will be equally useful, and he and his family far more contented, I think they should be permitted to return, especially after being secluded from the circle of their friends for six or seven years.[14]

Yet, with all this background of yearning for home, Gustavus did not lightly make the final decision to return. He writes:

On the 10th of August, 1845, notice was given by Captain Sylvester, that the Brig *Chenamus* would sail from the Wallamette River for Boston by the way of the Sandwich Islands about the 1st of September, and that a few passengers might be comfortably accommodated on board. Mr. Gary began already to consider that his work in Oregon was accomplished, and he felt quite solicitous to avail himself of the opportunity offered, to return home; but kindly proposed to leave it altogether with the writer, to say which, whether the latter, or himself, should be the favored one, at the same time assuring me, that if he left, and I should remain in the country, he should leave the superintendency of the mission with me. This, after a night of the utmost solicitude, brought me to the conclusion to close up my missionary labors, and leave the scene of toil and danger, and set my face towards my native land. Rev. Mr. Gary, as the superintendent of the mission, made arrangements with the Captain for my passage, and that of my family, consisting of Mrs. Hines, her sister, Miss Julia Bryant, and Lucy Anna Maria Lee, the daughter of Rev. Jason Lee, who had already returned to the United States.[15]

So after more than five years of mission work in Oregon, Gustavus accepted Gary's offer, and the Hines family set sail for home. Their journey touched Hawaii, China, and South Africa before they completed a circumnavigation of the globe in May 1846, when they returned to the New York harbor they had departed in 1839.

There must have been considerable disappointment on the part of Gustavus in the extremely limited success he had experienced toward his goal, in his own words, "...to bear the tidings of Salvation to those that have long sat in darkness..."[16]

But he had participated in establishing a provisional government, and in founding a first educational institution, the Oregon Institute, later to become Willamette University.[17] In so doing, he assuredly had helped lay groundwork for the successor to the dying native culture, and wittingly or not had paved the way for his own return to Oregon, with others in his family, just a few years later.

Although it gets little notice from our three principal chroniclers,[18] Gustavus and family were not the only ones in the 1853 party who had been to the West Coast earlier. In the spring of 1850, Holden Judson, who was then wed to Phoebe for less than a year, set out with Phoebe's parents, Jotham and Anna Goodell, and several of Phoebe's siblings for Oregon. Either because of a late start, or problems along the route, they determined that it was too late in the season to attempt passage of the last mountain ranges, so they opted to stay over the winter in the valley of the Great Salt Lake, the new home of the Mormons. After an unhappy stay near the inhospitable Latter-day Saints, they completed their journey in the spring, reaching Portland in June 1851. Holden separated from the Goodells on the way out of the Salt Lake Valley and went on to California, but evidently unsuccessful in finding his fortune there, he rejoined Jotham and others in Oregon before returning home to Ohio in 1852, only to repeat the Oregon trek, this time with Phoebe and daughter Annie, in 1853.[19]

---

[1] F. W. Conable, *History of the Genesee Annual Conference of the Methodist Episcopal Church,* Sec. Ed., (New York: Nelson & Phillips, 1885) 432.

[2] Gustavus Hines, *A voyage round the world,* 9.

[3] *Christian Advocate and Journal,* March 15, 1839.

[4] The girl was Julia Bryant, younger sister of Lydia Bryant Hines.

[5] Gustavus Hines, "Account of last days in the East, 1839," the current editor's transcription of a handwritten manuscript, at the Oregon Historical Society.

[6] Gustavus Hines, *A voyage round the world,* 36-37.

[7] Gustavus Hines, A *voyage round the world,* 47-48.

[8] F. W. Conable, *Genesee Annual Conference,* 432.

[9] N. Rounds, "Outlines of the Life of Mrs. Lydia Hines," *Pacific Christian Advocate,* April 2, 1870.

[10] Margaret Jewett Bailey, *The Grains, or, Passages in the Life of Ruth Rover,* (Portland, Oreg.: Carter and Austin, 1854) 132.

[11] Cornelius J. Brosnan, *Jason Lee: Prophet of the New Oregon,* (New York: Macmillan, 1932) 259.

[12] Jason Lee, in a letter to the Methodist Board dated Fort George, August 12, 1843, courtesy of the Oregon-Idaho Conference Archives, Salem, Oreg.

[13] Gustavus Hines, A *voyage round the world,* 151, 152.

[14] *Christian Advocate and Journal,* May 21, 1846.

[15] Gustavus Hines, A *voyage round the world,* 244.

[16] See Gustavus' letter of March 28, 1839, on page 11 of this chapter.

[17] Gustavus Hines, *Oregon and its Institutions,* (New York: Carlton & Porter, 1868).

[18] See, however, Chapter 14 for Celinda's diary entry of August 28.

[19] David L. Bigler, Editor, A *Winter with the Mormons.–The 1852 Letters of Jotham Goodell,* (Salt Lake City: Tanner Trust Fund, J. Willard Marriott Library, University of Utah, 2001).

2

December 1852: The Decision

> *And yet what wonder that there was a drop of*
> *relenting in his heart as he stood there that day. He were*
> *less or more than man not to have felt it. With redoubled*
> *power the ties of home and love of kindred were tugging at*
> *his heart strings.*[1]
> —Harvey (as "Mr. Cathard") in December 1852

Of the four Hines brothers who decided to leave New York in favor of Oregon in 1853, the one who provides us with the most insight into the circumstances of his decision is Harvey, the youngest. The first four installments of his *On the Frontier* paint the picture for us.

Harvey (as "Mr. Cathard")[2]

Seated in the pleasant parlor of the neatly furnished parsonage of one of the most popular stations in [Genesee] Conference, near the Atlantic seaboard, a young pastor and his wife were spending alone an evening of early December, 185[2]. There was a warm, cheerful, homelike glow to the grated fire, and a like cheerful repose to the glow in the contented and happy pair of hearts that beat near each to other as they two sat and talked, full of plan and prophecy for their future. Out of doors the snow of a cold winter night was being whirled in driving eddies by the singing wind, but no cranny nor crevice let the wind nor snow chill into the warm and happy room. It was such a night as, in northern winters, is consecrated to the free and select companionships of home.

Listen! With clanging bell and roaring wheels the evening express of the B[uffalo] and N[iagara] railroad rushes by the door and stops in the depot a few rods away. A half hour passes. The noise of the train had been only like a passing dream flashing through a sleep, scarcely observed by the two, so filled were they of their own thoughts, and so intent on the airy visions of the future that they had just been weaving out of their hopes and fancies. It may be suitable that during this passing half hour we give some further description of these people, who are, in some sense, to be central figures in the story which is to follow. We do this now because this half is a pivot hour of history for them and for others through them.

The man is of New England blood; his veins being reddened, through the maternal flow, by that which [John] Carver brought to Plymouth Bay, and through the paternal by the blood of all the Hopkins'. Like all his race, though not overgrown in stature, he is compact, lithe, agile and enduring. With a subdued dash of enthusiasm, he is yet calm and self-poised, with somewhat unusual command of all his powers. Dark and dilating eyes look squarely and steadily out from beneath somewhat projecting brows, from which heavy hair, approaching black, is thrown away over the right temple by a careless brush of the hand. With no bold self assertion in words, there is yet that impress of self-trust in action that marks men with whom to decide is to do.

The woman is, for a woman, somewhat taller than he for a man, with a pale white face, and a deep blue eye that looked inward and outward with a fathoming vision. Hers was also a New England descent; and the staid and solid depths of a well-built Massachusetts life were seen in hers. Without ostentation or pretence, there was the dignity of conscious character in all her movements, and the mild firmness of womanly will in her words.

Only a few months before they had been married.[3] Theirs was a union into which the clear purpose of the life and work of the Methodist itineracy entered as a chief factor. That was to be their life; chosen, understood, accepted; with all its possibilities of either joy or sorrow.

Before them, in this December night, in this pleasant parsonage home, on this delightful station, was the prospect of a happy, useful, successful, popular future. They were beloved by their people, and the beginning of their life was on heights that many true men and women *never* reach.

The train that roared by the door a half hour ago brought the evening mail. Rising and drawing on overcoat and gloves the young minister stepped out into the night, passing quickly down the village street, took from the post office letters and papers, and in a few minutes was again seated by the glowing grate in the light of the astral lamp upon the center table. Letters first. They have more of home in them; and these two persons had not been long enough from the home hearth to have the heart seared with forgetfulness of the dear ones yet around it. The letters were read, talked about, and if some tears, half joyous and half sad, were dropped upon their pages the reader may not care to know it. There were letters from the "old folks at home;" from dear ones from other pastoral charges. Memories stirred. Heart ties tingled. Old songs sang themselves through the heart again.

At length the letters were all read; all talked about; all folded and laid away to keep. A few moments of wordless communion with absent ones, and a package of newspapers was opened and each began to read.

A newspaper is often full of destiny. One of these was. Opening the *Christian Advocate*, a letter dated Salem, Oregon, and signed by W[illiam] R[oberts][4] arrested the eye of the young minister. In it was a cry impassioned and pleading for men; ministers; a deep Macedonian prayer, "come over and help us." It was read over and over again.

Laying aside the paper, that cry, touched with the sad wail of want, repeated itself again and over through the awakened heart of him who had just read it.

The writer of the letter he had never seen. He had known of him, some years before, in a general way, as a young minister of high position and brilliant preferment. He had known, too, that only a few years before, he had sailed away from the popular pulpits of the metropolis, disappeared around Cape Horn, and had covered himself in the shadowy depths of some wide western wilderness. The land from which he now wrote was three thousand miles away; close by the pulsing tides of the western sea. But still this cry for "help" sounded all the same through the young minister's heart.

Turning, and looking into the face that fronted his, he took up the paper again and said: "hear this," and read the letter again; laying the paper aside with the half question, half assertion of a purpose already taking form in his mind:

"Why can't *we* respond to this call?"

There was a far away look in the eyes that confronted his as these words were spoken. For a moment no answer was made. Then came the calm reply:

"Well I do not know *why* we cannot."

In the moment the visions of the future that filled the earlier evening in that parsonage began to dissolve and disappear; others, dim and distant and different, began to creep out of the unknown tomorrow. The "whys" and the "why nots" were weighed. The hopes and the fears were balanced. The losings and the gainings were measured. Duty and desire were estimated. While yet that night was on the earth the dim and distant and different visions that had so suddenly come into their sky—evoked out of an unthought-of future by that cry from a far away want—had become the fixed lights of guidance and life.

Oregon; then the distant, the shadowy, almost the unknown; was chosen—have and hold what it might under the cover of the unrevealed —as home, toil-field and resting place at last.

Not an impulse.—Visit to Presiding Elder.—His letter.—Another link forged.—A Sabbath.

It may be thought by the reader that the resolve of the young minister and his wife–whom hereafter we will call Mr. And Mrs. Cathard–was only a sudden impulse, but it was not. It was a result of moral growths and convictions that only needed the occasion to manifest themselves in action. The occasion had come; and though apparently sudden, yet the decision was really mature. But to will is one thing; to perform that which is willed is another.

According to the plan and polity of the Methodist Episcopal Church, not only the consent but the actual appointment of the authorities of the church must be obtained before such a work as that now contemplated by Mr. and Mrs. Cathard can be undertaken. This was now to be secured.

The Presiding Elder of the district in which Mr. Cathard was stationed, lived in the city of R[ochester], and the Bishop then in charge of the far distant Oregon was the then venerable, and now sainted W[augh]. The endorsement and recommendation of the first must be had before the Bishop would make so important an appointment. The city of R[ochester] not being very distant from N[iagara Falls], where Cathard was now stationed, he resolved to visit it in person and put the whole case before the Presiding Elder. Two hours ride on the cars[5] and a walk of a few blocks in the city brought him to the Elder's residence. Admitted, welcomed, and the one thing for which he was there was at once understood. He said:

Myself and wife have decided to offer ourselves for the missionary work in Oregon, and I have come to ask you to say what you feel that you can and ought to the Bishop in regard to the matter.

The Presiding Elder was himself a man of intense missionary spirit. Broad in view, energetic and decided in action, strong in faith, he had the moral and physical daring of an apostle. He had only just passed thirty-four, and his greatest life was yet before him. His great, deep, gray eye dilated a moment as though he were looking into the undiscovered. Faith flamed on his face. At length, after a space of silent thought he said—

Well, Cathard, you gladden me and sadden me at once. I am glad you are led to this work; though I shall be sorry to lose you from my district and the conference.

Seating himself at his table he began to write. Cathard thought: Every moment now was putting the past further away and more out of sight, and bringing the future nearer and more into vision. The cycles of destiny were rapidly revolving before his mind as he waited and thought.

In a few minutes the Presiding Elder had completed and placed in Cathard's hands the following letter.

R[ochester] Dec. —, 185[2].

My Dear Bishop W[augh]: — Rev. Brother Cathard of my district and now stationed at N[iagara Falls], has just called upon me and informed me that he and his wife have decided to offer themselves for the missionary work in Oregon. Brother Cathard stands in the first class of our best young men, and is fully competent for any place in the regular work to which you may wish to assign him. His wife is well adapted to sustain and help him in his work. He is [24] years of age and has good health. We know not how to spare him from our conference, but if you should appoint him to that distant field, I will supply his place as best I can until conference, and we will trust the Lord of the harvest thereafter.

Yours, ever, C_____.[6]

He placed this letter in the hand of Cathard who read it silently. A thrill was in his heart; a tear in his eye. With thanks, and an acknowledgment that the recommendation was beyond his deserts, he placed it in his pocket and arose to depart. Receiving the helpful "God bless you, my brother" of the Presiding Elder, he stepped beyond the threshold.

By and by, in other scenes, and thousands of miles away these men will meet again. They will meet amidst the founding of empire; the uprisings of Christ's Kingdom; amidst the joy of songs and the chill and shivering of tragedy.[7] But we must not anticipate.

A few hours brought Cathard to his own home and the side of

his wife.

Well? Was the significant monosyllable with which she asked "what of the night?"

The letter of the Presiding Elder was produced, read, commented on, and they sat down to frame a suitable one to accompany it to the Bishop. This was not so easy. Nothing seemed quite good enough for the occasion. They felt this to be, as it was, one of the great hours of their life. There is always something thrilling in the hour that makes or unmakes a life. There is an ecstasy in deciding and doing such as never is found in drifting. A letter was written, then laid aside. Another shared the same fate. It seemed impossible to leave unsaid that that ought not to be said. At length, in despair of a better, one was folded over that of the Presiding Elder, taken to the office and–it was on its way to its destination. They had forged another link in destiny. They must wait to know how well or ill.

Up to this moment all that had been decided or done was between God and the parties in direct interest. The time was not yet come to have it otherwise. Wait.

The Sabbath bells are sounding their call to worship over the town. Hundreds of people are rapidly walking through the clear sunlit winter morning toward the churches. As the last bell began its toll Cathard entered the pulpit to behold before him a sea of faces with longing looks as though hungry for the words he brought them.

There was a strange, unusual tenderness in his tones, and a glittering drop on his eyelid, as he announced his hymn–Wesley's grand soul-burst—

> "O for a thousand tongues to sing
> My great Redeemer's praise"—

And how the words

> "To spread through all the earth abroad,
> The honors of His name,"[8]

leaped with the accents of a great passion, from his lips. And yet what wonder that there was a drop of relenting in his heart as he stood there that day. He were less or more than man not to have felt it. With redoubled power the ties of home and love of kindred were tugging at his heart strings. Possibly it was more for himself than for the people, that he read, "But none of these things move me, neither count I my life dear unto myself so that I might finish my course with joy and the ministry I have received of the Lord Jesus."

And all through that sermon *he* saw the future and the far away. All through that sermon the *people* saw the present and the near. So variously, as men have need, does God speak to different hearts the same truth.

As the Sabbath service closes, with what unusual warmth and tenderness do the people grasp the hand of the pastor. He is nearer to them, they nearer to him than ever before. They did not know that they were offering to him then the sweet bribe of their love to buy him from a stormy, distant, perilous future. It is no shame nor sin that his heart dallied with it for a moment.

Letter from the Bishop—Its effect—Two homes—Letters sent— An evening scene.

"I hear a trumpet in the distance pealing news

Of better, and Hope, a poising eagle, burns

Above the unrisen morrow."[9]

The few days that were passed before an answer could be had from the Bishop were days of excited anxiety. When, at last, the train that should bring the response came rolling into the depot, Cathard could scarcely wait the few moments that must pass before he could receive it from the mail. With an excited air that evidently attracted the attention of those who stood near he took the letter and ran rather than went to his home. He did not dare read it alone and there. His wife met him at the door; her usually calm face flushed and expectant. Standing by her side, with trembling hand he opened and read:

B[altimore?] Dec. __, 185[2]
Rev. ___ Cathard. Inclosed you will find your transfer to the conference in Oregon. As you will need time to prepare for so long a journey, and for so complete a separation from your friends, the transfer takes effect immediately, and you are hereby relieved from your present charge. You have my sincerest sympathy and prayers in your great undertaking.

Affectionately yours,   W[augh].

Whether it was joy of sorrow, hope or fear that held these two hearts in speechless spell just then, we cannot tell. There is something that crushes and yet strengthens; that kills and yet gives a greater life. It was this that had come to them.

With the letter of the Bishop the old life ends and the new life begins. The heart could not but feel the blow of the words that cut at once the ties that had bound the hearts and hopes of Mr. and Mrs. Cathard to home and friends and native land. In some sense it was all the keener that it was invited. They fully realized that those words had all the pathos of a separation; perhaps an endless separation; from all that had entered into the plans and work of former life. They were a voice out of the future, echoing that voice of the past "go ye." There was some struggling with the question, have we not answered too hastily? Can we bear the strain and trial of the hour in which the farewells are said without relenting? Wait.

Yonder, a hundred miles away, is a quiet home where an aged couple are living who have borne the toils of clearing away a wilderness, and contemporaneous with that toil, rearing a family of sons and daughters, all of whom had gone out from them. It was to them a great parental pride that their children had graduated from their home life to conditions of honorable influence and respectability in the world. These parents were bending low now under the weight of almost three score years and ten. These were the parents of Mr. Cathard.

In another direction and not quite the same distance away was another home from which, years before, the husband and father had been borne to a neighboring cemetery, and where a widowed mother had cared for and trained to honor and piety a family of daughters. This was the home and circle from which, a few months before, Mrs. Cathard had been taken, a bride–a minister's wife. She had fully consented to what and all that relation involved. Still, in neither of these homes was there a thought that such a world-wide and life-long separation from those so dearly loved was impending.

Besides these there was the wide circle of friends and Christian associates whose fellowship was so dear to their hearts, all of whom were to be left behind. Then Mr. Cathard was a pastor of a successful year, among a loving people, on a popular station, and the hopes of his church were highly elated by the success of the past months. These were all ties that may be spoken of but cannot be described. It would be futile to attempt it.

Is it a wonder that Mr. and Mrs. Cathard hid these things in their own hearts for a time, and pondered them deeply in the light of the past? How to cover the edge of what they knew would be to so many a smiting blade with roses to conceal its sharpness was not so easily found.

At last letters full of tenderness were framed, stating the facts with their reasons, and sent them to the distant parents.

The evening lamps had just been lighted in the quiet sitting room of a farm house only a short distance from a small village.[10] A woman somewhat advanced in years, yet vigorous and alert, is sitting by the center table with an open bible resting upon it, her eye tracing the oft read, long-loved story of Infinite Love. A light and rapid step whose echo has answered out of her heart for more than fifty years is heard coming up the walk. "Father" is coming–how well she knows it. He enters and lays on the open bible by her hand a letter. Her mother's eyes could not be deceived; it was from her absent boy. She opened it and read aloud as follows:

Niagara [Falls], Dec. ___, 1852.

Dear Father and Mother
    I know with what joy you will open this letter, but fear that joy will turn to sadness before its reading is completed. Still, I know that through a long life you have both learned how to bear what may appear to be great trials. "All things work together for good to them that love God" though we may not see from the beginning how it can be so. When you sent your boy out into the work of the gospel ministry with your blessing, you understood from your long and intimate relation with Methodism, what it involved. To me it seems to have brought its extremest changes, and it becomes a duty, as sad to me as to you, at the order of the church, to go to a distant though not exactly a foreign field. I am transferred to Oregon Conference, and we shall be compelled to leave our work in the early spring. I am now closing up my work here, and will soon visit you and can tell you better than I can write all that has led to this complete change in the relations and work of my life. I need not say to you that the greatest pain of my heart today is from the fact that this will take me from my parents to whom I owe so much.
    I need not write more as I shall soon see you. Your affectionate boy.
C.

The mother's spectacles, dimmed by the flooding tears, were often wiped, and sighs and sobs punctuated the reading of the letter. A silence, not all sadness, followed its reading.

Of course the mother spoke first; for a mother's heart is always first to respond to a boy's want or prayer.

I have half expected this for years; she said. The prophesy of such a day has whispered through the dreams of many a night. I have tried to sow the seeds of a true obedience to the divine will in the heart of my son, and I must not murmur now to reap what I have sowed. But must I so soon look on *his* face for the last time?

Is it a wonder that those dimmed eyes wept again?

The father was a man of few words. His tears answered hers; but his was the consent of silence. Yet he was brave and strong, and neither then nor thereafter spoke a word of remonstrance against the Divine will on the decision of his son.

This father had toiled hardly for many a weary year to give his sons some better advantages than he had ever enjoyed; to fit them for wider fields of usefulness than his limited privileges as an orphan boy whose boyhood almost touched the years of "the revolution," qualified him to fill. There was something of fatherly pride in his heart that God had seconded his hard toil in some degree, and now his boy was to represent him in a wide and distant and honorable; even if self-denying field.

At this point parents often mar and spoil the possibilities of their children's life. The few years, or days perhaps, that they can have their children near them, are weighed against all that their children could do or be if they were pointed to their own destiny by their parents. At this point these parents were strong where so many are weak.

Another home scene—What it teaches—The unknown land—An incident—last Sabbath at N[iagara Falls].

> Scouts upon the mountain peak –
> Ye that see the Promised Land,
> Hearken us! For ye can speak
> Of the country we have scanned,
> Far away![11]

On the summit of a high hill overlooking a wide sweep of valley and rolling uplands, dotted here and there with white farm houses, stands another home where a scene even more touching than that just described is being enacted. It is the same hour; evening. A mother whose silver hair flows away from her temples, and two or three daughters,[12] all in early womanhood, are in conversation about the only one of the circle now absent, when a letter is put into her hand from the absent one. Exclamations of pleasure greeted it, and in a moment a pair of younger eyes were doing service for the failing ones of the mother, in reading it. In gentle, daughterly, sisterly words the harshness of the great and awful fact that in a few weeks that absent daughter and sister would be on her way to a land that to them was only a shadow across the sunset sky was sought to be disguised. To the sisters the romance that so lures the young heart away from the sorrows of the present relieved the fact; even draped it with an ideal beauty. But the mother's heart was too deeply read in the sad mysteries of life, had been too chastened and clarified in struggles of loneliness, not to read the truth through the tender gauze that the words of the letter had thrown over it. Between the written lines the unwritten fact that this meant a final earthly separation from the loved one glared out. Her silver temples throbbed; her heart stood still a moment in the thrall of this new and living bereavement.

When the reading of the letter was ended a hush fell upon the group. Faces were pale and eyes had distant and thoughtful looks. The mother's one hand rested on the page of the letter which seemed to throb under her fingers with its pulse of sorrow; the other supported her aching brow while a tear drop dewed her flushed cheek. To say that there was sorrow is to speak only half a truth. There was triumph in the trial. For what do mothers bear and train daughters and sons if not for what these sons and daughters may be and do in the world? And what sends so proud a thrill through the mother's heart, or kindles such exalted light in her eye, as to see that son or daughter in the way of imperial doing? Sad, therefore, as was the first sense of bereavement and personal loss, the higher sense of the exalted sphere of life and work which was thus and now opening before her child mastered the sadness, and subdued the grief. The true motherhood conquered the false, as she saw God's will in her daughter's destiny.

But why attempt to paint these heart throes and triumphs? We have spoken of them only that the reader may see, as we gently draw aside the curtain but a little through what and how many struggles and sacrifices the leal sons and daughters of the church have gone at her bidding to do her work in the uttermost parts of the earth.

It would not greatly interest the reader to follow the routine of preparation that filled the months from December to March. A few incidents only will here be given and they because they serve fitly to introduce the reader to the real history that lies beyond.

It was not until the Sabbath after he received the letter of the Bishop containing his transfer to the Conference in Oregon that Cathard acquainted his congregation with the fact, and announced that he should close his labors with them the Sabbath succeeding. The week that intervened was filled with much that was said, much that was joyful, and some things that bordered the ridiculous. Mr. and Mrs. Cathard were very human beings, and so they were disposed to accept the ordinary happenings of life in a very practical way. Into their leave-takings there was woven a woof of threads both sable and golden. The better, higher piety and intelligence of the church gave them words of cheer and hope and God-speed for their distant field. These were the golden threads. The lower and least intelligent piety saw only the dangers of the way; the deprivations after Oregon was reached; the perils of death that were everywhere; and spoke only of these. These were the sable threads.

In this long-ago time of which we write, Oregon was an almost entirely unknown land, especially in the region of country where Cathard was stationed. Of course considerable information of all the Pacific Coast had touched the fringes of the western settlement, and as far east as Illinois and Indiana; but Cathard was in the heart of the East. To most people there the very name, Oregon, was as a sound out of another world. This was illustrated during the week of which we now write.

Passing down the street one day Cathard met, on the sidewalk, a member of his church; a farmer living a little distance from the town; who grasped his hand with unusual warmth and said:

They tell me, brother Cathard, that you are going as a missionary to the heathen. Is that so?

Well, not exactly that; said Cathard, smiling; but the Bishop has transferred me to Oregon, and we expect to leave N[iagara Falls] in a few days.

To Oregon! To Oregon!—let's see—I almost forget what part of Africa Oregon is in; half answered, half queried the good brother.

O, said Cathard, Oregon is in the United States, over beyond the Rocky Mountains. It's a new country, and the people are not heathens at all. There are some Indians, but we go to labor among the white people who are rapidly settling the country.

After a moment's thought the farmer, who was a Vermonter by birth and early training, said: Well it must be a long ways or I'd heard more about it. Is it as far as Vermont?

Said Cathard, if one goes by land it is about four thousand miles; if by water perhaps eight thousand. A somewhat lengthy conversation followed in which the journey to Oregon was discussed; the condition of society there spoken of; all of which only served to more deeply inspire the good brother's mind with the utter desperation of such a venture as Cathard's; a feeling which he freely expressed. Cathard replied to it quietly that the Bishop had called for some young men for that field, and he had accordingly offered himself.

Well, replied the farmer, with an emphasis that meant what the written words can hardly communicate, I think nobody but a *very* young man would answer to such a call as that. Cathard; who saw such things from the comical side, laughed heartily at the brother's covert compliment, and went home to tell it over to his wife. The walls of the parsonage of N[iagara Falls] heard a great many pleasantries and laughs during the next few days about "heathens," and "Africa," and "very young" men, which served to lighten and brighten the hours of preparation.

The last Sabbath of Mr. And Mrs. Cathard at N[iagara Falls] has arrived. Several of the other churches of the village had given up their services that their people might join the Methodist Church in this last day with their pastor. The crowded seats and aisles; the frequent tearfall; the rapt listening of the multitude, all tokened the deep interest of the people in the occasion. The text for the hour could hardly have been other than the words of the risen Christ: "All power is given unto Me, in heaven and in earth. Go ye therefore and teach all nations, baptizing them in the name of the Father, and of the Son, and of the Holy Ghost; teaching them to observe all things whatsoever I have commanded you; and lo, I am with you always, even unto the end of the world. Amen."

Cathard could speak but little. The pathos was in the hour itself, and in the future to which it pointed. When the services of the hour were over, and the pastor and his wife had spoken hundreds of tearful farewells and received many words of blessings, they felt that God's blessed angels were bearing the bleeding heart-bonds that now were severed here far westward to an unknown land, and uniting them to —; What? The future can only answer.

Gustavus

We recall from the previous chapter that his family's dissatisfaction was a large part of Gustavus's decision to leave Oregon and return to New York.

Did Gustavus by then have his fill of missionary work? Not according to the feelings he expressed in an article in the *Northern Christian Advocate* in 1849, in which he described returning to the village of his boyhood, West Winfield, N.Y.

After having a sermon in the morning, an appointment was circulated that, at four o'clock, I would give an account of our missionary expedition to Oregon. Considerable interest was excited, a large congregation assembled, among which were some who remembered me only as the wild, flaxen headed urchin, gamboling in the streets, and others, as the vain and trifling apprentice, and subsequently, as the sedate and thoughtful journeyman in a shoemaker's shop; but by the help of God I was enabled for two hours to discourse on the subject of the Oregon Mission, in such a manner as to secure the profound and unbroken attention of the congregation, and to leave the most favorable impression upon the mind, as to the great utility of Christian missions—I am led to make this remark concerning my own labors, not from any egotistical feelings, but for the purpose of correcting those who may have entertained the opinion that, because I have voluntarily abandoned the mission field, I therefore look upon the missionary cause as unworthy to be sustained; than which a greater error can scarcely be embraced. No! It is a cause that still lies near my heart; and if I were left now to my own selection, I would say, let me go back to Oregon; let me assist in planting the gospel along the shores of the Pacific Ocean! Let my life, my death, my grave, my crown, be that of a missionary of the cross of Christ.[13]

So it appears that Gustavus was primed and ready for the slightest nudge that might send him back to Oregon and the mission field. Perhaps younger brother Harvey's decision provided just that nudge. We note too, that the Oregon of 1852 was already far different from the Oregon of the 1840s which Gustavus' wife Lydia had found so unappealing. Population figures alone—over 20,000 Americans in the Oregon Territory in 1853 in contrast to fewer than 100 in 1839—implied a far less lonely prospect for Lydia, and perhaps she also found the promise of an overland journey less forbidding in contrast to the long sea voyage of 1839.[14]

Phoebe Judson

The motive that induced us to part with pleasant associations and the dear friends of our childhood days, was to obtain from the government of the United States a grant of land that "Uncle Sam" had promised to give to the head of each family who settled in this new country. This, we hoped, would make us independent, for as yet we did not possess a home of our own—all of which meant so much to us that we were willing to encounter dangers, endure hardships and privations in order to secure a home that we might call "ours."

The many air castles that I built concerning my "ideal home" while the preparations for our long journey were being made, are still fresh in my memory.

It should be built by a mountain stream that flowed to the Pacific, or by some lake, or bay, and nothing should obstruct our view of the beautiful snow-capped mountains.

True, it would be built of logs, but they would be covered with vines and roses, while the path leading to it should be bordered with flowers and the air filled with their sweet perfume.

> "Home, home, sweet home;
> Be it ever so humble,
> There's no place like home."[15]

My parents had already found a home on the banks of the Willamette, in Oregon.[16]

In fact, not only had Phoebe's parents settled in Oregon, but as we noted earlier, her husband Holden had accompanied her parents on their westward trip in1850-51. Although his side trip to California evidently uncovered neither a fortune nor a suitable place to settle his young family, the overall appeal of the West apparently endured, and the government's land grant program, according to Phoebe, was a major factor in their ultimate decision.

The Bryant Family

In December 1852, after their official transfer to Oregon by the M. E. Church, Gustavus and Harvey sought company in a letter of appeal, published in the *Buffalo Christian Advocate*. It seems likely that the Bryants, living not far from Buffalo, may well have seen this letter, and subsequently made their arrangements to accompany the Hines family.

To the Editor of the *[Buffalo] Christian Advocate.*[17]
Spencerport, Dec. 17, 1852.

The undersigned having been transferred by Bishop Waugh, from the Genesee Conference of the M. E. Church, to the Oregon Mission Conference, would respectfully give the following notice to all whom it may concern:—

We are to proceed to our destined field of future labor on the shores of the Pacific Ocean, by the usual route across the Rocky Mountains; and shall take our final departure from the frontiers of Missouri, about the middle of April next. We are desirous of enlisting for emigration to, and settlement in that fertile, beautiful and rapidly rising country, as many persons of good moral and Christian character as we can. It will be remembered that one of the subscribers has resided in that country as a missionary, for nearly six years, and is consequently qualified to judge of the character of the country with respect to its climate, and natural advantages. Too much cannot be said in commendation of that interesting portion of the world; but as a particular description of the country would not be admissible in a paper, we would refer the inquirer to a book entitled "Missionary Expedition to Oregon," which contains a full description of the Geography, History, and resources of the country, and which is peculiarly adapted to benefit the person desiring to emigrate thither. If, therefore, any persons are desirous of obtaining information concerning that country, they can inclose one dollar to Rev. G. Hines, Spencerport, Monroe Co., N.Y., and a fine book of 437 pages will be immediately returned to them by mail free of postage. It should also be remembered, that the law granting land to actual settlers in Oregon extends only to Dec. 1853. If, therefore, any man would have a farm of choice land in Oregon without paying for it, he must go without delay. Concerning the organization of a party for society, and mutual protection on the way, we can speak more definitely when a sufficient number shall decide to accompany us. Other information will be communicated through the papers as occasion may require.

Come brethren, preachers, exhorters, and members, whose hearts have dwelt in the regions of the setting sun, "come with us," to that land where the harvest is so plenteous, and the laborers so few.

Gustavus Hines.
Harvey H.[sic] Hines.[18]

Whether or not the Bryants saw the above letter, or its later copy in the *Northern Christian Advocate*, evidently many others did see it, and followed up with letters of inquiry to the Hines brothers, for the following appeared in the latter paper in late January.

OREGON
ANSWERS TO INQUIRIES

Since the publication of the article from us relating to Oregon, we have received so many letters of inquiry in reference to that country and the land journey thither, that we find it impracticable to do other than give general answers to the more important of them through the *Northern*. Many others may also desire the same information, and will be able to obtain it through this published medium. Information will be found below in questions and answers.

Ques. 1. When will you leave New York state for the frontier of Missouri?

Ans. By leave of Providence, we purpose to leave the city of Buffalo, Monday, the 7th day of March. But it is not absolutely necessary for all who go to leave at so early a date. But all should give themselves time in Missouri for thorough preparation for the journey.

Ques. 2. What will be the probable time of starting from the frontiers of Missouri?

Ans. This we cannot answer definitely, but the proper time to start is as soon as there is sufficient grass to sustain the animals on the way.

Ques. 3. From what place in Missouri do you intend to start?

Ans. We cannot positively state at the present, but so far as preparation is concerned, this will make no difference. We will communicate this information in due season.

Ques. 4. With what sort of teams would it be best to perform the journey?

Ans. Ox teams are generally preferred, from two to five yoke of cattle to each wagon. Emigrants often take cows in their teams, and drive others.

Ques. 5. What will be the probable expense of an outfit for five adults?

Ans. We cannot answer this definitely, but think it would require five hundred dollars, beside expenses to Missouri. The outfit embraces four yoke of cattle, wagon and provisions for the journey.

Ques. 6. How long will it probably take to perform the journey?

Ans. About one hundred days from Missouri. To perform the journey expeditiously, very little loading, except provisions and clothing, should be taken.

Many are inquiring concerning the climate, soil, and many other things in Oregon. It will be seen to be impossible for us to furnish in this way, or by letter, this lengthy information. It may be obtained from the book (*Missionary Expedition to Oregon*) spoken of in our former articles, which can be procured by inclosing one dollar to the subscribers at Spencerport, Monroe Co., N.Y.

Persons wishing to do so can send boxes, at the expense of seventy-five cents per cubic foot from New York, consigning them to F. and D. Fowler, No. 86 West-street, New York. The vessel will probably leave about the first of March for Oregon, direct.—Boxes should be sent by the middle of February.

Many inquiries are made in reference to the company. We cannot state definitely its number and character, but many persons in N. Y. state and the West have certified to us their intention to accompany us; principally preachers and members of the M. E. Church.

Gustavus Hines, Harvey K. Hines.

Spencerport, Jan. 16, 1853.

P. S.—*Western* and *North Western Christian Advocates* please publish.[19]

Obadiah

We have no direct evidence concerning the decision by Obadiah Hines and his family to join the company headed to Oregon. An aside in a letter of 1854 written by Gustavus to a minister friend in New York suggests, however, that it may have required some persuasion from others to convince Obadiah. Gustavus says, in referring to Obadiah's drowning, "A beloved brother, whom we had induced to accompany us,…"[20]

And in another letter, Gustavus provides this bit of insight as to Obadiah's motivation: "He was sanguine in the hope of making himself and family a comfortable home in Oregon…"[21]

---

[1] H. K. Hines, "On the Frontier," *Pacific Christian Advocate,* January 19, 1882, 2.

[2] Were we to doubt "Mr. Cathard's" identification as Harvey, it is illuminating to consider the teasing reply Harvey had for a reader in 1882: *"A lady writing from an important charge in Columbia River Conference, says: 'I see my time is about out for the* Advocate, *and I don't want to miss a number, I must hurry and send in my money. I find so many good pieces for my scrap book. I never miss anything on tobacco or temperance; and such fine poetry. But we are anxious to know who Mr. Cathard is?"*

This sister is one of "the pioneers." She has held a faithful fealty to the church through all the years—and they are many—that we have known her "manner of life." Of course we cannot gratify her woman's curiosity to know "who Mr. Cathard is," but it would be strange indeed if he had not eaten at her table either in the Willamette valley, or in her home by the "birches" of the little creek that flows by her later dwelling. We thank Sister L___ for words of cheer." H. K. Hines, "Notes on Letters," *Pacific Christian Advocate,* June 22, 1882, 2.

[3] Harvey married Elizabeth Jane Graves June 26, 1852, in Wyoming, N.Y. A. J. Joslyn, "Mrs. E. J. Hines," *Pacific Christian Advocate,* February 12, 1890. (This was his second marriage; his first wife, Angeline Seymor, died June 19, 1851. Thomas Carlton, "Angeline S. Hines, wife of Rev. H. K. Hines," *Christian Advocate,* July 30, 1851.)

[4] Rev. William Roberts was superintendent of the Oregon Methodist Mission in 1852. Although we have not located a letter matching Harvey's description, a notice in the *Advocate* in late October details the new conference assignments, with many stations "to be supplied," and the editor notes "... how many men are needed there yet to supply the work." "Oregon Conference," *Christian Advocate and Journal,* October 28, 1852, 174.

[5] This ride was probably via the Rochester, Lockport & Niagara Falls railroad, formed in 1850 by a merger of two smaller railroads, and thereby connecting Rochester and the Falls by a seventy-seven-mile rail route—a trip that could not unreasonably be completed in two hours in that day. National Railway Historical Society, New York Central Historical Information, http://www.crisny.org/not-for-profit/railroad/nyc_hist.htm; accessed April 8, 2007.

[6] In a later chapter of *On the Frontier,* Hines refers to this same presiding elder as T___, which is consistent with (Rev. Eleazer) Thomas (1814-1873), who was Hines' own presiding elder in 1852.

[7] The tragedy to which Harvey refers was the gunning down of Rev. Thomas and Gen. Edward Canby by Modoc Indians as they were engaged in a peace mission to these Indians during the so-called Modoc War or Lava Beds War (1872-73), the last of the many nineteenth century Indian wars in Oregon or California.

    This followed by a couple of years a joyous reunion of Harvey with Rev. Thomas in Oregon. For the story of the fatal final mission of Thomas and Canby, see "Modoc War," *Wikipedia* entry, http://en.wikipedia.org/wiki/Modoc_War#Thomas-Wright_Massacre; accessed April 8, 2007.

[8] "Wesley wrote this hymn to commemorate the first anniversary of his conversion to Christ. This origin is reflected in the lyrics, 'On this glad day the glorious Sun of Righteousness arose.' The stanza that begins 'O for a thousand tongues to sing' is verse seven of Wesley's original poem. This work first appeared in *Hymns and Sacred Poems* in 1740." The Cyber Hymnal; http://www.cyberhymnal.org/htm/o/f/o/oforl000.htm; accessed June 9, 2007.

[9] Harvey quotes here from Tennyson's *The Princess,* Canto IV. Project Gutenberg, 1997; http://www.gutenberg.org/dirs/etext97/prncs09.txt; accessed April 8, 2007.

[10] Harvey's parents, James and Betsey Hines, then aged 72 and 69, respectively, lived near the small town of Brockport in Monroe County, N.Y.

[11] Writing in 1882, Harvey quotes here from a school reader, Charles W. Sanders, *Sanders' Union Fourth Reader* (New York: Ivison, Blakeman, Taylor, & Co., 1863). (Project Gutenberg, 2005), http://www.gutenberg.org/dirs/etext05/sread10h.htm; accessed April 8, 2007.

[12] In 1850, Elizabeth Graves, the future wife of Harvey, lived in the household of Philena Bainbridge, age 57, along with sisters Alma, 26; Martha, 19; and Celina, 17. Also listed is

Hester Bainbridge, 12, a step-sister. 1850 U.S. Census, Middlebury, Wyoming County, New York; image copy at www.Ancestry.com; accessed April 9, 2007. As will be seen later, Elizabeth's younger sister Martha joined the Hines company on the trip to Oregon.

[13] Gustavus Hines, "Notes of Travel," *Northern Christian Advocate,* August 1, 1849.

[14] After writing the preceding speculation about Gustavus' decision, we came across the following revealing commentary in Lydia's obituary. "While residing in the latter place [Spencerport, New York]…, very unexpectedly to her husband she informed him that she would be glad to return again to the Pacific Coast, and there spend the remainder of her days. Sympathizing in this feeling, Mr. Hines asked of Bishop Waugh and obtained a transfer to the Oregon Conference, with the privilege of returning to the country by way of the Plains." N. Rounds, "Outlines of the Life of Mrs. Lydia Hines," *Pacific Christian Advocate,* April 2, 1870, Vol. XVI, No. 14.

[15] The lyrics for the song, "Home Sweet Home," were written in 1822, over a century before Phoebe Judson wrote her reminiscences, by John Howard Payne (1792-1852), as part of an operetta, *Clari, or the Maid of Milan.* The song was also published separately, and sold about 100,000 copies in the first year. Long Island Our Story, http://www.newsday.com/community/guide/lihistory/ny-history-hs510a,0,6109116. story; accessed April 9, 2007.

[16] Judson, *A Pioneer's Search,* 9.

[17] Their masthead identifies this newspaper as the "Christian Advocate," while the running title includes the "Buffalo" prefix.

[18] Gustavus Hines and Harvey H. [sic] Hines, "An Appeal for Oregon," *Buffalo Christian Advocate,* December 1852.

[19] Gustavus Hines and Harvey K. Hines, "Oregon, Answers to Inquiries," *Northern Christian Advocate,* January 26, 1853, 14.

[20] Gustavus Hines, "Oregon," *Northern Christian Advocate,* April 19, 1854, 61.

[21] Gustavus Hines, "Letter from Oregon," *Northern Christian Advocate,* December 7, 1853, 194.

3

February 16–March 7, 1853: Getting to Buffalo

> *We not only expected to have enjoyed your society from time to time, but as our heads are silvering over with age, and as we shall soon be unable to engage in the active concerns of life, we fondly hoped that you would have been the support of our declining years. But as you have been called by one who has a higher claim upon you than we possibly can have, we will cheerfully acquiesce in the dispensation, and bid you go. May the God of peace be with you.[1]*
>
> —Betsey Hines, saying good-bye in 1839

In February 1853 the Hines family were scattered about western New York, poised, knowingly or not, for emigration westward. Celinda, her father Obadiah, and the rest of their family were in Hastings, Oswego County. The other brothers destined for Oregon, Gustavus and Harvey, having been dismissed from their pastoral duties to prepare for their trip, were evidently living with their respective families in or near Spencerport, Monroe County. (This supposition is based on the Spencerport address given on their joint letters of December 1852 and January 1853.) Joseph, who was to learn of his own transfer later in the spring, was stationed at Warsaw, Wyoming County. The parents, James and Betsey Hines, had moved from Hastings in the late 1840s and were living in Brockport, Monroe County, as was their son, James R. Hines, and family. The eldest son of James and Betsey, Adolphus, was living in Rochester, Monroe County, and a daughter, Malissa Hines Robinson, along with her family, were in the process of moving from Hastings to Monroe County.[2]

Celinda

Wednesday, February 16, 1853—Left Hastings, Oswego Co., N.Y. after dinner & arrived in Syracuse about dark.[3] Stayed all night at Cuddebeck's.[4]

Thursday, February 17—Started on the 7 o'clock train of cars for

41

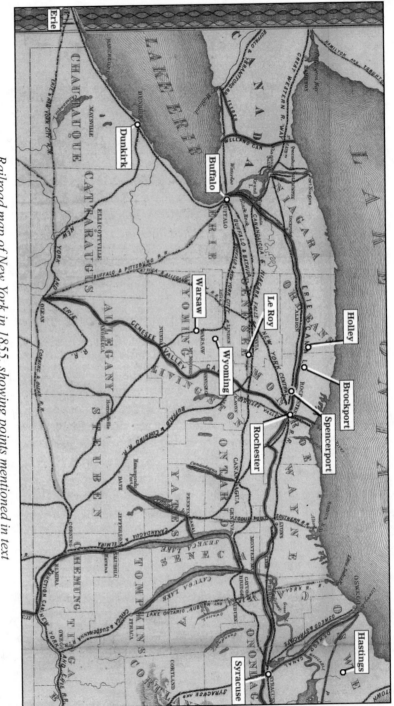

Railroad map of New York in 1855, showing points mentioned in text

Rochester where we arrived about one PM. Hired a carriage to take us to uncle Adolphus'.[5] Found all well but Nelson.

Friday, February 18—It is quite snowy...

Saturday, February 19—Started on the morning train for Brockport arrived about 8 o'clock. Found grandpa who took us home with him all well. Uncles G & H with their families and uncle James gone to Warsaw. Received a letter from uncle J. Bennett[6] all well.

Sunday, Feb. 20—Very quiet all day.

Monday, February 21—Uncle Gustavus and family together...came ...

Tuesday, February 22—Stormy.

Wednesday, February 23—Stormy & cold. Uncle H & wife came in the eve. from Wyoming.[7]

Thursday, February 24—Boxed up our things.[8]

Friday, February 25—Cold. Went with Uncle Harvey and aunt Elizabeth to Warsaw, Wyoming Co. Stopped at Le Roy. Went to Wyoming took dinner at the Havens...went to...Joseph...all well but the little boy.[9]

Saturday, February 26—The little boy is better.

Sunday, February 27—attended service at the baptist church forenoon & afternoon. Uncle Joseph preached.[10]

Monday, February 28—Boy still better. Uncle Harvey called.

Tuesday, March 1—Went out at eve.

Wednesday, March 2—Went to see Uncles...

Thursday, March 3—Uncle Joseph and myself started for Brockport. Stop at Le Roy. Roads very muddy. Arrived in B. just before dark, found Uncle Robinson's family at grandpa's, aunt Malissa sick in Syracuse. Uncle Joseph starts immediately to see her. Find a letter from Cousin M L Higgins all well but uncle...Clarissa...[11]

Friday, March 4—Uncle Gustavus and family leave for Buffalo. Affecting scene. Uncle Joseph arrives in the evening from Syracuse. Aunt is a little better, but can not sit up without fainting.

Saturday, March 5—Pa receives a letter from L. F. Devendorf—all well.[12]

Harvey

Having received from our Rev. and dear Bishop Waugh, a transfer from the Genesee to the Oregon Annual Conference of the M. E. Church, and completed our preparatory arrangements for our long journey across the Rocky Mountains, on Saturday, March 5th, 1853, Mrs. Hines, her sister, Miss M. M. Graves, and myself took our tearful leave of the parental home of Mrs. H. and seated ourselves in the carriage which was to convey us to the home of my brother, Rev. J. W. Hines, of the Genesee Conference. Three miles brought us to the pleasant village of Wyoming, where for two years past, I had exercised pastoral charge. We halted here but for a moment, and taking a hasty leave of the friends we met, resumed our route, and arrived at Warsaw, my brother's charge, at 3 o'clock p.m. Here we were to spend the Sabbath. Our people at this place are engaged in the erection of a fine church, and consequently now worship in the Baptist edifice. On Sabbath morning I endeavored to preach to the people, from, "Searching what, or what manner of time, the Spirit of Christ which was in them did signify, when it testified beforehand of the sufferings of Christ and the glory that should follow." In the afternoon, Rev. Bro. Eddy, the Congregational clergyman, being absent, I yielded to an urgent solicitation, and preached to his large and interesting congregation. Thus passed away the last Sabbath that for the present we are to spend with our friends in Western New York. But we shall find God's Sabbath to observe wherever we go, and I trust be disposed to preach Christ's Gospel upon it.[13]

Celinda

Sunday, March 6—Receive a visit from cousins Lydia and Sylvester Flansburg.[14]

Monday, March 7—W...

Harvey

Monday, March 7th.—Early in the morning we bade adieu to brother and family, and repaired to the cars on the Buffalo and New York Rail Road, and were soon rapidly whirling away towards the former city. Before 10 o'clock p.m. we met at the depot in that city, my brother, Rev. G. Hines, who was to be our company to Oregon. We had accepted an invitation from Mr. and Mrs. Alexander Miller[15] to make their home our home during our stay here, and accordingly repaired to their mansion, and were greeted with generous hospitality. After sharing the same until the morning of Tuesday we seated ourselves in the carriage, and soon found ourselves at the depot of the Buffalo and Cincinnati rail-road. Here we met Rev. Bros. Wilbur, Stiles, and Roberts,[16] stationed preachers in Buffalo, and received their parting benedictions.[17]

Celinda

Tuesday, March 8—Uncle James takes us to Holley (after parting with our friends), and we start on the 8 o'clock train for Buffalo. On arriving find Uncles Gustavus and Harvey waiting for us. Get our baggage taken to the state line road depot, where we find the rest of our company in waiting. Start…immediately…where we arrive just after dark. At Dunkirk we met a Mr. Force directly from Oregon. Speaks very favorably of our going the overland route. He is going to drive sheep to Oregon this spring. Our route from Buffalo to Dunkirk is very pleasant & we have occasional view of the lake. Erie, Pa. is a very pretty place…Clea…

Notice that Celinda makes only a parenthetical reference to "parting with our friends." In this context, "friends" included at least the extended family. To capture the poignancy that must have attended this farewell scene, we cite Gustavus's description of his parting with family fourteen years earlier when he left for Oregon on his first trip in 1839.

Having a large circle of friends in this place [Hastings], and it being quite probable that after this visit they would see my face no more on this side [of] death, we continued with them for two weeks, receiving their tokens of friendship, and preaching to congregations in various places.

On Monday the third day of June, we took leave of my beloved Parents, having the evening previous received their benedictions. The remarks of my Mother on the occasion of our parting were not only characteristic of the true state of her mind, but were remarkably affecting to all present. Said she, "We not only expected to have enjoyed your society from time to time, but as our heads are silvering over with age, and as we shall soon be unable to engage in the active concerns of life, we fondly hoped that you would have been the support of our declining years. But as you have been called by one who has a higher claim upon you than we possibly can have, we will cheerfully acquiesce in the dispensation, and bid you go. May the God of peace be with you."[18]

How much emotion was Betsey Hines bravely shielding with these words? Here is her later letter to Gustavus and his wife Lydia in September 1839, while the missionary party were still awaiting departure of their ship from New York City:

Hastings Sept. 8, 1839

My dear and ever beloved children i now sit down with a heart full of the deepest anxiety to try to rite a few lines to you doubtless for the last time that i ever shall be privileged the blessed opportunity. but i fear i cannot compose my mind so as to convey anything that will be worth your perusal.

i have undergone some very close trials since you left here on account of your arduous undertaking and have felt sometimes as tho i could not have it so. at other times i have felt perfectly resined to the will of God and i feel now while i rite with brim full eyes that it is the will of God that you should go and that your motives are pure and i bles the na[me] of the Lord i feel as much of a reconciled mind as i do. and i hope and it is my continual prayer that you will conduct you[rself] with the rest of the mishinary family safely to orragon and that your labours may be blest to the advancement of Christ's kingdom. this is the sincere prayer of mother.

we recieved your mishinary box very thankfully. Mallissa felt some-what grieved that her name was not rote in some one of the books, but with your consent i shall give her my hymn book as i have one that Lydia gave me that will last me while i live. farewell, Betsey Hines[19]

How much more difficult must it have been for the now older mother to bid farewell to not just one, but three sons (and later in the spring, still another) and their families in 1853!

A third group, the Bryant family, of Wyoming County, N.Y., were also headed west. Charles Bryant was a distant cousin of Lydia Bryant Hines, Gustavus' wife. Prior to departure the Bryants had made arrange-ments to meet with the Hines party in Kansas City and join them for the journey on the Overland Trail. Little Alta Bryant was three years old in 1853, and years later recalled the trip for her daughters, from whose notes the following extract is taken.

Alta Bryant

[I recall] the old homes, Grandpa Bryant's home and Grandpa Fay's home, and the house father built to go to housekeeping in, 30 miles from North Java.[20] I was born in Grandpa Bryant's home. Pa didn't get the house done in time.

Early in March, Pa's brother, Joseph, and Amos Fay, Ma's brother, took freight, provisions & belongings—trunks, to Buffalo. Carriage was brought back just for Uncle Am & Uncle Joseph to take us to Buffalo, 30 miles. Grandpa Bryant wanted to keep me, but I said "Don't cry Cap home tomorrow."

Went to Buffalo, stayed all night, went on boat (Lake Erie) to Toledo —went to Michigan City and took boat across Lake Michigan to Fort Dearborn (now Chicago).[21] Took train to Peoria, went down the Illinois and Ohio [should have said Mississippi] rivers to St. Louis. Changed boats and went to West Port (Kansas City) on the Missouri river—others of party waited at West Port till "Pa" got there.

---

[1] Gustavus Hines, "Account of last days in the East, 1839," the current editor's transcription of a handwritten manuscript, at the Oregon Historical Society.

[2] The obituary for James Robert Robinson (1836-1916), eldest son of Samuel and Malissa Hines Robinson, states that the family moved to Monroe County, N.Y., near Brockport, in the winter of 1852-3, and then in September of 1853 to Eaton County, Michigan. *Grand Ledge Independent,* December, 1916. In 1860 Malissa's mother Betsey lived with Malissa's family, her father James having died in 1859. 1860 U.S. Census, Eaton County, Michigan; image copy at www.ancestry.com; accessed April 9, 2007. James and Betsey are buried in Delta Center Cemetery, Eaton County; it is assumed that they moved to Michigan with Malissa and family in 1853. James R. Hines and family moved to Eaton County in 1856.

[3] In 1853 there was no rail service from the Hastings vicinity to Syracuse (see map), so they must have traveled by horse-drawn vehicle. And since the distance from Hastings to Syracuse is about twenty miles, the "dinner" must have been an early meal in order for them to have reached Syracuse by dark.

[4] In the 1850 Syracuse census, there is but one Cuddebeck/Cuddeback family listed, that of Joshua C. and Lovina Cuddeback. 1850 U.S Census, Syracuse Ward 3, Onondaga County, N.Y.; image copy at www.ancestry.com; accessed June 9, 2007. Perhaps this is where Celinda and family stayed.

[5] For Hines relatives, see the James Hines and Betsey Hines Family Tree on pages 410-411.

[6] J. Bennett is probably a relative of Celinda's step-mother, Eliza (Bennett) Roth Hines.

[7] Harvey's wife Elizabeth's family, the Graves, lived near Wyoming, N.Y.

[8] It is clear from Celinda's entry of March 31 that some of the "things" boxed were their disassembled wagons. Household goods not needed for the trip, however, were shipped on the ocean, according to Harvey's comment in Chapter 17.

[9] An Internet posting may shed some light on who these Havens might have been. "I am looking for info on James Debbs Havens, Sr. He was married to Elizabeth Bennet, who was born 4/19/1796...Their son, James Debbs Havens, Jr. was born 6/6/1826 in Eagle, Wyoming County, N.Y." Havens Family GenForum, http://genforum.genealogy.com/cgi-bin-pageload.cgi?wyoming::havens:: 187.html; accessed April 9, 2007. Obadiah's second wife (Celinda's stepmother) was Eliza (Bennett) Roth, so they may have been visiting her relatives here.

[10] Warsaw, in the town of Wyoming, was Joseph Hines' station assigned by the Genesee Annual Conference of the M. E. Church for 1852-53. "Genesee Conference Appointments," *Christian Advocate & Journal,* September 23, 1852.

[11] This may have been Clarissa, a daughter of the oldest Hines sibling, Adolphus, who would have been 7 years old in 1853. 1850 U.S. Census, 9th Ward of Rochester, New York; image copy at www.ancestry.com; accessed April 9, 2007.

[12] Lewis F. Devendorf was listed on the same census page as Obadiah Hines and family, from which we infer they were neighbors. 1850 U.S. Census, Hastings, Oswego County, N.Y.; image copy at www.ancestry.com; accessed April 9, 2007.

[13] H. K. Hines, "Incidents of Travel, En Rout to Oregon," *Northern Christian Advocate,* April 13, 1853, 58.

[14] Lydia Carley Flansburg's mother was Catharine Hines Carley, sister of Obadiah (Celinda's father), Gustavus, Joseph and Harvey. Personal communication, Mildred Clark, great-granddaughter of Lydia.

[15] Alexander Miller is listed with his family in the 1860 census, with ample evidence of his wealth: $18,000 in real estate and $6,000 in personal estate. 1860 U.S. Census, Buffalo, Erie County, N.Y.; image copy at www.ancestry.com; accessed April 10, 2007.

[16] These were Rev. A. D. Wilbur, Rev. Loren Stiles, and Rev. Benjamin T. Roberts, stationed at Swan St., Pearl St., and Niagara St. M. E. Churches, respectively. *Buffalo Christian Advocate,* Sept. 16, 1852. According to Conable, Rev. B. T. Roberts, at about this time in 1853, was one of the leaders of the maverick "Nazarite Band," who eventually were expelled from the M. E. Church, and ultimately formed the beginnings of the Free Methodist movement. F. W. Conable, *Genesee Annual Conference,* 628.

[17] H. K. Hines, "Incidents of Travel, En Rout to Oregon," *Northern Christian Advocate,* April 13, 1853, 58.

[18] Gustavus Hines, "Account of last days in the East, 1839," the current editor's transcription of a handwritten manuscript, at the Oregon Historical Society.

[19] Betsey Hines, letter to Gustavus and Lydia Hines (September, 1839), the current editor's transcription of the handwritten original at the Oregon Historical Society.

[20] The 1850 census lists Charles Bryant, 28; Mary, 21; Alta, 8/12. 1850 U.S. Census, Town of Java, Wyoming County, N.Y. (recorded 14 Aug 1850); image copy at www.ancestry.com; accessed April 10, 2007.

[21] Actually, Chicago was incorporated as a city in 1837, but the "Fort Dearborn" name evidently lingered. "A City of Chicago Timeline," About.com, http://chicago.about.com/cs/history/a/hicago_timeline.htm; accessed April 10, 2007.

4

March 8–24, 1853: Gathering in Kanzas

> *Thoughtfully I gazed, with tearful eye, upon the*
> *minarets of the city of Buffalo, until they were lost in the*
> *receding distance. Shall I see them again?...When?[1]*
> —Harvey K. Hines, March 8, 1855, reminiscing in Oregon

On Thursday, March 10, 1853, the *Buffalo Christian Advocate* published the following notice.

> Rev. Gustavus Hines and his brother, Rev. H. K. Hines, left this city on Tuesday last for Oregon. They go by the way of the Plains. We are certain that many good wishes and kind feelings will accompany them through their long and perilous journey.[2]

So it was on March 8, 1853, that the Hines families departed Buffalo, New York, to begin their cross-continent trip. For the first leg of their trip, to Kansas City, Missouri, the party included the following eleven people.

Obadiah Hines, age 47, was accompanied by his second wife, Eliza Bennett Roth Hines, 50, and his two children from his first marriage,[3] Celinda Hines, 25, and Gustavus Hines, 14.

Accompanying the second Hines brother, Gustavus, 43, was his wife, Lydia Bryant Hines, 42, her younger sister, Julia Bryant, 17, and the daughter of the late Rev. Jason Lee, Lucy Anna Maria Lee, 11.

The third brother, Harvey K. Hines, 24, was accompanied by his second wife, Elizabeth Graves Hines, 23, and her younger sister, Martha M. Graves, 19.

The three young unmarried women, Celinda, Martha, and Julia, were near enough in age to enjoy each other's company, as will presently be seen in various of Celinda's diary entries. Celinda's Uncle Harvey, being a minister with some five years of experience, though younger than she, must nevertheless have commanded her respect. And, as she notes, both he and Gustavus were frequently preaching to one group or another throughout the trip.

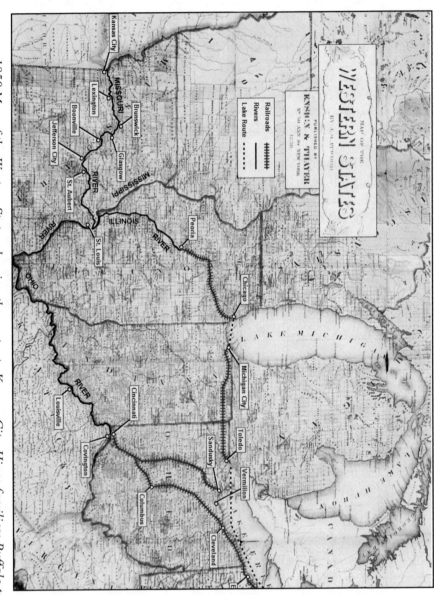

1850 Map of the Western States showing the routes to Kansas City; Hines families: Buffalo to Erie to Cincinnati to St. Louis to Kansas City; Judson family: Vermilion to Cincinnati to St. Louis to Kansas City; Bryant family: Buffalo to Toledo to Chicago to St. Louis to Kansas City.

Harvey (Reminiscing in 1884)

On the 8th day of March, 1853, the most of the company whose fortunes were to be carried so long and so far in an "Emigrant Wagon" left the city of Buffalo, N.Y., by way of the Lake Shore rail road,[4] bound for Oregon. Their route for the first 1,800 miles was by rail to Cincinnati, thence by boat down the Ohio and up the Mississippi to St. Louis, thence by another steamboat up the Missouri to Kansas Landing, now Kansas City, where the outfit for the wagon ride of 2,000 miles was completed.[5]

Thus Harvey, thirty-one years later in 1884, makes short shrift of the first half of the trip. He does go on to describe "one incident [that] may justify a moment's detention," and we will get to that shortly. In the meantime, we will follow day-to-day activities as covered by Celinda in her diary and by both Harvey and Gustavus in letters they wrote to the editor of the *Northern Christian Advocate*, Rev. William Hosmer. We begin with an excerpt from one of the letters from Gustavus.

Gustavus

Grand Prairie, near Shawnee Mission,
May 1, 1853.

Br. Hosmer:—I intended before this to have furnished you somewhat ample notes of our journey from Genesee to these distant frontiers, but the great press of business and cares upon me, have prevented my so doing. And at this time I shall only be able to give a brief outline. We left Buffalo on the morning of the 8th of March, in cars crowded to their utmost capacity, so that some of our company, which consisted of eleven persons, were obliged to stand up the entire way to Cleveland, at which place we arrived at 8 o'clock in the evening. At nine we were on our way to Cincinnati, where we "brought up" at eight on the morning of the ninth. We went immediately from the cars to the steamboat Hamburg, which was up from St. Louis, and secured our passage.[6]

Harvey (writing from the Missouri River in 1853)

The incidents of rail-road traveling are so common-place, and the scenery along the routes so imperceptible, that it would be useless to follow our tracks in this narrative. Suffice it, that on Wednesday at 10 o'clock a.m. we found ourselves, for the first time in our life, in sight of the Ohio River, and soon after entered the city of Cincinnati, one of the two great marts of commerce in the West. The city from the rail-road presents quite a forbidding aspect, nor is one's impressions of its order and beauty improved in passing from the cars to the steamboat landing, along the low damp streets, and crowded and bustling levee, yet one is impressed with its business importance. The levee is a broad open space, sweeping down from the street which bounds its top to the river at the bottom, where lay the steamboats, bound to all places on the Ohio, Mississippi, or Missouri rivers. It is literally crowded with all kinds of vehicles for the transportation of merchandize and passengers to and from the boats, and from early in the morning until late at night presents a scene of great and constantly varying interest. Passing up from the levee, you go up a considerable ascent, and are then on what appears to have been a bench of table land, a half mile or more in width, bounded on the north by an abrupt hill some hundreds of yards high. From this summit, Cincinnati, with the adjacent cities of Newport and Covington in Kentucky, and a large extent of country is before you; but the atmosphere is so loaded with smoke of coal, of which vast quantities are used in the city, as to obscure and almost destroy the view. Yet with this smoky veil over the city, Cincinnati is certainly an interesting, if not a beautiful city. By the number of blacks seen here, one is advertised that he is near the territory of slavery.—On some streets, quite one-fourth you meet are of some shade of African blood. Having satisfied our curiosity as far as we could expect to do in Cincinnati, Bro. G. and myself stepped upon a ferry boat, to pass over to Kentucky. At the shore we paid a trifling charge, and entered for the first time the dominion of slavery, in the city of Covington, Ky.—This place contains about 15,000 inhabitants, but seems to possess none of the enterprise observable on the other side of the river. The pulse of life, and noble aspirations, and high and man-like energy have been stagnated by slavery's poison touch, and will never thrill again until the decree goes forth from the high places of governmental rule, "break every yoke, and let the *oppressed* go free."[7] In Church, in State, in the wide world, slavery "is evil, only evil, and that continually."[8] But here I will close this hasty sketch. It has been written with my paper lying upon my knee, on board the steamer Delaware.[9]

Celinda

Wednesday, March 9—After having rode all night in the cars which are very crowded so much so that we have to stand part of the time we find ourselves at daylight starting from Columbus. The route from here to Cincinnati is delightful.[10] Arrived in Cincinnati about 10 AM. Stopped in the depot until they procured a boat…in fair…Majestic, Ohio, which I now see for the first time…The gentlemen have procured a boat to which we all hasten. On arriving we find it to be the Steamboat Hamburg, a very nice boat. The Captain appears very pleasant. We after dinner go out in the city (Julia,

Martha and myself), which is notwithstanding the smoke of burning coal …
We return in time for supper which is very good. There are now many
passengers but we have a very pleasant Stateroom. Julia, Martha and myself
occupy one room. It costs $75 to take us all to St. Louis. The Licking River
comes in at Covington, opposite Cincinnati.

      Thursday, March 10—After breakfast we go on deck and I count
…but could not count the steamboats but think there are twenty. There are
on the wharf any quantity of barrels, boxes and merchandise. It is the most
business place I was ever in. After dinner we all go out in the city, have a
very nice walk. Mother gets some tired as she was very seasick ["last night
before last" all crossed out] yesterday morning. We pass through a very
pleasant part…return to pass another night on the boat.

Gustavus

      At five of the 11th, we were on our way down the far famed Ohio, a
river beautiful in name and nature, and of vast importance to the states whose
borders are marked by its crystal waters. Walking one evening on the deck of
the boat, I approached a respectable looking colored man, and asked him if
he had ever been a slave. He replied, "I have been a slave all the days of my
life." Are you now a slave? "Yes, but I have papers which will make me free
on certain conditions." What are those conditions? "I am to go to California
and dig gold for three years to purchase myself. I also have a wife and three
children, and when I succeed in purchasing myself, I intend, by the help of
God, to purchase my family." I found this man, who is a member of the M. E.
Church, South, to be much more of a man, and vastly better qualified for
freedom than was the drunken wretch with a white face, who claimed to be
his master.[11]

Harvey

      Friday, March 11th, 1853.—A little before dark, the noble steamer
Hamburg, on which we had taken passenger for St. Louis, left her position at
the foot of the levee, and turned her bow down the Ohio. The evening was
cold and cloudy, an immense drapery of smoke shrouded Cincinnati, and
rendered it impossible for us to enjoy the hour of our departure. We arranged
our matters in our state-room, and early in the evening retired to rest. We
thought then of home and friends, or associations sundered, and sighed—yet
rejoiced that we were in our Master's business.[12]

Celinda

      Friday, March 11—Awake and find all confusion on the boat as usual pass the time in looking about and making observations on the passengers until 3 o'clock PM., when we start for St. Louis. Some of our passengers are very agreeable, but there are all together too many and too many children.

Harvey

Saturday, March 12.—On arising this morning, we found ourselves at the Levee of the city of Louisville, Ky. This is considered as the fourth city in the west. We did not find it possible to go into the city, as the boat stopped but a little time; but it presented, along the river, quite a business like appearance. On leaving the city we ran the rapids known as the "Falls of the Ohio."[13] The scene was exciting enough, and perhaps dangerous enough, but I like something occasionally stirring enough to break the monotony of life, and was glad of the privilege of going over the falls rather than running through the stupid canal dug around them.[14] We floated to-day with Ky. on the south, and Ohio and Indiana on the north, and while viewing the scenery on either hand, appreciated something of the feeling which dictated for this stream the name "Ohio, the beautiful river."[15]

Celinda

Saturday, March 12—All confusion as usual about 500 passenger berths, strewn all over the floor. Arrive this morning at Louisburg, Ky.[16] Find it a very nice place, go ashore. Regret very much that we passed North Bend in the night, as a General Harrison's residence and tomb are in full view of the river. At Louisburg we pass…[the falls] of the Ohio which is rather exciting. Get acquainted with some of the passengers find them (some) very agreeable. Am particularly interested in a lady from Virginia, which much resembles my mother and her family. A young gent from Mass. is particularly attentive to us, lends us some papers. People notice his partiality and we have…at his expense….Evening passes very pleasantly. We have during the day passed by many little villages but there is a marked difference between the country here and N.Y., and also a great difference between the people and houses. The contrast is as great as between N.Y. and Canada.

Harvey

Sunday, March 13th.—At about 11 o'clock, by the agency of some of the passengers, consent was obtained from the captain, to hold religious service on board; and brother G. preached to the passengers from, "Searching what or what manner of time the Spirit of Christ which was in them did signify, when it testified beforehand, the sufferings of Christ and the glory that should follow."[17] Good attention was given to the Word of Life. In the evening I preached from, "Seek those things which are above." It is pleasant to hope that bread thus literally cast upon the waters, shall be gathered again after many days.[18]

Celinda

Sunday, March 13—Very pleasant here…with the passengers. Am particularly interested in a negress who has a little babe. She is a slave. Her master is with her. He is a very pretty appearing man very kind to her. They are from Virginia. She does not wish her liberty. This morning we have an introduction to Dr. Burwell, who is going to California driving sheep. He…Virginia and attends the lady with whom I was so much interested. She tells me she has been a widow 4 years, has two children is going to visit a brother in Missouri. The Dr. seems very attentive to Julia. He is very fluent in conversation. Uncle Gustavus preaches this morning. All very attentive. I become somewhat acquainted with…from Illinois, returning from the Eclectic Medical college at Cincinnati. He is a graduate of the Ohio Medical college— appears very agreeable. He informs me that Gen. Lane, Ex Gov. of Oregon is at St. Jose [St. Joseph?], or rather, his family are, waiting to return to Oregon this spring. He is well acquainted with the rout[e] and it would be very fortunate if we could get in company with him. Uncle Harvey preaches this evening all seem very attentive especially Dr. B. Aunt Elizabeth is sick and we exchange rooms with her as hers is by the wheels. Dr. B. lends us a book to read and the other Dr. lends me one, a medical journal. I am also reading The…which a lady from St. Louis has lent me.

Harvey

Monday, March 14th.—Just before daylight this morning, our boat passed from the waters of the Ohio to the Mississippi, and turned her bow upstream.—The junction of these two rivers is about 620 miles below Cincinnati, and 80 below St. Louis. One is quite disappointed when entering the river called the "father of waters." It has not that majestic appearance here, one may have been led to expect. No wider than the Ohio, muddy and boiling, it presents to the voyager a prospect of unpleasant navigation, which is not greatly decreased by the immense number of snags lifting their black heads above the water in various places. So many of them appear in one place, and so many boats have been destroyed by them, that that portion of the river is known as "the grave yard." On this river we sailed all day, and retired to rest, hoping to be in St. Louis in the morning.[19]

Celinda

Monday, March 14—Awake to find ourselves on the Father of Rivers, "Mississippi". Have just been called to see a high bluff which some resembles Niagara, but it is not so high, neither, so majestic. We saw some turkey buzzards for the first time. About 11 o'clock called to see some rock islands, the most beautiful to be imagined. One of a circular form composed of solid rock, perpendicular all around, and I should think 200 feet in height. While on the mainland near are two pillars very small in circumference, but equally as high as the islands, looking like pillars of solid masonry, truly wonderful to behold. This is in Missouri, and I no sooner retire to write than I am asked to go the other side of the boat to view a similar scene in Illinois. Have been transcribing Katy Darling[20] from a book of Miss Gilbreath's. Pass the evening very pleasantly in singing songs and hymns. Meet a gentleman from St. Lawrence….in every state of the Union

Gustavus

Three days of beautiful sailing brought us into the Mississippi, "the father of rivers;" and the next day we arrived in safety at St. Louis. We went immediately from the Hamburg to the Robert Campbell, that was up for the Missouri river. Before leaving, we made the acquaintance of our brethren, Houts, Denison, and Trotter. The latter is the editor of the "Central Christian Advocate."[21]

Gustavus and Harvey

Having arrived at St. Louis on our way to Oregon, we would say to those designing to join us in our journey: our rendexvous will be Kansas [City], Missouri; lying twelve miles above Fort Independence and four miles below Weston, immediately on the border of the great plain stretching from this point nearly to the Rocky Mountains. Probably the best route by which to reach this point is, by railroad from Buffalo to Cincinnatti, thence by steamboat to St. Louis, and thence also by steamboat to Kansas on the Missouri river. We wish to be ready to leave Kansas, by the fifteenth of April. No time is to be lost, brethren. —Prospects are encouraging, if you are here in *time*. If you bring your wagons, give them a start immediately; they should have at least a week's precedence of you from Buffalo. Direct them to Cincinnati, then take them on the same boat with you and then bring them on. Box the entire wagon, and it will come much cheaper. Give yourselves two weeks from Buffalo to Kansas.[22]

In the *Missouri Republican* of March 16, 1853, for the Port of St.

Louis arrivals (of the preceding 24 hours, presumably) is listed "Steamer Hamburgh, Malin, Cincinnati,"[23] thus signaling the Hines' March 15 arrival at St. Louis.

Harvey

Tuesday, March 15.—At about eight o'clock this morning, we came in sight of St. Louis, the great city of the West. A dense cloud of smoke hangs over the place, so that with the exception of the row of buildings bordering the Levee, none of the city can be seen from our boat. But turning our eyes from what little could be seen from the city, we found it necessary to give attention to preparations for embarking. We had enjoyed a pleasant trip down the Ohio, and up the Mississippi; had been treated by the officers and crew of the Hamburg courteously, and felt reluctant to exchange our position here, for a doubtful one upon another boat. But every thing arranged, we left the boat, and secured passage on the Robert Campbell, to Kansas, Mo., with the exception of myself, it having been decided that I should remain in St. Louis and purchase our outfit for the plains. This being arranged, I went out to seek an acquaintance, Rev. C. J. Houts, Presiding Elder of the St. Louis district of Missouri Conference. On inquiring, I was directed to the house of Rev. L. B. Dennis, pastor of the Ebenezer Chapel, of *our* Church. Here I met Br. Houts,[24] and from both these brethren received a real Methodist preacher's welcome. 'Tis grateful to meet *brethren* in a land of strangers. And you know, Br. Hosmer, as far as *Methodist* preachers are concerned, "we *be* brethren." I am to stop with Br. Dennis, during my stay in the city. In the evening I met Rev. W. D. R. Trotter,[25] editor of the Central Christian Advocate, a Methodist paper recently established in St. Louis, who reported some prosperity, and fair prospects for the enterprise. It ought to succeed, and in such hands as those to which it has been committed, there can be no such thing as a failure. Here, as I shall not have room to conclude what I wish to say about St. Louis, I will tie up this budget of incidents, and forward it to the loved and much missed Northern, and through it to all my friends.[26]

Celinda

Tuesday, March 15—Arrive in St. Louis soon after day break. All confusion on board. Feel rather disconsolate on parting from those with whom we had formed an acquaintance on the Hamburg, especially Mrs. Grea, Mr. and Mrs. Higgins, Miss Elizabeth and others. Take passage on the Robt. Campbell for Independence.[27] Find the boat very nice…large as the Hamburg. Some on board who are bound for Oregon. In the P.M. take a walk up town very much pleased with the city. Uncle Harvey concludes to stay here and buy provisions and stores for our journey, and also be in readiness if our boxes should arrive, be ready to send them to us. In the evening take another turn about the city. Am more than ever charmed with the city and with the superb appearance of everything together with the rich and tasty apparel of the ladies we saw in the street. Go with Uncle Harvey to the preacher's, who has kindly offered to take him into his family. Returned to the boat.

Harvey

In my last communication, I spoke of designing to say more about St. Louis, but for want of time, must let it be only a desire, at the present, and proceed with my journalizing.

Wednesday, February [He means March!] 16th.—On going to the wharf this morning, I found that the "Robert Campbell,"[28] on which our party was embarked, had not left her moorings, and going on board, I found Mrs. Hines sick. In consequence of this, it appeared proper that we should so far change our arrangements as to allow me to go up the river with her, while brother O[badiah] should stop at St. Louis in my stead. Consequently, we took leave of this great center of commerce in the west, deeply impressed with the immense resources of this portion of our great country. We had before us from this point, 444 miles of travel by the Mississippi and Missouri rivers, to Kansas, the most westerly town in Missouri, and within one and a half miles of the territory of the Wyandotts.—Our boat left her position at 4 o'clock p.m., and turned her bow up the majestic Mississippi.[29] The evening was exceedingly beautiful, and the scenery along the river sufficiently interesting to keep us upon deck until some friendly passengers announced to us that we were likely to lose our tea, unless we were soon at our places, which speedily brought us down. Supper over, we again went on deck. At about 8 o'clock we were at the point where the two mightiest rivers of this land of mighty rivers whelm our waters.—The Mississippi sweeping down from the north, and the Missouri rolling in from the west, lay, as they glistened in the moonlight, unrippled by a breeze, like a fringing of silver, skirting the low and dusky wilderness which stretched far away on either bank. We entered the mightier stream, Missouri, and were headed directly towards the Rocky Mountains, and our Oregon home.[30]

Celinda

Wednesday, March 16—Aunt Elizabeth sick all night. Julia and I pass the morning on deck reading. As yet have made but very few acquaintances. Have spoken a few times to a Miss Finny, who is with her sister and husband, going to Oregon. Pa concludes to stay instead of Uncle Harvey on account of Aunt Elizabeth's sickness. At noon receive a visit from Dr. Burwell, or rather Julia did. he stayed until the boat started. We rush on deck. The scene is beautiful. Remain on deck awhile. Our passengers are mostly emigrating to Oregon or California, and I see but very few with whom I would care to cultivate an acquaintance. There is at my back a slave who has her husband and mistress on board. Her mistress is a very cross lady. There is also a criminal who has committed murder, although it is said in self-defense. And altogether I think no more motley throng can surely be seen than one can see on board a steam boat on the Ohio or Mississippi rivers. Pass the evening on deck. Scenery at the confluence of the Mississippi & Missouri enchanting. Regret very much that it is not daylight. But as it is the scenery is very nice. Pass the eve. very pleasantly.

Harvey

Thursday, 17th. —Mrs. H. was sick all night. The morning was quite pleasant, but the scenery along the river, for the most part, too uninteresting to invite us much on deck. The banks are low, and so exposed to overflow, that they are almost uncultivated, and it is quite seldom that we see human dwellings. They are sedimental deposits, rich, but miasmic.—Sycamore and Button-wood appears to be the principal timber.[31]

Celinda

Thursday, March 17[32]—Passed rather an uncomfortable night. Martha...sleep in one berth. Am sick this morning. The channel of the Missouri is very precarious. The sandbars are so changing that it is not known one day where the channel will be on the next. And the river is also filled with logs & snags which we are in danger of running onto.... The scenery along the Missouri is beautiful in some places enchanting. On one side the eye will be greeted by large plains called bottoms, while on the other perhaps rise rocks from 100 to 200 feet high. We sometimes on the sandbars see large quantities of wild ducks. Mother, Martha, Aunt Libby, Julia and myself all well.Have considerable sport at the expense of the passengers, their conversation, etc. Such expressions as "I reckon that needs a powerful heap sight of fixing."

Gustavus

On our way up the Missouri we ran afoul of a snag, and stove a hole in the bottom of the boat, and if we had been in deep water we should have gone down. As it was, we had four feet of water in the hold in a few moments, but the bow of the boat was on shore, and the stern was on the snag, and she could not sink deeper. However, we were all put ashore, in the forest, about 150 miles above St. Louis, with the not very comforting assurance from Capt. Edes,[33] that it was all he could do for us. We felt a little like rebellion, but there was no remedy, and we submitted coolly to our misfortunes. Here we camped, and remained two days, when another boat came along, and took us on board, and three days more brought us to Kansas, the place we had fixed upon at which to make our preparations for our journey across the plains.[34]

Harvey

Friday, 18ᵗʰ.—This morning at about 6 o'clock, I was awakened from a troubled sleep, by Mrs. H., who informed me that the boat had snagged and was sinking. I cautioned her to be collected, and then hurriedly dressing, went out to ascertain the truth of the report. I found the passengers in great confusion, and rapidly going on shore, which was easily done, as the boat rested her bow on the land. Her hold was already full of water, and though there was cause for fear, after consultation we decided to remain on board, until all should be known. At length, it was decided that the cargo should be landed, the passengers put off, and the boat return to St. Louis, for repairs. As it would take nearly two days to unship the cargo, the captain allowed us to remain on board during the day and the next night.[35]

Celinda

Friday, March 18—Awoke this morning by the cry, "The boat is sinking. There is a hole in the boat as large as a man's head. Give us your blankets to stop the leakage." Find that the boat was snagged, but is near the shore on the north bank of the Missouri. No particular danger. Deck passengers and some of those in the cabin rush in affright to the shore. Ladies remain very quiet. One says she never knew of the circumstance of a white horse, a red one and a preacher being on board a steamboat without some accident taking place. Aunt Elizabeth sick yet…us off the snag, breaks one of shafts and disables the boat so that we must all leave.

Very fortunately we are near inhabitants at a place call St. Auburt. People are seeking board and lodging wherever they can be found. The captain says we may remain on the boat until tomorrow morning, when they will start back for St. Louis. We avail ourselves of the opportunity. Many are camping on the shore. Some Germans are singing merrily on the shore. Evening very pleasant. Many are dissatisfied with the captain. He charges an exorbitant price for those who wish to pay for the distance they have come and run the risk of procuring another boat, but if we remain here until he returns he will take us on as he agreed to. Says he shall return on Monday, but we think it is impossible.

Harvey

Saturday, 19th.—Went on shore this morning with all our party and effects, and on looking about us, found about 250 passengers landed in the woods, without possible entertainment near, for one-fifth the number. But all set about making ourselves as comfortable as possible. Having with us some eighteen blankets, we soon had a small tent erected, in which the ladies could shade themselves from the sun, which shone as in July, in New York. The ladies began to knit or sew, and brother G. and myself strolled off into the pathless wilderness, concluding to enjoy this strange interlude in the harmony of life. We succeeded in obtaining some food, and at night a place in a house nearby, for the ladies to sleep, while G. and myself, after I had preached to the people, rolled ourselves in our blankets, and lay down upon the ground to sleep, thanking God that we were not sunk to the bottom of the river.[36]

Celinda

Saturday, March 19—Waiters awake us, saying we must leave immediately, for they are going to start. Dress as soon as possible. Have hardly time to take off our things before the planks are being hauled up, although it is nothing but pretense for fear we intended to stay till after breakfast. We get our things out as best we can. Uncle Harvey, Aunt Elizabeth & Martha have gone to seek themselves lodgings. Our things are all piled up on shore. Uncle H returns. Has got a place. He goes back to see if we can have breakfast there. Returns with the welcome news that we can. We go and for the first time are entertained at a planter's house in Missouri, and also the first time we have ever been in a slaveholder's house.

We find the family to consist of a Mr. Robison and two daughters, one of them married to a man by the name of Towner the gentlemen are merchants. They have one maid servant 17 years old, who is about to marry. Her master expects to buy her husband. They have…Negro men. The house is very prettily situated. It is built mostly of logs and is the best house in the village of St. Aubert.[37] The village is built in a forest of Cotton-wood, elm & sycamore trees, which are many of them encircled by grape vines and it would, were it not for logs and rubbish, be a delightful place, but there is danger of overflowing, which retards the growth.…It is in Caliway Co. 16 miles from Jefferson city. We have been more disappointed in coming up the Missouri, as we had expected the banks to be studded with villages & farmers' residences, but we were mistaken, for the banks of the Missouri as far as we have come are high, and precipitous rocks on one side and on the other low bottoms covered with primeval forests and occasionally, but few and far between, is the sight relieved by a settlement or a single dwelling.

Another striking feature of this country is that whenever we come to a settlement we invariably see more or less negroes. The manner, customs & conversation of the inhabitants here are very different from what they are in N.Y. I wish some of our friends in N.Y. could look in at our boarding place, especially at meals, and yet we consider ourselves very fortunate in securing the best place in St. Aubert. The house is a two-story log one, with one room on the ground and one above, with a back kitchen where Mary does the work. The rooms are both carpeted with ingrain carpeting. There are two beds above & one below. They have also a piano on which the oldest sister plays. The beds are in the French style as is also….There are two divans below & one sofa above. The people appear anxious to do everything for our comfort. After breakfasting we return to our baggage and sit by it while the men go hunting. They are gone till afternoon. On their return we go to dinner, which is composed of a great variety, all very different from a dinner in N.Y. After dinner the men employ themselves in constructing a tent out of fifteen blankets, which were placed in uncle's care by a Mr. Grey [William H. Gray],[38] whom we met at St. Louis. He is directly from Oregon and is going to return this spring with some friends and drive a drove of cattle. Uncle Harvey preaches in the evening. Very attentive and nice. The females return to the house while the men remain in the tent to watch our baggage and to be on hand if a boat should come. Many are going to sleep in the camp.

Harvey

Sunday, 20ᵗʰ.—To-day is the holy Sabbath. I doubt if its light ever shone upon a stranger scene than is here displayed, when the multitude rises up from its ground-bed to greet the morning. The first sound we hear is the voice of a Methodist, (I know he is) singing that good old Methodist hymn:–

"He dies, the friend of sinners dies,"[39]

and the voice of the multitude is heard in all the strains, and all the languages. At about 11 o'clock, brother G. preached from, "They seek a better country." The day passed quietly, and at dark we were gladdened by the sight of a steam-boat coming up the river.—She proved to be the Delaware,[40] and though already crowded, we obtained passage upon her to Kansas.—We could only obtain rooms for the ladies, and as the cabin floor was entirely filled, G. and I rolled our blankets around us and slept on the deck.[41]

Celinda

Sunday, March 20—Weather calm and pleasant, not so uncomfortably warm as yesterday. Nearly all of us sick or unwell. It rained last night and the men had to move the baggage into an old blacksmith shop about midnight. Uncle Gustavus preaches this morning, but being somewhat ill I remained...Lucy Anna at the blacksmith shop to watch our things. They return from meeting and we go to the house dinner nearly ready. After dinner Martha and myself being indisposed go to bed. The rest go and take a walk. Awoke somewhat refreshed. Weather so delightful. Just before sitting down to tea Gustavus [her younger brother][42] came running in saying there is a boat coming. Mr. Towner goes to see while we remain to secure our supper. He returns saying the boat is some four miles distant. Those who have supped go to the landing to remove the baggage near the shore. We go down to the shore. They have secured passage, but can have no promise of a stateroom. Suppose we will have to remain on deck. We go on board, Uncle Gustavus carrying most of the trunks. We sit down on deck as best we can. Many gentlemen interest themselves in our behalf, and succeed in getting us a stateroom while the men construct a bed outside.

And now Harvey's 1884 reminiscent account of hitting the snag. We note, relying on the greater credibility of the details in the three contemporaneous accounts above, that Harvey's version below, in which he places them on the *Delaware* immediately out of St. Louis, and then on an unnamed steamboat after the accident contradicts his own account above, and is undoubtedly in error. This is further substantiated by the following news item of March 20, 1853.

Accident.—The steamer Wenona, down from the Missouri yesterday afternoon, reports having passed the Robert Campbell lying to at St. Aubert, discharging her freight. She had encountered a snag Thursday night which caused a leak which resulted in her shipping four feet water before it was discovered. Nearly all her freight was much damaged. She had broken her doctor in the endeavor to pump the water out of her hold.[43]

It seems clear that they departed St. Louis on the *Robert Campbell*, and finished their trip on the *Delaware*.

Harvey

There was little on that part of the journey from Buffalo to Kansas that was outside of the ordinary incidents of such a voyage. One incident may justify a moment's detention. We had left St. Louis on the steamer, Delaware expecting to reach Kansas Landing in about four days, but just toward morning of the second day out our steamer "snagged" at a "landing" on the north side of the river, and sunk until her bow rested on the bottom of the river, the stern remaining on the "snag." Three or four hundred passengers; emigrants mostly; with all their baggage, were incontinently tumbled on the shore among the cottonwood trees, without shelter, and mostly with very little food. There was one small log cabin on the bank of the river, but it afforded neither shelter nor food. Here we were compelled to remain from Wednesday [should be Friday] morning to Sunday night, extemporizing a shelter with a few blankets and bushes, and obtaining a little bacon and hominy from the scanty store of a "settler" a mile away from the river. The weather was delightful, so that our discomforts were not great, though we were glad just at dusk of Sabbath evening when the light of a steamboat swung into sight on the river a few miles below, the first that had appeared bound up since we were stranded. Before the boat reached the landing we had all our "truck" lying just at the water's edge, and when the gangplank was run ashore, without asking anybody's consent, we put them on the fore deck ourselves, and then made our own way on board the already crowded boat. Nearly all who were with us on the shore went aboard to negotiate, and the result was that the captain refused to admit any, as his boat was already crowded almost to suffocation, and the boat moved off and left them.

In an hour or two we went to the captain's office, told him who we were and how we came on board. He took it pleasantly, telling us however that he would not have admitted us if we had applied for passage, but saying that we would have to take care of ourselves as best we could. That we were willing to do. Some gentlemen gave up their places on the cabin floor for the cots of the seven ladies, and G[ustavus] H[ines] and myself spread a blanket on the outer deck, and thus we rested the three nights we were on board the boat. Each evening, by request of many of the passengers, and the consent of the captain, we held service and preached a sermon. It was somewhat unusual indeed to us to be preaching in one end of the long cabin and a dozen tables surrounded by gamblers for money and card playing for amusement at the other, but we enjoyed, nevertheless, the privilege of telling them that the ways of wisdom "are ways of pleasantness, and all her paths are peace."[44]

Harvey (back in 1853 once more)

Monday, 21st.—Soon after morning, we passed Jefferson City, the capital of Missouri. It is situated on the southern bank of the river, on an elevation rising abruptly from the shore. Like all other places along the river, it presents quite an indifferent aspect. Many of our New York villages wear a much more city-like garb. The State House is finely situated, fronting the river, and is a respectable looking edifice. We could not go ashore, as our boat stopped but a moment. At dark, we passed Booneville, on the same shore. Yielding to the solicitation of some of the passengers, I preached in the evening from John 1:14, and then again lay upon the deck to sleep.[45]

Celinda

Monday, March 21—Awake early. Feel sick, Martha sick also. Very pleasant. Think I shall like the boat very well. Name of boat is Delaware. Passengers speak well of the captain & crew.[46] Some of our friends of the Robt. Campbell are on this boat. Go to breakfast, eat very little. Soon after pass the mouth of the Osage river. Scenery very fine. Go on deck. Soon come in sight of Jefferson City. The capital is situated on a bold & prominent eminence near the river, which may be seen from a great distance. Am considerably disappointed in the appearance of the city as seen from the river. Have a very good view of the penitentiary. It is a small affair in comparison to the N.Y. prison at Auburn. And the capitol comes far below my ideas of what the capitol of Mo. should be. We stop but a few moments at Jefferson City. Pass the afternoon very pleasantly on deck. At evening arrive at Boonville, which is the largest place since St. Louis. Am well, which I have not been before in a week.

Tuesday, March 22—Very pleasant. Boat not so crowded as usual. Arrive at Glasgow soon after breakfast. The river is very serpentine. Have been much disappointed in the Ohio, Mississippi and Missouri rivers. I had expected they were clear & placid and withall much broader than they are, but I find their waters very turbid and the Missouri especially foaming & boiling similar to the foaming springs which are so common in the sandy parts of New York. Have seen since we left St. Louis thousands of wild geese and ducks. Have seen no bluffs today, consequently the shores of the river are more inhabited. Below the high rocky bluffs which invariably present themselves on one bank and the low land subject to inundation on the other, retard the progress of civilization. In the afternoon arrive at Brunswick, a town much in keeping with some I have seen in Canada. At dusk we go on deck and sing. At eve (uncle Harvey having preached last night) uncle Gustavus preaches.

Wednesday, March 23—Very pleasant but windy. Behold a prairie for the first time. Arrive at Lexington in the evening. The city is situated mostly on an eminence & but very little of it can be seen from the river. It is said to contain eight or ten thousand inhabitants & to be the most beautiful city in the state. A steamboat was blown up here last season, by which many lives were lost, fragments of bodies being strewn for many rods around & the river being one gore of blood.[47] We stopped here most of the evening, but did not go on shore, which we certainly should had we known our stay here would have been so lengthy. Passed the evening near the guard, mostly in conversation with Volney Hobson[48] & Nathan Caroll, both young men from Indiana, on their way to California. Conversation, the evils of profligacy, especially gambling.

Harvey

Thursday, 24ᵗʰ.—The weather still continues pleasant; except a slight rain at Cincinnati, we have had uninterrupted good weather, since leaving Buffalo.—Indeed, it appears that we have "stolen a march," of time, and stepped at once from February to April.—Soon after noon, we reached the landing, four miles from the city of Independence. It appears for the river, to be difficult to reach the place, and quite impracticable for passengers to stop here; yet many outfit here for the plains. At about 8 o'clock p.m., we reached the city of Kansas, and were glad to leave the boiling, muddy Missouri, and find ourselves at the point where, for the present, our journeying ceases.

Kansas is nearly seventeen hundred miles from Buffalo, by the way of Cincinnati, yet is regarded as somewhere east of the place the whole world is seeking for—"the West." Indeed it is east of the center of Uncle Sam's dominions, which is located at the point where the two main forks of the Kansas (Caw) river unite, about one hundred and forty-one miles above its mouth.

At this point I will close the communication, promising to write up before leaving for the plains, which are only five miles distant.[49]

Celinda

Thursday, March 24—Very pleasant. Gustavus [her brother] had his cap taken from under his head last night. Pass Richfield this morning. Arrive at Independence landing before noon the town is south of the river about four miles. The lost cap was in the cabin boy's berth. Write a letter to Maria Wightman.[50] We arrived at Kansas in the evening. The ladies remained on the boat until the gentlemen had removed the baggage to the shore, & then we all went to a hotel near – the Union Hotel – where we found everything very comfortable & nice.

Holden and Phoebe Goodell Judson and family, of "the little town of Vermillion, Ohio, located midway between Cleveland and Sandusky, on the shores of Lake Erie," were also on their way to the Pacific Northwest. They, too, traveled to Kansas City, and from there intended to depart on the overland route, although they had no prior plans as to which wagon train they might attach themselves. Like Celinda Hines, Phoebe kept a diary as they traveled, and many years later wrote down her reminiscences of the trip. Here begins Phoebe's account.

Phoebe

It is the oft repeated inquiry of my friends as to what induced me to bury myself more than fifty years ago in this far-off corner of the world, that has determined me to take my pen in hand at this late day.

Did I come around the Horn, cross the Isthmus, or come across the plains? Was I not afraid of the Indians, and much more they ask. So I have decided to answer them all and singly by writing a short history of our pioneer life, and to affectionately dedicate my book to the memory of the late Holden A. Judson, my dear husband, who journeyed with me for half a century in the wilderness.

This will be but a condensed narrative of events which I shall endeavor to recall out of the mists of the past, written with no attempt at literary display, containing no fiction, but simply a record of the homely, everyday incidents of a plain woman, who has now exceeded her three score years and ten, and who has roughed it in the early fifties on the extreme northwestern frontier.

Time has passed so rapidly I can scarcely realize that I have already attained the number of years allotted to mortals on earth.

The romance of frontier life beyond the confines of civilization with its varied, exciting and interesting experiences among the children of nature—both human and brute—has caused the years to fly swiftly, as on the wings of the wind.

If I am permitted to occupy the body that has served me well for so many years until this chronicle is completed, I shall be satisfied, and consider my work upon this planet finished.

Our pioneer story begins where love stories (more is the pity) frequently terminate, for Holden Allen Judson and Phoebe Newton Goodell had been joined in the holy bonds of matrimony three years before we decided to emigrate to the vast and uncultivated wilderness of Puget Sound, which at that time was a part of Oregon.

Little did I realize how much it meant when I promised the solemn, but kindly faced, minister in the presence of a large assembly of friends, to obey, as well as to love, the one whom I had chosen for a partner through life, for the thought of becoming a pioneer's wife had never entered my mind; but it is not surprising that a girl of only seventeen summers, romantically inclined, should have chosen from among her suitors one possessing a spirit of adventure.

Mr. Judson was five years my senior. Seldom were two more

congenially mated to travel the rough voyage of life. Both were endowed with vigorous health, fired with ambition and a love of nature.

Our childhood days were spent together in the little town of Vermillion, Ohio, located midway between Cleveland and Sandusky, on the shores of Lake Erie, on whose beaches we strolled, and on whose blue waters we sailed in company, little dreaming our future lives were destined to he passed together on the far away shore of Puget Sound.

We attended the same church and the same district school. It was "Hopkins' choice," [she means "Hobson's choice"] for there was only one of each in town. These two buildings stood side by side....

The parting with my husband's parents and only sister was very affecting, as he was their only son and brother, and our little two year-old Annie their idol.

The time set for our departure was March 1st, 1853. Many dear friends gathered to see us off. The tender "good-byes" were said with brave cheers in the voices, but many tears from the hearts. After we were seated in the stage that was to carry us forth on the first part of our journey into the "wide, wide world," little Annie put out her hands and asked "Fazzer," as she called her grandpapa, to take her. He begged us to leave her with them— mother and Lucretia seconding his request with tearful eyes. Her sweet young life was interwoven with theirs, and well I knew the anguish that rent their hearts at the parting with their little darling. Deeply we sympathized with them in their grief, but how could we part with our only treasure?

Amid the waving of handkerchiefs and the lingering "God bless you" the stage rolled away—and we were embarked on our long and perilous journey.

Our route lay along the lake shore road as we journeyed, and as the distance increased between our loved ones—father, mother, sister and the dear home environments, my heart grew heavy. I realized we were for the last time gazing upon the waters of beautiful Lake Erie, upon whose sandy beaches I, with my twin sister, had whiled away many, many happy hours gathering the little periwinkles and other shells, or rowing upon its placid waters; never tiring of watching the steamers and other vessels sail into the harbor, or hastening to the islands of Put In Bay for protection in time of storm.

These beautiful islands were a place of resort, and also of renown—steamers making many delightful "picnic" excursions to the place where Commodore Perry captured the British fleet, about which be sent the famous laconic message to General Harrison, "We have met the enemy, and they are ours."

My mind was occupied with many sad reflections until we reached Sandusky City, where we boarded the train for Cincinnati. 'Twas here we parted with my dear brother, William, who had accompanied us this far on our journey. From my car window I saw he was weeping, while I could scarcely refrain from sobbing aloud. He was but two years my senior, and we were both much attached to each other. He was married a few days before our departure, that we might attend his wedding, and with his young wife emigrated to this coast the following year.[51]

Riding on the train was a new experience for me—the interest and novelty of the trip served in a measure to alleviate the sadness of parting. It was before the day of fast trains, and, though owing to my inexperience, we seemed to be moving very rapidly, the trip consumed the entire day; and it was long after dusk when we reached Cincinnati. The depot was some distance from our hotel and the deafening rattle of the cab wheels over the cobble stones frightened little Annie, and she cried piteously to be carried back home.

The hotel accommodations were luxurious. As we rested in the pleasant parlor a short time before retiring to our rooms, a lady played the piano and sang that pathetic song, "The Old Folks at Home."

The sentiment of the sweet old song harmonized with my feelings and caused the tears to flow afresh, as I thought of the dear father and mother we had left in their lonely home. The music soothed Annie's fears. She sat in my lap and talked about poor "Fazzer, mozzer and Aunt Trecia," as she called them, until she fell asleep.

In the morning we boarded a steamer. I have forgotten her name, but she was a floating palace for those days, and was loaded with passengers bound for the "far west."

We steamed rapidly down the Ohio and up the Mississippi. The pleasure of this voyage would have been without alloy, but the third day little Annie was taken very ill, and for a time we were much alarmed; but with simple remedies and good nursing she recovered without the aid of a physician.

The deafening whanging and banging of the gong startled us from our slumbers in the morning, calling us to a bountifully spread table. We greatly enjoyed the luxurious meals with which we were served on these river boats.

To while away the time, many of the passengers indulged in

dancing and simple games of cards, which seemed innocent amusements; but after awhile, to my horror, I learned that others were gambling—risking their fortunes, many times beggaring their innocent families by a single throw of the dice. Although there were no bloody affrays on the boat, still I knew that gambling frequently led to murders, and the iniquity of this awful practice filled my soul with terror and I was in constant dread that the vengeance of an angry God would be visited upon us, by the blowing up, or sinking, of the boat, with all on board. My religious training had taught me fear, instead of trust. My heart was filled with thankfulness when we reached St. Louis in safety, where we remained but one day and night.

Transferring our baggage to the little steamer "Kansas," we began the ascent of the Missouri river, which we found was a very difficult and dangerous stream to navigate. Only light draft steamers were able to stem the current of its turbulent waters and make their way around the many jams and snags with which it was obstructed, and over the logs which made the little steamer bend and creak as though she was breaking in two. Our progress was slow and we were ten long days in reaching our destination, feeling greatly relieved when we disembarked at what was then called "Kansas Landing," where now stands the large and flourishing city of Kansas City.

A number of our fellow travelers, who were emigrating to California and Oregon, went on to Council Bluff to purchase their "outfit" for the journey over the plains. They urged us to go on with them, which would have pleased us well, for they were enterprising and intelligent people, with congenial qualities, well fitting them for good citizens in a new country. But we were only too glad to leave the muddy Missouri.

We had made our arrangements, before leaving home, to purchase our outfit for our journey at this place, which seems quite providential, for the news came to us here that the steamer Kansas struck a snag and sank before reaching her destination—the unfortunate emigrants losing all of their baggage.

We were thankful to get this far without accident, not knowing what lay before us. We little realized this was a pleasure trip in comparison with the journey across the plains.[52]

Alta Bryant

Went to Buffalo, stayed all night, went on boat (Lake Erie) to Toledo

—went to Michigan City and took boat across Lake Michigan to Fort Dearborn (now Chicago) [Actually, Chicago was incorporated as a city in 1837, but the "Fort Dearborn" name evidently lingered.]. Took train to Peoria, went down the Illinois and Ohio rivers to St. Louis. Changed boats and went to West Port (Kansas City) on the Missouri river—others of party waited at West Port till "Pa" got there.[53]

Departure Postscript

How emotional was the departure from New York? Some of the accounts we have seen, in their very matter-of-factness, fail to reveal much of an answer. Consider, for example, Harvey's 1853 description:

> The incidents of rail-road traveling are so common-place, and the scenery along the routes so imperceptible, that it would be useless to follow our tracks in this narrative. Suffice it, that on Wednesday at 10 o'clock a.m. we found ourselves, for the first time in our life, in sight of the Ohio River, and soon after entered the city of Cincinnati, one of the two great marts of commerce in the West.[54]

and his equally unemotional 1884 reminiscent comment:

> There was little on that part of the journey from Buffalo to Kansas that was outside of the ordinary incidents of such a voyage.[55]

In striking contrast, he lets down his emotional guard dramatically —although still not completely—in a letter to the editor of the *Northern Christian Advocate*, written in March 1855, two years after their New York departure.

> Sadly, two years ago this day, in company with a small band of uncompelled exiles, I seated myself in the car which was so rapidly to roll me away from the land of my youth. Thoughtfully I gazed, with tearful eye, upon the minarets of the city of Buffalo, until they were lost in the receding distance. Shall I see them again? and when? were the questions I asked, but could not answer. Desire pointed down the future, and whispered in my heart, you may; but a dark uncertainty stayed my vision and I could not see the when. On, on, unceasingly on, the steaming car bore me cruelly away. Away from what? I will not open the sanctuary of my soul or the eyes of my curiosity and say from what.[56]

Grand Tower and Devil's Bakeoven on the Mississippi, 1853

Steamboat Ben Campbell *on the upper Mississippi, 1852*

United States Illustrated

St. Louis from the Mississippi, 1853

The Early History of Greater Kansas City, 1928

Snags in the Missouri River

[1] H. K. Hines, "Two Years from Home," *Northern Christian Advocate,* May 23, 1855.

[2] *Buffalo Christian Advocate,* March 10, 1853.

[3] More likely, young Gustavus was Eliza's son by her first marriage. In one of his accounts of Obadiah's drowning, Harvey refers to Obadiah's "adopted son" standing on the river bank. H. K. Hines, "An Incident of 1853," *Pacific Christian Advocate,* January 27, 1881, 4.

[4] "Buffalo and State Line Railroad Company, with 68 miles of line, was incorporated October 13, 1849, and road opened from Dunkirk to State Line on January 1, 1852. February 22, 1852, road opened from Buffalo to State Line." History of The Lake Shore and Michigan Southern and its predecessors from the 1913 Annual Report of The New York Central Railroad System. http://www.s363.com/dkny/lsms.html; accessed April 10, 2007. Harvey refers to the "Lake Shore rail road," but this section did not acquire that name until merger with another more western line in the 1860s. He may simply be recalling his own more recent trips on that line.

[5] H. K. Hines, "Emigrant Wagon," December 11, 1884, 2.

[6] Gustavus Hines, "Correspondence, Grand Prairie, near Shawnee Mission," *Northern Christian Advocate,* May 25, 1853, 13:21, 82.

[7] This quotation is attributed to the abolitionist Rev. Samuel Webster Salisbury in 1769, cited in George W. Williams, *History of the Negro Race in America, 1619 to 1880,* Vol. I (New York: Putnam, 1883), 218, 219. Google Book Search, http://books.google.com/books?; accessed May 3, 2007.

[8] The phrase Harvey quotes, evidently a paraphrase of Genesis 6:5 in the King James Version, appears in many religious texts in the form used here. The earliest we have found is in a sermon of John Wesley—something Harvey likely would have seen. Global Ministries; the United Methodist Church: The Sermons of John Wesley, "The Deceitfulness of the Human Heart," Sennon 123. http://new.gbgm-umc.org/umhistory/wesley/sermons/123/; accessed May 3, 2007.

[9] H. K. Hines, "Incidents of Travel En Rout for Oregon," *Northern Christian Advocate,* April 13, 1853, 58.

[10] For the Cleveland-to-Cincinnati leg of the trip, they probably patronized the Cleveland Columbus and Cincinnati Railroad Co. This company was originally chartered March 14, 1836. The charter was allowed to lapse, and was revived March 12, 1845, and February 21, 1851, the first train ran through from Cleveland to Columbus. "History of The Lake Shore and Michigan Southern and its predecessors from the 1913 Annual Report of The New York Central Railroad System." http://www.s363.com/dkny/lsms.html; accessed April 10, 2007.

[11] Gustavus Hines, "Correspondence, Grand Prairie," 82.

[12] H. K. Hines, "Incidents of Travel En Rout for Oregon," *Northern Christian Advocate,* Apr. 20, 1853, 13:16, 62.

[13] In 1993 an Indiana state park was established at this location. The narrative at the park website, has this to say about the falls: "Although the name seems to imply waterfalls at this new state park, in actuality, the Falls are cascading rapids, or cataract falls. They cause the Ohio River to drop 26 feet in elevation over a two-and-a-half-mile stretch. Early explorers found this area the only navigational barrier on the entire Ohio River—historic records refer to the "Rapids" or "Falls" of the Ohio River.

Many visitors, some famous, have graced the Falls throughout the past 200 years. After General George Rogers Clark returned here from conquering the Northwest Territories during the Revolutionary War, John James Audubon arrived to render more than 200 sketches of birds in the Falls area. Mark Twain endured the Falls and recorded, "We reached Louisville—at least the neighborhood of it. We stuck hard and fast on the rocks in the middle of the river, and lay there four days."

After experiencing a boat trip down the Falls, Wait Whitman wrote that "The bottom of the boat grated harshly more than once on the stones beneath, and the pilots showed plainly that they did not feel altogether as calm as a summer morning.

When Meriwether Lewis and William Clark began their famous 1803 expedition to chart an overland route to the Pacific Ocean, they didn't start out in St. Louis, but rather, from the Falls of the Ohio. The Falls provided a natural stopping point for all river travelers in those early days. Native Americans, explorers, pioneers, and travelers loved to stop and marvel at the "petrifications" at the Falls." Falls of the Ohio State Park, http://www.fallsoftheohio.org/park-history.html; accessed April 10, 2007.

[14] This statement by Harvey gives us a revealing glimpse of his personality. His thirst for adventure emerges repeatedly in the course of the journey. Compare with Celinda's comment about the falls in her March 12 diary entry.

[15] H. K. Hines, "Incidents of Travel," 62.

[16] It is evident from the context that Celinda means Louisville, Ky. We find no indication that Louisville was ever called "Louisburg" elsewhere.

[17] Gustavus' text is from I Peter 1:11 and Harvey's is from Colossians 3:1 (King James Version).

[18] H. K. Hines, "Incidents of Travel," 62.

[19] H. K. Hines, "Incidents of Travel," 62.

[20] Celinda, like most others in the family, evidently enjoyed singing. "Katy darling," (Boston: Oliver Ditson, 1851) was a popular "Irish" song of the mid-nineteenth century. Library of Congress, American Memory, http://memory.loc.gov/cgi-bin/query/D?mussm:4:./temp/~ammem_Kjq5::; accessed May 3, 2007.

[21] Gustavus Hines, "Correspondence, Grand Prairie," 82. For further information on the three "brethren," see notes for Harvey's later mention of them.

[22] G. Hines and H. K. Hines, "Oregon," *Northern Christian Advocate*, March 30, 1853, 51.

[23] "Arrived," *Missouri Republican*, Mar. 16, 1853, 2.

[24] The 1850 census lists C. J. Houts, 38, Methodist Episcopal minister, along with his wife and two children. 1850 U.S. Census, Hannibal, Marion County, Missouri; image copy at www.ancestry.com, accessed May 3, 2007.

[25] The 1850 census shows W. D. R. Trotter, 43, Methodist minister, living with his family in Jacksonville, Illinois, about sixty miles north of St. Louis. 1850 U.S. Census, Jacksonville, Morgan County, Illinois; image copy at www.ancestry.com, accessed May 3, 2007. No census information is available for L. B. Dennis/Denison, as Harvey and Gustavus, respectively, refer to the third minister.

[26] H. K. Hines, "Incidents of Travel," 62.

[27] According to the *Missouri Republican*, the steamer *Robert Campbell*, Edds master, had arrived on March 14 and was preparing to depart on the Missouri River. Also reported under "River Intelligence," "The steamer *Robert Campbell* lost four days on her upward trip by the breaking of the shaft of her doctor [water pump]," which in retrospect did not bode well for the Hines' upcoming trip. "Arrived," *Missouri Republican*, Mar. 15, 1853, 2.

[28] This steamboat was named for Robert Campbell (1804-1879), who came to America from Ireland in 1822 and entered the fur trade soon thereafter. He quickly rose from trapper to brigade leader to partner, all within a half dozen years. In the mid-1830s, Campbell retired from the mountains, having already amassed considerable wealth, and embarked on a new career. He returned to St. Louis and built up a business empire that embraced mercantile, steamboat, railroad, and banking interests. Through these ventures he not only gained more wealth but also became a leading force behind the development of the region's economy. His home still stands in St. Louis. Robert Campbell, The Free Dictionary by Farlex, http://columbia.thefreedictionary.com/Campbell,+Robert; accessed April 10, 2007.

[29] According to the *Missouri Republican*, "The *Robert Campbell* and *Isabel* both left for St. Joseph yesterday evening crowded with passengers, a large number of whom are bound for California and Oregon." "River Intelligence," *Missouri Republican*, March 17, 1853, XXXI:65, 2.

[30] H. K. Hines, "Incidents of Travel, En Route to Oregon," *Northern Christian Advocate*, May 4, 1853, 13:18,70.

[31] H. K. Hines, "Incidents of Travel," 70.

[32] In the *Missouri Republican* of March 17, 1853: "The steamers *Delaware*, *Patrick Henry* and *St. Paul* having been withdrawn from the New Orleans trade, are all three receiving freight for the Missouri river. The *Robert Campbell* and *Isabel* both left for St. Joseph yesterday evening crowded with passengers, a large number of whom are bound for California and Oregon." "River Intelligence," *Missouri Republican*, March 17, 1853, 2. It is the *Delaware* that will come to the aid of the Hines party when the *Robert Campbell* hits a snag in the river.

[33] See note 27, wherein the *Missouri Republican* identifies "Edds" as captain. It should not be surprising that that this ship captain, William Eads/Edds, would have his name spelled

differently in different places; he used two spellings, Eads/Edds, interchangeably himself—evidently to avoid possible charges of bigamy based on his marriages to two different women (in Virginia and St. Louis) without benefit of an intervening divorce. About Riverboat Captains, http://www.riverboatdaves.com/aboutcaps/capse.html#WEADS; accessed April 11, 2007.

[34] Gustavus Hines, "Correspondence, Grand Prairie," 82.

[35] H. K. Hines, "Incidents of Travel," 70.

[36] H. K. Hines, "Incidents of Travel," 70.

[37] In 1853 St.Aubert was a small village in St. Aubert Township, Callaway County, located on the Missouri River, about fifteen miles south of Fulton, and about twenty miles downriver from Jefferson City. Today the township remains, but the village has dwindled, disappearing from recent maps. History of Callaway County Missouri, published in 1884 by the St. Louis National Historical Company, St. Aubert Township, http://callaway.county.missouri.org/l884history/townships/staubert.html; accessed April 11, 2007.

[38] William H. Gray, in fact, was about to make his third overland trip westward, having gone previously with Marcus Whitman and others in 1836, and with another missionary party in 1838. Merrill J. Mattes, *Platte River Road Narratives* (Urbana: University of Illinois Press, 1988). He had returned east by the Panama route in 1852 and was in St. Louis buying sheep to take with him back to Oregon when he crossed paths with the Hines party. He joined the rest of his party in Independence (and visited the Hines group near there—see Celinda's May 1 note in Chapter 5). Although they started overland from there in early May, as did the Hines families, they made slow progress the first couple of weeks. They later made up the difference and caught up with the Hines train in eastern Oregon. (See Chapter 14.)

[39] "The Friend of Sinners Dies!" Isaac Watts, The Cyber Hymnal, http://www.cyberhymnal.org/; accessed April 11, 2007.

[40] The *Delaware* was a side-wheeler used on the Missouri River until 1857 when it was wrecked on a snag in the river. Riverboat Dave's Paddlewheel Site, http://members.tripod.com/~Write4801/riverboats/d.html; accessed April 11, 2007.

[41] H. K. Hines, "Incidents of Travel," 70.

[42] This is Celinda's first reference to her young brother. Whenever she is referring to her uncle of the same name, it is in the form of "Uncle Gustavus," or simply "Uncle G."

[43] "River Intelligence," *Missouri Republican,* Mar. 20, 1853, XXXI:68, 2.

[44] H. K. Hines, "Emigrant Wagon," December 11, 1884, 2. Harvey's quotation is from Proverbs 3:17 (King James Version).

[45] H. K. Hines, "Incidents of Travel," 70.

[46] According to a list of steamers departing St. Louis on March 18, Captain Baker was in

charge of the *Delaware*. "Departed," *Missouri Republican,* March 18, 1853, 2.

[47] This would have been the steamboat *Saluda*, which exploded on April 9, 1852. This was the worst such disaster on the Missouri River, with an estimated 80-100 deaths. Many of the passengers were Mormons headed west. William G. Hartley and Fred E. Woods, "Explosion of the Steamboat Saluda: Tragedy and Compassion at Lexington, Missouri, 1852." *Missouri Historical Review,* Vol. 99, issue 4, 281-305.

[48] The 1860 Federal Census for California shows a "day laborer," V. Hobson in Sacramento, age 29, birthplace Indiana. He would have been about 23 in 1853, and could well have been one of the young men Celinda mentions. There is no comparable census listing for Nathan Caroll (or Carroll) in California in 1860, but there is one in Indiana. Perhaps he returned home to Indiana, as did so many other men disappointed after seeking their fortune in California. 1860 U.S. Census, Sacramento County, California; image copy at www.ancestry.com; accessed April 11, 2007.

[49] H. K. Hines, "Incidents of Travel," 70.

[50] The 1850 U.S. census lists a Mariah Wightman, age 13, as part of the Dennison Wightman (inn keeper) household on the same page as the Obadiah Hines listing, suggesting they were neighbors. Given her age, she may have been a pupil of Celinda's. 1850 U.S. Census, Hastings, Oswego County, New York; image copy at www.ancestry.com; accessed April 11, 2007.

[51] The "young wife" was Anna Maria Goodell. She kept a diary on her 1854 trip, a typescript of which is at the University of Washington Library in Seattle. Mattes, *Platte River Road Narratives,* 438.

[52] Judson, *A Pioneer's Search,* 7-13.

[53] Mrs. Eugene D. Funk, *Trip to Oregon in 1853,* May 27, 1953, typescript, courtesy of Funk family.

[54] H. K. Hines, "Incidents of Travel, En Rout to Oregon," *Northern Christian Advocate,* April 13, 1853, 58.

[55] H. K. Hines, "Emigrant Wagon," December 4, 1884, 2.

[56] H. K. Hines, "Two Years from Home."

5

March 25–May 3, 1853: Waiting for the Grass to Grow

> *There was a misty weirdness over the unknown*
> *before us as we stood on that gray May morning and looked*
> *over the billowy prairie-sea that rolled away westward we*
> *knew not how far. Behind us were the steepled villages*
> *and templed hills of "home;" before us the songless*
> *solitude. Behind us blossoming civilization, before us*
> *petrified barbarism. Behind us the friends and friendships*
> *of the years, before us strangers and loneliness. Who thinks*
> *that underneath the smile on our face there was not a sigh*
> *in our hearts knows nothing of humanity's profoundest*
> *deceits.*[1]
> —Harvey K. Hines, May 1853

By late March 1853 the three Hines families had reached the frontier and were poised to begin their long journey via the overland trail. Three matters detained them. First, they had stock and supplies to buy. Second, they awaited the arrival of other families to supplement their small party and increase its security for the perilous trip. Third, they dared not start until the vegetation along the route had reached a stage sufficient to support their own stock, along with that of thousands of other emigrants.

During these final preparations Celinda's diary continues to provide a day-by-day account, while the others give more of an overview, with Harvey in particular focusing on the emotional and spiritual aspects of their activities.

Some clarification is in order regarding the place names frequently cited by Celinda and the others. When she or others use the name Kansas they invariably are referring to the Missouri city located on the Missouri River at the far western edge of the state, and which has grown into the Kansas City, Missouri, of today. (Harvey sometimes refers to the city as "Kansas Landing."[2]) When she uses the phrase, "the Kansas," she refers to the Kansas River, which flows into the Missouri River at Kansas City.

After a several-week stopover in Kansas City, the party traveled south to the town of Westport and then west into Indian Territory, what is

The Kansas City, Missouri, area, adapted from an 1855 map, which still has this city shown as simply "Kansas." This and other Missouri cities mentioned in the text are highlighted. Locations of the Shawnee Mission and Grinter Place (at Delaware Crossing) in Indian Territory are also labeled. Wyandot City, now part of Kansas City, Kansas, was the site of the Wyandot Methodist Mission.

The light area on the left side of the map is all part of present-day Kansas, but in 1853, the area south of the Kansas River was Indian Territory and some maps designated everything north of the river as Nebraska. Such a map presumably was what led Celinda to state that they had landed in Nebraska when they crossed the river at the Delaware Crossing and reached Grinter Place.

now the state of Kansas. (Note that the Kansas-Nebraska Act was passed by Congress the following year, in 1854.) Thus it is at first confusing to the modern reader when, as the families are encamped in Indian Territory, now Kansas, Celinda speaks of her uncles "going back to Kansas," by which she means returning to Kansas City.

We begin with a report from Gustavus to the *Northern Christian Advocate.*

Gustavus

Here [Kansas City area] we arrived on the 23rd of March [actually the 24th, according to Celinda and Harvey], and since then have been busily engaged in outfitting. You may be aware that besides Br. Harvey, I have an elder brother who is emigrating to Oregon. For the conveyance of our three families we have purchased thirteen yoke of cattle, two mules, and three horses. We have two common two horse wagons, and one light carriage. We put five yoke of cattle to each of the lumber wagons, and harness our mules to the carriage. The horses are designed for riding. We have procured extra cattle, so that in case of the failure of any, we shall have a supply. Our cattle have cost us sixty-five dollars per yoke, horses from eighty to one hundred dollars, mules two hundred and twenty five dollars a pair. We have a good outfit, good health, good courage, good company, and enough of it, and an Almighty protector, and if none of these fail us, we are sure of success.—We are now encamped in the Indian country, about three miles from the line of Missouri, on the borders of the Grand Prairie. We expect to leave our present quarters, and put out on the great prairie sea before us, between this and the fifth inst., after which it is doubtful whether you will hear from us until we bring up on the shore of the Pacific. The emigration of human kind the present year, is not so large as last, but that of cattle kind is said to be larger. It is the opinion of some that not less than 100,000 head of cattle will start to cross the plains the present spring. —The principal danger to be apprehended arises from the amount of stock which may be greater than the supply of grass. Be this as it may, when you receive this letter we shall be slowly moving on towards our home in the west. We hope to be permitted to do some service to the cause of truth and holiness in Oregon, before we go to occupy "that better country that is, the heavenly."[3]

Harvey

At Kansas landing we remained about two weeks. Here we purchased oxen, horses, cows, and other such things as we had not already provided for the journey to Oregon. One incident only of our stay here needs to be recorded.[4]

Once again, Harvey has succinctly summarized this interval in their travels. His description of the "one incident" is inserted in Celinda's day-by-day chronicle that follows.

Celinda

Friday, March 25—Received last evening a telegraphic dispatch from Pa. It was written on monday. The boxes had not yet arrived at St. Louis. Uncles telegraphed back to Pa. It is very cloudy this morning & looks like rain. Uncles have procured a house & we remove to it. It is a small log house & we make ourselves as comfortable as we can. We have a fireplace & by using a little stove which was given to Lucy Anna in Buffalo we get along as to cooking very well. We enjoyed ourselves very well during the day it being very pleasant, but at night it became very windy, & having no beds we camped out as best we could on the blankets.

Saturday, March 26—Passed the night very uncomfortably, Being very much crowded & very cold. Pass the day in cooking & making preparations for the Sabbath. The village is situated on a high bluff rising from the river. The Houses are very much scattered, extending over considerable space, Making the place, from a distance, appear as if containing much more inhabitants than it in reality does. The houses are mostly log, with nice brick chimneys on the outside. The streets run every way without regard to form, & the houses are scattered hither and thither over the hills and in the vallies.

Sunday, March 27—Very pleasant. I went to church. Uncle Gustavus preached. The congregation looked very respectable. Indeed, I was quite pleasingly disappointed. After tea Julia, mother & myself took a walk. We ascended a high hill where we had a very pleasant view of the river. We attended church in the evening preaching by Uncle Harvey.

Monday, March 28—We have concluded to take in turns doing the work, so as to give each one more time to sew. Aunt Lydia & Julia are to do the work today. In the afternoon received a call from Mrs. Troost[5] & another lady. Find there are many going to Oregon from Missouri. In the evening some of our washing, which we had put out, came home. It was not very well done.

Tuesday, March 29—Very pleasant. Aunt Elizabeth & Martha do the work today. We received call from Mrs. Rice & Mrs. West.[6] In the evening pa came from St. Louis. We were very much pleased. He started wednesday, consequently did not receive our telegram & had not heard anything from us since we left St. Louis, only by the papers[7] that we were wrecked on the Robt. Campbell and by the officers of that boat that they left us on the bank. He knew that Kansas was our destination, but whether we had arrived there, or where we were, he knew not. He had been sick nearly all of his stay at St. Louis, but had found it necessary to remain on the levee nearly all of the time to watch the boats which came in from Cincinnati so that if our boxes came in they might not be put into some warehouse where he could not find them. Monday night they came.[8] On Tuesday he ordered the stores for our journey & wednesday he started on board the Fanny Sparhawk. He was sick most of the way and when at Wayne city[9] the boat was wrecked,[10] he remained on board one day & the next came to Kansas in a hack, leaving the boxes to come on the Fanny Sparhawk when she was repaired. During Pa's stay at St. Louis he received no intelligence from our friends at home.

The Hines' boxes mentioned by Celinda and attended to by Obadiah evidently arrived aboard the steamer *Hindoo*, which was the only ship listed in the *Missouri Republican* as having arrived on Monday, March 21. In this newspaper's "Receipts" column, for the cargo of the *Hindoo*, shown below,

> Cincinnati—Per Hindoo—H Thayer 10 pkgs; F B Chamberlain & co 67 bdls paper 11 bxs butter 10 bbls saleratus 50 boxes cheese; S McCartney 10 cks coal; Ckck & Reo 100 bxs starch; Scott & Bro 19 pkgs; Rosenburger & Cook 23 do; Newbury & co stoves and castings; Pottle & Bayley 100 bxs cheese; S Humphreys 25 pkgs; Donaldson & Hall 12 to; Horton & May 418 do; Bridge & Rao 45 do; T & J Card 1 do; Geo G Hines 3 do; E A Macay 3 do; Greenfield, Sluder & co 1 do; Mudd & Hughes 17 do; Hill & McKee 20 bdls paper; O Wales & Sons 10 cks coal 10 bbls cider 28 bags dried apples; Rasenkamp & co lot bedsteads; Jno McWeehan 72 bxs wax; W S Gilman 228 do; T Smith & co 12 pkgs; Pettus & Sexton 1 do; W M Morrison 5 do; Wm M Morrison 5 do; Fisher & Bennett 2 do; Greeley & Gale lot furniture; R Thompson 6 pkgs; A C Williamson 2 do T W Hoit 1 do; J E Elder 3 do.[11]

there is an entry "Geo[!] G Hines 3 do," which we interpret as representing three packages shipped by Rev. G. Hines.[12] The full listing provides an interesting view of steamship cargo of that era.

Wednesday, March 30—Weather pleasant. Mother and myself did the work. We found it exceeding uncomfortable to work over the fireplace. After tea Julia, Martha & myself took a walk. After we had retired for the night we heard a steamboat bell ring the men got up & went down to the wharf to see if the boxes had come. They found that it was indeed the Fanny and our boxes had safely arrived. They returned & we all feel better for knowing that we had some beds, although they were yet on the wharf.

Thursday, March 31—It looked some like rain last night but it cleared off. Aunt Lydia & Julia do the work. The men engaged a man to bring up the boxes but they were so heavy they had to be taken to pieces before being brought up. When the bystanders saw the wagons as they were taken from the boxes they remarked that none but Yankees would have thought of boxing them up, or especially sawing the tungs into. They said they had counted we were city folks & did not know how to take care of ourselves, but they were now convinced we would arrive safely in Oregon & if they were going they would wish to go with us. One company asked to be admitted into our company. Our men have bought twelve yokes of oxen. We have now many conveniences which we did not have before the arrival of our boxes, but most of all we prize our beds.

Friday, April 1—Very pleasant. Aunt E & Martha did the work. We slept much better the night before for having our beds & mattresses, than we did on our bed of leaves. Some men were taken up for breaking open a store. They were suspected and a gentleman went in with them, learned their plans and secrets and then exposed them. It was their intention to burn Kansas [city] and steal all they could. There were eight of them. In the afternoon Martha and myself called to see Mrs. Dr. Troost. Had a very pleasant call. Uncles went in the morning to the Mission—Indian territory—and returned in the evening. They found the country delightful. They purchased a horse.

Saturday, April 2—Mother & myself officiated as cooks. In the morning we received a call from Mrs. & Miss Armstrong from the Wyandotte Mission, I. T.[13] She is the widow of a lawyer who was employed by the Wyandotte nation to do and settle their business. He died on his return from Washington about a year since, where he had been to arrange some affairs for them. Mrs. A. called to make our acquaintance & also to see if she could induce one or both of my uncles to preach to the Wyandottes on the Sabbath, as their missionary was absent. She invited us to spend some time with her during our stay. She is, as far as I could judge, an accomplished lady. In the afternoon, Martha, Julia and myself called to see a Mrs. Gear,[14] a merchant's wife in the place. We had a very pleasant call & they invited us to take tea with her on Tuesday. She gave us some butter & some apples to bring home.

Harvey

One Saturday afternoon there came into the little log cabin in which we were temporarily domiciled a lady of less than forty years, evidently cultivated and intelligent, and introduced herself as Mrs. Armstrong, the daughter of Russel Bigelow,[15] with whose name we were familiar as one of the most eminent Methodist preachers the west had ever produced. She said she was an Indian by adoption into the Wyandotte tribe, and had become so from a sense of duty to aid in their Christianization and civilization. Her father had been missionary among them in Ohio, and she had married an educated Indian, a lawyer, by the name of Armstrong, the more fully to identify herself with their interests and destinies. The Wyandottes had been removed from Ohio to the Indian Territory, and were now settled on a reservation just across the Kansas river. She had followed the fortunes of "her people," as she had given up her life for them, in a sense that few would be willing to give up their life. She had heard of us, and had come to urge us to spend the following day with her Indian brothers and sisters, as they had, at that time, no missionary among them. Of course we went, met them in their little log chapel, preached to them, through an interpreter, sang and prayed with them, held a class meeting, and left them, ourselves greatly refreshed and benefited by this then novel incident of ministerial work. Dining with Mrs. Armstrong we learned more of her history and work than we can attempt to recite. We found that her influence among her people was almost supreme, and almost supremely good. They had given her a name – which we have forgotten – signifying the "white rose;" a beautiful emblematic representation of the purity of her life and the fragrance of her influence among them.[16]

We have often thought of this woman; of what she surrendered and did for Christ's battered and beaten ones: how she gave a life that was well fitted by nature and cultivation for the best spheres of society for these poor outcasts, to bring them to a better life and nobler humanity. Surely here was something in the line of Him of whom it was said, "He was rich, yet for our sakes he became poor that we through His poverty might be rich."[17]

Celinda

Sunday, April 3—Pleasant, but rather cold. Uncles went to the Wyandotte Mission to hold meeting. Aunt E., M., J., G. & myself went to hear Mr. Scarritt.[18] Uncle G. preached in the evening. I remained at home. Lucy Anna was sick all day. Mr. Lykins called to see about the meeting & gave us a newspaper with some very cheering intelligence in regard to crossing the plains.[19]

Monday, April 4—Weather rather cold. Aunt E. & M. did the work.

Aunt L., J., Mother & myself sewed on the waggon covers. In the afternoon we recieved calls from Mrs. Perry & Mrs. Northrop. Mrs. P. is a Methodist preacher's wife[20] and Mrs. N. is a merchant's wife & a Wyandotte.[21]

Tuesday, April 5—Weather very pleasant. Mother & myself did the work. At noon Mr. Flint called and took dinner. He wishes to go in our company.[22] Martha, Julia & myself spent the afternoon at Mr. Geer's. We had a very pleasant time met Mr. Conant,[23] a merchant, who boards there. Mrs. G. invited us to visit at Mr. Walker's[24] at the W. Mission on Thursday.

Wednesday, April 6—Pleasant weather. I sewed on the tent nearly all day. In the afternoon Miss Dawson called. In the eve. Mrs. Geer. On Tuesday Kansas was made a city & Dr. Lykins mayor.[25]

Thursday, April 7—Pleasant weather. We did not go to the Mission because Martha was sick. Aunt E. and M. did the work. After tea J., M. & myself called at Mr. Perry's & had a very pleasant call. I worked on the tent all day.

Friday, April 8—Pleasant yet. Aunt Lydia gave Julia & myself materials for some breir...[sombrero?] bonnets. We busied ourselves in making them. In the evening (people here begin to call evening after dinner), Martha and I called at Mr. Geer's. Met Mr. Conant. Were very pleasantly entertained.

Saturday, April 9—Received a letter from Uncle James, all well. Uncle Samuel & aunt M. arrived from Syracuse the day we left Brockport. Aunt was almost well. Uncle S had concluded to go to Ohio & buy a farm in about a year.[26] Uncle G also received a letter from Mr. Moore[27] saying that in eight days (it being dated the 28th of March) he should start for Oregon with his family & intended to join us at Kansas. After tea Martha, Julia & myself called for milk at Mr. Geer's. Lucy A. sick.

Sunday, April 10—Uncle H preached in the morning. I went to church. Dr. Lykins visited us before meeting. He has spent 30 years in the Indian country as missionary & physician. I attended church in the eve. uncle H officiated.

Monday, April 11—Mother & I did the work. In the night it rained very hard, with much wind.

Tuesday, April 12—Aunt Lydia & Julia did the work. I finished my bonnet. Aunts L & E visited at Mr. Geer's mother was not well enough to go. We received a call from Mrs. Northrop & Mrs. Coots.

Wednesday, April 13—Martha, Julia, Lucy A visited at Mrs. Perry's. Became acquainted with Mrs. P's daughter, Mrs. Boughton, also Mr. B. & brother. We had a very pleasant time. The younger Mr. B. walked home with us & spent the evening. Mr. P.'s family is a sad representation of the folly of cousins intermarrying.

Thursday, April 14—Uncles went to the Shawnee Mission[28] & found the house to which they intended to remove taken. Julia & myself went shoping after dinner and in the eve. called on Mrs. Geer. She refused to take pay for milk although we have had milk of her nearly all the time since our stay.

The Kansas City Public Library

These emigrant wagons, photographed in Kansas City near the Missouri River in 1869, were probably similar to the Hines' wagons of 1853.

Friday, April 15—The cattle which uncles had purchased were delivered in the morning & we made preparations to move to the Shawnee

Mission, I. Territory. Julia & myself called on Mrs. G. who gave Julia a ring
& me a fancy box. We saw there Miss Walker from Wyandotte & were very
much pleased with her. Mrs. G. engaged us to write to her at Ft. Laramie. Our
preparations, packing, etc., being completed, about noon we commenced our
journey, that is the overland part of it. The provision wagon has five yokes of
oxen attached. The baggage wagon four, the light one three. The females,
mother excepted, walked nearly all of the way, six miles. We were afraid to
ride as the men were unaccustomed to driving oxen. The light wagon was
behind, and being so much lighter the oxen were frequently running ahead in
spite of all pa could do to prevent them. We had gone about two miles, aunt
E, mother & M being in the wagon. They were going up a hill when the oxen
attached to the light wagon rushed ahead, ran upon a bank pa ran to prevent
the wagon from upsetting as it was running onto the bank on one side and
coming into collision with the provision wagon on the other. As he was
trying to hold it up, it upset, jamming him against the other wagon & bruising
him very much. He could not tell us how much he was hurt and we feared he
had received some internal injury which in the end would prove fatal. Mother
aunt E & Martha were tipped out uninjured. The wagon was not materially
broken, but things were strewed all along the road. As soon as pa was able to
ride & uncles had engaged a young man who was present, Mr. Collins,[29] to
take pa's place in driving, we started on. At length we arrived at Westport,
which is a very pretty village 4 miles from our destination. There we saw
numbers of Indians in their uncultivated state, half dressed. We drove on &
presently crossing the line between Missouri & I. T. As we came into the
latter country we became struck with its beauty & loveliness. Never before
had our eyes beheld so delightful a scene. The broad, rolling prairie (Grand
Prairie) is stretching for many miles. Here, covered with fruit trees of almost
every variety, currant, gooseberry & whortleberry bush, together with the
rose bushes of almost every kind growing spontaneously & there miles of
grass with not a fence or a house to change the scene constituted the most
romantic view imaginable. We arrived at our destination before night it was
on the prairie near a little rivulet along which were trees & brush as I have
described. The men took the oxen to the Methodist Mission about a mile
distant. We then prepared supper, when for the first time I ate seated on the
ground in the open air. Our tents, or Uncles' had previously been pitched.
After their return from the mission and supper being cleared away, we retired
for the night.

Saturday, April 16—Awoke, found ourselves none the worse for having
slept in a tent, although I was suffering from pains & weakness in the chest,
which I suppose was brought on by lifting & then walking beyond my strength.
I had slept but little. Pa was better than we had expected, although it was with
great difficulty that he could move. Our tent was put up & we arranged them

to our taste. The baptist mission church was the only house in sight. In the afternoon some California emigrants came & camped just out of sight of us & some Spaniards were also near. Julia & I called at the house of a Mr. Parish who resides near. He has an indian wife.

Sunday, April 17—Very pleasant. I enjoyed camping very much, but was sick yet. We received a call from three Indian girls from the M. E. mission. In the eve. Mr. and Mrs. Parish called we liked them much. She is educated and has traveled much. Pa is no worse.

Monday, April 18—We made preparations by packing everything in the middle of our tents for rain, which we saw was approaching. Uncles went away with a team to get some corn. The storm proved to be more wind than rain. Uncles' tents were both torn by it & had to be taken down & mended. Uncle G's was also burned considerable. The men returned very much fatigued. I went with the girls to Mrs. Parish's to borrow her wash tubs. Mr. P. informed me that the Shawnee nation consisted of about seven hundred & seventy five (775) while the Wyandotte of only five hundred (500) also that the Shawnees are a harmless people if well treated. He said that the country of the W's was unhealthy & consequently they diminished rapidly.

Tuesday, April 19—Aunt L & Julia washed in the morning & in the afternoon M, J and I went to the methodist mission. The farm consists of about six hundred acres. There are three large brick buildings. We went to the female department and saw forty Indian girls in school—it consists of sixty. The teacher Mrs. Chick[30] is the mother of Mrs. Scaritt and also of Mrs. Perry, who has charge of the girls out of school. Mr. Johnson is Supt. We were pleased with the progress the girls had made, but think they labor under disadvantages. The mission is beautifully situated. The buildings were built about fifteen (15) years ago. The children appear happy. In the evening Uncle G and Mr. Collins returned from Kansas no news from home.

Wednesday, April 20—Aunt E washed in the morning and I, with Julia's assistance, in the afternoon.

Thursday, April 21—It rained very hard in the night & we had to get up to protect ourselves it cleared up about noon & then we had a real time drying our things.

Friday, April 22—Uncles went to Kansas & returned at night. The afternoon was very warm. It began to rain in the eve. & rained all night. It was the hardest thunderstorm I ever witnessed. Everything was drenched through. Puddles of water were standing on the beds. Thunder & lightning played in all their awful sublimity just above our heads.

Saturday, April 23—It cleared off in the morning & our bedding & sacks of clothing, being wet, we spread them on the bushes clearing the tents of everything we could, so that the ground might dry. I went to Mr. Parish's to bake. In the night we were alarmed by Mr. Leonard[31]—who, by the way came with his family in the afternoon & tented by us. They are going to Oregon. The bell in the baptist church had been ringing for an hour or more. It was about one o'clock. Mr. L thought we might better get up and await the result of what the alarm might be. Mr. L & uncles went to the church, but saw nothing, neither did the bell ring. We went to bed again and were not disturbed.

Sunday, April 24—Very cold. We suppose that the alarm was caused by some drunken person. In the afternoon the teachers at the M. E. Mission called with about 18 of their pupils afterward Mrs. Leonard & her sister called. Mrs. L appeared to be a good sort of a woman.

Monday, April 25—Warm & pleasant. Aunt E did the work. We got our beds & clothes all dry.

Tuesday, April 26—Uncles went to Kansas, brought back two horses now we have three. Mr. Parish's dogs bit Lucy Anna's dog very bad. He died in the night. In the night it rained. Pa is not so well as usual.

Wednesday, April 27—Very pleasant. A gentleman who has been across the plains twice advised us not to start in a week.

Thursday, April 28—Rainy weather. Mother was sick. Mr. Bryant, from N.Y., on his way to Oregon, called. He wishes to go with us. Mr. Long came.

Friday, April 29—Pleasant. Uncles and Mr. Collins went and drove the cows (five and four calves), which they had purchased, home. Mr. Charles Long, who had previously engaged to go to Oregon with us, being left here to take care of the oxen. He appears to be very handy. Some Californians came in the PM and camped near us. They are rather rough.

Saturday, April 30—Uncles went to Kansas heard nothing from our friends. In the eve. Mr. Bryant & family came and camped near us.

Sunday, May 1—It rained nearly all day. Mr. Grey came.[32]

Monday, May 2—Pleasant. Mr. Judson, a presbyterian missionary came & camped by us. He is going with us.

Tuesday, May 3—We are very busy preparatory to starting. Pa went to Kansas. Received no news.

Phoebe

The emigrant rendezvous was at a small trading post called West Port, two miles from the landing, but is now included in the great city of Kansas City.[33] Here we found a comfortable boarding place, where all the work was performed by slaves. Eggs were only five cents per dozen, and were served to us in some shape at every meal by the black waiters. The cook was a large, good-natured negress, who prepared all the food in a little shanty separated from the main building, where she lived with her husband and pickaninnies.

This was my first, and only, experience in a slave state, and as "Uncle Tom's Cabin" had just been published, my sympathies were so strongly excited in behalf of the poor slaves in their hopeless bondage, and consequent afflictions, that I became engaged in some warm discussions with the landlady of the hotel.

Here we were occupied five weeks in making the final preparations for our journey. Mr. Judson ordered our wagon made with a projection on each side of one foot in width, which enabled us to cord up our bed in the back end and to stow away our provisions under it, leaving room in front for our cooking utensils, where they would be convenient to lift out and into the wagon.

Straps were attached to the hoops, overhead, for the rifle. Our wagon cover was made of white cotton drilling, which I lined with colored muslin to subdue the light and heat of the sun while crossing the desert plains.

Cattle were brought here for sale from New Mexico. Mr. Judson purchased two yoke of well broken oxen, and a cow. A young Scandinavian who had offered to go with us and help to drive the team, to which we had consented, bought two yoke of unbroken steers for leaders.

We now considered ourselves fully equipped and in readiness to roll out to the emigrant road and join some company, without the most remote idea as to who would be our fellow travelers, when one day, while arranging things in the wagon to make it, if possible, more "home-like," two gentlemen came to us and introduced themselves as Revs. Gustavus Hines and Harvey Hines, brothers, Methodist missionaries from New York. On hearing the name of Gustavus Hines we surmised at once that he was the author of a history of Oregon in which we were much interested before leaving home, and upon inquiry found we were not mistaken.[34] He informed us that he was returning to Oregon with his family, accompanied by his two brothers and their families, and were camping out while waiting for a better growth of grass.

When they invited us to join their company we were much pleased and gladly accepted their invitation. Mr. Judson and young Nelson managed, after many vain attempts, to yoke the cattle, hitch them to the wagon, and drive around to the door of our boarding place, where Annie and myself were waiting to take possession of this house on wheels, that was to be our abode for a number of months.

After bidding "good-bye" to our landlady and the black waiters, who had been very kind to us, and in whom we had become much interested, we climbed up over the heavy wheels, entered our tiny house and were off, headed for Hines' camp.

The greater portion of our journey across the plains seems more like a dream than reality, but this, my first ride in a "prairie schooner," is as fresh in my memory as though it had occurred yesterday.

The yoke of leaders were wild steers and were bent on running away. For a time all four yoke were on the stampede. Mr. Judson on one side of the team and Nelson on the other made free use of their great ox goads, and succeeded in controlling them. I held on to little Annie with one hand and the wagon hoops with the other, while she was struggling to hold a pet kitten in her lap; and the old cow that was hitched to the back end of the wagon, in her vain efforts to keep it from moving forward, shook her bell furiously.

Although much amused at the novelty of the experience, we were somewhat relieved to reach Hines' camp without further accident than the loss of Annie's pet kitten, over which she was much grieved.

Hines' camp was on a lovely prairie in the Indian Territory. The hills were green and dotted with cattle. The absence of human dwellings and the improvements of civilization made the scene one of a wild, weird nature, to which we must now become accustomed.

The three Hines brothers and their families, together with another New York family by the name of Bryant, gave us a hearty welcome.

There were three young ladies in the company. One, the daughter of Jeddadiah Hines,[35] the eldest of the three brothers, and the other two were sisters of the wives of the younger brothers. And then there was Lucy Ann Lee, the sweet ten-year-old child of Rev. Jason Lee.

The little one was bereft of its mother when a tiny babe, and her father died soon after. She was fortunate in finding loving and devoted parents in Gustavus Hines and his wife, who adopted her as their own. Lucy Ann's father and mother were among the first missionaries to Oregon.

We had but three small children in the company, Alta and Lee Bryant and Annie Judson. Alta and Annie were of the same age and proved loving companions during the journey. Three young men completed our number.

Before breaking camp, another family by the name of Leonard, from Missouri, joined the "caravan," but only remained with us a few days.

It was now the first of May—two months since we left home, and we were becoming impatient to get started on our journey "over the plains."

Alta Bryant

Stayed [in West Port] three weeks—left about the 18th [sic] of May—assembled wagons—hunted around and bought oxen (bought 5 yoke of oxen) and a cow for milk for the babies—a dog, "Towser" brought from N.Y—brought flour.

Gustavus Hines was made Captain of Company. He had made the trip before and knew the way. [Note: Gustavus' earlier trip had been by ship! On the other hand, according to Celinda, Holden Judson had in fact been across the plains before—see Chapter 11.] Cattle ready then—Pa had 2 men to help him—they had their own tents—they guarded the cattle—they rode the horses —most of them walked. Five wagons—one or two freight wagons—10 oxen—others had more—one had horses—every wagon had one or two helpers. Obidia [Obadiah] Hines (Uncle Dyer we called him) his daughter Celinda Hines (Mrs. Shipley), Aunt Eliza her mother. Uncle Dyer's son helped him.[36]

Judson Wagon	Mr. & Mrs. Judson
	Alma [Annie] Judson 3 yrs and a baby
	Bob Nelson helper

In Gustavus	Gustavus Hines
Hines Wagon	Lydia, his wife
	Julia Bryant (her sister)
	Lucianna [Lucy Anna] Maria Lee (Jason
	Lee's daughter, 10 yrs old)

"Charley"   a helper

Obediah Hines   Obediah [Obadiah] Hines
                   His wife, Eliza
                   His daughter Celinda
                   His son the helper

Harvey Hines   His wife—Eliza [Elizabeth]
                   His wife's sister—Martha Graves
                   Helper

Charles Wesley   His wife, Mary E. Fay Bryant
Bryant   Alta Bryant   (3 yrs old)
                   Lee Bryant   a baby
                   Martin and Miner (helpers)

Harvey

We will now ask the reader to take his station with us on the morning of the 9th day of May, 1853,[37] on a little spring run that winds down from the north from some high prairie rolls that lie just westward of the little town of Westport, Missouri, about four miles from the then Kansas Landing, which was just below where the Kansas river debouches into the Missouri, and only a mile outside of the state of Missouri in the then Indian Territory. On the east bank of the little rivulet is an "Emigrant Camp." Down to the south, a half mile, the "Shawnee Indian Mission" of the M. E. Church South, under the superintendence of Rev. Thomas Johnson,[38] is located.

A little eastward is the timber of the Missouri bottom and a couple of miles to the north that of the Kansas river. The hills are green as emerald. Straying over them, cropping the rich herbage is a band of near a hundred cattle, while near the tents and wagons are tethered a few horses and mules.

At this point has gathered the company of men and women who are to be *companons du voyage* for a few months, whom, in a few words, we will a little more formally, introduce to the reader. Two of the men were Methodist preachers, G[ustavus] H[ines] and a brother nearly twenty years his junior—the writer of these sketches. The former had spent several years in Oregon, in missionary work, but when, by the direction of the Missionary Board Rev. George Gary closed up the Indian Missionary work, he had returned to his former

Conference, the Genesee, and had spent six years in the pastoral work there. The younger brother had spent four years in the work of the ministry in the same conference and both were now transferred by Bishop Waugh, who then had charge of the work of the Pacific coast, to the Oregon Conference which was about to be organized by Bishop Ames. With them and their families was a yet older brother who with his family had determined to accompany them to the coast. These three families had reached Kansas Landing alone, and after purchasing their outfit had occupied the "Camp" we have described. While waiting a few days for the grass of the spring to become more mature, there joined them, first a family from Western New York consisting of Mr. And Mrs. B[ryant] and a daughter. Soon after one from Ohio, Mr. And Mrs. J[udson] and a daughter, and then Mr. And Mrs. L[eonard] of Missouri with their children. These latter were accompanied and introduced to the company by Rev. L[erner B.] Stateler, then a veteran in frontier missionary work, and yet, we think, in active work in Montana in the ministry of the M. E. Church South. Mrs. L[eonard] was his sister, and he had come with her to the borders of the great wilderness into which she was to disappear.

Six large white covered wagons, to each of which are hitched from four to six yoke of "steers" many of them wild and unbroken, are standing in a line, while fifty or more "loose cattle" are gathered in a band near by. It had taken a good half day to get the yokes on the oxen, and hitch them to the wagons. It was new work and men and beasts were strangers to each other, and not a little shy of each other besides. But at last all was done, and, thus prepared we stood, our backs to the rising, our faces towards the setting sun.

There was a misty weirdness over the unknown before us as we stood on that gray May morning and looked over the billowy prairie-sea that rolled away westward we knew not how far. Behind us were the steepled villages and templed hills of "home;" before us the songless solitude. Behind us blossoming civilization, before us petrified barbarism. Behind us the friends and friendships of the years, before us strangers and loneliness. Who thinks that underneath the smile on our face there was not a sigh in our hearts knows nothing of humanity's profoundest deceits. We had—we *must* have—a bold seeming, but stolen glances into each others eyes discovered hidden tears that challenged our own, and but for the pride of our resolve we should have broken down at the outset. So, tossing to each other some light badinage, we swung the great ox-whips on the heads of our teams, and, with empire on our wheels, started westward.

Addendum to Chapter 5: Letter from Oregon

Celinda's diary entry of April 3 refers to a newspaper item, "*Mr. Lykins...gave us a newspaper with some very cheering intelligence in regard to crossing the plains.*" From our study of newspapers that may have been available in the area in the spring of 1853, the best candidate for the item Celinda saw appears to be a letter from Rev. J. L. Yantis sent from Oregon in November 1852, and published in the *St. Joseph Gazette*[39] in March 1853 (but copied from the *Warsaw Review*).[40] Given the upbeat appraisal of Yantis's own trip across the plains in 1852, his letter may well have been the "cheering intelligence" cited by Celinda. We include the letter here in its entirety both for that reason and because it sheds further light on what the Hines party faced on the trail and in Oregon.

From the *Warsaw Review*.

From Oregon.—We offer our readers, as an apology for the lack of our usual variety of general reading, this week, the publication of a lengthy and intensely interesting letter from Oregon, by the Rev. Mr. Yantis, addressed to Maj. James Dunn, of this vicinity. Its perusal will amply repay the reader, and those interested in the affairs of Oregon, or desirous of emigrating to that country, it will be doubly interesting. A vivid description of the route, country, climate, products, &c., &c., is given in which implicit confidence may be placed. The letter follows:

Portland, Oregon Territory,
Nov. 30, 1852.

My dear Brother: I fear you are beginning to grow impatient with my tardiness in writing to you; but you will fully excuse me when I tell you that, until within the last ten days, I have not been able to write or even read a line for nearly two months. One of the families of our train brought us an epidemic sore eye of the most malignant type with which I was attacked not long after passing Fort Hall, and from which I am only now recovering.

I could give you a long chapter of incidents of travel, but I wish to fill my sheet with matter which may be more profitable. We reached this place, the largest town in the Territory, during the first week of October, after a travel of five months and a few days. At least one month of this time was consumed by harassing delays. We have reason to be profoundly thankful, that our families came safely through, having had no disaster, and no case of alarming illness. We were greatly favored in the preservation of our stock; it is a remarkable fact that I did not lose a single ox from the three teams I set out with, or one which I bought on the road. This was owing partly to the excellence of my teamsters; (all of whom I selected from good families and were first rate young men) and partly to the constant supervision of my own eye; but mainly to the fact that I had the very best teams on the road. It would have gratified you to have seen the performance of my Osage cattle and to have heard the remarks made about them. I expect to get from $150 to $250 a yoke for the cattle I sell. I am satisfied now that cattle such as you bought for me can always be got through in good condition.

I have not been able to see much of the country, but I have seen enough to feel profoundly thankful to God that He has directed my footsteps to this lovely land. The only objections that I can see to the country are, first, that it rains too much in winter, and the second, that it so hard to get to it. The last of these objections does not effect me now, only as it will be in the way of many friends coming. It has been about a month since the rainy season set in, and I declare to you, I think I have seen more rain in twenty four hours in Missouri, than I have seen here during the month. The rain descends so gently that unless you are watching you would not know it frequently—no thunder, no lightning, no wind.—Then the remarkable evenness of the temperature; it is cooler now than when we arrived, but when it got so, or how, I do not know. I am confident that the mercury has not passed over five degrees up or down the scale during any twenty-four hours since we have been in this Valley. The old settlers say that thus gradually the cold will increase until about Feb. 1, and then it will as gradually decline, till spring comes on in all her clemency and glory. —I am delighted with the climate. I am pleased also to the clear evidence borne to the healthfulness of the country by every man's appearance whom I have seen in this country. They are the most vigorous and healthy looking men I ever saw, no dull, languid eye; no pale, tallow face; no heavy dull motion to be seen. I have not seen a sickly, feeble looking man in the Territory who has been here twelve months.

The extent and beauty of the country far exceeds my expectations—this valley alone is said to be much more extensive than I had supposed. Then the Rogue River and Umqua River Valley's to the South, the Puget Sound and Chehalis country to the North, and the Tilmuke, &c., on the coast are opening, wide and exceedingly promising districts. I have not selected my location—from all I can learn I am strongly inclined to select near Marysville, on the Willamette. This is the seat of the Territorial University, said to be rich and beautiful country, adapted in a remarkable degree to the growth of wheat, oats, potatoes, melons; and that the domestic fruits, such as apples, peaches, pears, quinces, plums, grapes, &c., &c., prosper here beyond anything we have known in the Western States.

Another charm this country possesses over any other I have known—you can sow your wheat at any time from June to March with a certainty of a crop of from 20 to 35 and even 40 bushels, which you can harvest without haste and without fear of damage from a rainy spell, and then you can sell every bushel at from $1 50 to $3 00 per bushel. Potatoes here are at home, never saw such anywhere, from 150 bushels to 300, and even more are expected from an acre, they are selling here at $2 00 per bushel. Turnips are finer both as to size and quality than I ever saw—what would you think to see a man give $1 00 for a bushel, and to save trouble measuring take two turnips for his bushel? I have not seen this but I have no doubt it has been done. I have given a dollar for three cabbage heads, and made better bargains than I have sometimes made in Missouri at five cents a head. Suffice it to say, that I have never seen a country, where the laborer was so richly recompensed for his toil, or where it was so easy to live and thrive.

A man who can start with ten or twelve cows can hardly fail to grow independent in a few years, having no other trouble to take than see after his cattle—no feeding to do. Now, these are the things which I fully believe, after the most careful and diligent endeavor to know the truth.

If I were not here and knew all I do, I would get here some how, if I could. I advise no body to come, and there are many who ought not to think of coming—but I am glad that I am here and I hope when I have to go hence to my last home, to rejoice that it is my privilege to leave my children here.

The storms gave us no trouble, and I have no doubt the wonderful tales we hear on this subject, are pretty much gassy. We suffered considerable from dust during the last month, because we started too late—our cattle never suffered materially for want of grass or water—those terrible tales of waterless deserts, are all stuff—mere stuff. The fact is we did not happen to come by the places where you had to let your cattle down perpendicular precipices of many hundred feet by the tail!—or where your tongue would swell with thirst till you had to find room for it out of doors. We saw no great marvels, made no hair breadth escapes, and we do not feel that we deserve a high place on the roll of fame as heroes or heroines. The fact is, that coming to Oregon, is a very plain, matter of fact sort of business, in which the adventures are few, and from which the wonders all vanish, just before you get to see them. As to the road, you may have some idea of it when I tell you that my most unruly team was driven every alternate day by a 15 year old black boy, who regularly took a nap of two or three hours every day, and yet, in all our train there was not a single upsetting all the way. It is amusing to think of some of the terrible anticipations which almost deterred me from making the trip. One of these it is laughable to remember, viz.: the crossing of the South Platte, a stream full half a mile wide, and muddy and tumultuous as the Missouri—this stream had to be forded and the bottom was one wide spread quicksand, on which, if wagon or horse should stop it [...] Well the fact is, the South Platte is full half a mile wide, muddy and mad, but there is about as much alarm in crossing it as in crossing Cole Camp, or little Teho, in July. I remember that about the middle of the stream I dropped the whip from the stock, and had the temerity to risk every thing and jump out to save it, when the waters of the hissing, roiling stream came all the way up to my ankles! So of many of the awful passages you have to make.

There is generally more or less disease, almost always very manageable, diarrhea, some slight fevers, &c., &c.

It may be of service to give some directions as to the preparations, &c., necessary to be made. If I were yet to come, I would be careful as to the wagons I would bring. I found by experience that there is often at least the difference of a good yoke of steers in waggons of the same burden. The Chicago waggons are the best. I would have at least five yoke of steers, and two of cows to each wagon, using four yoke at a time, and I would not start with a steer about which I felt any fears. I would have my wagon cloths so fixed at the ends and sides that rain could not beat in and so that they could be easily drawn up to admit the air; I would have my yokes lined with lead or zink to keep from galling; I would get some three hundred ox shoe nails (half the size of horse shoe nails) and a few iron shoes; I would use stout harness leather for shoeing the lighter cattle. I would have one wagon body made very tight to ferry in (the simplest thing in the world) otherwise there is great imposition. I would get Walker's guide[41] to Oregon; I would put up with my provisions several hams of bacon and several of venison to serve in case of sickness; I would get my family physician to put up my medicine, and if I had a son-in-law who was a physician, I would bring him along if I could, I would lay in a good stock of patience and perseverance, I would commit myself and family to God with prayer and fasting; set out by the 15th April if possible not later than the 20th travel regularly consulting the capacity of my cattle; and then, resting every Sabbath; I would make the journey; I would endeavor to be as near ahead as possible, so as to get the best grass, to avoid dust, epidemic diseases, and I would try to get to the Cascade Mountains by the 10th September, and would cross the mountain instead of coming by the Dalles. There is more expense, more trouble, more danger to persons and stock more delay and more vexation from the Dalles to this place, than in all the rest of the journey. Mark that well.

I would bring at least two pounds Gum Arabic (pulverized), with which to clear coffee; it is an excellent preventative used in this way, against bowel complaint.

Very affectionately; yours

J. L. Yantis.

---

[1] H. K. Hines, "Emigrant Wagon," December 11, 1884, 2.

[2] In various secondary sources we have seen more frequently the name "Westport Landing," a natural designation because of its riverfront location just to the north of the town of Westport. See, for example, Louise Barry, *The Beginning of the West*, (Topeka: Kansas State Historical Society, 1972), 1289.

[3] Gustavus Hines, "Correspondence, Grand Prairie," 82.

[4] H. K. Hines, "Emigrant Wagon," December 11, 1884, 2.

[5] This was Mary Troost, wife of Dr. Benoist Troost. "Dr. Troost, born November 17, 1786 in Bois Le Duc, Holland, was a graduate physician. He had served as hospital steward in the Army of Napoleon." In early Kansas City, he was a "city father and early entrepreneur. At the sale of lots of the Town Company of Kansas in 1846, he bought five. In 1849 as the California gold rush peaked, Troost and his wife's uncle built the town's first brick hotel, the Gilliss House." Kansas City Library biography, Dr. Benoist Troost, 1786-1859. http://www.kclibrary.org/sc/bio/troost.htm; accessed July 3, 2003.

[6] Given that Celinda and the others became acquainted with Dr. Johnston Lykins, soon to be elected mayor and council president, this Mrs. West could well have been the wife of T. H. West, also elected to the council in early April, 1853. Barry, *Beginning of the West,* 1143.

[7] Obadiah probably read of the *Robert Campbell's* fate in the Missouri *Republican,* which published steamboat news in a daily column, "River Intelligence." The *Robert Campbell* item was reported in this column on March 20, 1853, as cited earlier.

[8] The only steamboat arrival in St. Louis from Cincinnati on Monday March 21, 1853, as reported in the Missouri *Republican* in its March 22 issue was the Steamer *Hindoo,* Burke master. "Arrived," Missouri *Republican,* Mar. 22, 1853, XXXI:70, 2.

[9] Wayne City Landing, or Independence Landing as it was sometimes called, was a small community situated on the Missouri River on the northern edge of Independence. Today the community, now having a population of less than 5000, is known as Sugar Creek. Sugar Creek is nearby, but there is nothing at the Wayne City landing but a cement company. Sugar Creek, Missouri: History, http://www.sugar-creek.mo.us/about/history.asp; accessed April 11, 2001.

[10] The Missouri *Republican* of April 1 reports, "The steamer El Paso, from the Missouri,… met…Fanny Sparhawk at Wayne City, repairing plumber block." "River Intelligence," *Missouri Republican,* Apr. 1, 1853, XXXI:80, 2.

[11] "Receipts," *Missouri Republican,* Mar. 22, 1853, XXXI:70, 2.

[12] "Geo." very likely is someone's mistranscription of "Rev. " The "do" in the cargo list is the then commonly used abbreviation for ditto. Thus the "3 do" in the Hines entry must mean three packages, if we work our way back to the "Scott & Bro 19 pkgs" and interpret the intervening "to" as an intended "do."

[13] The Wyandot Methodist Mission was located in the vicinity of what is now the intersection of Tenth St. and Freeman Ave. in present-day Kansas City, Kansas, i.e., across the Kansas River to the west from where the Hines party were staying in Kansas (City, Missouri). Barry, *Beginning of the West,* 729. It is interesting that no mention is made, by Celinda or the others, of Mrs. Armstrong's means of crossing the river for her visit, nor is there any discussion of river crossing when Gustavus and Harvey visit the mission to preach. Perhaps there was a routine ferry. In any case, it must have been a relatively uneventful crossing in contrast to their later arduous transit of the river at the Delaware Crossing.

[14] This was probably Emily Gear, wife of Samuel Gear, a grocer. 1850 U.S. Census, Kaw, Jackson County, Missouri; image copy at www.ancestry.com, accessed May 4, 2007. In several later diary references, Celinda spells the surname, "Geer." Her April 9th entry, "… called for milk at Mr. Geer's…" is consistent with the grocer identification.

[15] Russell Bigelow is listed as a delegate from the Ohio Conference to the General Conference of the Methodist Episcopal Church. in 1832. Nathan Bangs, *A History of the Methodist Episcopal Church,* Volume IV—Book V, Chapter 11.
    A contemporary of Bigelow in Ohio described him this way: "He was a good speaker; an eloquent man, mighty in the Scriptures. He was a very large, muscular man had

a voice like a lion: sharp, piercing eyes that when he became excited seemed almost to flash fire. He preached a great deal of hell fire: was a very successful preacher, and an exemplary Christian in his deportment. His influence with the people was such that he got many name-sakes, the old ladies readily believing it would have a good influence over their sons to be called after such a powerful man as Russell Bigelow." History of Crawford County," http://www.heritagepursuit.com/Crawford/crCh5.htm; accessed April 11, 2007.

[16] "Mrs. [Lucy] Armstrong, the daughter of Russell Bigelow, the venerable missionary, married J[ohn] M[clntire] Armstrong in Mansfield, Ohio, in 1838, and was adopted into the nation...J. M. Armstrong, the United States interpreter, of whom mention has previously been made, had, with his family, become the happy occupant of a little log hut sixteen feet square, near the corner of Wawas and Fifth streets [in Wyandotte City, i.e., present day Kansas City, Kansas], a short distance southeast of the present residence of his widow. The Armstrongs moved into their house December 10, 1843, and then and there occupied the first house ever erected on the present site of the city...J. M. Armstrong taught the first free school in the Territory, which was opened July 1, 1844. The building was a frame one, with double doors, which but a few years since stood on the east side of Fourth street, between Kansas and Nebraska avenues, Wyandotte City...Mr. Armstrong taught until 1845, when he went to Washington as the legal representative of the nation, to prosecute their claims." William G. Cutler, *History of the State of Kansas,* (Chicago: A.T. Andreas, 1883).

     J. M. Armstrong died on April 15, 1852 in Ohio, while en route to Washington, D.C. Barry, *Beginning of the West,* 1077. Thus Mrs. Armstrong had been a widow for a little more than a year when the Hines family met her.

[17] H. K. Hines, "Emigrant Wagon," December 11, 1884, 2.

[18] Rev. Nathan Scarritt had been principal of the high school at the Shawnee Methodist Mission from 1848 to 1851 and was apparently continuing to serve as a missionary to the Shawnees, Delawares, and Wyandots. Barry, *Beginning of the West,* 776, 1012. Scarritt was also first pastor of the Kansas City Methodist church when it moved to its first permanent non-temporary home, a new brick building located on Fifth St. between Delaware and Wyandotte in 1852. Kansas City chapter, Daughters of the American Revolution, comp., *Vital Historical Records of Jackson County, Missouri* (Kansas City, Missouri, 1934), 191.

[19] See addendum to this chapter.

[20] This was probably the wife of Rev. John T. Peery, one-time missionary to the Wyandots. Barry, *Beginning of the West,* 537. In her diary, Celinda sometimes spells the surname "Peery" and sometimes "Perry." One census index mistakenly has "Pury."

[21] The 1850 Census lists H. M. Northrup, 32, merchant; Margaret, 20; and two males, 4 and 1. 1850 U.S. Census, Kansas Twp., Jackson County, Missouri; image copy at www.ancestry.com; accessed April 11, 2007. Barry reports, "Married: Hiram M. Northrup (a Westport, Missouri, resident since 1844), and Margaret Clark (part Wyandot;...) ...Northrup first established a mercantile business in the new town of Kansas, Missouri..." Barry, *Beginning of the West,* 566-7.

[22] Flint evidently did not get his wish. There is no further mention of his name by any in the Hines party. Louise Barry mentions a Dr. Flint who was in this vicinity headed west in the

spring of 1853 (Barry, *Beginning of the West,* 1161), but according to Dr. Flint's diary, on the evening of April 5, when Flint was dining with the Hineses, Dr. Flint was dining in the little village of Chili, Hancock County, Illinois. Thomas Flint, *Diary of Dr. Thomas Flint: California to Maine and return, 1851-1855,* (Los Angeles: Historical Society of Southern California, 1923), 16.

[23] This was very likely Franklin Conant, a merchant and hotel resident in 1850. 1850 U.S. census, Kaw, Jackson County, Missouri; image copy at www.ancestry.com; accessed May 4, 2007.

[24] William Walker was employed as an interpreter at the Wyandot Mission in 1853. Barry, *Beginning of the West,* 1189.

[25] Louise Barry explains further: "At the town's first municipal election—on Monday, April 4—William Gregory had been elected mayor, [Dr. Johnston] Lykins, council president... But Gregory had not lived at Kansas City, Mo., long enough to be eligible for office, so Lykins was named to replace him as mayor. Barry, *Beginning of the West,* 1143.

[26] In fact, before 1853 was over, Samuel and Malissa (Hines) Robinson and children moved to Eaton County, Michigan. Malissa Robinson obituary, *Grand Ledge Independent,* April 20, 1900.

[27] There is no further mention of this Moore family in the course of their trip. Perhaps they arrived too late or had a change of heart. On three different days, August 30, September 14, and September 25, the immigration roster at the Umatilla Agency lists single Moore men, without families. Linn County History Websites, http://linnhistory.peak.org/l853/1853imregis_9.html; accessed May 18, 2007.

[28] Some of the buildings housing the Shawnee Methodist Mission in 1853 were rehabilitated in the mid-1980s and are open to the public today, as part of the Shawnee Indian Mission State Historic Site, 3403 West 53rd Street, Fairway, Kansas 66205, just off the Shawnee Mission Parkway in the greater Kansas City, Kansas, area. Kansas State Historical Society: Shawnee Indian Mission State Historic Site: History, http://www.kshs.org/places/shawnee/history.htm; accessed April 11, 2007.

[29] This Mr. Collins stayed on with the Hines party as a driver until May 25, when he departed, after an apparent dispute with Gustavus. (See Celinda's diary entry for May 25.)

[30] This Mrs. Chick was Ann Eliza Chick, wife of Colonel William M. Chick, a longtime Missouri resident who opened his home to the early Methodist missionaries in Kansas (City). One daughter, Matilda M. Chick, married Rev. Nathan Scarritt on April 29, 1850. Another daughter, Mary Jane (Chick) Johnson, widow of Rev. William Johnson (who had died in 1842), married, second, Rev. John T. Peery. Barry, *Beginning of the West,* 537, 919. See also Kansas City chapter, Daughters of the American Revolution, comp., *Vital Historical Records of Jackson County, Missouri* (Kansas City, Missouri, 1934), p. 191. While returning to this area, Francis Parkman mentions Col. Chick, "At length, looming through the rain, we saw the log-house of Col. Chick, who received us with his usual bland hospitality..." Francis Parkman, *The Oregon Trail,* (New York: Random House, 1949), 9.

[31] This is evidently Joseph Leonard and family. Phoebe later indicates they were from Missouri, and Harvey in Chapter 18 indicates they settled in Linn County, Oregon. The 1850 U.S. census shows Joseph Leonard, 42; Mary 45; Sarah, 18; Catharine, 10; Cyrus 8; Lucinda, 6; and Joseph (Josiah?), 3. 1850 U.S. Census, Clark County, Missouri; image copy at www.ancestry.com; accessed April 11, 2007. The 1860 census for Oregon lists Joseph Leonard, 50; Mary, 55; Lucinda, 16; and Josiah, 13. In both censuses, Joseph's birthplace is given as Maryland, Mary's as South Carolina, and all the children's as Missouri. 1860 U.S. census, Linn County, Oregon; image copy at www.ancestry.com; accessed April 11, 2007.

[32] This was William H. Gray. See note 38 in Chapter 4.

[33] "Westport was actually about three miles south of Westport Landing, also called Kanzas Landing. Westport predates Kansas City, but was annexed to Kansas City in the 1870s." Personal communication, Gregory M. Franzwa.

[34] Gustavus's book, A *Voyage Round the World, etc.*, published in 1850, was already in its third printing in early 1851 (See "Voyage Round the World," *Northern Christian Advocate*, Feb. 12, 1851, 11:7), with favorable notices and frequent ads in the *Northern Christian Advocate* (See, e.g., "The Oregon Mission," *Northern Christian Advocate*, Nov. 27, 1850, 10:35, p. 138, and "Book Agents Wanted," p. 139 in the same issue). The newspaper was widely read by many thousands of Methodists of New York and as far west as Michigan, and the book evidently was seen by many potential emigrants throughout the region. The Judsons may very well have seen the following ad for the book, placed by its publisher, Derby, in their local newspaper. "Oregon, its History, Condition and prospects, containing a description of its Geography, Climate, and productions, with personal adventures among the Indians during a residence on the plains of the Pacific, embracing extended notes of a voyage around the world, by Rev. Gustavus Hines." *The Daily Sanduskian*, February 1851. Note that this refers to the second edition, with a changed title.

[35] It may well be that Phoebe always heard Obadiah referred to as "Diah," as that seems to have been his accepted nickname. Thus, when writing her reminiscences, over seventy years after the fact, she may have made the understandable inference that his full name was Jedediah. Holmes evidently saw no instance of "Obadiah" in any of his research and accepted Phoebe's "Jedediah" without question. Holmes, *Covered Wagon Women*, 79. The "Jedediah" error also appears in Barry, Faragher, and perhaps elsewhere. Barry, *Beginning of the West*, 1149. John Mack Faragher, *Women & Men on the Overland Trail*, 2nd Ed. (New Haven, 2001), 33. But the testimony of direct descendants, census records, and the writings of Gustavus and Harvey leave no doubt that the actual name was indeed Obadiah, and as far as we have been able to determine, the present work is the first book-length publication with the correct identification.

[36] A nearly complete roster for the group constituting this small "train" can be assembled from several sources: Celinda's diary (and Holmes' edition of the diary), Phoebe Judson's book, and the Bryant family information cited here. Leading the group was the elected captain, Rev. Gustavus Hines, accompanied by his wife, Lydia Bryant Hines, Lydia's sister Julia Bryant, and Lucy Anna Maria Lee, the daughter of Rev. Jason Lee, who had been in the Hines' care since her early childhood. (Holmes erroneously ascribes the surname Graves to Lydia and Julia.) Gustavus' older brother Obadiah (mistakenly identified as "Jedediah"

by Holmes, repeating Judson's error), his daughter Celinda, the diarist, his stepson Gustavus, and Obadiah's second wife, Eliza Bennett Roth Hines (Celinda's stepmother, whom Holmes misidentifies as her mother). Holmes, *Covered Wagon Women*, 78, 79. The youngest Hines brother, Harvey, was accompanied by his wife, Elizabeth Graves Hines, and her sister Martha M. Graves. Charles Wesley Bryant of Wyoming County, New York, a distant cousin of Lydia and Julia, was accompanied by his wife, Mary Fay Bryant, and their daughter Alta and son Lee. The Judson family of Vermilion, Ohio, included Holden Allen Judson and Phoebe Newton Goodell Judson, and their daughter Annie. A son, LaBonta, was born on the journey. A young Swede, Robert Nelson, accompanied the Judsons as a driver. Two young men, a Mr. Martin, and a Mr. Miner, assisted the Bryants. Joseph and Mary Leonard of Missouri and their family left the group after about a week of travel. Charles Long, a wagon maker, accompanied the train for several months.

[37] Here and in many other places, Harvey's dating of entries in his reminiscent account are in accord with neither the calendar, nor with Celinda's diary entries for matching events. Given that Celinda's diary is contemporaneous with the events, and that it consistently matches the calendar, we accept her date designations in favor of Harvey's.

[38] This Thomas Johnson was later in 1853 to be elected as a delegate to Congress from this territory, although the election was disputed and he ultimately was banned from a seat in the House of Representatives. Barry, *Beginning of the West, 1184*. Years later, in 1887, while critiquing Bancroft's *History of Oregon*, Harvey relates an incident with which he links himself indirectly (through Johnson) to Jason Lee. "This writer has stood in the very room in which Jason Lee was reposing when the sad intelligence of the death of his wife reached him; and in that room conversed with the very man, Rev. Thomas Johnson, who was his host on the memorable night when the iron of bereavement and sorrow entered his soul." H. K. Hines, "Bancroft on the Early Missionaries and their Work," *Pacific Christian Advocate*, May 19, 1887. Harvey's encounter with Johnson undoubtedly took place in the spring of 1853 as the Hines party awaited their departure.

[39] It is not unlikely that Mr. Lykins would be familiar with a St. Joseph newspaper. His name appeared on a list of people for whom mail was being held at the St. Joseph Post Office. *St. Joseph Gazette*, April 13, 1853, Vol. VIII, No. 26, 2.

[40] *St. Joseph Gazette*, March 30, 1853, Vol. VIII, No. 24, 2. According to Rev. J. Dudley Weaver, pastor of the First Presbyterian Church of Portland, "John Lapsley Yantis stands as a prominent, albeit short termed, figure in the life of this congregation. It was he who was authorized by the Presbytery of Oregon, which consisted of five pastors and one elder to organize a Presbyterian Church in Portland, Oregon—then a village of approximately 500 residents." Private correspondence from Rev. Weaver.

[41] This is a tantalizing clue as to what printed guide the Hines party may have had available to them in 1853. If, as speculated, they did indeed see this published letter, then they might well have followed the writer's advice. Regrettably we have been unable to locate anything more with regard to this guide.

Westport Landing (also called Kanzas Landing), in 1853, the year it was incorporated as Kansas City, Missouri. Lithograph from United States Illustrated. *The rock ledges, partially obscured by the shrubbery, made this port preferable to Wayne City Landing, and is where the Hines party landed. One of the buildings along the levee is probably the Union Hotel, where they lodged briefly, and another may well be the home of Col. William Chick, with whose family they became acquainted.*

Celinda's description: "Saturday, March 26...The village is situated on a high bluff rising from the river. The Houses are very much scattered, extending over considerable space, Making the place, from a distance, appear as if containing much more inhabitants than it in reality does. The houses are mostly log, with nice brick chimneys on the outside. The streets run every way without regard to form, & the houses are scattered hither and thither over the hills and in the vallies."

6

May 4—14, 1853: Starting Across the Plains

> *Each advanced step of the slow, plodding cattle*
> *carried us farther and farther from civilization into a*
> *desolate, barbarous country, where for several months we*
> *would be at the mercy of the treacherous savage. But our*
> *"new home" lay beyond all this and was a shining beacon*
> *that beckoned us on, inspiring our hearts with hope and*
> *courage.[1]*
>
> —Phoebe Judson, May 1853

Celinda

Wednesday, May 4—Forenoon rainy. Uncles went to the Kansas [River] where we intended to cross at the Delaware ferry & found that they could ferry our company across thursday morning. Consequently on their return we made preparations to start although it was yet raining. I paid Mrs. Parish three dollars ($3.00) for what had been got of her by our family that is our company. At length we were ready seven (7) wagons (one remaining to find stock) & started on. Pa drove the light wagon. Passing over a very good road on the prairie we soon arrived at the quaker mission. Directly the road became hilly, rough & muddy. The heavy wagons were in much jeopardy. We were alarmed for the safety of those within, but no one was hurt. The mules being gentle, we were not in much danger. At length after passing over three & a half miles of the worst road imaginable we arrived at the river & encamped for the night. The men guarded the cattle by turns all night. We could get no water but river water, which was very muddy. The men were completely tired out.

Harvey

When, after hours of wearying preparations, "the train" of five wagons, drawn by twenty yoke of oxen and one carriage drawn by a span of mules, with quite a band of loose cattle driven by men on horseback, moved forward, we all felt that the great journey was now begun. Henceforth there must be no looking backward.

The teams were wild, the drivers unpracticed, and many of the incidents of the early part of the journey were decidedly of the ludicrous order. Our

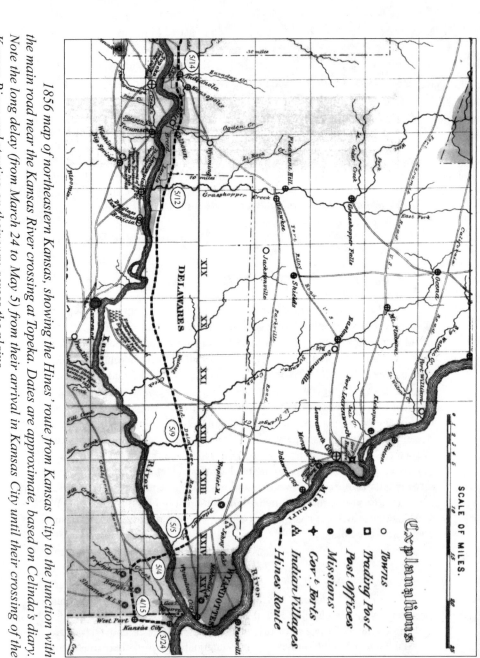

1856 map of northeastern Kansas, showing the Hines' route from Kansas City to the junction with the main road near the Kansas River crossing at Topeka. Dates are approximate, based on Celinda's diary. Note the long delay (from March 24 to May 5) from their arrival in Kansas City until their crossing of the Kansas River and starting on their way across the plains.

chosen route was a little aside from the usual one for the first hundred miles, being a little more to the east and north. We crossed the Kansas river at the Delaware Crossing—the old "Choteau Landing"[2] of Fremont's narrative— about twelve miles from the mouth of the river, and on the Reservation of the Delaware Indians, who owned and operated the ferry. Reaching the river late in the afternoon our first encampment was made upon its bank among the great cottonwood trees that covered the bottom lands. It was a wild, weird scene, this first camp. The white-covered wagons were standing about among the great trees, the tents scattered here and there through the forest, the horses and mules tied to the trees, the cattle gathered into a body and guarded by sentinels, and over all the great camp fires sending lurid glares and weird and wavering shadows. The excitement of the "start" was such, both to people and animals, that all were restless and wakeful, and there was a constant hum of movement among them during all the night. Besides we were in a forest, and no animal could be permitted to wander from the camp or we might be detained for days before it could be found. So the guards paced their assigned beats all night, and all were glad when the night had gone westward out of our sight.[3]

Phoebe

At length, early one bright morning, our camp became a scene of great commotion. The final preparations for our departure were in progress. Tents were taken down, tin dishes and cooking utensils were packed away. Men were excitedly running to and fro, hallooing at the cattle, who decidedly objected to being caught, as if they suspected what was before them—as some of them were unbroken steers, and there was not a practical ox driver in the crowd. With much difficulty they were finally collected, yoked and attached to the wagons.

The sunbonneted women watched the operations with intense interest, patiently awaiting the time to move forward.

It was nearly noon before the whole train, consisting of six wagons, each drawn by four yoke of oxen, one carriage drawn by a span of mules, and a band of loose cattle driven by the young men on horseback, were ready to begin the journey. At last the teamsters began shouting "gee Tom," "haw Buck," "up there Tom and Jerry,"'with various other names they had given to their oxen—and the start was made.

What a sense of relief possessed our hearts as the heavy wheels made their first revolution on the forward march.

Each advanced step of the slow, plodding cattle carried us farther and farther from civilization into a desolate, barbarous country, where for several months we would be at the mercy of the treacherous savage. But our "new home" lay beyond all this and was a shining beacon that beckoned us on, inspiring our hearts with hope and courage.

This hope was mingled with fear, for I had many forebodings, with but little trust in those days that "He who gives his angels charge over us, would keep us in all our days." I could only hope that we would get through safely, and was much gratified that we were at length en-route for Puget Sound—our watchword "Westward Ho!" A few hours' travel brought us to Kansas river crossing, just at nightfall, where we camped on its banks, amid the cottonwood trees. As we were in the forests, the horses and mules were tethered to the trees, and the cattle gathered into a body and guarded by the men to prevent their straying.

The men soon had the tents pitched, and the cheering blaze of the camp fires cast their fantastic shadows high among the dark cottonwoods. Our bed was so comfortably arranged that we preferred sleeping in our wagons.

I prepared the food in the wagon, then passed it down to Mr. Judson, who cooked it over the camp fire. When the bacon was fried and the tea steeped our meal was ready. A flat top trunk in the front of the wagon served as our dining table, and the foot of the bed for seats for Annie and myself. Mr. Judson and Nelson made themselves as comfortable as possible on the front board of the wagon.

There was but little sleep in the camp that night. The novelty and excitement of our environments drove slumber from our eyelids. My excited nerves kept me wide awake; the shouting of the men to the cattle, and the jingling ox chains on our journey during the day still rang in my ears, mingled with the noises of the camp, the steady tread of the guard, the stamping of the horses, the continued, though subdued movement all through the camp, and the occasional braying of the mules— all combined, were not conducive to sleep.

Oh, those mules; every tortured nerve of my being cried out in protest as their ear-splitting brayings rent the air. Our camp lay on the reservation of the Delaware Indians, who owned the ferry.[4]

Celinda

Thursday, May 5—Very pleasant. All right at the camp. It took almost all day to ferry the teams & cattle across. Some of the cattle swam the river & one cow got mired, but at length we were all safely landed in Nebraska at Little St. Louis.[5] I purchased a pair of shoes as cheap as I could in New York. We went out a mile & camped for the night. Plenty of grass & good water. Julia sick, all the others well.

Harvey

The work of crossing the river occupied nearly the whole day. It was done by ferrying the wagons and people on a flat boat, and swimming the horses and cattle. The Kansas is a large river, and at this season of the year, May 10th, was feeling the swell of the melting snow of the Rocky Mountains, so that it was a roiled and angry flood three hundred yards wide that swept before us.[6] It was the work of many hours, even with the help of several of the Delaware Indians, to make the cattle cross the river, and it was almost night again before, wet and weary and hungry, we were all across and in camp again not more than a mile from our camp of the night before.

The Kansas River near the Delaware Crossing, photographed by the editor from near Grinter's Place in July 2003, when the river level was much lower than during the May 1853 crossing by the Hines party.

Again we drove our pickets in the forest that margins the lower Kansas, and were compelled to stand out another night in guard of the stock, or allow them to stray away to the great delay of our journey. As it was, when the morning came our two mules were missing, and a part of the company were compelled to remain in the same place for another day and night, when a Christian Wyandotte Indian—"Gray Eyes"—whom we had met on the Sabbath spent with these people of which mention has been made, brought them to our camp, having tracked them twelve miles before overtaking them.[7]

Phoebe

The next morning we, the women and children, with the wagons, were safely ferried across, while the men swam the stock. This was a difficult undertaking and not without dangers, as the river was much swollen by the melting snow, being about three hundred yards wide at this point, with a very rapid current.

One of our large wheel oxen, in some way, got one foot over the yoke. We were afraid he would drown; it seemed almost impossible for him to escape that fate, but greatly to our joy he managed to swim out, in spite of his awkward position.

Years after, while recalling this incident, I attributed this remarkable feat to "old Tom," but Mr. Judson said no, it was "old Jerry." Well, it does not matter, they were both faithful creatures, and we depended more upon them than any other yoke in our team to carry us safely over the rough and dangerous places, for they were very large, strong and obedient.

It was nearly night before the arduous task of swimming the stock was accomplished, and with thankful hearts we again took up our line of march, only traveling one mile, when the falling shades of night compelled us once more to make our camp among the cottonwood trees that fringed the Kansas. Although still among friendly Indians, we were obliged to guard our stock to keep them from straying.[8]

Celinda

Friday, May 6—A.M. pleasant P.M. rainy. Some cattle of Mr. Leonard's & one of our mules gone. We started on & left them uncle H & pa remained. Mr. Stateler who by the way is a missionary at West Port & brother-in-law of Mr Leonard—and his wife having come so far with us & Mr S's horse having gone off with the mule, Mrs S & pa remained with the wagons. Uncle H. & Mr. S. hunted for the lost. Mr. S did not return at night & Mrs. S. Uncle H. & pa stayed all night in the wagon having no supper nor any covering except the wagon cover although it was very cold & rainy. We went out on the prairie about six miles ahead & pitched our tents. Water & no wood.

Saturday, May 7—Pleasant, but cold as winter. Uncle H came no news as yet. He went back with pa's breakfast and with the intention should not the mule be found to go back to the Shawnee mission & purchase another but during his absence the indian White Crow had bought him back. They payed him $1.00 & then came to the camp. Mr. L had not yet found his cattle. A very intelligent Delaware chief came to the camp. He wore a beautiful wampum belt exceeding every thing I had ever seen of the kind. He advised us to take the divide route instead of the government road by Ft Leavenworth as it is nearer & they say a better road. Uncle G captain.

Harvey

Those of us who had remained in the old forest camp overtook the remainder of the train a few miles beyond the line of the river timber at evening of the second day. We were then not more than six miles from our starting point, three days before, but we had disentangled ourselves from the floods and timber of the Kansas river and were now fairly afloat on the prairie sea that rolled its emerald waves westward.

Here the organization of the train was effected, a captain elected, guards and reliefs appointed, and all that seemed necessary to arrange for the journey attended to.[9]

Phoebe

In spite of our vigilance, the mules made their escape from the camp. It was two days before they were restored to us by a friendly Indian, named "Grey Eyes—he had tracked them twelve miles. Though my nerves rejoiced in the absence of their discordant voices, I was pleased that their owners did not suffer loss. Only six miles of our journey had thus been accomplished. Here the organization of our company was affected.[10]

Gustavus Hines was elected captain; we could not have made a better choice. As a leader, he was qualified by experience, and his personal appearance and manners commanded our admiration and respect, inspiring our little band with hope and courage. When leading the train, mounted on a magnificent gray horse, I looked upon him more as a general than a captain— often mentally comparing him to General Winfield Scott. On him devolved the duty of selecting our camping places. On Saturdays he was particularly careful to select a suitable situation for our Sabbath encampment, which would afford water and grass for our cattle, these being of the first importance.

Celinda

Sunday, May 8—Weather cold. Some Californians camped near Jonny Cakes house lost one of men

Monday, May 9—Cold. Started about half past eight. Found the road bad. Collins wagon got almost tipped over. Julia Martha & I rode upon Charles' wagon. M jumped out every bad place. We went about 15 mi camped in a beautiful place....

Tuesday, May 10—Pleasant. Found some bad road in the morning afterwards it was good. Scenery delightful went about 13 miles....

Wednesday, May 11—Pleasant. road good except crossing ravines scenery delightful.

Thursday, May 12—Rainy. Crossed the Grasshopper in a ferry. The wagons had to be unloaded & let down the bank with ropes it being too steep and high on both sides and the river so deep that we could not ford it. It took all day to cross it. It rained most of the time. We stopped at an indian house. The woman was very good looking. She wore a broad-cloth blanket round her for a shirt a calico sash round her waist & broad-cloth pants trimmed with ribands. Her feet were small & she wore morocco shoes. She wore what looked to be tin ornaments for dress pins & steel ones—in her ears—which resembled eight or ten small keys.

Friday, May 13—One cow not to be found. Passed over a level prairie good road most of the way camped near a ravine. Plenty of wood & water

Saturday, May 14—Pleasant. Road good with the exception of a number of ravines which we had to cross before noon. We were obliged to stop at one while the men constructed a bridge as we could not cross without. In the P M. we were on a level prairie road good. Just before night we intersected the southern road which crosses the Kansas at the upper ferry camped near the junction.

Harvey

The trail we were traveling was an unfrequented one, chosen because it swung us loose from the great caravan of the emigration for the first hundred miles, and led us westward up the [north] side of the Kansas river, and across the Stranger, Soldier, and Grasshopper creeks, uniting with the main road between the Kansas and the Vermilion.[11]

Phoebe

Our route for the first hundred miles lay westward, up the Kansas river, away from the great line of emigrant travel. During the first week we crossed four small rivers, the Kansas, the Stranger, Soldier and Grasshopper.

Over the last named river our wagons and provisions were carried in a very large canoe. The entire day was consumed in the tedious operation of unloading, crossing and reloading the wagon.[12]

Prairie in eastern Kansas

[1] Judson, *A Pioneer's Search*, 18.

[2] It appears that Harvey is confusing things here. According to Franzwa, the two sites known successively as Chouteau's Landing were on the Missouri River—not the Kansas—and were several miles to the east of the Delaware Crossing of the Kansas River. Gregory M. Franzwa, *The Oregon Trail Revisited* (Tucson: The Patrice Press, 1997), 99-100. Other than the sites known as Chouteau's Landing that Harvey mentions, there was also an establishment known as the Chouteau Trading Post, and this was indeed located on the Kansas River, but again somewhat east—about two miles downstream—from the Delaware Crossing. Views of the Past 1: Old Wyandotte, http://www.kckpl.lib.ks.us/KSCOLL.lochist/views/views1.htm; accessed October 8, 2007.

[3] H. K. Hines, "Emigrant Wagon," December 18, 1884, 2.

[4] Judson, *A Pioneer's Search*, 1820.

[5] Note that although both Harvey and Celinda refer to this as the "Delaware Crossing," which by modern maps would leave them still in the state of Kansas after crossing the river, Celinda writes, "...at length we were all safely landed in Nebraska at Little St. Louis."

Why "Nebraska?" This region was not to be designated as part of Kansas until the Kansas-Nebraska Act of 1854. Prior to that, efforts in Congress to establish a Nebraska Territory west of Iowa and Missouri embraced a region as far south as the present southern boundary of the state of Kansas, although the area south of the Kansas River was generally designated "Indian Territory." Celinda was giving voice to what was likely the common understanding that anything in the region west of the Missouri River and north of the Kansas River was part of Nebraska. Kansas historian Louise Barry cites another 1853 account in a newspaper, regarding a steamboat that "came up to [St. Joseph, Mo.] and landed on the opposite of the river, in Nebraska..." Barry, *Beginning of the West*, 1161.

Why "Little St. Louis?" Barry's reference to this same quotation from Celinda's diary, "...at length we were all safely landed in Nebraska[!] at Little St. Louis [Delaware trading post]" seems to imply that "Little St. Louis" was one of the (several?) names for the settlement on the north bank of the Kansas river. Barry, *Beginning of the West*, 1149. The settlement later became known as Grinter Place, named after Moses Grinter, who operated a trading post there from 1855 to 1860, and also operated the ferry. Kansas State Historical Society, Grinter Place History; http://www.kshs.org/places/grinter/history.htm; accessed May 25, 2007.

[6] Celinda records May 5th as the crossing date, and given that hers is a diary entry as contrasted to Harvey's reminicense of some thirty years later, we take May 5th as the more likely date.

[7] H. K. Hines, "Emigrant Wagon," December 18, 1884, 2.

[8] Judson, *A Pioneer's Search*, 20, 21.

[9] H. K. Hines, "Emigrant Wagon," December 18, 1884, 2.

[10] It is difficult to miss the frequent, striking parallels in phrasing between Harvey's and Phoebe's accounts. The most plausible explanation is that Phoebe, writing her reminis-

cences in 1925, had access to Harvey's 1884 account, and used it along with her own diary, as a reference when writing her book. From a reference Harvey made to "Sister Judson" in the *Advocate* while he was editor, it appears likely she was a regular reader, and certainly his published account therein of their shared trip experiences would have been a good candidate for her keepsakes:

"Brother J. A. Tennant, from Ferndale, W.T. [Washington Territory], under date of June 6th, adds the following P.S. to a communication:

"Our camp meeting commences at Femdale July 11th, and continues one week. A steamboat will come direct from Seattle, leaving there on Sunday evening, the 9th. Come over and *rest*, and we will give you such a rousing welcome and show you what wonders God has wrought among the poor Indians that you will be astonished. Bring no *preacher in charge* to take *charge of* you; well, you can have a good time. Sister Judson will most likely have a tent on the ground, and we will allow her to take charge of you. Why not get a few good workers and come? Will be a good vacation, and do you good and benefit us and help on the cause. Just put a line in the glorious old *P. C. Advocate* and say yes, and make us glad. Pray for us, that the Great Shepherd will be present in power. I think Sister Hines might do some good temperance work here.

"Most reluctantly do we say to Bro. Tennant that it is impossible for us to go. 'Sister Judson' and Bro. Judson were members of our company in the long, trying joumey of five months, with ox teams from Westport, Mo., to Portland, Oregon, in 1853. Our memory sweeps the years, as we write this line, and rests on the events of that weary way with unspeakable thrill. How delightful it would be to sit down in the "tent" again and talk over, in the old familiar way, the pains and perils past. But work, not inclination, keeps us from it now." *Pacific Christian Advocate*, XXVIII, No. 25, June 22, 1882, 4.

[11] H. K. Hines, "Emigrant Wagon," December 18, 1884, 2.

[12] Judson, *A Pioneer's Search*, 21.

7

May 15–29, 1853: Keeping the Sabbath

> *Mr Collins left at noon Uncle Harvey drove his team. He was angry at Uncle Gustavus…*
> —Celinda Hines, May 25, 1853

> *All were in fine spirits and we were making good time, when all at once, just as we were about to camp on a little creek for our noon lunch, every spoke in the hind wheel of Harvey Hines' wagon gave away at once. "There," ruefully remarked my husband, "is one wagon already that will have to be left behind."*[1]
> —Phoebe Judson, May 29, 1853

Sunday, May 15, marked, in Harvey's words, "the first Sabbath on the plains," welcomed by nearly all—including the animals—as a day of respite from "the hard toils of a life of labor." We say "nearly all" because Mr. Leonard felt he could not "lose one day in seven" if he and his family were to make it to their destination before bad weather arrived. Harvey notes that Leonard, though evidently pious, could not be persuaded on religious grounds or otherwise, so he and his family moved on. Hinting that the incident is "full of moral teaching," Harvey reserves further comment until later down the trail.

Celinda's only comment on the incident is that no one expressed regret at the departure of the Leonards, perhaps because their large contingent of livestock added a great deal to the overall workload, with little in the way of added manpower to compensate.

Phoebe, on the other hand, indicates that she and her husband did indeed feel regret in losing the company of a congenial family. Furthermore, they shared the Leonards' reluctance to give up a day of travel every week. But in the end the Judsons bowed to the leadership of Gustavus, the company captain. Phoebe also points out that the day of rest is perceived differently by the women than by the men, the latter—in her view, at least—having endured a week of more wearying labor than the former. In any case, the break in activities sets Phoebe to introspection and reminiscence.

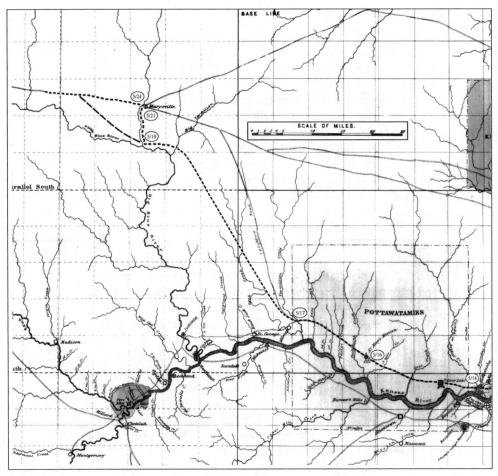

*1856 map of northeastern Kansas showing the Hines' route (short dashes)
from Topeka to the crossing of the ("middle fork" of the) Big Blue River. Dates are
approximate, based on Celinda's diary. River names on this map (and modern maps)
do not all correspond with river names in the diary. For example, what is called "Lost
Creek" on this map probably is the "Cross Creek" of modern maps, and the "Kross
Creek" of the diary.*

*The line marked with long dashes denotes the path taken by some emigrants
from the Big Blue crossing near Alcove Springs to what Celinda calls the "junction
with Ft. Jo road." (See Appendix.)*

Harvey

By Saturday night we had made our junction with the main road, and on a beautiful prairie we made our camp for the first Sabbath on the plains. A more laborious week than this we had then never spent. It was the first of the journey and nothing had yet dropped into easy grooves. Besides the crossing incidents related we had been obliged to ferry our goods and wagons over the Grasshopper in a canoe, consuming a whole day in unloading and loading them again, so that that bright May Sabbath seemed a bit of Eden thrown down to us amidst the hard toils of a life of labor. Oxen and horses seemed to share our sense of rest, and lay contentedly near the wagons and tents. Here occurred one of the incidents of the journey that we have ever looked upon as full of moral teaching.

Nothing had been said at the organization of the company about traveling on the Sabbath. My brothers and myself not thinking of it as a thing necessary to be spoken about. So, about ten o'clock, as we were standing together conversing about the pleasure the day of rest was bringing us, Mr. L[eonard] approached us and inquired when we were going to "hitch up." We told him Monday morning. "But," said he, "those who have crossed the plains say we must never camp two nights in a place; and besides I am out on these plains with my family and I cannot lose one day in seven in crossing them. If you are not going to move on I must say good-bye to you." We expostulated with him, as he was a Methodist as well as ourselves, but after a little he and his men went out and gathered his stock from ours, and about eleven o'clock moved onward. There was no disagreement except in regard to travel on the Sabbath. In fifteen minutes his white wagon tops had disappeared over a roll of prairie. We reserve any remarks or reflections until we meet further on and months ahead.

The hours of Sabbath rest helped us, man and beast, back to our wonted vigor, and when Monday morning came we were astir, and with a cheerful swing the oxen drew us onward.[2]

Celinda

Sunday, May 15—Very pleasant. The Co, all but Mr. Leonard wishing to camp over Sunday did so but Mr. L left. He having a good many cattle & but three men & two wagons none at least expressed sorrow at his departure. In the P M. Martha Julia Charles & myself walked out had a very pleasant time. All were alarmed at our prolonged stay.

Phoebe

The first Sabbath of our journey over the plains found us encamped on a beautiful rolling prairie, covered with a luxuriant carpet of grass, as green as a meadow. The wide spreading plains, as far as the eye could reach, presented a picturesque scene—whose silent beauty awakened solemn thoughts—that impressed one with awe and reverence. Here we were isolated from the world, and in this secluded, romantic spot we were free to worship our Maker according to the dictates of our conscience. It is Emerson who says, "We are as much strangers to nature as we are aliens from God."

Only one incident occurred to mar the harmony of the day of rest. Our Missouri family, though good Methodists at home, seemed to think they could not afford to keep the Sabbath day holy while traveling on the plains. When they found they could not prevail upon our good captain to break the Sabbath, they gathered up their stock, and, after saying "good-bye," pulled out. We were sorry to have them leave us, as they had the appearance of being a very nice family. Mr. Judson and I were as much opposed to camping two nights in the same place as they were, and our fears greatly inclined us to go with them, but we decided to abide by the decision of our captain, in whom we had much confidence, and afterward during our long journey were very thankful that we were so providentially led into his company.

During the week our men had been very busily employed driving their oxen, yoking and unyoking their cattle, standing guard at night, unloading and reloading the wagons at the ferries, and swimming the stock. Saturday night found them very tired and much in need of physical rest, so they lolled around in the tents and on their blankets spread on the grass, or under the wagons out of the sunshine, seeming to realize that the "Sabbath was made for man."

But the women, who had only been anxious spectators of their arduous work, and not being weary in body, could not fully appreciate physical rest, and were rendered more uneasy by the continual passing of emigrant trains all day long—most of them much larger than our own. To me, much of the day was spent in meditating over the past and in forebodings for the future. In my reveries I was carried back home to my childhood days, and listened to the waves of beautiful Lake Erie as they softly lapped the sandy beach. I saw the barefooted children splashing in its limpid waters. Happy children; childhood days are only too short. The snowballs and lilacs in mother's yard were in full bloom; how lovely they looked. The ringing of the church bell greeted my ear, and in fancy I joined the throng that wended its way to the church, and, ascending the flight of stairs that led to the gallery, mingled my voice as of yore with the choir in singing Old Hundred, Coronation, Boylston, and other grand old tunes. At the singing of each song the whole congregation rose to their feet, turned in their pews in order to face the choir, and listened attentively to the music. When again seated, the minister, with a dignified air and solemn countenance, arose in the pulpit (my father, the Rev. J. M. Goodall, pastor of the Presbyterian church, arose in the pulpit)—and announced his text: "Known unto God are all His works from the beginning of the world."[3]

By the time he had finished his discourse on creation, transgression, effectual calling, election, redemption, justification, adoption and sanctification—with all the benefits derived from firstly to last, I was aroused from my reverie, and, looking out upon God's glorious works of creation, concluded with Whittier "that the book, the church, the day, were made for man, not God, for earth, not heaven."[4]

Although so remote from civilization and haunted by many fears of the calamities that might overtake us on our journey through the wilderness, we passed a very pleasant day. It gave us a better opportunity to become acquainted with our fellow travelers.

Monday morning we were up bright and early, our men much refreshed by their day of rest, and all were in fine spirits. After camp duties were performed and the oxen yoked and attached to the wagons, we were ready to jog along on our journey.

By the departure of our Missouri family our train was reduced to five wagons, and each took its turn in leading the train, like an old fashioned spelling class—the one that was head at night took its place at the foot next morning.[5]

As the now-smaller Hines party proceeds, we note with Celinda that by May 19, four days after leaving the Hines to forge ahead faster, Mr. Leonard is spotted only "...*about a mile & a half ahead.*"[6]

Gregory M. Franzwa

Oregon Trail ruts still visible in 1997 north of Blaine, Kansas.

Monday, May 16—Rained in the A M & hailed the largest I had ever seen. Pleasant. Passed the catholic mission of the Pottawatamies. Found there to our surprise quite a pleasant looking village there. Country—rolling prairie consequently many ravines. The worst one bridged. Went about 17 miles (Kross creek)[7]

Tuesday, May 17—Warm. Crossed the Vermillion[8]—bridged— Overtook a Co. of Californians: one lady & maid in the Co. & a drove of cattle. Camped in a delightful place near which was a grave. The bones had been dug up. H. A. Blinn Michigan died …27, 1852—three marks on the board. The eve. was very rainy.

Wednesday, May 18—Very cold. Country uneven. Crossed the Little Vermillion.[9] See dead cattle every day along the road. Saw two men who were 50 miles behind their Co. gave them some sea bread. Overtook another Co. of Californians with a drove. Camped near a ravine. Traveled 24 miles.

Thursday, May 19—Very pleasant & warm. Saw Mr. Leonard about a mile & a half ahead. [Crossed?] Salt creek the banks of which are very high. The oxen were not detached from the wagons but ropes were hitched to the wagons to let them down. All crossed over in safety. Soon after we arrived at the Middle Fork of the Blue. Aunt Lydia, Julia, Lucy Anna & myself were in Charles wagon as we were going down the bank the wagon tipped over none were much hurt but L A & myself being behind the others & the things coming upon us we could not move. I could stir neither hand nor foot. Julia & Aunt jumped out in the mud & water. L A. & I remained until the cover was removed & some of the things taken out. Everyone was very much frightened. Some Californians were near & assisted us. The wagon was injured a little. The contents of the provision chest were mostly emptyed into the stream. But on the whole but little damage was done. The wagon was reloaded & we proceeded. Camped near the Blue. Made the acquaintance of a Mr Ferguson[10] a Santa Fe trader who had lived ten years in Mexico & crossed the plains six times. We could not cross the river for high water. Mr F's Co. were making a raft.

Friday, May 20—Thirteen head of cattle were missing 7 of our work oxen. They were found P M. Mr F's raft went down stream. River continued to rise. We washed in a ravine. People camped in every direction waiting for the water to fall. Impossible to cross unless it did.

Saturday, May 21—Very warm Concluded to go north to the ferry about 7 miles came to a ravine which we could not cross went round came to a crossing. I rode Mr. F's pony across the water. Charles wagon run against a tree in consequence of the breaking of a chain. Detained a little but no damage done. Mr. F's Co with us. I drove loose stock part of the way. Camped about two miles from the ferry in a beautiful place. This week our route has been over a rolling prairie beautiful to behold. We frequently see wolves or those who guard do & 7 rattle snakes have been seen by the Co since we started. We find Leeach [leek?] lillies & star of Bethlehem wild here. Wagon ran over Mrs Bryant's foot.

Sunday, May 22—It rained hard in the night we got up [all but?] one tent. Morning cold. Martha & Mr Miner & I took a walk after noon.

Monday, May 23—Remained in camp because our turn had not yet come to cross the Blue. Many camps in sight. Mr Jones[11] Co from Kansas has arrived.

Gregory M. Franzwa

The Big Blue River was crossed in the area of this photo, taken in 1973.

Each large river encountered posed problems for crossing. The unusually high water of the Big Blue presented the Hines party with a long wait and particular problems for crossing their stock. The Hines' solution was unique, and caused somewhat of a stir, although Celinda says simply, "...almost impossible to swim cattle but we had no difficulty with ours we all crossed in safety & camped on the other side."

The clever Hines stratagem is attributed by Phoebe to "our captain," i.e., Gustavus, but Harvey implicitly claims at least part of the credit through the phrase, "…*we* hit upon…"

Celinda

Tuesday, May 24—Struck our tents & went to the ferry. Many wagons were before us some who were booked before us & some who were not. I should think there were a hundred wagons in sight during the day. The river was falling but yet very high. [It was] almost impossible to swim cattle but we had no difficulty with ours we all crossed in safety & camped on the other side. We were now in the Pawnee country.

Harvey

At Big Blue occurred another little episode, somewhat vexing in its delay but pleasant in its outcome. We transcribe the record made at the time:

Big Blue, generally fordable, we found swollen so much from heavy rains upon its sources that we were obliged to wait five days for our turn upon a ferry boat doing business there at the rate of three dollars per wagon. We ferried the wagons and swam the stock. For five days we had watched men endeavoring to force their cattle over the angry flood, but the brutes obstinately refused to face the boiling current, and the men had given it up in despair. Seeing they could not be *driven* over, we hit upon the following expedient. Three of our cows had calves. These we tied on the stern of the boat behind our wagons, huddled our whole band of cattle close down by the ferry landing and as the boat shoved off drove them all rapidly in after it. The calves called their mothers, who followed them as rapidly as possible, the oxen followed the cows, and in ten minutes all were safely on the other shore. The bystanders, among whom were men who had crossed the plains more than once, shouted and hurrahed, and one old graybeard frontiersman said to me: "You uns'll git to Oregon."[12]

Phoebe

In a few hours we reached the Big Blue river and were somewhat crestfallen when we found there were several large trains ahead of us awaiting their turn to be ferried over. The facilities for crossing were so inadequate that we were detained five days, awaiting our turn to be ferried over.

The time seemed long to wait, and I, for one, was quite impatient at the delay, but not a murmur was heard censuring "our Moses," who, no doubt, had he known the situation, would have made another day's travel and not allowed so many trains to pass us. There was nothing for us to do but "possess our souls in patience" and wait.

One would naturally suppose that traveling after the slow, plodding cattle would have been sufficient to thoroughly inculcate that Christ-like quality, but it was evident, at least in our case, that additional lessons were required. So here we were, mixed up with other trains in the greatest confusion on the sandy banks of the Blue, where a perfect bedlam reigned. Men hallooing from one side of the river to the other, cattle bellowing, calves bawling, and a woman on the opposite side of the river screaming at the top of her voice, "Oh, Papa, mam says them cows can't swim with their bags full of milk." The poor woman was nearly frantic for fear the cows would drown. The prolonged sound of the "O" indicated that they were western people, or at least were not Yankees.

Many trains were distinguished by having the names of their states painted on the covers of their wagons, and some were loaded with "a right smart chance of truck," with many of the belongings of its inmates dangling from the outside.

The women and children of each train were ferried over on the flatboat with the wagons, where they anxiously awaited the swimming of the stock. The river was much swollen from the melting snow, and it seemed utterly impossible to drive the poor, dumb brutes into the cold water of the rapid stream.

Our captain finally devised a successful plan which proved a solution of the difficulty. Placing three young calves on the stern of the ferry boat, he huddled the cattle together on the bank, and when the boat started the calves bawled for their mothers, who plunged into the river after them—the other cattle following. They were all soon over on the opposite bank of the river, when a shout of victory went up for the shrewd "Yankee" captain.

One of the Missourians was so pleased with this successful scheme of the captain that he gave utterance to this encouraging prophecy, "You ones will git to Oregon," which implied that he had some lingering doubts that the others would attain the goal of their ambition.

The expense of the ferriage was three dollars per wagon, but we did not stop to parley—we were only too glad to take up our line of march again at any price.[13]

Celinda

Wednesday, May 25—Pleasant. Started early & traveled about 24 miles across a rolling prairie. Passed four graves. Mr Jones Co joined us in the morning five wagons. Mr Collins left at noon. Uncle Harvey drove his team. He was angry at Uncle Gustavus. Camped on…prairie. Saw 2 wolves A.M.

Thursday, May 26—It rained some in the night. Morning pleasant & warm. Crossed a number of ravines. Passed them all in safety. Camped after crossing a very bad place where we saw a wagon which was broken. Two companies in sight. Saw three graves.

Friday, May 27—Very pleasant & warm Crossed Otter creek A M. In the P M. crossed Little Sandy having about noon crossed the Big Sandy. Saw five graves. See dead cattle often. Saw some elk hornes. Encamped [near?] the Little Sandy. Heard a pack of wolves barking near by. Two camps in sight.

Not long after crossing the Blue—Harvey implies it was the very next day, although Celinda's diary suggests it was several days later—Harvey's wagon suffered a breakdown. Our three chroniclers have similar accounts of the incident, but with some distinct differences. We start with Celinda's contemporary description, which implies the repairs were carried out mainly by Charles Long, "a wagon maker," and Mr. Jones, "a blacksmith," while others, presumably including Harvey, provided incidental help. Harvey's reminiscent account portrays himself in a more central role, and Phoebe appears to endorse that view. We suspect that Harvey's retelling of this incident over the intervening years may well have introduced embellishments, and he may have found it simply less complicated to describe it as a repair he made with a little help from others. And as we have noted before, Phoebe undoubtedly had Harvey's account in hand as she wrote and she may have relied on it for describing details of this incident.

Celinda

Saturday, May 28—Cloudy. Crossed some 15 ravines before noon when in crossing one, one of the hind wheels to Uncles large wagon broke, all of the spokes coming out. No other damage was done. On examination it was found that the spokes in all the wheels were loose. We camped to repair it. Some timber was found not far off which was thought would answer the purpose.

Sunday, May 29—About ten at night I was awakened by a violent storm of rain. Water poured in torrents & we were soon drenching with rain. We succeeded in keeping some of our clothes & bedding comfortably dry. After about an hour the rain abated in a measure (although it continued raining some all night) after which we lie down as best we could & I slept most of the time till morning which the storm having ceased was cold & cloudy. Mr Long who was a wagon maker went to work at the wheel the others assisting as much as they could. Mr Jones being a blacksmith set the tire & before night all was repaired. Many trains passed during the day. After tea M, J & myself went to see a grave. It was a young lady. The body had been dug up by wolves. Bones & clothing were scattered around. Prickley pears wild.

Phoebe

All were in fine spirits and we were making good time, when all at once, just as we were about to camp on a little creek for our noon lunch, every spoke in the hind wheel of Harvey Hines' wagon gave away at once. "There," ruefully remarked my husband, "is one wagon already that will have to be left behind." But the owner of the wagon had not given up hope. After dinner he went up the creek to a thicket of ash which we had passed a short time before and brought some of the wood to the camp, with which, and the aid of willing hands, he had the wheel filled, and the tire reset ready to resume our journey with thankful hearts in the morning.[14]

Harvey

At noon of the next day, as we were turning a little away from the road by a little creek for our dinner halt, the hind wheel of my wagon, which was what wagon makers call rimbound, broke down, every spoke giving away at once, and the rim and tire of the wheel running clear away from the wagon. "There," said Mr. J[udson] of our train, "is one wagon to be left," and it seemed a safe prophecy. But, dinner over, I told the company that I only desired the train to lay by until morning and I would be ready to move onward again. To this they consented, so, taking an ax, I went a mile or so up the creek on which we had stopped to where I saw a few green Ash trees, and cutting one down split out spokes enough to refill the wheel and brought them down to the camp, heated them for an hour or two over a fire, while, with help volunteered by others, I bored and chiseled the broken tenons out of the hub, then shaved and drove the new spokes, knocked the tire off the rim, and fitted the spokes to the rim, then built a fire and set the tire back on the wheel again, and at dark was ready to move forward once more. We had taken the precaution to bring with us an ax, a drawing knife, two or three augers, and two or three small chisels. In boyhood I had learned to use them.[15]

---

[1] Judson, *A Pioneer's Search*, 27.

[2] H. K. Hines, "Emigrant Wagon," December 18, 1884, 2.

[3] This text is from Acts 15:18 (King James Version).

[4] Phoebe's quotation is a paraphrase of a passage in Whittier's "The Meeting." Project Gutenberg; http://www.gutenberg.org/dirs/etext05/witl4l0.txt; accessed May 5, 2007.

[5] Judson, *A Pioneer's Search,* 22-24.

[6] "While most of those abstaining from travel on the Sabbath did so for religious reasons, it is a fact that the day of rest was so rejuvenating to the draft animals that such teams often made better time than those traveling seven days a week." Private communication, Gregory M. Franzwa. See Harvey's comparison of Leonard's and Hines' travel times in Chap. 18.

[7] "The beauty and fertility of the Pottawatomie reserve, and the fact that it was traversed by the California and Oregon road, one of the great highways of the Territory, made it an especially desirable location, but while an Indian reservation, of course, no title to any land could be obtained except through marriage relations with the tribe. Those who settled in the vicinity of Cross Creek in 1847-48, were nearly all connected with the Pottawatomies in this way. Among those settlers were John Bassho, Stephen McPherson, William Martel, Alexander Rodd, Francis Bergeron, Anthony Tacier, Lawton and William Nasseau. *(Metsepa* signifying the "cross" was the Indian name of the creek—so called, because at its junction with the Kansas the angles formed by the two streams bear a resemblance to a cross.)" William G. Cutler, *History of the State of Kansas,* (Chicago: A.T. Andreas, 1883), Shawnee County, Part 44. Kansas Collection Books, http://www.kancoll.org/books/cutler/shawnee/shawnee-co-p44.html; accessed April 12, 2007.

[8] Also called the "Red Vermillion." "[This] area is the site of one of the great tragedies of the trail. Late in May 1849, a huge outfit camped around the ford on the east bank of the river. Asiatic cholera took over and before the week was over many were dead. Fifty emigrants are believed to be buried on the river bank." Franzwa, *Oregon Trail Revisited,* 141.

[9] Also called the "Black Vermillion."

[10] Louise Barry identifies him as "Alexander C. Ferguson," but gives no further details. Barry, *Beginning of the West,* 1149.

[11] Celinda later mentions that this Mr. Jones from Kansas [City] was a blacksmith. The 1850 U.S. census for Kansas Township (i.e., Kansas City) lists a Joseph Jones, 30, blk smith. This was perhaps the same man, although we have no further confirmation. 1850 U.S. census, Kansas Township, Jackson County, Missouri; image copy at www.ancestry.com; accessed April 12, 2007.

[12] H. K. Hines, "Emigrant Wagon," December 18, 1884, 2.

[13] Judson, *A Pioneer's Search,* 24-26.

[14] Judson, *A Pioneer's Search,* 27.

[15] H. K. Hines, "Emigrant Wagon," December 18, 1884, 2.

8

May 30—June 10, 1853: Fort Kearny and Beyond

Rev. Harvey K. Hines, who possessed a daring
spirit of adventure, wandered off one pleasant afternoon,
accompanied by a young man of the train. Ascending a
high hill they were lured so far away by the grandeur of
the scenery that on their return they were overtaken by
darkness, and it was midnight before they found their way
into camp, where we were still up, anxiously waiting with
lanterns on the wagons for beacon lights. Mr. Hines found
his young wife in tears, and indeed we were all terror
stricken for fear they had been captured by the Pawnees.[1]
—Phoebe Judson, June 1853

Harvey

Up to this point our journey had been in comparative safety. We had passed through the territory of three tribes of Indians, the Shawnees, the Delawares, and the Pottawatomies, all of whom had been long under the teaching and influence of Missionaries, and already quite on the way to civilization. With many of them we became somewhat acquainted, among whom was a Delaware who had been one of Fremont's trusted guides in his explorations of eight or ten years before, over the Rocky Mountains, and among the Sierras, and through the valleys of He was with that explorer on the night of the 9th of May, 1846, near the Klamath, when the treacherous Klamaths assaulted his camp and came so near destroying his entire command. We met him at the Grasshopper, and he cautioned us about the Pawnee's territory we were soon to enter. He was a man of splendid physique, with an open, generous face, and inspired us with trust in his kindness and integrity. Between the Blue and the Republican[2] we entered the Pawnee's territory, and henceforth our march must be more guarded and military.[3]

Phoebe

The prairie over which we moved so slowly with our horned steeds was covered with a coat of living green. Springs of pure, cold water came bubbling forth from ravines in abundance. An occasional patch of timber,

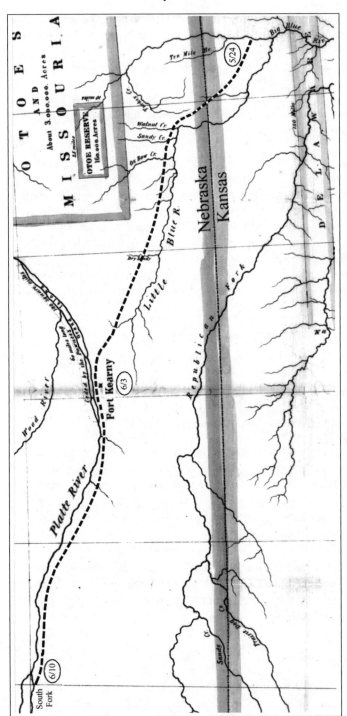

Section from an 1854 map of northern Kansas and southern Nebraska showing the Hines' route along the Little Blue River to Ft. Kearny—the classic Oregon Trail—and then along the Platte River to the South Fork of the Platte. Dates are approximate, based on Celinda's diary. Map scale can be estimated from the dimensions given for the Otoe Reserve (25 miles by 10 miles).

snow capped mountains, lake or bay, I fancied, until we had experienced one of the terrific thunder storms and hurricanes peculiar to that locality, would have made it the "ideal home" of my dreams.

So far we had been free from the fear of Indians. We had passed through the territory occupied by three tribes—the Shawnees, Delawares and the Potawotamies, all of whom were friendly. One of the Delawares had been the faithful guide of the explorer, Fremont. He was with him when his party was so nearly annihilated by a treacherous tribe.

This same friendly Indian kindly warned our captain to beware of the Pawnees, as we were now entering their territory, which lay between the Blue and Republican[4] rivers. Now that we had entered the Pawnees' hunting grounds, it behooved us to exercise great vigilance. Our company was so small that two of our men had to take their turn standing guard six hours every other night. Each was armed with a rifle and revolver, which they kept in readiness for instant use, in case of attack. We kept aloof from the great body of emigrants, that we might have the advantage of the little patches of grass and pools of water that lay along our way—which enabled us to advance more rapidly than in a larger company.[5]

Celinda

Monday, May 30—Pleasant. Arrived at the Blue or rather the Republican Fork.[6] Our route lies up the river 50 miles. The country is level but we have as many ravines as we did where the prairie was more rolling. Saw two antelopes AM.

Tuesday, May 31—Rainy. Mr. Jones Co & ours came to the conclusion that we could go faster & get along better separate so our Co, that is Mr. Judson, Mr Bryant and their families together with ourselves went on & left them. It stopped raining before noon. At noon Mr Jones Co. came up. The country is rather level. Camped near the river

Wednesday, June 1—We had a stampede in the night but they went only a short distance. It rained in the night. I rode on horse back all the A M. liked it much. Crossed a very bad stream all got over well. Camped near it. Rained very hard during supper.

Phoebe

One night, while encamped in a rather exposed place, and all were asleep, with the exception of the guard, we were suddenly aroused from our slumbers by the stampeding of our stock. Oxen, cows and horses came rushing "pell mell" through the camp, making a terrifying noise which threw us into the wildest consternation. The men rushed after the frightened animals, and fortunately found there were none missing. The Indians, after they had stampeded them, were foiled in their purpose of securing any. They are cowardly, and seldom fight without a decided advantage in position and numbers. After this alarm we were more vigilant in watching for these stealthy miscreants, for pitiable indeed would have been our plight had they succeeded in capturing our teams.

Not long after our first alarm, while all were enjoying a sermon from our captain on a fine Sabbath day, and at the same time keeping an eye out for the stock, which were feeding but a short distance away, Indians were spied crawling stealthily upon them. For that once the "Doxology" was omitted, and our men went full speed after them, with their firearms—in time to save them from stampeding. These alarming incidents were quite frequent in this region of the country.[7]

Celinda

Thursday, June 2—Cold. Two young men of Messrs Martin & Miner's acquaintance on their way to California came. They had lost six horses worth about 1400$. We traveled about 25 miles. Country level. Roads good. Camped within sight of the Platte or rather the forest skirting it.

Gregory M. Franzwa

The Platte River, just east of Fort Kearny.

Friday, June 3—[Morning] pleasant. Rains some after noon. Passed Ft Kearny about four O'clock. Camped about 2 miles beyond. People are forbidden to camp within three miles of the Ft. No wood & nothing but rain water standing in puddles on the prairie.

Saturday, June 4—The men went to the Ft. in the morning to shoe the horses & mules. Government has a blacksmith shop there for the accommodation of emigrants but at present there is no smith. Aunt E., M., J. and I went with pa in the [carriage.]…There are four large [buildings]…two small ones built of wood. The barracks are made of mud. There is a store where they sell about the same as in Kansas. There are sixty soldiers there. They have no fortifications & it was probably built more for the accommodation of emigrants & to awe the indians than for a defence. The seargeant invited us to his house where we were pleasantly entertained. The captain informed pa that there had passed here 85000 head of cattle & 8000 men who were crossing the plains this year also that most of the emigration [was going to] Oregon. Took up camp after dinner & started up the Platte. Our route lies up the river to South Fork on the south side. Many go on the north. The road is level being between the bluffs & the river. The Bluffs are very high & picturesque. The river ranks among the first class as to width but is very shallow as indicated by the many islands with which it is filled. The water partakes of the same laxative properties of the Mo. & Miss.

Sunday, June 5—Road not very good. [No] water but from the river. Camped about the middle of the P M. I rode on horseback. It rained & was very windy. Saw five snakes.

Monday, June 6—Pleasant. Saw some of the most beautiful Cactus I had ever seen. Camped near the river in a very pretty place.

Tuesday, June 7—Pleasant. Road leads along by the river. Scenery pleasant. Camped not far from the river. No wood.

Wednesday, June 8—It rained in the night and we got very wet. Scenery pretty. Camped near the bluffs. After tea we went out on to a very high one. Scenery delightful. The [bluffs] are in a chain but each [one is large enough to] be a mountain by itself being disconnected from its neighbor while between & around lie the sweetest little vales imaginable. From the summit of the one we ascended, the river is to be seen for miles. No scenery I had ever beheld bears any comparison to it. They seem to be of sand formation with neither rocks or stones to be seen. On the perpendicular side of one we saw many names written. Saw a new kind of cactus.

Thursday, June 9—Pleasant. Road very good. The Bluffs are now on the other side of the river. We drove to the crossing of the South Fork. Camped by a very good spring preparatory to crossing the river. Many were camped [near?] Among the rest was [Mr. Leonard?] We took another...

Friday, June 10—Made preparation to cross the Platte by fording or rather the South Fork. The river is about a mile & a quarter wide in low water it is shallow but now it was high water. Yet it was thought that we could cross without raising the wagon beds as was usual in such times. We drove to the river & as our turn came—for there were many waiting. They put all the oxen on the wagons. Ten yokes were attached to one of our wagons (Mr Longs) and Martha, Julia & myself rode across. Water came into the box some but we had no difficulty in getting across. The men waded to drive the teams. They went back with them & hitched on to the other wagons pa following with the mules. In the river a chain broke which detention caused the mules to become so restless as to be almost unmanageable & in the meantime a team which had been trying to get ahead ran against the carriage & almost upset it. They however got through without any very serious difficulty. We drove on about five miles & camped near a good spring. We unpacked the wagon to dry out the things as they needed airing much. Saw the first drove of sheep I had seen. Pa packed our wagon so that our family might sleep in it. We did so & found it very comfortable.

Phoebe

A few more days of travel, going through the same monotonous line of camp duties, brought us to the Platte river valley. We made our encampment opposite Grand Island, some ten miles below Fort Kearney,[8] whose adobe building could be seen in the distance, and as this was the first land mark of importance it was a satisfaction to know we had reached this noted point in our journey.

The river extended at the head of the island into a broad, shallow stream, flowing over a bed of sand, making the water very roily. We were compelled to allow it to settle before using. We found water and grass in abundance, but wood was very scarce, except in places near the margin of the river. The river bottom land was so soft and muddy that we were in constant fear of losing our teams, and for many days the cool north wind made traveling very unpleasant.

As our guide book pointed to the places where we would be obliged to make our camp without wood, we managed to carry a few sticks along with us—just enough to boil the coffee and fry the bacon.

When out of bread we made "hard tack" and crackers take its place.

How much we missed our camp fires at night in these cheerless places, not only for culinary purposes, but to brighten the dreariness of the way. But my sympathies were more with our men, who were wading through the mud and sloughs, day after day, driving their teams. There seemed but little rest for them night or day, except when we were camped for the Sabbath.

Buffaloes were often seen at a distance, in droves, but we had no time to capture them. One day we were so fortunate as to come across two that had been slain by the train ahead of us, and as they had carried away but a small portion, we helped ourselves and left an abundant supply for the next train. Our buffalo steak compared favorably with beef, and better relished on account of it being the first fresh meat we had tasted since we began our journey.

Antelopes were frequently seen, but were so fleet of foot we did not get a shot at them.

The captain's youngest brother, Rev. Harvey K. Hines, who possessed a daring spirit of adventure, wandered off one pleasant afternoon, accompanied by a young man of the train. Ascending a high hill they were lured so far away by the grandeur of the scenery that on their return they were overtaken by darkness, and it was midnight before they found their way into camp, where we were still up, anxiously waiting with lanterns on the wagons for beacon lights. Mr. Hines found his young wife in tears, and indeed we were all terror stricken for fear they had been captured by the Pawnees. This was the only time that any of our party ventured on so hazardous an expedition.

For many days we traveled in sight of long emigrant trains on the opposite side of the river, and we judged that the heaviest portion of the emigration was on the north side of the Platte, which made it all the better for our stock. The white tops of these "prairie schooners" creeping so slowly in the distance reminded me of the sailing vessels that I had so often seen on Lake Erie, beating against a light head wind. They were the trains that had fitted out at Council Bluffs, and I presume were making as good time as ourselves.

On reaching the south fork of the Platte we found that the river was rising caused by the melting snows from the Rocky mountains, and was one and a half miles wide. Many of the trains went farther up the river before crossing, but our captain concluded it was best to cross here. We were obliged to double teams, making eight yoke of oxen to each wagon. The beds of the wagons were raised a number of inches by putting blocks under them. When all was in readiness we plunged into the river, taking a diagonal course. It required three quarters of an hour to reach the opposite shore. After starting in we never halted a moment, for fear of sinking in the quicksand, of which there was much danger. We found the river so deep in places that, although our wagon box was propped nearly to the top of the stakes, the water rushed through it like a mill race, soaking the bottom of my skirts and deluging our goods. The necessity of doubling the teams for each wagon required three fordings, consequently by the time the last wagon was brought across the whole day was consumed. Thankful were we when night found us all safely encamped on the west side of the Platte, where we remained a day in order to dry our goods.[9]

---

[1] Judson, *A Pioneer's Search*, 30.

[2] See note 6.

[3] H. K. Hines, "Emigrant Wagon," December 18, 1884, 2.

[4] See note 6.

[5] Judson, *A Pioneer's Search*, 27.

[6] What Celinda here calls the "Republican Fork" was probably the Little Blue River. After the Hines party had crossed the Big Blue River on May 24, and continued westward (or perhaps somewhat northwestward), there were two major rivers to the west: first the Little Blue, and then the Republican, or Republican Fork. Inasmuch as the river mentioned here by Celinda is the first they had encountered since the Big Blue crossing, we conclude it must be the Little Blue. They then traveled along this river until they were near Fort Kearny on the Platte. Again, this is in line with the Little Blue identification. And in the mileage notes in her diary (See Appendix) Celinda identifies this river as the Little Blue. Morris W. Werner, a student of Kansas trails, notes that "...sometimes the Little Blue was identified as the Republican Fork [by emigrants]." Kansas History websites, http://www.ku.edu/heritage/werner/undone/werner2l.txt; accessed April 12, 2007.

[7] Judson, *A Pioneer's Search*, 28, 29.

[8] Phoebe's misspelling of Fort Kearny probably is based on the name of the nearby town. In a personal communication Gregory Franzwa notes, "... a clerical error spelled the name of the town north of the Platte to Kearney, but the correct spelling of the fort should be Kearny."

[9] Judson, *A Pioneer's Search*, 29-32.

The Oregon Trail, Federal Writers' Project, 1939

Arapahoes, ca. 1868

The Oregon Trail, Federal Writers' Project, 1939

Along the Trail

Tim Frodsham

Chimney Rock

The Oregon Trail, Federal Writers' Project, 1939

Scotts Bluff

9

June 11–23, 1853: Chimney Rock; Fort Laramie

...when we reached the fort we found letters from "home" awaiting us; the first we had received since leaving the Missouri river, and the last we received until we reached Oregon. So, amid visions and memories of the times departed and of the friends far away we camped; and read and re-read our letters and lived over the old life that now seemed so far away; so utterly gone never to return.[1]
—Harvey K. Hines, June 1853

Along the Platte, the party encountered buffalo. On a Saturday Celinda notes that "a fine buffalo came near," and further, that a member of their party, a Mr. Miner, managed to kill one. The carriage must then have been commandeered for a "meat wagon," because she reports that "The women got out of the carriage & took out the things & the men started for some buffalo meat." For the next day's travel the young women must ride in another wagon.

The buffalo encounter no doubt excited the adventurous young Harvey, whetting his appetite for a buffalo trophy of his own, and setting the stage for his own sighting the following day. Unfortunately for the would-be hunter, the day is a Sunday, with hunting proscribed. Harvey and Phoebe both describe the incident, although with somewhat contradictory details; Celinda is silent on the subject.

But even though it is Sunday, when travel, too, would be normally prohibited, the party is on the move because of water conditions. Harvey notes that this is their first Sunday travel of their journey so far, but Celinda makes no special mention of that circumstance.

Celinda

Saturday, June 11—Our road lies along by the river & was very good. Before noon a fine buffalo came near. I saw him distinctly. At noon we came where there had been two buffaloes killed. The head of one was there it was very large. In the P. M. Mr Miner came hurrying to us with news that he had killed one buffalo & wounded another. The women got out of the carriage &

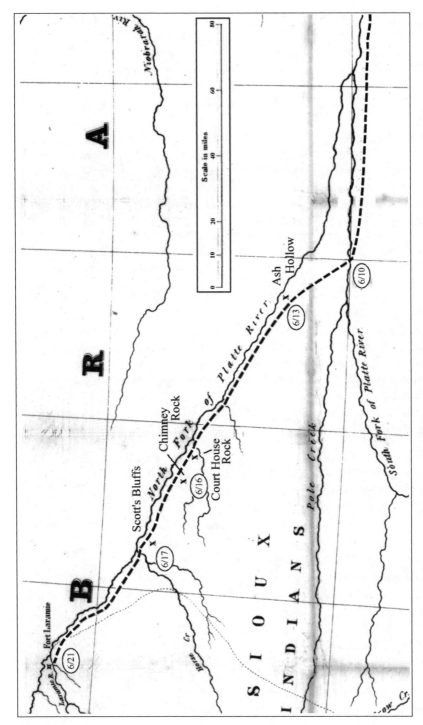

Section of 1854 Nebraska map showing Hines route from the crossing of the South Fork of the Platte Rive to Fort Laramie (shown in what was then western Nebraska but is now Wyoming).

took out the things & the men started for some buffalo meat. They did not get up to the camp until nearly dark. Mr Smithers killed a badger & as our camp was in a prairie dog village some one killed a dog. Their bark resembles that of a puppy but they look more like rats. Mother & I washed.

Harvey

The crossing of South Platte was an important event in the journey. It seemed to put between us and civilization another and greater barrier than any we had passed, and we felt much nearer our destined home—Oregon— than we did the day before. It was with cheerful hearts, therefore, we moved onward the following day up the valley of North Platte. Wild sage begins to appear. The valley is narrow, the sandy hills pushing close upon the river and crowding the road over their sterile points. Being unacquainted with the road we found ourselves compelled to encamp on Saturday night, June 12th [Celinda's diary assigns June 11 to this Saturday, and this agrees with the 1853 calendar], where there was only a little brackish water and no grass for our stock. The next day, therefore, for the first time during our journey, we found ourselves compelled to travel on the Sabbath. Our road led over a succession of sandy ridges and was very dusty and uncomfortable. In the afternoon I had stepped into our wagon for a little rest as the oxen moved leisurely forward when the barking of a dog near by arrested my attention. Looking out I saw Mr. B[ryant]'s dog following a magnificent buffalo directly parallel with the train and only about thirty or forty yards distant from our wagon. Instinctively I reached for my rifle, which hung on the wagon bows just at my right hand loaded and capped, feeling that my time to kill a buffalo had come. Seeing my eager movement, and divining its cause, Mrs. H[ines], who was sitting in the wagon reading, quickly said: "Mr. H[ines], it is Sunday." I did not take down the gun and the buffalo sheared off and in a few moments disappeared among the sand hills.[2]

Phoebe

One of the dreaded obstacles on the journey had been successfully overcome, and we proceeded on our way up the valley of the North Platte with lighter hearts. We found the water, if possible, more roily than that of the South Platte.

In many places along the route we found the water so strongly impregnated with an alkaline substance as to make it poisonous for both man and beast. Having reached a place of this description one Saturday night, we continued our journey, for the first time, on the Sabbath, and as we crept wearily along the dreary way not a stick, stone, bird or flower to break the monotony—the cattle poking along more slowly than usual on account of being deprived of their day of rest, we were suddenly surprised by seeing a great buffalo coming directly towards the train. Crossing the road in front of Harvey Hines' team, that was in the lead, Harvey seized his rifle with the intention of killing it. The wagons were simultaneously halted, as we waited for the shot; but before Mr. Hines could pull the trigger his wife reminded him that it was the "Sabbath," and he immediately returned the rifle to its place. Mr. Judson sarcastically remarked "He would not have hit it anyhow." Mr. Bryant's dog chased the buffalo out of sight, and we proceeded on our way, passing down into a grove of ash trees, appropriately named "Ash Hollow,"[3] where flowed a sparkling rivulet, from whose transparent waters we were delighted to drink.

How refreshed and comforted we were by our sojourn in this beautiful spot, for here we remained a whole day, while Mr. Hines reset his tire.[4]

Sunday night brings a thunderstorm, complete with rain and hail of such intensity that both Harvey and Phoebe describe it at some length. Harvey in fact reports, "This was the hardest single night of our journey ..." Celinda, though, says only, "In the night it rained and hailed."

Celinda

Sunday, June 12—Arrangements were made for us girls to ride in the other wagon so we arranged our seats accordingly. Road very good. We had no water for dinner. In the night it rained and hailed.

Gregory M. Franzwa

Windlass Hill at Ash Hollow, photographed in 1973.
The gorge at left is the eroded remains of one of the many
paths the trail took down the hill.

Harvey

Just before sunset we turned down a steep gorge[5] towards the river, passed through a grove of ash, which gave name to the place—"Ash Hollow" —and emerged again into the river valley encamped just after having passed a row of eighteen or twenty graves, whose silent occupants were nearly all victims of the cholera the summer before, and all buried within two or three days, as their rude head-boards testified. They were a lonely company, and they seemed a sad presence to us in this wide desolation. The day had been exceedingly sultry. As night came on dark thunder-clouds, swinging and swaying and scudding before the driving wind began to gather in the west, growing deeper and blacker as the lightning zigzagged across and down and up their embattled front. The storm hung away in the west for a while, and after guard mount the remainder of the camp retired to rest. It was not my guard that night, so I retired also, but the lightning blazed and shot and quivered so in the west, and the very atmosphere seemed so charged with electricity that my nerves vibrated as though strung and struck by unseen forces. In a little time the storm broke the tethers that bound it to the range of hills twenty or thirty miles to the west and came leaping and roaring and screaming down the valley. It came under a canopy of fire, and discharging torrents of rain and tempests of hail such as we had never seen. The men on guard, M. and N., fled to the shelter of the wagons. G. H[ines] came to the door of my tent and said: "The cattle are frantic, the guards have left them, you and I must keep them or they will all be lost." I was already up and dressed with rubber coat on, and a shawl tied tightly around my head. Stepping out into the tempest we took our beats, about ten rods each, directly in front of the herd of frightened, bellowing cattle, and with our long whips in our hands paced and ran up and down in the face of the hail and rain and driving wind through all that lightning-illumined night. There was scarcely a half minute during the whole night when we could not distinctly see each other and all of the cattle by the glare of the lightning. The cattle stood, their backs bent against the tempest, but apparently assured by seeing us, their masters, standing out the night and tempest with them. In the morning the hail lay in great drifts, every hollow was a pool of water, and everything in the camp as though it had been in a [flood]. This was the hardest single night of our journey, but, when the time came to move forward again we had all our stock in hand, while all the trains near us had allowed theirs to be driven away by the storm, some not finding them for many days, and then from ten to thirty miles distant.[6]

Phoebe

Most melancholy indeed was the scene revealed as we journeyed through this valley—the road was lined with a succession of graves. These lonely resting places were marked with rude head boards, on which were inscribed their names, and "Died of cholera, 1852."

Many of these graves bore the appearance of being hastily made. Occasionally we passed one marked "killed by lightning," which was not surprising to us after having witnessed one of the most terrific thunder storms it had been our fortune to experience. This storm broke upon us after we had retired for the night. One after another, terrific peals of thunder rending the heavens in quick succession, roaring, rolling and crashing around, above and below, accompanied by blinding flashes of lightning, illuminating our wagons with the brightness of noonday, while the rain came beating down upon our wagon covers in great sheets. It was simply awful. Annie cried piteously to be "carried back home of Fazzer's house."[7]

William Henry Jackson's sketch of a prairie thunderstorm he experienced on a trip west in the 1860's. The Hines train was much smaller than this, and Gustavus and Harvey fought the elements alone.

Our guard, being insufficiently protected, fled to the camp. The captain and his brother, having gum coats and everything necessary for such an emergency, sallied forth, and by indefatigable efforts succeeded in keeping the frightened animals from stampeding. I have often thought of this noble deed of these courageous missionaries braving the terrors of that appalling storm for the welfare of the company who were sheltering themselves as best they could from the raging elements.

In the morning we found there was not a head of our stock missing, while other trains that were camped near us had allowed theirs to be scattered for miles away. Our bedding and clothing were as wet as water could make them, but the sun came out brightly in the morning, and we were again compelled to lay over a day to dry them.

The dearth of timber along our route heightened our appreciation of this beautiful grove. I love the timber, and this beautiful wooded spot in a prairie country will never be effaced from my memory.[8]

Continuing her description of Ash Hollow, Phoebe echoes Harvey's commentary on the cholera deaths from an earlier year, and muses about how her concept of death has evolved in the seventy-plus years since the trip.

Coming down again onto the river bottom, we passed a row of twenty graves. By the inscriptions on the rough head boards we learned that they died within a few days of each other of cholera. This dreadful scourge brought the journey of many poor emigrants to a sudden close, resulting in numerous pathetic incidents.

It was my privilege in after years to become acquainted with a refined lady who had buried her husband here, and she, besides caring for her two little children, drove her team through to the coast, and did as much, and more, than many of the men in helping to develop a new country.

A mother was also buried here, leaving five helpless children, the youngest only six weeks old. The father brought the little family safely through, and they lived to become useful citizens of this country. The sight of this little cemetery, so isolated and lonely, brought many gloomy reflections. Death to me was a shocking event, even at home, attended by all that love could devise to take away its gloom, and the thought of burying one of my dear ones here, or of myself being left by the wayside where only the savages and wild animals roamed, was awful to contemplate. I had yet to learn that the mystery which we call death is but a transition of the spiritual from the mortal, and it matters but little where the body lies; buried on the mountain top, in the briny deep, or consumed by fire, it is of no more account than the shell, or chrysalis, from which the bird or butterfly have flown; for we shall be clothed with a glorious spiritual body and be more ourselves than ever before. "I go away," said Jesus "that I may come again," but the story of "the women was an idle tale."[9]

And so we find it today, those who are immersed only in material things of this world are "slow to believe."[10]

We have seen in the foregoing that Harvey and Phoebe, in their respective reminiscent accounts, recall the fierce thunderstorm occurring after they arrived at Ash Hollow. Celinda's diary, however, records the storm on Sunday night, prior to their arrival at Ash Hollow on Monday. (See page 143.)

Celinda

Monday, June 13—In the A. M. the road lies along by the river. P M. arrived at a good spring the road soon leaves the bottom & leads upon the bluffs which are here of a rocky formation which seems to be a mixture of sand & lime. In about three miles we came to Ash hollow so called from the ash trees which grow there. We had looked to this place as one where we should have plenty of wood & water. Another road comes in here & we saw some companies which we had not before. Every Co but Mr Caulie's which we had seen were now behind us. The glen is very picturesque rocks rise almost perpendicular two hundred ft. or more. We had scarcely encamped in a prettier place.

Tuesday, June 14—Warm & pleasant. The men set the tire on one wagon wheel before starting. The road lies along by the river. We see many trains on the other side who started from Council Bluffs. In the afternoon we came into a hollow & saw many trains just before us. Camped near the river. After tea Martha Julia, Lucy Anna, Gustavus & myself went on the bluffs. It was some distance and they were hard to ascend but the scene which was unfolded to our view amply repaid us for our fatigue. We saw three antelopes & two wolves. Castle Bluff was near but we had not time to visit it & we thought by the looks that we could not ascend the dome if we were to go there.

While his brothers and their families were making their way across the plains—and quite unbeknown to them—Joseph W. Hines, second youngest of the twelve siblings, was also belatedly transferred to Oregon. Because of the lateness of the transfer, however, it was decided he should go by ship via Panama, rather than overland. Traveling with Joseph was his wife Elizabeth and their two children, Melissa and George.[11] Their journey began on this day, June 14, 1853.

Joseph

LETTER FROM KINGSTON, JAMAICA

Br. Hosmer:—Thinking that a few lines from one who has read with interest and profit the excellent "Northern," would not be entirely unacceptable to its columns, I snatch a few moments from the press of family cares, in order to give you a brief sketch of our journey hither. Having been transferred by our venerable and excellent Bishop Waugh from the Genesee to the Oregon Conference, after a hasty preparation, I started for that far-off, yet interesting and inviting field. It being quite too late to think of taking the overland route, in company with my brothers, it was decided that I should go by the Isthmus. All things being ready, on the 14th of June we bade adieu to home and friends, and took our passage on board the cars for New York—the appointed place of our embarkation. The incidents of railroad travel are too familiar to your readers to demand even a passing notice;[12] and suffice it to say, that, after making several stops with friends on the route, we found ourselves, on the evening of the 17th, pleasantly quartered at the Merchants' Hotel, at which place we were to remain during our stay in the city. Here we met brothers Heath[13] and De Vore,[14] of the Rock River Conference, who having likewise been transferred, the former to California, and the latter to the Oregon Conference, were to accompany us on our voyage.[15]

Celinda

Wednesday, June 15—Our route was mostly near the river & in the A M. the road was very sandy. In the P M. it was better. We passed a number of trains. Weather very pleasant. Came in sight of some trees but did not near them. Camped on the bank of a stream. Had a fine time washing.

Farther along the North Platte the emigrants come upon the first of several spectacular natural phenomena, Courthouse Rock,[16] and shortly thereafter, Chimney Rock.[17] Harvey, Celinda, and several others take a moonlit tour of the latter, and both describe it glowingly. Phoebe does not appear on either of the slightly different excursion lists given by Harvey and Celinda, but she mentions their tour. (Just a few days later, Phoebe gives birth to a son!)

Celinda

Thursday, June 16—The weather was fair. We soon came in sight of Courthouse rock. About noon we came near it & within about 4 miles the nearest point where the road approaches to it. It is a massive pile of rocks on the level prairie & not even a stone in miles of it. It is very appropriately named from its appearance. We soon after came near a Sioux village. It consisted of 25 Lodges made of buffalo hides with poles projecting at the top. Many of the inhabitants came out to see us. Most of the males had no clothing but a sort of apron. They are the most pleasant agreeable looking indians I have ever seen. They can not talk with us. At night we came to Chimney rock which had been visible to us for 15 miles. It is a pillar of rock

& sand 250 ft. in hight & wholly detached from the neighboring hills. We camped near the river about two miles from the rock. After tea uncles, Mr Long, Julia, Martha & I went to see it by moonlight. The sight was awfully sublime. The sides of the base on which the pillar rests are so steep that it was with the utmost difficulty we could climb up it at all. We however succeeded in climbing up some distance. We found it covered with names We got back to the camp about 10 O'clock.

Harvey

We were now among noted landmarks. On Tuesday [Celinda's diary says "Thursday."] at noon we passed "Courthouse Rock," and at night encamped near the Platte directly north of "Chimney Rock." The moon was at its full, and that, in the latitude and at the altitude where we were, means a light more soft and beautiful than that of day. Desiring greatly to visit the "rock" we formed a party, consisting of G[ustavus] H[ines]; Mr. M[arti]n; Mr. M[ine]r; Miss B[ryant], now Mrs. T[erry], of East Berkley, Cal.; Miss G[raves], afterwards Mrs. W[alts], of Portland, and who now sleeps the sweet sleep of the just in "Lone Fir Cemetery;" Miss H[ines], now Mrs. A.R.S[hipley] of "Hazelia," near Oswego, Oregon, and myself to visit it by moonlight, as we had no time to do it by day. We went on foot, finding it about three miles from our camp to its base. We found it to be, first, a huge pyramid of marl and limestone standing on the top of some broken, serrated hills, the pyramid being, we judged, from ten to fifteen hundred feet in diameter at its base, and rising towards an apex about two hundred feet, when a perpendicular shaft forty or fifty feet in diameter shot upward a hundred or more feet high. We all ascended to the base of this shaft, or "chimney," and for an hour or more contemplated the beautiful scene spread out in the moonlight night before us. We transcribe a sentence written there:

But this monument of nature's own building will not always stand. The marks of the warfare of the elements are upon it, and when the heavens have poured their fury a few more times upon it, its thunder-marred and blackened summit will be level with its base.

This is now a fact; its stately shaft has fallen, and only the pyramid remains.[18]

Phoebe

The next noted land mark to which we came was Chimney Rock, the tall chimney having been in view, and seemingly quite near, for several days, the peculiarity of the atmosphere causing distances to be quite deceptive. We camped within two miles of it, giving a number of our party the pleasure of paying a moonlight visit to this curious freak of nature, with its chimney-like shaft rising to a height of one hundred feet.

These land marks indicated our progress and helped to break the monotony—like the mile stones along the journey of life, there was one less to pass.

Celinda

Friday, June 17—Warm. All day the scenery was most enchanting entirely surpassing in loveliness & originality any thing I had ever beheld. Bluffs the most picturesque and resembling to the life some old castle of ancient times. About noon we came to Scotts Bluff[19] which much resembles an old fortification. It takes its name from the circumstance of a Mr. Scott & Co. traders who were robbed by the indians. Mr S was wounded. On reaching this place he was unable to travel farther. His companions remained with him until they could stay no longer. They & he knew that he could survive but a short time. He begged them to leave him & they did so. Afterwards human bones were found there, supposed to be his remains.[20] Went up the valley about 6 miles & camped in a most romantic spot near a spring brook. Martha & I went to find a spring. Mr. Martin & Mr. Long went with us. We went on up the ravine expecting any moment to find the spring at length we came upon what we supposed to have once been a trading post.[21] There were several log buildings connected together in them were remnants of wagons & other things which emigrants would want. In one had been a blacksmith shop. The whole was now deserted. Near by was one of the most beautiful springs I have ever seen. The scenery here is most romantic. At length we tore ourselves away from this delightful retreat & returned to camp. Our people had been much concerned about us. They knew not that the men were with us & thought perhaps we were lost.

Saturday, June 18—Very warm. Drove to Horse creek. Over a high valley. Passed some indian villages. Camped near one. Pear cactus very thick & troubling.

Although Celinda does not mention Harvey as a member of their little group that explored the abandoned trading post, he describes his own visit there, finding it equally as intriguing as she did.

Harvey

On Friday, the 17th day of June, we turned southward from the Platte, just before reaching "Scott's Bluffs," traveled a few miles up the valley of a "dry creek" that comes down from some wooded hills, and after leaving the road a mile or more came to a beautiful stream of clear, cold water flowing among the open glades and wooded slopes of the hills. After the camp was adjusted several of us wandered a mile or so further into the hills where, in one of the most beautiful retreats we had ever seen we found an abandoned post or fort of some hunting party of the preceding year. Thousands of buffalo horns and hoofs and skulls were scattered about the building, broken casks, wagon wheels, wagon irons, an old forge, and many other things that showed that this had been where thousands of buffalo, elk, antelope, bear

Gregory M. Franzwa

This dirt road over Robidoux Pass is within feet of the Oregon Trail, and at times right over it.[22]

and other skins had been prepared for market. Some of us had a passion for adventure, and almost desired to remain here, in what looked like a hunter's paradise, and try our prowess among the shaggy denizens of these glorious hills. But "the King's business required haste,"[23] and so we could only remain in the most beautiful camp of our entire journey thus far to give ourselves and oxen a few hours rest. Before ten o'clock of Saturday morning the teams were slowly swinging down the valley, retracing the steps of yesterday, and then, crossing a sandy divide that connects Scott's Bluffs with the timbered hills among which we had encamped, we entered and crossed the valley of Horse Creek, passed a couple of Sioux villages of perhaps a hundred lodges each, and crossing the creek opposite one of them, and not more than sixty rods from it, pitched our tents at about five o'clock of Saturday afternoon for our Sabbath rest[24]

Sunday, June 19, despite being a self-imposed day of rest for the party, is a most eventful day. All three of our chroniclers describe an exciting buffalo hunt carried out by the nearby Sioux Indians, and Phoebe adds an amusing tale of young children and homemade bread.

Celinda

Sunday, June 19—Remained in camp. Rained some in the night. P M. Saw some indians chasing buffalos. It was said that there were 50 in the herd. They succeeded in killing a number of them. The chase was very interesting to us. The indians had nothing but halters of their horses. One [buffalo] was killed a little way across the creek from us. We went to see it. Mr. Martin & Mr Long carried us across. A very small boy insisted in swimming it seemingly an expert as his father. We examined some bows & arrows with which they killed them. The Sioux gave Charles a quarter & offered him another but he took but one. Martha & I took off our shoes and waded back. Many Sioux came to the camp that day for food. I wrote a letter to cousin Licotta Higgins. Mr Martin wrote in my album. Our horses were stampeded but they got them again.

Harvey

Sunday, June 19th. As had been our wont after crossing South Platte we left the cattle during the night to roam of their own sweet will through the green meadows of Horse Creek, only staking our horses near the tents, and posting a single guard for the entire camp. We had left the territory of the Pawnees, and were traveling among the Sioux; nearly the whole tribe being encamped along the line of our march. We had learned that there was danger from the Indians only when there were none about, and as we were now camped within half a mile of about two hundred lodges filled with women and children we felt entirely safe in relaxing even our usual vigilance.[25] The result justified our confidence, for when morning came, after one of the sweetest night's rest of the whole journey every thing was safe. The oxen were resting as though conscious it was Sunday, and when we walked among them after the morning toilet, they lay contentedly chewing their "cuds" and looking upon us with their great, soft, beautiful eyes, never stirring from their grassy couches, as much as to say "this is Sunday; here we rest." We were all in splendid health. The day was as calm and soft and perfect as Eden. The camp was a perfect repose; some reading, some singing, groups in converse, all happy.

Just after the dinner hour had passed, as G[ustavus] H[ines] and myself stood at the door of my tent conversing, we noticed that the Sioux village just across the creek from us was amid a scene of intense excitement. The women were catching the horses and rushing up to the lodges with them, the men were casting off their blankets, throwing their quivers full of arrows on their backs, seizing and stringing their bows, then mounting and dashing away southward until the line of mounted, galloping warriors seemed interminable. Turning our eyes south-west we saw a great cloud of dust rolling rapidly down the valley, coming directly towards our camp. When it had come within a quarter of a mile of us the Indians broke into its dusty folds, and at the same instant we saw that another band of Indians had driven a band of two or three hundred buffalo directly to their village, and here they were making "a surround." They were so near us that when the band of buffalo was scattered by the charge of the Indians, we could see every movement. A stalwart Indian would put his flying steed within three yards of the right side of a buffalo, and, with both on the jump drive the steel-pointed arrow to the feather in his quivering side. A half grown boy would rival the skill and daring of the sturdiest man. As soon as a buffalo would stop at bay the hunter would leave him and be off for another, while the beast would lie down and die. The tremendous melee, the mad confusion sent the blood bounding though our veins, but "it was Sunday" again, and so we took no part in the fray.[26]

Phoebe

We were now nearing the territory of the Sioux Indians, and we shortly passed several of their villages, of more than a hundred lodges each. Many of the braves were parading around, fancifully arrayed in their Indian toggery, with an air of great independence—the buffalo, which constituted their wealth, being very plentiful at that time.

We camped over Sunday by a little creek on the suburbs of one of these little Indian cities. While our men and cattle were resting, some of the women improved the opportunity of making light bread, asserting that it was right to "do good on the Sabbath day." I baked my bread in a flat kettle, made expressly for the purpose, called a "Dutch oven," by heaping coals on the cover and underneath, replenishing when needed. Bread can be baked very nicely by this method. It was very light and I felt quite proud of my success. When done, I turned it out on the grass to cool, while I attended to my housework in our wagon home. Hearing the merry laughter of the children, I glanced in that direction, and what was my dismay to see little Annie standing on my precious loaf. I found that she and little Alta Bryant had been having a most enjoyable time rolling it on the grass.

The outcome of Mrs. Bryant's baking was even more ludicrous. She set her sponge in the bread pan to rise and left it in the wagon, where her little boy, less than two years old, was sleeping, while she, with others, went for a short stroll. When she returned to the wagon she found her little boy in the bread pan, up to his knees in the dough.

Another incident transpired that day that I must not forget to relate. While a party of Indians were pursuing a band of buffalo, they surrounded them within plain view of our encampment. The buffalo dashed around furiously in a vain effort to get away, but to whatever point they galloped they were met by the Indians, who were mounted on active little ponies and armed with bows and arrows, with which they slaughtered over thirty buffaloes. When one would break through the circle it was quickly overtaken and brought down by the arrows of the dexterous Sioux. This was a very exciting scene and greatly enjoyed, especially by the men of our company.[27]

Celinda and Harvey agree that they reached the Laramie River on Tuesday, June 21, but they disagree on the crossing date. (Phoebe gives no date, and Gustavus, writing a letter back home on Sunday, implies they may actually cross the river and reach Fort Laramie on Monday.) Harvey says they cross right away on Tuesday; Celinda says they wait until Thursday for their turn at the ferry. When they do reach the fort, they make purchases, pick up mail, and write letters to friends and relatives back home.

Wisconsin Historical Society, Image 1840

Fording Laramie Creek, 1849, by James Wilkins.

Phoebe

The next river that we forded was the Laramie. This river was narrow, but so deep that the water covered the backs of the oxen. When across, we found ourselves at Fort Laramie,[28] another "landmark" on our journey, where we remained two days and dried our goods. Here Mr. Judson purchased a very fine buffalo robe, which added much to our comfort in the cool region of the Rocky mountains.[29]

Harvey

On Monday morning we purchased from the Indians some fine pieces of meat, paying therefore in sugar; a little sugar buying a great deal of meat. The Indians used only bows and arrows, not a gun being fired during the hunt, and yet twenty or thirty choice buffalo lay with a few rods of the Indian village when it was over. The Indian women soon had their shaggy hides off, and the meat cut up for drying and jerking.

At noon of Tuesday we reached and forded Laramie river. The stream was clear and swift and deep, about fifty yards in its width, and the middle over the backs of the oxen. But we passed it without detention and in a few minutes reached Fort Laramie. A few hours before an enterprising express-man carrying a mail had passed us, and when we reached the fort we found letters from "home" awaiting us; the first we had received since leaving the Missouri river, and the last we received until we reached Oregon.[30] So, amid visions and memories of the times departed and of the friends far away we camped; and read and re-read our letters and lived over the old life that now seemed so far away; so utterly gone never to return.[31]

Wisconsin Historical Society, Image 3935

Sketch of Fort John (known as "Fort Laramie"), 1849, by James Wilkins.

Celinda

Monday, June 20—Pleasant. Passed some sioux villages & also some trading posts mostly temporary ones. Camped near a gorge. We have had no water but river water & no wood since leaving the cold spring near the old trading post.

Tuesday, June 21—Warm & pleasant. Went to within two miles of Laramie Fork which we could not ferry as there were 150 wagons ahead of us in waiting. Camped near the river.

Wednesday, June 22—Cold & windy. Hailed some. Remained in camp all day. Uncles exchanged the mules for a heavy wagon, three yokes of oxen & two cows giving $200 to boot. Uncle G took the new wagon, Harvey the broken one & fixed their beds in them.

Thursday, June 23—Went to the ferry. Uncles sold the carriage & harness. We crossed without difficulty. Made the acquaintance of a Mr. Donaldson of St. Louis going to California.[32] Soon arrived at the Ft. Stopped for noon near it. It is on the north Side of Laramie river & is overlooked on the north by a hill where stands the burying ground. I visited the Ft. & was much surprised at seeing no fortifications. There are at present 64 soldiers. We made an acquaintance of the quarter-master Mr Flemming a young gent. but 9 months from West Point & a native of Erie Pa. He walked to the camp with us making himself very agreeable.[33] I received 3 letters one from Marie Wightman one from R E Prescott & one from C E Robinson.[34] Camped near a pond of water.

Gustavus

Dear Brother—We are spending a very quiet Sabbath near two villages of the Sioux Indians, in one of the most magnificent countries spread out before the face of heaven. There is a sublimity in the scenery of the ever-varying and almost boundless prairie, not unlike that presented by the majestic ocean. [Gustavus had familiarity with the "majestic ocean," having circumnavigated the world in his first trip to Oregon and back.] But I shall not attempt to describe it, for I should come so far short of giving it a life-like representation, that I should leave a very erroneous impression on the minds of any that may read this letter. My chief object in writing is to inform you of our progress and circumstances. We shall probably reach Fort Laramie tomorrow, and as a mail leaves that place periodically, I avail myself of the opportunity of writing you this. We have made very good progress on our journey, our train having outstripped nearly every one that left the frontiers at the time we did. Though we have met with some detention by accidents, such as breaking down and tipping over wagons, yet nothing has occurred to detain us more than one day in any one place since we left the frontiers. We are now advanced nearly six hundred miles from Kanzas [i.e., the present Kansas City, Mo]. Our cattle are in excellent order; none of them appear to be footsore; and while I write this, they are luxuriating in grass equal to most of our New York meadows the first of July. I am thus particular regarding our cattle, as one might as well be cast away at sea as to lose his team on these plains.

Keeping the Sabbath—Our company is not as large as when we left the frontiers, two wagons leaving because we would not travel on the Sabbath unless it was absolutely necessary. He said that he must get along faster than we possibly could if we did not travel every day. We are now in advance of him one or two days' journey!

Our company is in excellent health and spirits, and, indeed, there has been but very little sickness on the Plains the present season. How it may be on the other end of the route remains still to be settled. But we are in the care of a kind Providence, and we feel perfectly secure in trusting him under all circumstances. We have just crossed the Laramie Fork of the Platte, and are now halting a few moments near the fort.[35]

While Gustavus and company were in the vicinity of Fort Laramie, Joseph was just nicely started on his alternate route; after departing New York on June 20, he reached Kingston, Jamaica, on June 22.

The Panama route he was on was not an unusual one in 1853. In the course of that year, according to John H. Kemble in his comprehensive work, *The Panama Route*, over 17,000 passengers traveled from New York to the West Coast of the U.S. via Panama, and almost 10,000 went by the closely related route through Nicaragua.[36] This total of nearly 27,000 traveling mainly by water exceeds by a sizeable margin the estimated 20,000 who traveled overland in 1853, according to Mattes.[37] Unruh arrived at a higher estimate for the total number of overlanders in 1853, namely 27,500.[38] Even this figure, however, still puts the fraction traveling by sea at nearly fifty percent of all bound for the West Coast.

The advantages of the Panama route as compared with going overland seem obvious. Gustavus and company started their overland trip in early March and arrived at their destination in early October, some seven months later. In contrast, Joseph departed home in mid-June and arrived in mid-August, a mere two months in transit, including layover time in New York, Panama, and San Francisco.

The Panama route was by no means trouble-free. According to Kemble, there were complaints of bad food, overcrowding, disease, and many hassles in getting across the isthmus itself, not excluding the terrible tropical heat. Fortunately for Joseph and family, such problems were minimal for their voyage. His letters make no mention of the food, and even though cholera had taken many lives in the preceding year, there is no mention of disease.

With the steamer *Illinois'* capacity nominally rated at 500 passengers, the "nearly three hundred" cited by Joseph hardly speaks of overcrowding. (Other trips on the *Illinois* must have been less comfortable —Kemble reports that 1,150 passengers left New York on the *Illinois* in 1856.)

All things considered, to the modern observer the Panama route appears far preferable to the overland. It's interesting that Harvey, in his 1882 semi-fictional story of "Mr. and Mrs. Cathard," leaves us in doubt as to their choice of route, instead offering a comparison, which we quote in full here.

It will not concern the reader to follow Mr. And Mrs. Cathard through the weeks of preparation for, and the subsequent journey to Oregon. It will be sufficient to say that the facilities for travel, in that long-ago day, had no semblance to those of the present time. It involved an uncomfortable and generally stormy trip from New York by steamer to the Isthmus of Panama, then a canoe or boat ride up the Chagres River in hourly exposure to all kinds of danger to person and property, and then a mule or mustang ride to the Pacific side of the Isthmus, with another steamer ride to San Francisco, and yet another from that port to the Columbia River; a journey of discomforts and danger from beginning to end. If this route was not taken there remained the alternative of a journey to the limits of civilization along the Missouri River, then through the great wilderness of the Rocky Mountains for two thousand miles, generally performed with oxen and wagons, through powerful and often hostile tribes of Indians, and with not a single white man's habitation to relieve the savage monotony of the route. This, too, was always full of perils.

On the one there were diseases and deaths, births and burials, on the ocean or amidst the pestiferous marshes of Panama. On the other, contagions and pestilences, the Indian's arrow or the robber's bullet, starvation or drowning, brought sadness to tent and camp. The scenes of bereavement and suffering along the line of either journey would make a chapter of most tearful pathos. The integrity of our story would permit Mr. And Mrs. Cathard to have reached Oregon by either route as they represent a character and a work rather than personalities; and, also, as both routes at about the time of which we write were traveled by those who bore equally honorable and important parts in the events and incidents that are to follow.[39]

We now turn to a further excerpt from Joseph's first letter to the *Northern Christian Advocate* during his trip. Other excerpts from his letters will appear in later chapters.

Joseph

LETTER FROM KINGSTON, JAMAICA

Monday, June 20th, having been fixed upon as the time of our departure, we had an opportunity of spending a Sabbath with our brethren in New York. In the morning, having excused ourselves from pulpit labors, we passed over to Brooklyn, to hear the celebrated H. W. Beecher; but were well paid for our idle curiosity, by finding his pulpit filled by a stranger. In the afternoon, arrangements having been previously made for a missionary meeting at Allen Street church, we enjoyed a very pleasant interview with Br. Scudder's congregation, who worship there, and in the evening preached for Br. Reed, at the Seventh Street church. Thus closed the labors of the last Sabbath we shall soon enjoy in our own native state.

The last few hours of our sojourn in the city flew rapidly away, and the time of our departure was soon upon us, when, accompanied by Dr. Durbin, and Br. H. Mattison, we repaired to the vessel that was to convey us from the scenes and associations of our past life. This proved to be the U.S. Mail Steamer *Illinois*,[40] commanded by Capt. Heurtstem, of the U.S. Navy. All things being soon ready for our departure, we took a final leave of our brethren and friends, and the dashing wheels of our majestic steamer bore us rapidly from the harbor and bay of New York, and soon nothing but the blue waves of the broad Atlantic greeted our eager vision. Very pleasantly indeed passed a few hours, and we had almost begun to flatter ourselves that nothing would disturb the even flow of our joyful emotions, when all the internal machinery of our physical being commenced such an awful and unaccountable commotion, that we really concluded all the combinations of earthly would not be sufficient to set them right. O the horrors of that twenty-four hours! Never, no, never shall we forget them. All sick at once, all that we could do was to give up entirely, and be satisfied to wallow in our own filthiness. Only think, Mr. Editor, nearly three hundred human beings all heaving and vomiting at once. Why, sir, we almost drowned the bellowing of old Neptune himself. But our troubles were soon over, and the remainder of the voyage, thus far, was one of great pleasantness, with the single exception of a stormy and dangerous night spent off Port Royal, on the coast of Jamaica.[41]

[1] H. K. Hines, "Emigrant Wagon," January 1, 1885, 2.

[2] H. K. Hines, "Emigrant Wagon," January 1, 1885, 2.

[3] Ash Hollow is south of the North Platte River, just off U.S. 26, about five miles southeast of Lewellen, Nebr.

[4] Judson, *A Pioneer's Search*, 32-34. "Wagon wheels were soaked when crossing the South Platte, but dried so quickly in the hot, dry air of the high plateau between the rivers that the iron tires frequently rolled off the felloes. Emigrants dug shallow circular pits, a bit larger than the tire, built hot fires (frequently of buffalo chips) scattered the coals around the rim of the pit and placed the tires on the coals. The heat quickly expanded them so they could slip back on the wheels, where shims were placed." Personal communication, Gregory M. Franzwa.

[5] "[This] "steep gorge" is Windlass Hill, leading to Ash Hollow. Wheels had to be roughlocked, and trees felled to serve as drags, to send the wagons down safely. Ash Hollow is a Nebraska State Historical Park today, with a fine interpretive center." Personal communication, Gregory M. Franzwa.

[6] H. K. Hines, "Emigrant Wagon," January 1, 1885, 2.

[7] "Even today, visitors from states east of the Missouri River are shocked at the ferocity of the Kansas or Nebraska thunderstorms." Personal communication, Gregory M. Franzwa.

[8] Judson, *A Pioneer's Search*, 32-34.

[9] Phoebe alludes here to Luke 24:11 (King James Version) wherein Jesus' desciples scoff at Mary Magdalene and the other women who return from the empty tomb telling of his resurrection.

[10] Judson, *A Pioneer's Search*, 35-36.

[11] This is surmised from the 1860 U.S. census, which lists Melissa, age 9, and George, age 7, both born in N.Y. 1860 U.S. Census, Fairfield, Solano County, California; image copy at www.ancestry.com; accessed April 12, 2007.

[12] The similarity to Harvey's phraseology in his letter of April 13, "The incidents of rail-road traveling are so common-place…" suggests that Joseph has read that letter to the *Advocate* prior to writing his own.

[13] This was Rev. N. P. Heath. "N. P. Heath…was a man of marked character, a very good preacher, and with a snap and vim which would naturally seem to fit him for this field. He had been about seventeen years in the work before he came to California. But he was never contented with the country, and in 1856, or at most early in 1857, he returned. He filled important charges in Illinois after that." C. V. Anthony, *Fifty Years of Methodism, A History of the Methodist Episcopal Church within the bounds of the California Annual Conference from 1847 to 1897* (San Francisco: Methodist Book Concern, 1901) 135.

[14] This was John F. DeVore who settled in Washington Territory. From Yarnes we learn of DeVore: "J. F. DeVore is probably the man, above all others, who should be mentioned as the Circuit Rider of the Puget Sound region. In August, 1853, the people of Steilacoom received word that a Methodist minister was expected to arrive by ship to establish a church at Olympia. However, they decided that their little village of about 100 inhabitants should have a church so they sent a delegation to intercept the ship and try to induce this preacher to come to Steilacoom. They prevailed upon Rev. DeVore to organize a Methodist church which he did and before the next conference he built the first church of any denomination north of the Columbia River. This was in 1853, a year before the Methodist Church was built in Jacksonville." Thomas D. Yarnes, (Harvey E. Tobie, Ed.), *A History of Oregon Methodism,* (Parthenon Press, 1958?), 120.

[15] J. W. Hines, "Letter from Kingston, Jamaica," *Northern Christian Advocate,* July 20, 1853.

[16] Courthouse and Jail Rocks are visible to the south of Highway 92, near Bridgeport, Nebr.

[17] Chimney Rock can be seen to the south of Highway 92 near the junction with Highway 26, south of Bayard, Nebr.

[18] Harvey is incorrect. About ten percent of the chimney of the nineteenth century is gone, but most of it remains today. Personal communication, Gregory M. Franzwa.

[19] Scotts Bluff lies to the north of Highway 92, just west of present day Gering, Nebr.

[20] According to Mattes the story of Scott's demise took many forms; he takes nearly ten pages to describe the various versions, concluding with, "Celinda Hines, Rebecca Ketcham, and Abigail Duniway, all of the 1853 migration, heartily agree with the part that the dying Scott prevailed on his companions to abandon him and save themselves. This version was more palatable to the emigrant ladies, apparently." Merrill J. Mattes, *The Great Platte River Road* (Lincoln: Nebraska State Historical Society, 1969), 432.

[21] This was evidently the Robidoux Trading Post. See, e.g., Gregory M. Franzwa, *Maps of the Oregon Trail,* Third Edition (St. Louis, 1990), 101-103.

[22] Franzwa, *Oregon Trail Revisited,* 214.

[23] Harvey's quotation is from I Samuel 21:8 (King James Version).

[24] H. K. Hines, "Emigrant Wagon," January 1, 1885, 2.

[25] The Hines family was fortunate to hit a peaceful interlude. They were beneficiaries of a treaty signed less than two years earlier, in September 1851. The Horse Creek Treaty (also known as the Fort Laramie Treaty of 1851, because it was originally to be negotiated at the fort) was signed near here (about four miles west of present day Morrill, Nebr., on Highway 26) with some 10,000 Plains Indians in attendance. A year after the Hines family passed through in 1853, hostilities again broke out between the Army and the Indians, ignited by a "triggerhappy" second lieutenant, John L. Grattan. The officer and his attacking force of thirty were killed several miles west of here, near present day Lingle, Wyo. Franzwa, *Maps*

of the Oregon Trail, Third Edition (St. Louis, 1990), 104-107. See also the later note regarding Lt. H. B. Fleming of Fort Laramie.

[26] H. K. Hines, "Emigrant Wagon," January 1, 1885, 2.

[27] Judson, *A Pioneer's Search,* 36-37.

[28] "The old stockaded fort, named Fort William by its founders (Robert Campbell and William Sublette) was built in 1834; replaced by the adobe Fort John a few years later, was bought by the U.S. government in 1849, naming it Fort Laramie officially." Personal communication, Gregory M. Franzwa.

[29] Judson, *A Pioneer's Search,* 37.

[30] It is remarkable that any mail would find its way to them on the trail. A note in the Liberty (Mo.) *Weekly Tribune* points out one problem: "Great numbers of letters intended for emigrants to Oregon and California while on the route, never reach their destination in consequence of the wrong direction given to them.—The Post Office Department itself seems to know nothing about it, for in the Official Register it is put down 'Fort Laramie, Clackamas Oregon.' Generally, however, the mistake is committed in directing letters, 'Fort Laramie Oregon route.' In the haste with which these letters are distributed at the various offices in the United States the eye catching the word 'Oregon' it is at once supposed that it is to be sent by the California steamers, and off it goes in that direction. To ensure its getting to 'Fort Laramie,' nothing more is necessary than to direct it 'Fort Laramie, via Independence, Mo.'" "Mail for Fort Laramie," *Liberty Weekly Tribune,* March 18, 1853.

[31] H. K. Hines, "Emigrant Wagon," January 1, 1885, 2.

[32] This may well have been Dr. A. C. Donaldson, age 52 in 1853, who appears in the 1850 U.S. census for St. Louis (1850 U.S. census, St. Louis County, Missouri; image copy at www.ancestry.com, accessed April 13, 2007); and the 1860 U.S. census for California (1860 U.S. census, Granite, Sacramento County, California; image copy at www.ancestry.com, accessed April 13, 2007). The Sacramento area was a magnet for gold seekers. Donaldson was instrumental in starting a school and a church in the area.

[33] Hugh Brady Fleming, graduated from West Point in June 1852, and had served in the Sixth Infantry at Fort Laramie for about a year when Congress confirmed his appointment as a second lieutenant on June 9, 1853. Less than a week later, just a couple of weeks before the Hines party arrived at the fort, Fleming had been assigned to follow up on an incident of Indian provocation at the army-administered river ferry. In an encounter at the nearby Indian camp, Fleming's detail killed several Indians, and worse, came away with mistaken impressions regarding what a small army contingent could do in intimidating Indians. A year later, in 1854, these misperceptions held by then-commander Fleming, were partly responsible for the massacre of thirty soldiers led by 2nd Lt. John L. Grattan (see note 24). Fleming continued to serve in the regular army until his retirement in 1870. D. C. McChristian, *Fort Laramie and the U S. Army On the High Plains 1849-1890,* National Park Service Historic Resources Study, Fort Laramie National Historic Site, February 2003. http://www.cr.nps.gov/history/online_books/fola/high_plains.pdf, accessed April 13, 2007.

[34] The 1850 U.S. Census for Hastings lists a Sheldon Prescott (age 28), Experience (51), Albert D. (17), and Caziah (30), but nothing that would correspond to R. E. Prescott. C.E. Robinson would be Celinda's cousin, Clarissa E. Robinson, age 18. 1850 U.S. census, Hastings, Oswego County, New York; image copy at www.ancestry.com; accessed April 13, 2007. About Marie Wightman, see Celinda's diary entry for March 24 in Chapter 4.

[35] "Rev. Gustavus Hines, on his overland route to Oregon, writes us," *Christian Advocate and Journal,* Sept. 22, 1853, 150. On this same page, just above Gustavus's letter, is the notice: "Revs. J. W. Hines, J. F. Devore, and N. P. Heath left New York June 20th, and brother Hines was in Portland, Oregon, aiding brother Kingsley August 3rd." The Hines party on the trail knew nothing of this at the time; they assumed their brother Joseph was still home in New York.

[36] John H. Kemble, *The Panama Route 1848-1869,* (Berkeley: University of California Press, 1949).

[37] Mattes, *Great Platte River Road,* 23.

[38] John D. Unruh, Jr., *The Plains Across,* (Urbana: University of Illinois Press, 1979) 120. Of the 27,500 travelers, Unruh estimates 7,500, or only about a quarter, were headed to Oregon. Of those traveling by sea, probably an even smaller fraction were Oregon-bound.

[39] H. K. Hines, "On the Frontier," *Pacific Christian Advocate,* February 9, 1882, 2.

[40] At a comprehensive website for California-bound steamship travel, we find "SS ILLI-NOIS: Wooden side-wheeled steamer, built by Smith and Dimon of New York, for the United States Mail Steamship Company. Entered the New York-Chagres service for the USMSC on August 26, 1851, and remained in it until the spring of 1859. Although not suffering complete destruction, the *Illinois* did run aground on a reef near Havana in August, 1857. She was sold at auction to Cornelius Vanderbilt in 1860 and placed on his New York-Havre run that year. She was chartered by the War Department during the Civil War and from October, 1863, to June, 1864, she again ran between New York and Aspinwall for Marshall O. Roberts. After the Civil War the *Illinois* served as a quarantine ship at Hoffman's Island in lower New York Harbor until about 1900." California Bound, http://www.pt5dome.com/ships.htm; accessed April 13, 2007.

Elsewhere at the same website, we find a "Captain Hartstein" listed for the *Illinois* on the same route in April 1853. We suppose this was the captain for Joseph's trip as well, and that Joseph has misspelled his name. http://www.pt5dome.com/ill042153.html; accessed April 13, 2007.

[41] J. W. Hines, "Letter from Kingston Jamaica," *Northern Christian Advocate,* July 20, 1853.

10

June 24—July 12, 1853: On to the Continental Divide

*On the 12th day of July, 1853, at noon, I stood on
the crest of the Rocky mountains, with a train of five yoke
of oxen by my side, an ox whip in my hand, and leaning on
my arm a stately, blue-eyed, golden-haired woman, the
queen of my heart and the crown of my life. From a single
filling of a tin cup we took our first quaff of the waters of
the Pacific slope—drank farewell to the land and the
friends behind, and hail to the land and the yet unknown
friends before. It was a happy, solemn, great epochal hour.
The old died and the new was born within us.*[1]

—Harvey K. Hines, reminiscing in 1898

From late June to mid-July, the Hines train was making its way
from Fort Laramie to South Pass on the Continental Divide. During the
same period Joseph and his family were sailing the Atlantic to Panama,
then crossing the Continental Divide 2,500 miles farther south on the
isthmus, and afterward making their way northward on the Pacific.

Harvey

We left Fort Laramie at noon of Thursday, June 23rd, and camped at
night on a little stream fringed with cottonwood and aspen, the scene of a
fierce battle between the Indians and a company of "mountain men," led by
Kit Carson as described by Johnson in "Leni Leoti,"[2] a story of the plains and
mountains which we were reading at that time. Here we began to ascend the
"Black Hills,"[3] a lateral range of the Rocky Mountains, which runs out from
the backbone of the continent north and west of "Laramie's river," and between
that and North Platte. The "Hills" are crowned by "Laramie's Peak" on the
sides of which great patches of snow were visible. The road over and among
the hills was good, except that it was a bed of sharp flinty rock, broken fine
and intermixed largely with a reddish clay, which wore and ground the feet of
the oxen like a huge file so that before night of each day it was with difficulty
the patient brutes could move forward. This range here abuts sharply against
the North Platte, indeed, is cut asunder by the river which here for twenty or
thirty miles flows through one of the most fearful gorges of its whole course.

164

In this gorge Fremont and his company were wrecked in 1843 in attempting to run it with boats.[4]

Phoebe

After leaving Fort Laramie we began the ascent of the Black Hills. Our route over these hills was a perpetual succession of ups and downs, and the aspect of the country drearily barren. The soil was of a reddish clay, intermixed with fine, sharp stones. These stones cruelly crippled the feet of the oxen. Old Tom, one of our heavy wheel oxen, became quite lame for a time. The poor fellow was obliged to limp along, as it would not do to lay over among these barren hills.

Laramie Peak towered above the hills, and there patches of snow were visible.

We reached La Bonta Creek on Saturday, a little before sundown, and made our encampment on its banks, among the cottonwood trees, one of the most charming spots of the whole route, where we found good water, grass and wood—which was greatly appreciated.[5]

Celinda

Friday, June 24—Warm. Came to the Black Hills. Laramie Peak has been in sight for a week. Some of the road was very rough, some very good. Landscape wild & romantic. On the bluffs we were by cedar & pine trees. Was advised by a trader to take a cut off thereby shunning the Black Hills & also 20 miles where there was neither wood or water. He represented that by going this new way we should have good water at intervals of 4 or 5 miles also a better road & 30 miles nearer. We took it. At noon a man gave us some ice. We camped near a small clear stream in a bed of larkspur the most beautiful.

Saturday, June 25—Warm. Country peculiar. Passed Horse creek a beautiful stream before noon. Heard a waterfall near the crossing. AM rode on a horse. I walked about 5 miles P M. Passed a place where the Platte passes through the mountains. Camped near the river about 2½ miles from the gorge.

Harvey

At the end of two days ascending and descending these hills we came out on a summit on the afternoon of Saturday, June 25th and saw before us and at our right a beautiful valley two or three miles across, enclosed on the west, south and east by a circle of rugged mountains, while on its north the

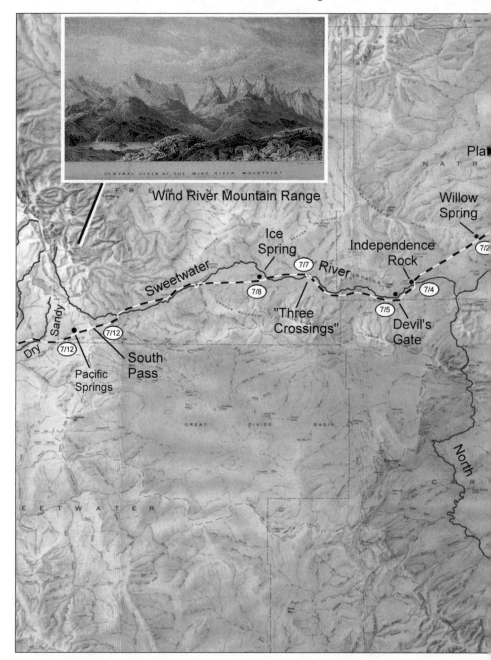

Topographic map of southern Wyoming showing the route of the Hines

Inset: *The Wind River Mountains from John C. Fremont's* Report of the Exploring Expediton to the Rocky Mountains in the Year 1842, and to Oregon and California in the Years 1843-44. *(Washington, 1845.)*

party along the North Platte and Sweetwater Rivers.

Inset: *Laramie Peak, based on the 1870 painting by Albert Bierstadt. http:/ /people.cornell.edu/pages/sab56/layout/intro.html*

broad, silver flow of the river, margined by a few cottonwood trees bounded the loveliness. We had been told at Fort Laramie that we could reach "La Bonta" before Saturday night, but we did not suppose that "La Bonta" would be such a paradise of beauty as was sleeping at our feet. The tired oxen, whose food for a few days had not been abundant, seemed to snuff the fragrance of the green pasture near the river and moved with willing steps down the hill and off through the meadow-like grass of the valley towards the river bank, where, long before the sun was down, we had driven our wagons into a circle and pitched our tents for our Sabbath's camp and rest.[6]

Judging from the descriptions of all three principal chroniclers, Sunday, June 26, was one of the more memorable days of the journey, both for the stunning natural beauty displayed in bright June sunshine, and for the arrival of a "new emigrant." Referring to this latter event, Celinda says straightforwardly, "We returned to camp & found we had an addition to our company in a little boy named Labonte Judson."

Harvey's version is wryly humorous: "We found, on reaching the tents, that another emigrant, barefoot and empty-handed, had joined us during our long afternoon walk, and proposed to make the remainder of the journey with us *nolens volens*...

But only Phoebe can give the mother's warm account, "...I am certain of the date, for the day was made memorable to me by the birth of a son."

Celinda

Sunday, June 26—Pleasant. Some of our neighbors (Traders) killed an antelope. Charles went and got some meat. After dinner we went to see the gorge. The scenery surpasses for grandeur sublimity & peculiarity any thing we have yet seen on the road. The river passes through what seems to be a natural fissure in the earth I should think 700 feet in height. We went to the top of the bluff. How grand how magnificent. Several miles of the road with teams & camps. The river & its various windings with its valley & bluffs on either side Laramie Peak in the distance with its snow capped crest was before us in all the grandeur of which a landscape can be possessed. We returned to camp & found we had an addition to our company in a little boy named Labonte Judson. Mr Leonard had arrived. He had left his company. They were all right.

Phoebe

The Sabbath dawned most serenely upon us, a bright, lovely

morning, the twenty-sixth of June. I am certain of the date, for the day was made memorable to me by the birth of a son.

Monday morning our party were so considerate of my welfare, and that of the "new emigrant," that they proposed remaining in camp for a day or two. I assured them that we were both very comfortable, and, though reluctant to leave this most beautiful spot (the romantic birthplace of our baby boy) I urged them to proceed with the journey.

The next morning we found the name of Platt La Bonta inscribed on our wagon cover. The name was suggested by the captain in commemoration of the birthplace on La Bonta Creek, in the Platte valley.

The name did not exactly suit me, so we compromised by adopting half of it, adding his grandfather's name, Charles; so the little fellow took his place in the ranks of life under the name of Charles La Bonta Judson. Thirty years after his wife's sister, Miss Kathie Moore of York, Pennsylvania, wrote the following birthday verses for him.

A JUNE BIRTHDAY

One sweet and lovely summer-time in June,
One fair and tranquil day, near noon,
The great Creator thought a thought,
And lo! life's angel gladly brought
A baby boy on earth to dwell—
And thus it is the birthday fell
         In June.

Since then, in sweet array, the years
Have passed with far more smiles than tears;
But as some days are dark, some fair,
         In June,

So this life, too, held some of care;
Some rain-filled clouds have dimmed the sky—
But these drop blessings as they fly
         In June.

Still time goes swiftly on from, June to June,
While blossoms grow and glad birds sing in tune,

And that the flow of future years
May bring thee nothing more of tears,
But that new joy may speed thy way—
Is my great wish for thy birthday
      In June.

Sunday evening who should come rolling into camp but the Missouri family who had left us on our first Sabbath encampment, because they feared to take the day for rest. We supposed they were at least one week in advance, but here they were, one day behind. Truly we had been favored by traveling with a company who believed in resting one day out of seven.[7]

Harvey

Sunday, June 26. Nowhere on the green earth had we seen a more beautiful morning, or been surrounded by scenes that would stir the imagination to softer and sweeter musings. As the sun came up over the eastern summits of the Black Hills swimming like a great globe of softened flame into an azure as pure as a sea of glass, the bland air rolled softly down the hillside and flowed riverward with just current enough to sway the spires of the tall grass and make the aspen leaves quiver with a silver sheen. The tents and wagons of several "trains" dotted here and there the river margin of "La Bonta vallee." There was a gentle murmur of awaking life as oxen and horses started afield, and men and women began the duties of the day, or childhood bounded out into the glad morning with trilling song or rippling laughter. It was a scene and time to impress the memory of a life-time's remembrance.

As the morning wore on one train after another had moved forward, and early in the forenoon ours was the only one remaining. We felt that we were making better haste by keeping the Sabbath than by breaking it. However, after the sun had passed the meridian, some of our ladies—good, Christian women they were, too—after a little mysterious conversation together, proposed that nearly all the gentlemen and ladies of the train take a long walk to examine the head of a gorge where the river entered the "Black Hills," and to gather some of the beautiful flowers that bloomed on the hillside. So we wandered far down the valley, up among the rocks, gathering flowers and beautiful specimens of rock; the ladies never seeming to tire of the beauties of the place or the pleasures of "the walk." One lady sat on a boulder and drew a pencil sketch of "La Bonta vallee" and the surrounding mountains. It took a long while to make that sketch. But, as the sun began to drop quite to the hill-tops westward we all strolled slowly back across the couple of miles of grassy plain that lay between the hills and camp. We found, on reaching the tents, that another emigrant, barefoot and empty-handed, had joined us during our long afternoon walk, and proposed to make the remainder of the journey with us *nolens volens*.[8] Mr. And Mrs. J[udson] kindly took him into their wagon, fed and clothed him, and brought him safely through. The name of our camp that day stuck with him for life; and as Mr. And Mrs. J[udson] and "Bonta," away up in northern Washington Territory read these lines, they, and all that were with us that day will revisit in pleasant memory "La Bonta vallee."

Just as the sun was setting, a couple of wagons came rolling down the hillside, and directly towards our camp. On their coming up to us we were surprised to recognize Mr. And Mrs. L[eonard] and family, who had left our train on the morning of the first Sabbath of the journey because they thought it best to travel every day, including Sabbath, and whom we had not seen from that time to this. They had traveled every Sabbath; we had laid by every Sabbath but one when we were compelled to travel for want of grass and water, and yet at the end of seven weeks we were one day ahead of them. We were glad to meet them, for they were good people, and acting according to their judgment of what was best under the peculiar condition of life on the plains.[9]

Although not surrounded by the wondrous scenery encountered by his relatives on the overland route, Joseph and his family did have a pleasant Sabbath on the Atlantic Ocean, where they enjoyed the morning sun several hours before its rays reached the overlanders.

Joseph

On the 26th of June, we spent our first Sabbath at sea. Such had been the tide of mirth and hilarity on board, that we feared the holy Sabbath would fare slim in the hands of the passengers and crew of the *Illinois*. But we were happily disappointed. No sooner did the rising sun throw its golden beams across the heaving billows of our ocean-home, than nearly all on board appeared to pay an instinctive homage to the command of God, and, in conduct at least, exclaimed,

"This is the day the Lord hath made,
He calls the hours his own."

By the kind request of the Captain and passengers, we had religious service at half past ten o'clock, Br. De Vore preaching to the steerage pas-sengers, while we endeavored to press upon the attention of an intelligent and interesting congregation, upon the saloon deck, the 130th verse of the

119th Psalm. ["The entrance of thy words giveth light; it giveth understanding unto the simple."] It would have done your soul good, Br. Hosmer, to have been with us as our united voices echoed forth upon the mighty bosom of the deep, while we sung,

> Come, thou fount of every blessing."
> [From the CyberHymnal, the first verse:
> Come, Thou Fount of every blessing,
> Tune my heart to sing Thy grace;
> Streams of mercy, never ceasing,
> Call for songs of loudest praise.
> Teach me some melodious sonnet,
> Sung by flaming tongues above.
> Praise the mount! I'm fixed upon it,
> Mount of Thy redeeming love.]

All appeared to feel that God was in our midst. In the evening, we assembled upon the deck, and, led by Mr. Angel,[10] of Geneseo, who is on his way to the Sandwich Islands as American Consul, we spent a pleasant hour in singing a variety of spiritual songs and hymns.[11]

Phoebe

The captain decreed that our wagon should lead the train (although it was not our turn), saying if "our wagon was obliged to halt the rest would also."

It proved the roughest day's journey through the Black Hills. The wind blew a perfect gale, and while going down some of the rough sidling hills it seemed that the wagon would capsize; but I had little to fear, for Mr. Judson had become an expert in handling his team. Some of the ladies remarked that "he drove over the stones as carefully as though they were eggs."

When we halted for our noon lunch the ladies hurried to our wagon with anxious inquiries. Are you alive? etc. I quieted their fears by informing them that little "Bonta" and I were doing finely—that Annie held on to her little brother with both hands while going down the steepest hills, for fear that he would roll out of bed among the pots and kettles. Mr. Judson had buttoned and tied the wagon covers down so closely that I could not get a peep out, and I suffered but little inconvenience from the wind and dust.[12]

Celinda

Monday, June 27—Morning pleasant. We went out to the hills. The wind soon commenced blowing a perfect gale. Sand blew with such violence as to be painful even to our hands. We were almost blinded. The country was a barren waste of sand hills covered with short stunted grass. Towards night passed the Labonte. Were much refreshed at the sight of trees & water. Went 4 miles & camped near a beautiful stream skirted by trees.

Joseph

Monday, June 27, at about nine o'clock a.m., we entered the harbor of Kingston, the largest town in the island of Jamaica, where we were to receive coal, and then sail for Aspenwall, on the Isthmus. Here we must close for the time being, intending in our next to speak of the Island and the condition of the Negroes here.[13]

Joseph continues with his impression of Jamaica in his next letter.

CORRESPONDENCE

Kingston, Jamaica, June 28, 1853.

Br. Hosmer:—In my last, I promised to give you, in another communication, some reflections upon Jamaica and its inhabitants. I will now redeem that promise. As to the city of Kingston, at which we landed, I was greatly disappointed. Between it, and the cities of the United States, there is very little resemblance indeed. Its streets are exceedingly narrow and filthy, and the buildings appear weather-beaten and dilapidated. There is, I believe, about fifty thousand inhabitants, made up of representatives from almost every nation under heaven, and distinguished by almost any form of feature, and shade of complexion. The business of the place is quite considerable. One is completely astonished on entering an old and apparently unused building, to find it furnished in the most gorgeous style, and filled with costly and beautiful merchandize, yet so oppressive and ener-vating is the climate here, that little of the anxiety and bustle of our mercantile houses is seen. Every man appears desirous to do some-thing, but at the same time, makes no effort to accomplish it.

There are several churches here, nearly all of which contain large memberships. There are four belonging to the Wesleyans, who were the pioneers in missionary labors here, and have been as inde-fatigable and self-sacrificing as any other Church, in laboring for the moral elevation and improvement of the inhabitants of this island.

One of the Churches contains a membership of about two thousand, and they worship in an edifice that will seat at least three thousand individuals. Yet notwithstanding this apparent prosperity, the preachers inform us it is exceedingly difficult to produce any permanent and reliable impression, especially upon the native inhabitants. But still they keep toiling on, hoping, as the effects of former misrule and oppression are effaced, to see still greater fruit of their labor. You are aware, I presume, that this island is frequently referred to by the slave-holder, as an awful and affecting instance of the foolishness and *crime* of emancipation. Having a few of these gentlemen on board, and not having failed to let them know "what spirit I was of," the question was frequently put to me, "do you not think that the inhabitants of Jamaica are worse off than when slavery was practiced there?" Of course, I invariably answered no. And once I had the insolence to remark to a swaggering oppressor, that I did not believe that a condition of greater peril and horror than slavery could be found, until man found himself where there is "weeping and wailing and gnashing of teeth." This, with other remarks, greatly raised the ire of this graduate of the "peculiar institution," and he stoutly swore that if he should see me at the South advocating these sentiments I now entertain, he would be the first man to swing me on a tree. But what of all this? Suppose we admit that they are worse off at present than when in bondage; does that prove that emancipation was the cause of their increased degradation? By no means. I took occasion carefully to question an intelligent English merchant here, as to the cause of the slow movement of those who had formerly been in bondage on this island, and he candidly informed me that it was not altogether their own fault. "England," said he, "after having set us free, has abandoned us." The import of this remark is this. It is utterly impossible for Jamaica, or any other place, to compete with slave labor; and the mother country, patronizing as she does the slave labor of the United States, leaves her emancipated colonies to struggle on without encouragement or support. It must be understood that when the slaves of Jamaica were set free, they were poor and ignorant, and nearly all of humanity had been crushed out of them. No one could reasonably expect, therefore, that they would immediately rise to the refinement and practical industry of those who had long been free. Years of instruction and encouragement are needed, in order to [achieve] their full redemption. And this, I fear, they will never enjoy. The world is too selfish, and too much under the control of popular prejudice, to be found freely and readily extending the hand of support to those who have been maltreated and ruined. But will not the same effects follow in the states, should emancipation take place there? We think not; and for the following reasons: In Jamaica, the vast majority of the inhabitants were slaves, and upon being set free, those passions which had been cultivated in bondage, would, to a greater or less extent, exhibit themselves in retaliatory feelings and actions. And more: there was comparatively a small amount of intelligence and moral power developed in a state of freedom, into which the slaves could at once be brought in contact. Consequently the light retired before the darkness, and left it in possession of the field. The inhabitants were also of necessity confined to one or two departments of industry, and consequently, if these should fail, bankruptcy would immediately follow. But far different is the condition of things in the United States. There the white population is in the majority; the light vastly predominates over the darkness; and her widely extended domain furnishes almost every variety of industry and encouragement. No apology, therefore, can be found here, for our black and heaven-daring crimes to the colored race in our midst. There is nothing in the way of their freedom but the willful malice and black-hearted villainy of those who oppress them. "How long, O Lord, how long."[14] More anon.[15]

Back on the Oregon Trail, in the meantime, Joseph's relatives pushed on through the Black Hills, reaching Independence Rock in time for a Fourth of July celebration.

Celinda

Tuesday, June 28—Pleasant. Not so windy as yesterday. Country barren. Shall be very glad to get through the Black Hills. Camped at noon by a beautiful stream. Camped at night in a retired place by a stream. Gustavus came near being lost. He went after a pail of water & lost the camp.

Wednesday, June 29—Pleasant. Came on to the river. Have got through the Black Hills. The road is better now. Camped near the river. Uncle H caught a rabbit & a...

Thursday, June 30—Warm. I rode on horseback A M. Crossed some very bad places. Snow in sight on the bluffs all day. Camped near a ravine. Uncles, Mr Martin & Mr Miner went on to the bluffs & stayed all night.

Passed Mud creek PM…night. We heard wolves howling in the night nearer & louder than I had ever before heard.

Friday, July 1—Warm. I engraved my name on a rock near our camp. Hunters return unsuccessful. Crossed the North Platte on a bridge paying six dollars a wagon & 1 shilling a head for loose stock.[16] 5 miles very sandy. Some of the time we could not see the heads of the oxen. Camped near the Platte.

Saturday, July 2—Pleasant. Passed the Rocky pass about noon, afterwards passed Alkali swamps. Camped near the Willow springs.

Phoebe

During the week we crossed to the other side of the Platte on a bridge owned by the Mormons, paying them six dollars per wagon toll. Some of the trains refused to pay so exhorbitant a price, but paid more dearly in the end, by having their stock stolen from them by the Indians, who no doubt were instigated by the owners of the bridge, through a spirit of revenge.

The country over which we were passing was still a succession of barren hills; but, as it was shut out from my view I realized but little of its discomforts.

Saturday night found us at Willow Springs. Here a few scattering willows were struggling for an existence in a sandy desert, amid the gray sage and thorny cactus. The name "Willow Springs" had a delightful sound, suggestive of clear, purling water and grateful shade, but we were greatly disappointed to find only a small amount of brackish water, compelling us to take up our onward march Sunday morning. Before night we came to the Sweet Water valley, and, turning to the right, we traveled about two miles from the road, where we found good grass for our stock and made our encampment by a stream of pure water, very close to the celebrated Independence Rock, where we proposed to remain over a day and celebrate the Fourth of July.[17]

Harvey

From "La Bonta" to "Independence Rock" our road led us, for a couple of days, up and near the Platte, on its south side, then crossing it on a bridge owned by the Mormons for which we paid six dollars per wagon, toll, we bore away to the north-west over a very hilly and desolate country for three days when we struck the valley of the Sweetwater. Here Saturday night found us at a place called "Willow Springs" in the midst of a sandy desert on which gray sage and thorny cactus were the only vegetation. Only a little, poor, alkaline water could be found at the "Springs," so necessity compelled us to make a short drive on the Sabbath. Before the middle of the afternoon, however, we had come to the edge of the Sweetwater valley, and crossing the dry sandy bed of an intermittent stream, we turned up to the right towards some great, gray, rocky buttes north of "Independence Rock" to find a suitable camp in which to spend the Fourth of July. A mile or two from the road brought us to where the bed of the stream was covered two to three inches deep with cold snow water, melted in the icy banks in the gorges of the mountains a few miles to the north. Before night it was a bold stream, six inches deep, flowing to and across the road where we had crossed its dry bed a few hours before; but every night it is locked in the fetters of the frost. Here, in a fine meadow, we prepared to "celebrate" "Independence day."[18]

Celinda

Sunday, July 3—Warm & pleasant. I rode on horse back in the A M. Mr. Miner & Mr Martin for company. P M crossed Wire creek also Greese wood creek. Likewise Bad slue & Alkali region. Camped near Independance rock.

Monday, July 4—Very warm. Saw a buffalo chase in the morning. The water in a ravine near by seems to proceed from snow in the mountains as it flows by day and ceases by night. We got up an independance dinner all the company eating together. Very pleasant.

Phoebe

The morning broke brightly. The roaring of the cannon in our native country having failed to awaken us at the break of day, we had remained quietly, taking much needed rest. Awakening, greatly refreshed, we were now ready to enter upon the jollification of the day by a "picnic," the only method of celebrating that could be devised by our patriotic little band. We were isolated from all other trains, far from civilization, without the banner of our country to unfurl to the breeze, and there was no band of martial music to thrill us with its inspiring strains. But more loyal hearts never entered upon the festivities of the day with greater enthusiasm than did these pilgrim travelers through the wilderness. Each family contributed from their stores their very best.

I was able to sit in the little rocking chair my kind husband had thoughtfully purchased for my comfort the last thing before starting on our journey. An awning was attached to the side of our wagon to shelter the picnic party, and, with the curtains rolled up, seated in my little rocking chair, I gazed down upon the bountifully spread table and merry company surrounding it—heartily enjoying the delicacies constantly passed up to me.

The memory of the continual thoughtfulness of my fellow travelers to me glows with a brightness that can never be effaced. "Kind deeds can never die."

Our dinner was not so elaborate an affair as the customary Fourth of July dinners, but I doubt not was more keenly relished by all. As my readers may be curious as to our menu, I will give it: The crowning piece of the feast was a savory pie, made of sage hen and rabbit, with a rich gravy; the crust having been raised with yeast, was as light as a feather; cake of three varieties (fruit, pound and sponge), pickles, dried beef and preserves, rice pudding, beans and dried fruit. Beverages: tea, coffee, or pure cold water from the mountain stream, as we chose; while from the hearts glowed sparkling wit, in expressions of patriotic mirth well suited to the spirit of the day.

More than fifty of these national anniversaries have gone by since, but not one of them is so vividly portrayed upon my mind as the one celebrated by the little band of adventurers, so far from civilization. I imagine we must have been watched over and protected by an invisible army of the old Revolutionary soldiers, for "He giveth His angels charge over us to keep us in all our ways," or we could not have enjoyed ourselves with such a sense of safety in barbarous country.

How remarkable that so many of the old patriots should have been translated from their worn out bodies on Independence day.

I stood by the bedside of my grandfather, William Goodell, a Revolutionary soldier, eighty-six years of age, as his spirit departed from the body, while the cannons were booming at sunrise, the morning of July fourth, 1842.

Thomas Jefferson, the author of the Declaration of Independence, expressed a desire "that he might live to see its fiftieth anniversary ushered in," and his prayer was granted. In company with John Adams, they took their light to the spiritual realms on that memorable day. "Independence forever," exclaimed President Adams, as he passed from mortal view amid the rejoicings and festivities of a whole nation.

In looking upon the map, I find Independence Rock located in the center of the state of Wyoming, very close to Rattlesnake Mountain. I little thought while camped by its side that I should ever be able to define its position in so enterprising a state as that of Wyoming.

Fremont, "the great pathfinder," described it in the report of his expedition of 1842 as "an isolated granite rock, 650 yards long and forty feet high." With the exception of a small depression at one place on the summit, where a little soil supports a scanty growth of shrubs, and one solitary dwarf pine, it is entirely bare. It is surrounded by level ground, from which it appears to have emerged, and everywhere within six or eight feet of the base, where the surface was sufficiently smooth, the rock is inscribed with the names of travelers, most of which were very legible.

He estimated the rock as being "one thousand miles from the Mississippi."

We had many reasons to rejoice that this distance had been accomplished without serious misfortune to any of our number.[19]

Harvey

The great event of the Fourth was to be a "camp dinner" at which all expected to provide the best they had. Before the sun was up that morning, G. H[ines] and myself had taken our rifles and were off on foot for the mountains which lifted their rocky brows miles away to the north-west. Before an hour was gone herds of antelope which dotted the plains and hills had lured us away from each other, and as I could not tell the direction he had gone, I bent my steps alone towards the mouth of a large ravine between two granite summits five or six miles away. A couple of hours walk brought me to the place, which I found to be one of enchanting beauty. What appeared to be only a gorge was a wide, grassy vale, garnished with flowers and guarded with great sentinel peaks of naked gray granite. Down the center of the vale ran the stream on which our tents were pitched six or eight miles below. The sun was mounting towards meridian, but my feet were tempted to a further stroll up the valley, until I came to a great block of granite which some mighty convulsion had heaved from the mountain into the middle of the valley. It cast a cooling shade on the northern side, so, leaning my rifle against it, I seated myself on the grass at the base and gave myself over to the unhindered workings of my own mind; to thoughts of self, home, friends, my country, and my God. I was alone—nature only and God, were there beside. A delicious sense of their presence calmed and soothed me. I was experiencing the literal realization of the Prophet's type of God's all-sheltering love—"the shadow of a great work in a weary hand." I repeated aloud the poet's finely wrought verse:

"There is a pleasure in the pathless wood,
There is a rapture on the lonely shore;
There is companionship where none intrude,
By the deep sea and music in its roar."[20]

I sung:

"Here I raise mine 'Ebenezer;'
Hither by Thy help I've come."[21]

and felt a sense of that "help" as seldom before. Then my thoughts strayed eastward to the old home-roof; to the churches of my former care; to the friends whose tearful "good-byes" were still echoing in my heart. I thought of the roaring cannon and streaming flags and marching columns; of the eloquence and song that over the land were filling this day with gladness. Thinking, my heart thrilled with patriotic love for

"My own, my native land,"[22]

and my soul throbbed with silent worship of the Great "God over all; blessed forevermore."[23] It was with reluctance that I tore myself away from this spot and these reveries whose memory yet marks July 4th, 1853 as the sweetest "Independence Day" of my life.

At three o'clock I reached the camp. Our dinner was something of a novelty. Every wagon had yielded its best. We had of meats, bacon, and dried beef. We had a great chicken pie made of sage hen and rabbits. Of vegetables we had beans and rice. Of cake we had fruit, and pound, and sponge. Of pudding we had Indian and bread. We had pickles and preserves and dried apples. For drinks we had coffee, tea, milk, or water as we chose. And, for the rest we had health and happiness, and there was cheer and charity at our feast that day.[24]

Joseph and family spent Independence Day in the city of Panama, on the Pacific side of the isthmus. His letter of that date describes their trip across the isthmus. We noted in the last chapter that his overall journey for the most part was spared the difficulties associated with the Panama route. He was lucky to be traveling at a time, 1853, when years of experience had ameliorated many of those difficulties. But for the isthmus transit, Joseph's timing was in this respect less fortunate. The railroad across the isthmus was not completed until 1854; Joseph's party was able to take it only to

Barbacaos (Joseph spells it "Barbacoos."). From there it was fourteen worrisome miles upriver in a native-propelled boat, overnight in the open at Cruces because fire had consumed their bamboo-and-rushes building, and finally a twenty-hour mule-back ride over a 200-year-old road to the city of Panama.

It can be seen from the map of the two trips on page *xxi* that Joseph was at this time in the vicinity of the 80th west meridian, a milestone Gustavus and party had passed nearly four months earlier, on March 8, as their train approached Erie, Pennsylvania. However, it would not be many days before Joseph swept well past them as the steamer *Golden Gate* carried him rapidly north and west up the coast of Central and North America.

Joseph

Panama, July 4, 1853.

Br. Hosmer:—I will now, with your permission, furnish your readers with an account of our trip across the far-famed Isthmus. Friday morning, the first day of July, our noble steamer bore gallantly down from the Caribbean waves, and quietly rested herself on the placid waters of the harbor of Aspinwall. It rained at the time, a smart shower, and every thing indicated an unfavorable time. But soon the rain ceased, and a cloudy day sheltered us from the burning rays of a tropical sun. Assisted by the willing native "*hombres*," we soon conveyed our baggage to the boat from the cars, a distance of about a quarter of a mile. Here a season of hurry and confusion ensued, which baffles all power of description; but being soon over, we found ourselves started for Barbacoos, the present terminus of the road. The distance from Aspinwall to Barbacoos is about twenty-three miles, and took us about an hour and a half to accomplish it. The road would undoubtedly have been completed as far as Gorgona before this time, had not an unexpected rise in the Chagres River at Barbacoos carried away the bridge. They are now attempting to repair it, but when it will be completed, I will not endeavor to determine.

At Barbacoos, we were to take boats upon the Chagres River, and in them be pushed about fourteen miles by almost naked natives. About 1 o'clock p.m. we were quietly seated in our boat awaiting the signal to start. And now came the "tug of war." Such pushing and bawling, fighting and pulling, going up one rod, then floating down two, I never witnessed before, and I hope may never witness again. The river was high and rapid, and after the most laborious effort, which lasted until dark, we found ourselves but seven miles from the place where we started. Here we hauled up, and sustained of course by Christian patience, quietly sat in our boat until morning. Soon as the daylight broke in the east, stilling, as it did, the hissing serpent, and driving the ravenous crocodile to his den, we again started, and about noon arrived at Cruces, the place where we were to take the mules for Panama. This was Saturday, and the children being quite fatigued, and expecting the Golden Gate to sail on Monday, we were compelled to remain until morning and perform the remainder of our trip on the Sabbath. This, of course, was a source of regret to us, but under the circumstances could not be helped. The ass was in the pit, and we did not hesitate to pull him out. All things being prepared on Saturday afternoon, we retired to rest at night, intending at an early hour to commence our novel ride; but at about 1 o'clock found ourselves suddenly aroused by the cry of fire, and soon the building in which we lodged was enveloped in the devouring flames. It is astonishing how rapidly the fire spreads in one of these native villages; the walls of the buildings being made of bamboo, and the roofs of rushes, in ten minutes after the fire started the building was in ruins. But we all escaped unhurt, and without loss of a single article. The rest of the night we spent in almost every conceivable position. Of course we were up at an early hour, and at 8 o'clock were all ready for a start.

Now, Mr. Editor, I am not going to tell you how we looked when all mounted upon our mules. We were undoubtedly in the "regular succession;" but judging from our outward appearance, it was from Baalam[25] rather than St. Peter. But at all events we heard no angelic remonstrance, while with unsparing severity, we cudgeled the ass to the work. And now off we start, in a company of about a dozen, and in less than ten minutes, the "elephant" in all his giant proportions appeared in view. But to us, who had seen such animals before, he possessed no terrors; or in other words the road was not half so bad as we had expected. But, notwithstanding, it is a great curiosity. It is, I believe, about two hundred years old, and in its day was a fine thing; and even now, taken in connection with the animal used in traveling it, may be considered in many places rather passable. But we were informed that where we passed it was uncommonly good. We certainly had a delightful day, it being cloudy, cool, and refreshing. Our company consisted of brother and sister Heath, Mr. And Mrs. Farrar, myself, wife and brother [This brother of Joseph's wife was John Wesley

Meredith, who later in Oregon married Milley Ann Adams], and our two children; and we all passed over without a single mishap. When about half over, we brought up under a large and shady tree, and provided with some refreshments, partook a hearty meal. This being over, we again mounted our mules, and at about 4 o'clock a.m. we entered the gates of the ancient and venerable city of Panama. We put up at Booths' Hotel, situated near the Pacific shore, and there learned that the *Golden Gate* would not sail until Tuesday at 3 o'clock p.m. This arrangement gave us sufficient time to examine the city, which we did not fail to do with some care, and an account of which I will give you in my next. We are all well at present, especially the children, who have endured the fatigue of the journey in a remarkable manner. Pray for us, brethren, that we may be brought on our journey in safety, and arrive at our destined home with a hand and a spirit to work for the Lord.[26]

Celinda

Tuesday, July 5—Warm & pleasant but for the dust. 6 miles from camp came to Independance rock which is a large oval mass of primitive rock alone on the prairie. 6 miles from this is the Devils Gate, the place where the Sweet Water river passes through the mountains which are composed of solid primitive rock. The passage is nearly straight through the mountain. The rocks on either side are between three & 400 ft. in height perpendicular. How the water ever found a passage through this granite is very strange. Our road lies up the Sweet Water. We camped on the southern bank having crossed it in the morning near Independance rock. Fuel Grease Wood.

Phoebe

The fifth of July we reached another point of interest—the Devil's Gate, where the Sweetwater had cut its way through a spur of the mountain, rushing through a rocky gorge with perpendicular walls from three to four hundred feet high. Up these dangerous walls many foolhardy men had climbed, risking their lives for the mere pleasure, and supposed honor, of having their names inscribed upon these towering rocks. The larger portion of our party took time to inspect this place, so highly honored by the name of his satanic majesty. My curiosity was not at all excited, though I often concluded, when our way was rough and barren, that we must have traveled through his domain.

Passing over the ridge through which the river had cut its way, we again came into the valley of the Sweetwater, and had our first view of the Wind River mountains, whose snow-capped peaks glistened against the

Gregory M. Franzwa

The Sweetwater River flows through Devil's Gate.

western sky in shining lengths, as though arranged by design. Humboldt estimates the tallest peak to be 13,567 feet high. It bears the name of "Fremont, the man of the empire."[27]

Harvey

"Independence Rock"[28] is a huge block of granite lying upon the plain entirely detached from the mountains at a distance around it. Eight miles from it the Sweetwater has cut its way through a spur of the mountains, foaming for a mile or more through a rocky gorge with perpendicular or impending walls from two to five hundred feet high. The place has the name of "The Devil's Gate." Passing over the ridge through which the river has cut its way we again enter the valley of the stream, and had our first view of the snowy summits of the "Wind River Mountains—" the first mountains covered with perpetual snow we had ever seen. They set against the blue western sky in a long line of sharp serrated peaks, white and pure and cold.[29]

On Tuesday, July 5, in Panama, Joseph and family boarded the steamer *Golden Gate* and headed out onto the Pacific. A San Francisco newspaper later reported,

> The United States Mail steamship *Golden Gate*, C. P. Patterson, U.S.N., commander, left Panama on the evening of July 5th, at 9-1/2 o'clock. The *Golden Gate* brings a large mail but a small number of passengers— only about 300—among them are many of the old residents with families. B.F. Angell, Esq., Consul to the Sandwich Islands, with his family is among the passengers by the *Golden Gate*. The traveling on the Isthmus was the same as usual, the road being good and the Isthmus healthy.[30]

The steamship Golden Gate, *on which Joseph Hines and family traveled from Panama to San Francisco.*[31]

Celinda

Wednesday, July 6—Warm. Road up the river. Very sandy. Country barren. Sweet Water mountains lie parallel with the river on the north & near it. On the south they are farther off. They are one continued chain of granite rock. Camped near the river. Drove the cattle on the other side. Fuel sage. The men went over the river on the mountains, made a fire. Alkali all around south of the river.

Thursday, July 7—Pleasant. Men caught some fish in the morning & we had some for dinner. Crossed the Sweet Water three times in the P M. The first time the crossing was good, but at the next we had to raise the things in the wagon & the next was still worse. Mr. Bryant came near upsetting his wagon. Camped near the river where we were nearly encompassed by mountains of granite. We were on the north side of the river—on the south side the mountains are of a different formation, sand I should think.

Friday, July 8—Rather cold & windy. Camped at noon at Ice Springs. It is said that by digging two or three ft. under ground ice may be found. It rained very hard during our stay there so no one tried it. Before noon we came in full view of the Rocky mountains. Some of the Co. had seen them two days before. We camped at night on the south side of the river, having crossed it in the morning. We were in sight of the mountains.

Saturday, July 9—Warm & pleasant. Crossed the river once. The bluffs on either side of the river are of a grand formation & seem to have been thrown up by water. We made but one drive & camped on the north side of the river in a beautiful glen.

Sunday, July 10—Warm & pleasant. Uncle Gustavus preached at 2 o'clock. After tea all but Mr. & Mrs Judson & Messrs Miner & Nelson went on an adjacent bluff to view the scenery. The valley was at our feet with its river so serpentine that although near yet we could not trace its various windings. Many camps were strewed along its banks. Bluffs the most picturesque reared themselves on every hand while the snow capped Rocky mountains pierced the clouds in the distance.

On July 10, according to the *Daily Alta California*, the *Golden Gate* reached Acapulco.

At 9 P.M. arrived at Acapulco, and left July 11th at 9:1/2 A.M., detained 12-1/2 hours. Running time from Panama to Acapulco, 4 days and 23-1/2 hours. Not any vessels in port.[32]

Celinda

Monday, July 11—Pleasant. Passed one Co. who had lost two persons a man & a woman who left an infant also lost 88 head of cattle. And another company who by the sinking of a boat lost 3 wagons & all their provisions & some of their clothing & have since broke two wagons one yesterday. Camped at noon at Strawberry creek. Saw strawberries in bloom. Passed Willow creek in P M. Camped on the Sweet Water for the last time after crossing. Some indians came to the camp. One came riding up to another & pitched upon him seemingly with the intention of doing him harm pulling his hair & threatening him with an axe above his head. We thought that perhaps it was but a maneuver to attract our attention so that others might have an opportunity to steal. Mr. Bryant interfering they soon went away. The men guarded the cattle all night as we are among the Black Feet having left the Crows. Wolves howled terrificly near camp.

Tuesday, July 12—Pleasant but windy. Went 10 miles to South Pass then 3 to Pacific Springs near which we camped for dinner. Road good all the way. Soon after dinner a wagon just ahead of our train was upset but no material damage done. The same train have had two men killed by lightning. We drove till late without finding water but at length came to Dry Sandy where we found some water & camped. Fuel sage. Uncle H & Mr Bryant drove the cattle away to feed & remained with them all night. The water is very poor.

Phoebe

We had many hills to pass over that bordered the river, which we forded twice, and found the water deep and cold. Ice formed in the camps, and banks of snow lay by the roadside, making the air so chilly that we were obliged to wear heavy wraps to keep from shivering. I managed to keep my baby warm by cuddling him closely to me in bed.

At noon, on the twelfth of July, we reached the highest altitude of the Rocky mountains. The ascent had been so gradual that it was difficult to distinguish the highest point. From the beginning of our journey we had been wearily toiling on an upward grade, over vast prairies, up high hills, mounting higher and higher—not realizing the elevation to which we had attained, and now had nearly reached the region of the clouds, without being aware of the fact.

Many of the dangerous places which had loomed darkly before us were now things of the past. Safely upon this pinnacle, we could look down upon them as upon vanquished foes, with rejoicings, like those who have struggled for riches, fame and honor. When the pinnacle of success is reached, they look back upon the obstacles surmounted with a sense of pride and satisfaction.

But pride must take a fall, as we sadly realized, and all are sure to find the downhill grade is the hardest to travel.

The descent at first was so gradual as to be almost imperceptible, but became rougher and more precipitous as we proceeded on our journey. It was a satisfaction to know that we were now drinking from the waters that flowed to the Pacific. A number of great rivers have their source in this immediate vicinity—the Missouri, Colorado, Platte and Columbia.

Our first encampment on this side of the pass was made on the Dry Sandy, surely very appropriately named, for there was not a drop of water in the bed. We were obliged to dig down into the sand to obtain a little brackish water, and to drive our stock three or four miles up on the hillsides to find feed for them.[33]

Harvey

Up the Sweetwater, leaving the immediate stream occasionally to pass over hills that butted against it, and fording it a couple of times where the water was deep and cold, our road led us for five days more, when on the evening of the 11th day of July we encamped on it for the last time within nine miles of the summit of the Rocky Mountain range. Deep banks of snow lay near the road, and ice formed a fourth of an inch in thickness in vessels of water in our camp. Just before noon of the 12ᵗʰ we passed over the summit: a low ridge so gentle in ascent and descent that we could not tell exactly its highest point; and stopped for dinner on its western side; making our coffee out of "Pacific Springs" which send their waters to the Pacific Ocean through the Colorado of the West.[34]

On the summit of the continent. This is a place to pause, and look about, and think. We have climbed a weary distance. Three months and more the slow, patient ox has wheeled up the long slope down which the rivers flow towards *home*. We are on the crest of the world. If we cross it we follow the water-courses *away* from the old ties, old memories; away from *home*. To say that there are no regrets tugging at our heart-strings as these things sunk out of sight behind the crest of the Rocky Mountains would be to say that we had little of that human tenderness that would qualify us for the new life before us. But they were not our masters; we were theirs.

Years later, in a June, 1898 address to the Pioneer Association of Oregon, Harvey described the same scene as follows.

On the 12th day of July, 1853, at noon, I stood on the crest of the Rocky mountains, with a train of five yoke of oxen by my side, an ox whip in my hand, and leaning on my arm a stately, blue-eyed, golden-haired woman, the queen of my heart and the crown of my life. From a single filling of a tin cup we took our first quaff of the waters of the Pacific slope—drank farewell to the land and the friends behind, and hail to the land and the yet unknown friends before. It was a happy, solemn, great epochal hour. The old died and the new was born within us.[35]

As we stood on the noon of this twelfth day of July on this summit of the world and our vision swept the horizon there was an awe of the Great God resting on the soul. The vastness and the greatness of the outward universe deeply impressed the thoughts. We were in a vast depression in the summit of the range of mountains. North of us, up there in the sky, stood Fremont's Peak, white and cold and impending. Beyond were the icy pinnacles of the Wind River Range from beneath which broke the fountains of the Yellowstone and the Missouri. Southward, over a great stretch of gray, sage desert, perhaps twenty-five miles away, the frowning face of table mountain scowled upon us, and beyond that, the serrated ridges that fountain the Plattes and the Arkansas. East and west were down, down, down. Softly the waters of the Pacific Springs glided over their sandy bed westward. As we surveyed the scene it really began to seem that it would be a pleasant thing to glide out of the old life and world behind into the new life and world before.

Down a slope as gentle as we had ascended to reach the "Pass" we traveled during the afternoon, and at night made our camp in the bed of a waterless creek called "Dry Sandy"—certainly a very appropriate name. It was a dreary, desolate place. By digging some holes in the sandy bed of the creek three feet deep a little brackish water was obtained, but there was no grass for the stock, so, after supper Mr. B[ryant] and myself drove them some three or four miles away to the north on to the slopes of some high hills where we found a small supply of feed. The night was cold and frosty, but we built large fires out of dry sage and juniper, and, by rising frequently to replenish them, and "spooning[36] it" pretty closely in our blankets, we managed to have quite a comfortable night. It was not quite a safe place, as we were near the borders of the territory of the Snakes, and where war parties of Sioux, or Crow, or Blackfeet, or Snakes were liable to be prowling, and it would doubtless have been safer for us not to have built a fire, but we consulted comfort as well as safety. We lay with our rifles in the bed with us. In the morning gathering up our oxen as soon as it was light we reached camp just as breakfast was ready.

---

[1] H. K. Hines, "Rev. H. K. Hines Address to Pioneers," *Sunday Portland Oregonian*, June 19, 1898.

[2] Perhaps Harvey is recalling the author incorrectly, and instead means to refer to Emerson Bennett, *Leni-Leoti—or, Adventures in the Far West*, (Cincinnati: Stratton & Barnard, 1849).

[3] "The Black Hills, to which Harvey refers, are not related geographically to the Black Hills of South Dakota. However, both were named for the dark cedar trees on their slopes." Personal communication, Gregory M. Franzwa.

[4] H. K. Hines, "Emigrant Wagon," January 8, 1885, 2.

[5] Judson, *A Pioneer's Search*, 38, 39.

[6] H. K. Hines, "Emigrant Wagon," January 8, 1885, 2.

[7] Judson, *A Pioneer's Search*, 39, 40. See the discussion regarding the Leonards' departure from the Hines party on May 15 in Chapter 7.

[8] Displaying his erudition once again, Harvey here uses the Latin phrase for "whether willing or unwilling." *American Heritage Dictionary of the English Language*, 4th ed. s.v. "nolens volens."

[9] H. K. Hines, "Emigrant Wagon," January 8, 1885, 2.

[10] Benjamin Franklin Angel (1815-1894) was a lawyer and diplomat who served as American Consul in Honolulu, 1853-54, Ambassador to Sweden, 1857-61, and delegate to the Democratic National Convention in 1864. The Political Graveyard; http://politi calgraveyard.com/bio/andridge-anstine.html]; accessed May 6, 2007.

[11] J. W. Hines, "Letter from Kingston, Jamaica," *Northern Christian Advocate*, July 20, 1853. (Hawaii was a kingdom in these years.)

[12] Judson, *A Pioneer's Search*, 40-41.

[13] J. W. Hines, "Letter from Kingston, Jamaica," *Northern Christian Advocate*, July 20, 1853.

[14] Historian Prof. Michael McKenzie informs us that this quotation was commonly used by anti-slavery writers in the times leading up to the Civil War. Personal communication, Michael McKenzie. Among the many places Joseph may have seen it was the anti-slavery article, "Shall We Compromise?" *The Independent*, February 21, 1850. Making of America; Christian pamphlets, Vol. 13; http://quod.lib.umich.edu; accessed May 7, 2007.

[15] J. W. Hines, "Correspondence, Kingston, Jamaica, June 28, 1853," *Northern Christian Advocate*, August 17, 1853.

[16] There was evidently stiff competition for the emigrants' money at this crossing. According to Franzwa, "In 1847 the Mormons placed a ferry at the site of later Fort Caspar, in the western part of Casper, Wyoming. A model of the ferry is there. The following year it was moved eastward, operating at the site of a present Casper city park." Competitors built a bridge, at a cost by some estimates as high as $16,000, and advertised in the *St. Joseph Gazette* in early 1853 that the toll rates would be greatly reduced that year. But as Unruh notes, "Unfortunately, however, crossing fees did not decline: most travelers paid $6 for the privilege of driving their wagon across the once formidable Platte, plus up to $1 per draft animal." Unruh, *Plains Across*, 289-91.

[17] Judson, *A Pioneer's Search*, 41, 42.

[18] H. K. Hines, "Emigrant Wagon," January 8, 1885, 2.

[19] Judson, *A Pioneer's Search*, 42-44.

[20] This is from Lord Byron. George Noel Gordon, Lord Byron, *Childe Harold's Pilgrimage*, canto IV, st. 178.

[21] These are the first two lines from the second verse of the hymn, "Come, thou Fount of every blessing." (Some elucidation of "Ebenezer" can be found at I Samuel 7:12.) Note that this hymn was the same one as sung by Joseph and his shipboard congregation, as described earlier in this chapter. Apparently it was a favorite hymn of the Hines family.

[22] Here Harvey quotes Sir Walter Scott. Poets' Corner—Bookshelf, *The Lay of the Last Minstrel*, Sir Walter Scott; http://www.theotherpages.org/poems/minstrel.html; accessed May 7, 2007.

[23] As far as we have been able to determine, Harvey's quote is not directly from the Bible. The phrase did occur in several nineteenth century texts, according to a Google search. Searched May 7, 2007.

[24] H. K. Hines, "Emigrant Wagon," January 8, 1885, 2.

[25] Joseph alludes here to the Biblical Balaam, who, after three beatings of his disobedient ass, realizes, as God speaks through the ass, that the animal is wiser than he. Numbers 22:22-31 (King James Version).

[26] J. W. Hines, "Panama, July 4, 1853" *Northern Christian Advocate,* August 24, 1853.

[27] Judson, *A Pioneer's Search,* 45.

[28] "Travelers often stopped at Independence Rock to inscribe their names in grease, tar, and often cut into the hard granite. However, a comprehensive survey by Randy Brown fails to detect inscriptions from any of these diarists." Gregory M. Franzwa, Personal communication. It is interesting to note, however, that Celinda describes "engraving" her name on an earlier rock. See her diary entry for July 1.

[29] H. K. Hines, "Emigrant Wagon," January 8, 1885, 2.

[30] *Daily Alta California,* July 19, 1853.

[31] The Sinking of the *S.S. Golden Gate,* freepages.misc.rootsweb.com/-ssgoldengate/; accessed June 13, 2007.

[32] *Daily Alta California,* July 19, 1853.

[33] Judson, *A Pioneer's Search,* 45, 46.

[34] H. K. Hines, "Emigrant Wagon," January 8, 1885, 2. "There are nine crossings of the Sweetwater on the Oregon Trail. South Pass is about thirty-five air miles southwest of Lander, Wyoming. Pacific Springs, about 2.6 miles west of the pass. Today it a spongy slough, from which Pacific Springs Creek eventually emerges, flowing west." Personal communication, Gregory M. Franzwa.

[35] H. K. Hines, "Rev. H. K. Hines Address to Pioneers," *Sunday Portland Oregonian,* June 19, 1898.

[36] Here Harvey is using "spooning" in the sense cited in the OED: "4. To lie close together, to fit into each other, in the manner of spoons." *The Compact Edition of the Oxford English Dictionary* (New York: Oxford University Press, 1971) 2978. Note also the following entry from the on-line *Urban Dictionary.* "1. survival position. A position two people use when there is a need for warmth. The position is the same as spooning. Both persons are laying on their sides the back of one person touching the front of the other. Two men were lost on a snowy mountain. They had to stay in the cold overnight, so in order to stay warm they told the media they got in the survival position, in order to prevent hypothermia." *Urban Dictionary,* http://www.urbandictionary.com; accessed March 24, 2007.

11

July 13–26, 1853: From South Pass to Soda Springs

Uncle & Charles having a few words, Charles left
& went to Mr. Bryants...After tea Charles left and joined
another Co for Oregon.
—Celinda Hines, July 22, 24, 1853

Charles Long accompanied the Hines party for at least two months. Although he is not listed by Harvey or any of the others as a member of their train, Celinda, already on May 9, shortly after they had started on the trail, mentions that she, Julia, and Martha ride in his wagon. In his capacity as a wagon maker, he was also the one who Celinda credits with taking the lead in repairing Harvey's wagon wheel on May 29. His name is mentioned often by Celinda when she describes exploratory side trips she enjoyed. From the cryptic notes of July 22 and 24, however, it appears that his relationship with Gustavus became less than congenial, leading to his departure from the train.

After they crossed the Big Sandy, on their way from Pacific Springs to Soda Springs, the Hines party was faced with a choice: head directly west across a desert, following the so-called Sublette Cutoff, or head southwest along the Big Sandy, in the general direction of Fort Bridger. They chose the latter, departing from what Harvey calls the "main road" (that is, the Sublette Cutoff), so as to avoid as much of the open desert as possible. But they did not go all the way to Fort Bridger, as had some travelers in earlier years. Rather, after following the Big Sandy for some twenty-seven miles (according to Celinda), they then turned westward across the desert and after just sixteen or seventeen miles, reached the Green River. After crossing that river, they headed toward Slate Creek and followed what was known as the Slate Creek Cutoff until it merged with the Sublette Cutoff, and then proceeded westward to the Bear River.

Celinda

Wednesday, July 13—Warm & pleasant. Road good but sandy soil much of it has been, producing nothing but sage. We have seen no grass of

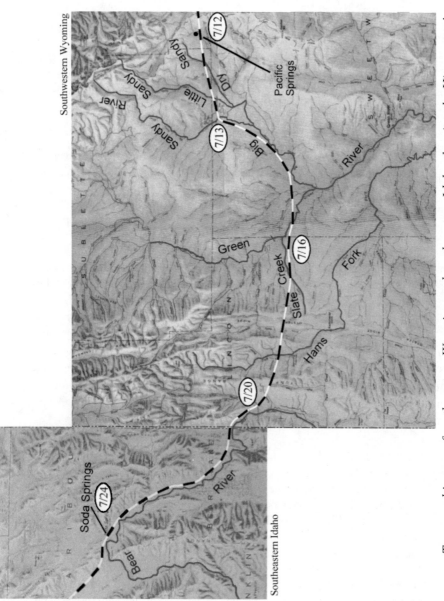

Topographic map of southwestern Wyoming and southeastern Idaho showing the Hines party's route from Pacific Springs to Soda Springs. Dates are approximate, based on Celinda's diary.

any consequence since we left Ft Laramie on the road. Passed Little sandy PM 12 miles from where we started. Camped on the Big Sandy 4 miles further. In the PM saw some mountains in the distance covered with snow.

Thursday, July 14—Warm & pleasant. Were detained in the morning by the cattle crossing the river. Took the road leading down the river although it is some farther; on account of the Green river desert which by the most direct road is 50 miles across & no water. Down the river it is 17 miles. We went 27 miles & camped on Big Sandy. Charles, Mr. Miner & Nelson went away with the cattle & stayed all night. The Desert is a rolling prairie producing nothing but sage.

Friday, July 15—Pleasant. Went to Green or Colorado river over the desert. Camped near a slew from the river. No grass for the cattle which have had nothing to eat since morning. Saw a N Y. Co.

Saturday, July 16—Pleasant. Crossed the river on the ferry paying $6.00 a wagon. They had to drive the cattle some ways up the river to swim them. They were loth to swim & it was necessary to drive them in with a drove to get them across consequently we were detained a good part of the day. But notwithstanding the cattle were very tired & hungry having traveled at least 27 miles the day before, we were under the necessity of driving 10 miles before camping in order to find grass. Camped on Slate creek.

Celinda's concern for the welfare of the cattle was shared by Phoebe and Harvey. All emigrants were aware that the viability of their teams was of fundamental importance to the successful completion of their journey.

Harvey

Through all the region lying between Pacific Springs and Green River the country is sterile and forbidding beyond description. The distance is about ninety miles and there are but two small streams, Little and Big Sandy, between. The main road led from Big Sandy across a waterless desert for about fifty miles to Green River, but we chose to travel a half day longer and avoid "the desert," as this dreary stretch was called. So after crossing Big Sandy we traveled down it, always near the water, for a day and a half, and then turning westward in sixteen miles we reached Green River just as the sun was setting on the evening of Friday the 15th day of July. The view from the top of the low ridge between the two streams was full of beautiful promise. The river shone like a silver mirror in the clear sunlight. On its banks the green cottonwood trees bowed to a gentle wind. A plain that looked as though green with grass lay on each side of the stream. With glad steps man and beast hastened toward the river. We reached it only to find, as is all too often found: "The distance lends enchantment to the view."[1] The river flowed through a grassy plain, covered with the thorny and bitter greasewood, upon which our stock must roam in hunger after the toil of the day. A bad camp for the stock is always a bad one for the people, for guard must be kept all night to prevent the cattle wandering miles away in search of food. So it was here.

Green, or Colorado, River is here about three hundred feet wide; deep and swift. As it could not be forded we were compelled to ferry the wagons on "the Mormon ferry" at $6 each, and swim the stock. This we found a difficult undertaking as the current was so swift and the water so cold that it was only after many trials that we could get them across. It was late in the afternoon of one of the most laborious days of the journey when we had our oxen yoked and hitched to the wagons on the west side of Green River, and then driving out about five miles over a high ridge, we descended into the valley of a little stream called Slate Creek, and, in good grass, encamped for the Sabbath.[2]

Phoebe

From the summit of the mountains to Green river our road led us through the most barren country of our experience, causing us much anxiety for our cattle. The nights were frosty, and the cold winds through the day made traveling very disagreeable. As we traveled along this barren ridge, Green river came frequently into view, flowing swiftly through the grassy plains. Cottonwoods waved their green branches by its silvery current. Our anticipation for the comfort of our cattle ran high. Already we could see them luxuriating on the succulent grass and slaking their thirst with the crystal waters.

Alas! for the poor cattle, when we reached the coveted spot, to our deep distress, the grassy plain proved to be but thorny cactus and bitter greasewood. Sadly we realized the truth set forth by the poet: "Distance lends enchantment to the view."[3]

The river at this point was about three hundred feet wide and the swimming of the stock was only accomplished after many ineffectual efforts to drive the reluctant animals into the cold, rapid stream.

The great anxiety experienced by the emigrants at these river crossings can hardly be realized. The lives of our men were in constant danger, as they forded these perilous streams on horseback—swimming the stock.

The Mormons owned the ferry, and we were again compelled to pay six dollars per wagon for crossing. It was nearly night when all were safely across on the west side of the river and our oxen attached to the wagons, ready to move forward. Driving but a few miles, and then descending into a valley, it was our good fortune to come to a small stream called Slate creek, where we found an abundance of grass for our cattle, that had toiled hard all day without a mouthful to eat. And as our six days of labor had been faithfully performed, we encamped by the side of the rippling stream for a day of rest.[4]

While his relatives struggled with "one of the most laborious days of the journey" as Harvey described it, Joseph was sailing toward San Diego, according to the *Daily Alta California*: "July [1]6th, at 3 P.M., arrived at San Diego, detained 2 hours; at 11 P.M., off Catalina Island, passed a schooner bound up."[5]

The steamship *Golden Gate* with Joseph and family aboard continued northward toward San Francisco on Sunday, July 17, but the Sabbath brought another welcome day of rest for the overlanders and their animals.

Celinda

Sunday, July 17—Went about 4 miles & camped for the day on the creek. Passed the day very pleasantly. Towards night it rained a little but it soon cleared off very pleasantly. Found some very pretty specimens of petrified wood.

Phoebe

As I look back on the stream of time, the only places my memory recalls with pleasure while crossing the plains, are the ones where we found pure water and good grass for our cattle, and allowed them to rest over the Sabbath. When God made a day of rest for the welfare of man, I'm glad that He did not forget the poor, tired animals, and said, "Thou shalt not work thy ox."[6] Had this commandment been observed, thousands of these poor creatures that were turned out by the roadside, in the sage brush and dust to die, would have been saved.

Memory vividly brings to view these patient servants of half a century ago. Our wheel oxen seemed more like rational beings than dumb brutes. The tears start as I see their great mild eyes, and think of the suffering they so patiently endured for our sake. It mattered not how tired, thirsty and hungry, when Mr. Judson lifted the yoke and said "come Tom and Jerry," they always came and obediently put their heads under the yoke. Buck and Berry were often found hidden away when it came yoking-up time, but they never shirked when pulling up the high hills and over the rough mountains. And as God was so merciful as to order a day of rest for them, He will surely reward them for their labor. Surely there is a heaven prepared for such faithful creatures, and I trust they are all on the "shining shore" where runs a pure stream of crystal water through a field of clover.[7]

Harvey

How the Sabbath as a day of *rest* drops into the weariness of a life such as this. How divine seems the order that prescribes it. From break of day till late at night, all the week, we toil on in wind and dust, in sweltering heat or chilling cold, the rest of the night being called to guard mount, or by the hundred alarms incident to this wild region, and when that one morning in seven comes in which tents are not to be taken down, nor the cattle yoked, but we can literally and absolutely *rest*, it seems an Eden oasis in an out-cast desert. I notice all faces are brighter and the very cattle look more content on these Sabbath mornings.[8]

On July 18, according to the *Daily Alta California*, the *Golden Gate* had reached San Francisco: "July 18th, 7 A.M., arrived at San Francisco making the passage in 12 days and 9 hours—running time 11 days and 19 hours."[9]

While Joseph and family took a week's break to explore San Francisco, the other Hines brothers and fellow emigrants were getting their first exposure to potentially hostile Indians.

But based on the accounts we have, practically all of the encounters the Hines party had with Indians were friendly. The scariest episode was probably the one that took place this following week in July, when two white men traveling east approached the Hines train, explaining that they were being pursued by Indians and that they were seeking shelter and protection. Whether the Indians were Snakes, according to Celinda, or Crows, according to Phoebe, it is clear that the young women were frightened. Harvey expresses a contrasting reaction, claiming that he "felt quite willing to fill up the diversity of our adventures by an Indian battle, if it were necessary to defend an imperiled man."

Celinda

Monday, July 18—Pleasant. Concluded to take into our Co a family with one wagon who had been with us two days. Another Co of two wagons wished admission but our Co declined. In the PM. uncle G went to find a camp. He came back with the report that there was trouble with the indians ahead. The story went thus: Two packers from Oregon to the states were overtaken & followed by 8 indians or people disguised as such who tried to entice them away into a ravine by saying there were emigrants there who wished to see them. Being unsuccessful in their efforts they attempted to drive off one of their pack mules. One of the white men told them that they must desist & stop following them. The indians said they would not & followed them for ten miles. One of the indians drew a pistol which the white man saw & dexterously aiming his rifle shot but not till after the ball which the indian shot grazed his breast. On firing the packer saw the blood spirt from the indian's side & the other packer fired but they supposed without doubt that the first shot mortally wounded him. The indians rode off & the packers came on & it was said that 800 or more were in pursuit & people were going on as far as possible to camp for fear of them. We camped near a small stream on a side hill, several camps being near, thinking if we were attacked we could all combine & resist it as we supposed the indians would take revenge on the emigrants as we were among the Snakes who are a blood thirsty nation. Soon after our stop these same packers came up & wished shelter & protection for the night. Some were in favor of retaining them & some were not but uncle concluded on the whole as there were a number of women & children & few men in the train it was best not to keep them but had no objections to them remaining at either of the other camps if they were willing to keep them. It seems the story was in the main true except that there were not more than 12 in pursuit. Yet it was expected that the whole nation would soon be in arms. A camp near by kept the packers & all prepared to resist should an attack be made. No women but 20 men in the camp.

Tuesday, July 19—We woke pleasantly surprised to find ourselves so happy & that we had not been molested. Mr. Judson was well acquainted with one of the packers. He went in the same Co when Mr J crossed the plains 2 years ago. He says that the packer is a fine man & would harm no one without provocation. Several of the emigrants saw the affray & justify the packers. They concluded to return with the emigrants at least until they should meet others with whom they could join so as to make it safe to proceed. Indians came around in the morning spying to find where they were & soon after starting others came up. Our road was hilly just before noon. They had to double team to ascend a very steep hill. I went around to get some snow & saw one of the packers. He appeared rather disconsolate but fearless & very pretty. In the PM. we ascended Quaking asp hill also passed Poplar grove on the top of the Green river mountains. The Co in which the 2 men had taken refuge was near us. The Co. consisted of 21 men well armed & no ladies.

Wednesday, July 20—Weather good. Road hilly. Two long hills to go up & 2 very bad ones to descend. I walked almost all day. Camped near Bear river. Some 2 indians came to camp & peeked into the wagons to see if the two men were there. Soon after, and while they were there, a trader came. After they went away he told us that the indians would not tell him what they were around for but that doubtless they were spies & that their object was to kill these men if they could find them. He also said that indians were coming together from different parts & that they were numerous as two or three tribes had joined together & they would visit every train as they had understood they were returning—until they found them & that any one in the tribe would know them if they should see them. We knew not whether the trader was sincere or whether he was trying to get some information. The packers camped near.

Phoebe

Monday morning we resumed our journey. The wind blew so cold from off the bald mountains that all who could walked, wrapped up in shawls and overcoats, in order to keep warm.

Two days of travel brought us to Crow creek. As we descended into the little valley a band of mounted Indians appeared in this distance, careening wildly across the valley toward our train—hair and blankets streaming in the wind. As they drew near at a terrific rate of speed, their hideous faces covered with war paint, struck terror to our hearts. It was a most terrifying spectacle, as they galloped furiously around and around the train, endeavoring to peer into the wagons. I still feel the thrill of horror that clutched my heart and curdled my blood as those bloodthirsty faces circled about us. We did not understand the cause of their threatening manifestations, and the only thing we could do was to conceal our fears and proceed quietly, as usual, to our encampment. Before we reached our camping place the Indians left us to bestow their unwelcome attentions upon other trains.

We were not long left in doubt as to the cause of these exciting maneuvers. Two men appeared, before we were fairly settled in camp, fleeing for their lives, seeking protection among us, feeling more assured of safety in the "missionary train." These men, who were on their way from Oregon to the states, got into trouble with the Indians and had killed one of the savages, as they claimed, in self defense.

On hearing this startling statement, our captain explained to them that "we had but eight men in our company" and advised them to seek protection in a larger train, which they readily consented to do. We greatly feared an outbreak from the Indians before morning, and all of the trains in that vicinity prepared for a battle, by coming together and forming a large circle with their wagons. The mounted guard frequently fired their rifles and revolvers, in order to give the Indians to understand that we were prepared to give them a warm reception, should they venture to molest us, keeping up a vigilant watch all night for the enemy.

The fear of being scalped before morning drove all desire for slumber from my eyes, but I lay down by the side of our precious little ones and prayed God to protect us from the hands of the ruthless savage. He, who heareth in secret, answered our prayers, and we were saved from the awful fate that seemed to await us, and which had befallen many of the emigrants while crossing the plains in the early days to Oregon and California.

The Crow Indians followed us for a number of days, bent on revenge, but feared to make an attack unless they had the advantage of an ambuscade. Had they possessed a little of the bravery of old Tecumseh, "the king of the woods," or the spirit of King Phillip, the illustrious Indian war chief of New England, there would not have been an emigrant left alive in Crow valley.

When safely out of the Crow Indian country, the two men emerged from their hiding places, where they had been so effectually concealed that the avengers of blood failed to find them, although they had peered into the wagons of every train. They returned to Oregon, as they were afraid to continue their proposed journey to the states, and no doubt some innocent party paid the penalty for the death of this Indian.[10]

Harvey

Monday, July 18th. Before us were high, bald mountain ranges, swept on this particular morning with a cold wind, so that an overcoat buttoned to the chin was a comfortable protection as I walked beside my oxen winding down and over the hills. The ladies, too, were clad in shawls and cloaks, and walked much during the day. The following day was a repetition of this, and towards evening we descended from the high ridges into the valley of Crow Creek, and descending it a couple of miles made our camp for the night.

As we came down into the little valley we saw quite a number of Indians, all very greatly excited, making unusual demonstrations of anger. As our custom was, however, we moved quietly to our camping place without exhibiting any tokens of apprehension though some of us did feel considerable alarm though as yet we did not understand the cause of the disturbance. Almost as soon as we were camped, however, Mr. M____ of one train, who had been at some other camps, came to us and said that an Indian had been shot and killed by a white man near by an hour or two before and it was apprehended that the trains in the vicinity might be attacked during the night. While he was yet relating the story two men came up to our tents and began to [several lines unreadable, but evidently these men were the ones being pursued by the Indians and were seeking protection] Some of the ladies were so alarmed that they urged our captain to ask the men to encamp in some other place, near a larger train where they would be more protected. They did so at once, saying that they would not stay near us if we felt that it endangered us. We did not all approve of the request, and felt quite willing to fill up the diversity of our adventures by an Indian battle, if it were necessary to defend an imperiled man. [Brave Harvey!]

All the trains in the vicinity mounted full guards all night and no Indian could have approached one of them without paying for it with his life.

The next morning all moved forward, but the two men were nowhere to be seen. Indians patrolled the road all day, armed and painted, and would ride up to the open end of the wagons and peer under the covers searching for the missing men. The trains moved forward with great caution, all arms loaded and near at hand. That night we encamped on Ham's Fork of Green River, and kept up the same vigilant guard. After a day or two more of the same search the Indians gave up the pursuit, and soon after the men came out of their hiding place in an emigrant wagon in safety. The Indians had looked into it several times, but they were too well hidden to be discovered.

These men were from the Willamette Valley and had started for the states. Some difficulty arose between one of them and an Indian because the Indian rode near him and appeared to be following him for some miles, the white man ordering the Indian not to follow him any longer. Both drew their rifles, the white man's exploding in an instant first, and the Indian falling dead. Of course they dare not proceed on their eastward journey, but, in the way we have related, turned back toward the west. We saw them often for a few weeks on the road, and in later years knew them well in Oregon. They are now [1884], we think, citizens of this state.[11]

Celinda

Thursday, July 21—Warm & pleasant. No one molested last night. Crossed the river on a bridge also three other streams. Road very hilly but not as bad as yesterday. Near night we had a long hill to ascend & then to descend. The descent was so bad in one place that they had to find a road for themselves. We went a short distance & camped by the river. We were annoyed very much by mosquetoes which were the largest I had ever seen. I do not remember where we have camped before when other camps were not in sight.

Friday, July 22—Remained in camp till near noon to recruit the cattle. A company of packers came along & we ascertained that the two fugitives had joined them & as the Co is large we think they are out of danger. Uncle & Charles having a few words, Charles left & went to Mr. Bryants. Mr. Martin took his place—We went on & it looking like rain, camped near a slew it soon rained a perfect torrent. We had to strain the water before using it. Grass was excellent. No wood.

Saturday, July 23—Pleasant. Crossed some bad slues from the river. Part of our road was hilly. Camped at noon near a fine spring. Called I believe White Mound spring. It commencing to rain we camped near the river in a very pleasant place.

Sunday, July 24—Pleasant. Remained in camp all day. Uncle H preached at 4 o'clock, it commenced raining & rained a few minutes. After tea Charles left and joined another Co for Oregon.

Monday, July 25—Pleasant. Our road was up the basin. We had a number of slues to cross & at about 11 o'clock we arrived at the far famed Soda Springs.[12] The first one we visited was clear & the water equalled the best soda water it was very strong. It boiled up out of the solid rock—as they all do—& in its ebullitions resembles the slakeing of lime. Placing the face near the surface the vapor has the same effect which the inhaling of hartshorn[13] produces. Two other springs were near which resembles the other except for the color of the water which is of another color. Two hills of soda are near. We camped for noon two miles ahead near the steam boat springs. We passed one spring on the bank of the river. Steam-boat spring is so called from the noise of its ebullitions resembling that of a steam boat pipe—as some fancy— This one is very clear and boils up about a foot above the surface it is strong with soda. Near this is another small one the waters of which does not at present run over the surface consequently it is dirty it is said to resemble steam boat whistle. These springs are near the river. They all come out of a basin of solid rock which where the water flows over is of a copperas color.

Many rocks around are of a deep yellow color. In the P.M. we passed the basin spring. Soda water bubbles up into a natural reservoir of stone which is a great curiosity. P M. passed through a volcanic region. There were large holes in the ground & rocks had been thrown up some times for rods in length. We camped near such a place. Stones looked as if they had been burned. Near here the California route leaves the Oregon trail but some of the California emigrants go up to Ft Hall. We went up the bottom & camped near a small stream we drove till after dark for water.

Tuesday, July 26—Road yet leads up the basin. Passed a great many slews. Camped near a stream near the termination of the valley [probably the Portneuf Valley]. This basin is productive. Have seen very little sage since we have been in it.

Phoebe

Our road led up a high mountain covered with fir timber. The descent was so steep that we were obliged to "rough-lock" the wheels of our wagons, by winding heavy log chains around the felloes and tires, allowing the chains to drag the ground. In this manner we made our descent into Bear River valley, where we turned our cattle loose to feed upon the luxuriant grass that carpeted the earth, filling the air with its fragrance. Here we experienced a delightful change from the frosty desert altitude to a lovely retreat, where the air was soft and balmy. A stream of pure water rippled through the valley, into which graceful willows dipped their drooping branches. Could foliage ever be more charming to the eye? It filled our souls with a spirit of perfect rest, inspiring us with the hope that the "ideal home" of which we were in search would be as sweetly enshrined by some mountain, or riverside, on the shores of Puget Sound.

How many delightful hours I passed, when but a child, building, rebuilding and furnishing the "ideal home" that should some day be mine—little dreaming that it would be located west of the Rocky mountains, and that to find it I would travel over two thousand miles in an emigrant wagon, through a country inhabited only by Indians and wild animals.

Traveling so far after the slow, plodding cattle nearly cured me of building "air castles," excepting those of a practical nature. I only hoped and prayed that we would live to get through with our little family, and now we press forward with all speed if we would escape being caught in the snow of the Cascade mountains.

We followed Bear river for a few days, finding good encampments all the way, until we reached the noted Soda and Steamboat Springs. These springs, lying about one mile apart, were natural phenomena—the water bubbling like a boiling pot. Steamboat Spring derived its name from the peculiar puffing discharge of its water. The waters were warm, with a bitter taste like some nauseous drug, being highly impregnated with mineral.

As we journeyed over a high ridge we had an extensive view of the surrounding country. The great panorama of nature presented a wide diversity of scenery. Mountains reared their lofty peaks, treeless and bare, far up into the sky; while others were capped with a soft mantle of snow, their broad sides clothed with timber.

As this constantly changing picture unrolled before us, in spite of our intense desire to reach the end of our pilgrimage, we were impelled to pause and contemplate this scene of wild and barren grandeur.

We crossed a few more small streams, usually finding good water and grass for our stock, but frequently a serious drawback to our comfort was a dearth of wood. Green willow, the size of a pipe stem, being the only substitute. Over this sizzling, smoky apology for a blaze we managed to heat water for our tea. I must say I preferred the willow to buffalo chips, which many emigrants used for fuel.[14]

Harvey

From Ham's Fork the road led up a mountain of about nine miles continuous, and often steep ascent, towards the eastern rim of the great basin of "Salt Lake." The summit of the rim, where our road crossed it is covered with a fine grove of fir and larch through which the road passes—the first of anything that can be called a grove since we left the Kansas River. It was about a mile through this one, and brought to us the memory of the old woodland paths along the Genesee and Allegany.[15] About noon of the 20th our train halted a moment on the summit of the ridge. Miles away westward, and perhaps three thousand feet below us, wound in emerald loveliness the broad meadowy valley of Bear River sweeping down from the south and finally disappearing among a wilderness of mountain peaks away in the north west. We were on the highest single mountain thus far of the route. The road dropped into the head of a sharp gorge just before us and we could see where it issued from the mouth of the gorge three or four miles below. My own wagon chanced to be on the lead that day, with five yoke of oxen attached. Rough locking both hind wheels by winding heavy log chains around the felloes and tires so that the chains would scrape on the ground we plunged down the gorge. Each wagon followed, and in hardly more than half an hour, without a moment's halt or slightest accident we drove out on the plain at the foot of the mountain. Ordinarily trains would stop on the summit, and, unhitching all the oxen but the "wheelers," four or five men would assist a wagon down, then return for another, and so on until all were down, consuming perhaps an entire day in getting down the single mountain.[16]

At the foot of this mountain is the junction of the South Pass road over which the emigrants from Missouri and the states north and east of it come, and that which crosses the Rocky Mountains by the Cheyenne Pass from Arkansas and the south west. Just as we approached the junction a train was approaching it on the Cheyenne Pass road. On one of the wagon covers was the name, "H. Cason."[17] Three months later we read his church letter in the old Taylor Street Church and put his name upon the church record. He can be found any Sunday in the M.E. Church in East Portland.

Bear River Valley is an oasis in the desert of the Rocky Mountains. Where our road reached it, it was a wide meadow-like expanse, covered with luxuriant grass, now in full head and waving before a gentle breeze, resembling a New York meadow of "red top" just before it was laid low by the scythe of the mower. We had just descended from the frosty altitude of the "South Pass," and almost in a single day had come out of a region incapable of producing anything but wild sage and greasewood, to one where flowers were blooming, meadows waving, and birds singing. The nights on the desert altitudes were all cold and frosty, here they were soft and balmy. Our whole train felt the happiness of the outward change, and our first camp on Bear River was a scene of nomadic romance. Our tents and wagons were scattered here and there on the green sod, the cattle and horses strolled lazily through the tall grass, some of the people were conversing, some reading or writing, some fishing, some gathering "curios," and all were in happy spirits.

The writer has often observed that people are much better in fair weather, and amid pleasant surroundings, than in bad weather and amid dismal surroundings. In the brightness of a spring Sunday, when the air is filled with the melody of birds and loaded with the fragrance of flowers a congregation will enter the church with faces [alive?] with joy, and they will speak of being happy, and perhaps mistake the influence of beauty and joy without for religion. We hardly ever have a poor class-meeting or even dull preaching on such a day. It is out of this fact that come our visions of an "Eternal spring-time?"

Just as into the gloom of the year drops the glory of spring, so into the cheerlessness of our past month's journey over the cold desert altitudes we had passed, dropped the beautiful contrast of this green and lovely camp.

We have entered here a new world—a continent in the middle of a continent. We have crossed the eastern "rim" and are now in the "basin" of Salt Lake; almost a very ocean in magnitude. Here are great rivers, pouring down from snowy mountains, and emptying into this interior ocean from which there is no outlet to the oceans that belt the world. Great mountain peaks, higher and grander than the Alleganies or White Mountains, spring skyward from the base of ranges hundreds of miles in length that lie entirely within this interior continent. At no point since our journey began have we so felt the greatness of the American continent as here.

The geology of this basin is as impressive as its geography. From the granite and sandstone and shale we have descended into a vast crater, now quenched, but once filled with an ocean of fire over which volcanic tempests swept their awful thunders. Walls and columns and escarpments of basalt stand everywhere. Lava, like slag from furnaces, in great fragments strew the ground. The imagination goes back into the eternities gone, and sees this mighty basin boiling and roaring, and vomiting its fire and smoke and ashes and melted rock, like a thousand Etnas towards the sky. The ages have passed. The fires have died to a deep slumber under the hardening crust of the globe. The mountains have been pushed upward by the force of the imprisoned gasses. The north winds have cooled their pinnacles; sunshine, rain, dew, the crystal snow-flake, the feathery frost work, the rolling season, all have wrought upon their flinty sides and dug into their crevices, until a tiny spring has bubbled to the surface, and spring after spring until the rivers run and the caverns of the sea are filled. And so the old world of fire and cinders and boiling gasses has passed away and the new world of prolific soil and running streams, and blooming flowers, and living men and women, and civilization, and, last but not least of "emigrant wagons" with their load of empire marching westward has come.

We entered Bear River Valley below the gorge through which it flows as it comes down the high summits of the Wasatch Mountains, and followed down it to the northward about sixty miles to where the river strikes against the northern rim of the "Basin" and its flow is turned back again southward toward Salt Lake. Just at this bend of the river the "Soda Springs" are found. Two considerable rivulets enter the main stream from the north—Smith's Fork and Thomas' Fork, on each of which we made pleasant camps. We reached the Springs on the evening of July 24th, and give a record written at the time as better than any drawn from memory could be.

The situation of the Springs is very beautiful. The mountains sweep around the northern end of the Bear River enclosing a large green basin, through which flows a beautiful stream of clear, pure water, near whose banks the Springs burst forth. The first thing that notifies a traveler of their presence is several red dome-like elevations of from two to four feet in height, and he will be surprised to find them hollow, with an open top, and the Springs boiling up in their center. These formations are rock formed by deposition from the water, and colored bright red by oxyd [sic] of iron. They are at present considerably higher than the water, which shows that the water has subsided since the elevations were formed. The water is reddish, highly charged with minerals, and kept constantly bubbling like a rapidly boiling pot by the escape of gasses. On putting my face near the water the gas instantly strangled me. There are a large number of these springs, bearing a close resemblance to each other, and constituting, with their surroundings, the most remarkable natural phenomena thus far on the route. We should be glad to examine this locality more particularly, but we are too far from the end of our journey to be beguiled into much lingering.

Steamboat Spring was about a mile further on, on the immediate bank of the river and bursts through the rock that forms the bed of the stream. It does not flow, but its water is discharged at regular intervals with a puff like a steam engine; whence its name. It is warm with a nauseous taste. Six miles further west the Oregon and California roads separate. The Oregon road swings slightly more to the north, and after passing over several ridges covered with *scoria*, and across some small streams that empty into Bear River, finally crosses the western rim of the great basin about forty-five miles from Soda Springs, and we are again on waters that flow to the Pacific.[18]

Somewhat earlier, on July 18, Celinda reported that the Hineses had decided to "take into our Co a family with one wagon who had been with us two days." It is apparently this same family to which Harvey refers when he recounts "A comical incident that somewhat relieved the somber monotony of the days and nights."

A very fine "Irish gentleman" and his family had joined our party a few days before—quite an intelligent and scholarly man, and his wife an excellent woman; but he was not raised to ox driving, and its worry wore on his nerves exceedingly. This night particularly he was much wearied as he drove into camp, and put his wagon alongside of mine. All had retired to rest and perhaps midnight had come, when Mr. B_____ began to vociferate quite vigorously: "Buck; you there, get oop wid ye." "Tom; why doos ent yees keep oop." By this time his wife was aroused. "Mr. B_____, Mr. B_____," said she in quite a loud voice, "do be still, you'll wake all the train." His answer was only more vigorous commands to "Buck" and "Tom." Again she expostulated, "Do be still Mr. B_____, I tell you there are no oxen here." By this time Mr. B_____ had begun to open his eyes, and crawling to the forward end of his wagon and looking out a moment in bewilderment he said, with a touch of disappointment in his voice—"And noo, wife, there's never an ox on this wagon." He crawled back quietly to his place in his wagon beside Mrs. B_____ and "Buck" and "Tom" never knew how near they were to a whipping for their misdemeanors that night.

Mr. And Mrs. B_____, as we have said, were most excellent people, and this little hallucination at which we laughed so heartily at the time only showed how the strain of those months of travel wore on strong nerves and brains. These people yet live in one of the most beautiful little cities of Oregon, respected and beloved by their neighbors. Mr. B_____ nongraduated to the degree of O.D., which, by interpretation means Ox Driver.[19]

Phoebe, too, recalls this family…

Phoebe

Our train was joined by an Irishman, with his family and team. I don't remember just when, or where, but have not forgotten that he nightly aroused the whole camp vociferating in his slumbers to his oxen to "Whoa, gee, and haw," and going for lazy Tom for not keeping "upp."[20]

Having arrived in San Francisco on July 18, Joseph recalled in his 1911 reminiscence, "I remained in San Francisco about one week, stopping with M.C. Briggs, the pastor of the Powell Street Church…We went on board the small steamer *Columbia* and sailed out of the Golden Gate about the 13 of July."[21] Clearly there is a date discrepancy. But both Joseph and the ship's log agree that they departed Panama on July 5, and given that eleven or twelve days was the shortest possible travel time in those days, the July 18 date for arrival in San Francisco seems reasonable. With Joseph's stated week-long stopover, this would suggest that he and his family left San Francisco on or about July 25.

[1] Harvey's quotation is from the poet Campbell. Thomas Campbell, *Pleasures of Hope,* pt. 1, (1799). See, for example, James Grant Wilson, *The Poets and Poetry of Scotland, Vol. II* (New York: Harper & Brothers, 1876), 5.

[2] H. K. Hines, "Emigrant Wagon," January 22, 1885, 2.

[3] Perhaps Phoebe is quoting directly from Thomas Campbell here, but more likely she has again mirrored some of Harvey's account.

[4] Judson, *A Pioneer's Search,* 46, 47.

[5] *Daily Alta California,* July 19, 1853.

[6] Phoebe has extracted from the fourth of the Ten Commandments the restriction against working animals on the Sabbath. See, for example, Exodus 20:10 (King James Version).

[7] Judson, *A Pioneer's Search,* 48.

[8] H. K. Hines, "Emigrant Wagon," January 22, 1885, 2.

[9] *Daily Alta California,* July 19, 1853.

[10] Judson, *A Pioneer's Search,* 49-51.

[11] H. K. Hines, "Emigrant Wagon," January 22, 1885, 2.

[12] "Most of the Soda Springs have been drowned by the Soda Point Reservoir. Hooper Spring, away from the river, remains." Personal communication, Gregory M. Franzwa.

[13] Hartshorn, or ammonium bicarbonate, was commonly used as a leavening agent before the ready availability of commercial baking powders. Ochef Archive; http://www.ochef.com/ 539.htm; accessed May 8, 2007.

[14] Judson, *A Pioneer's Search,* 51, 52.

[15] The Genesee and "Allegany" are rivers of western New York state.

[16] "They came down the steep hill to reach the Oregon Trail at Cokeville. The crossings of Smith's Fork and Thomas's Fork are near Montpelier, home of the splendid Oregon-California Trail Interpretive Center." Personal communication, Gregory M. Franzwa.

[17] This was Hilary Cason, who with his family was traveling with his sister, Mrs. Jesse Ward, and her family and others, according to Dillis B. Ward in his memoir of the 1853 trip, "Across the Plains in 1853." http://www.yelmhistoryproject.com/Yelm%20School/1860-1900; accessed July 15, 2007. Cason is listed as "Henry" Cason, born in Georgia, in the 1860 U.S. census for Oregon, along with a large family. 1860 U.S. census, Multnomah, Multnomah Co., Oregon; image copy at www.ancestry.com; accessed April 14, 2007. We surmise that the entry, "H. Carson, w, 1s, 3d," in the immigration roster at the Umatilla agency for September 21, 1853, is for the same family. J. Ward and family are listed on the

same date. Linn County History Websites, http://linnhistory.peak.org/1853/1853 imregis_9.html; accessed April 14, 2007.

[18] H. K. Hines, "Emigrant Wagon," January 22, 1885, 2. H. K. Hines, "Emigrant Wagon," January 29, 1885, 2.

[19] H. K. Hines, "Emigrant Wagon," January 29, 1885, 2.

[20] Judson, *A Pioneer's Search,* 58.

[21] J.W. Hines, *Touching Incidents,* 162.

12

July 27—August 25, 1853: Along the Snake River to Fort Boise

> *Nowhere before had the scene been so vast; but it*
> *was a scene frowning and desolate beyond descrip-*
> *tion…What emigrant, worn by his months of travel, with*
> *poor and jaded teams, his provisions getting short, and*
> *his money shorter, ever looked down this dark valley of*
> *Snake River without forebodings of peril? If there have*
> *been any we have not met them.[1]*
> —Harvey K. Hines, July 27, 1853

The Snake River, or the Lewis Fork of the Columbia River, as Fremont's journal refers to it, flows across nearly the full breadth of present-day Idaho, and represented perhaps the most trying stretch of travel for the already trail-weary emigrants. On his first viewing of the Snake Valley, Harvey senses "forebodings of peril," and Phoebe notes, "…first encampment on Snake river, a name ominous of treachery and tribulations." Added to Phoebe's misgivings is the realization that contrary to her expectations as they approached Fort Hall, they were still more than 800 miles from their ultimate destination.

There is some ambiguity as to just what constituted Fort Hall in the minds of our chroniclers. Phoebe writes simply of "Arriving at Fort Hall…" but both Celinda and Harvey imply that they took a "shortcut" that bypassed Fort Hall about twelve miles to the south, encountering instead a trading post affiliated with the fort. Perhaps this latter is what Phoebe thought to be the fort itself. The "Three Buttes" mentioned by both Celinda and Harvey are located about thirty miles to the north of the Fort Hall site, and therefore must have been over forty miles distant from the emigrants as they were viewing them from their trail.

We begin with an excerpt from Phoebe in which she recounts the journey of her parents through this region two years earlier, in 1851.

Phoebe

The name [Snake] was no misnomer, for these Indians were as treacherous, and their poisoned arrows as venomous as the reptiles whose

211

Topographic map of present-day Idaho showing the path of the Hines party as estimated from Celinda's diary and Harvey's reminiscent account.

Inset: *Photo of the Three Buttes (East Butte, Middle Butte, and Big Southern Butte, front to back) shows them as viewed toward the southwest. See the Digital Atlas of Idaho website at http://imnh.isu.edu/digitalatlas/*

cognomen they bore. Concealing themselves behind rocks, or in holes dug in the ground for that purpose, from which they assailed the emigrants and their stock with poisoned arrows, and were more to be feared than any tribe we had encountered.

My father, J. W. Goodell, who crossed the plains in 1851, with his family, experienced much trouble with this tribe of Indians. They followed his train the whole length of the valley, killing and stealing their stock; and, while camped near Fort Boise, very early in the morning the Indians attacked them in great numbers from the opposite side of the river, suddenly appearing from behind the rocks, which concealed them, long enough to shoot their poisoned arrows and fire their flint lock guns. One Indian, bolder than the rest, stepped out upon a rock and shook his red blanket in defiance, as a signal for war. A young man in the train (who, by the way, was the betrothed to my twin sister) was a splendid marksman, and possessed of a fine rifle, took a careful aim and fired—the bullet did not miss its mark; the Indian tumbled off the rock into the river, frightening the others so badly that it put an end to the battle.

For protection during the engagement, the women and children remained in the wagons, with their feather beds arranged around their covers as a barrier against the bullets and arrows. Not one of the company were wounded or killed, but I have heard my mother relate "they were so terrified that their tremblings shook the wagons."[2]

In late July, while the Hines train was beginning its long trek across what is now southern Idaho, Joseph and family were far west of them and departing San Francisco to head northward. Joseph records that they were on the steamer *Columbia*, and from this we estimate that that they reached Portland around August 1, based on the report of another family's trip on the same steamer a few months later in 1853.[3] Thus Joseph, despite starting from New York in late June, more than three months after his brothers' departure in early March, nevertheless reached his destination two months before their arrival in early October. It certainly leads today's observer to wonder what factors (cost, threat of disease or ship disaster) may have led so many emigrants to choose the overland option in favor of the much speedier Panama route.

Joseph

We went on board the small steamer Columbia and sailed out of the Golden Gate about the 13th of July [more likely about the 26th –see Chapter 11]. We crossed the storm swept bar of the Columbia in safety, and, sailing up the broad river, where the majestic fir forests crept down to the waters, and turning 12 miles up the beautiful Willamette, tied up our little steamer in front of the prospective metropolis of the North.

Our journey was ended. The varied scenes and checkered scenery through which we had passed had made a deep and lasting impression upon our minds, and I felt eager to acquaint myself with the field where I expected at that time to pass the remainder of my life. Everything seemed new and so roughly primitive in style that I questioned my power of adaptation, and felt at times a little feeling of homesickness creeping over me. But this I would shake off, and rush out into the field or forest and address myself to some enterprise that would tend to build up and beautify my new and future home.[4]

Celinda

Wednesday, July 27—Pleasant. Our road led through a kanyon [perhaps the Toponce Canyon between the Portneuf Valley and the Portneuf Range] over the dividing ridge between the waters of Salt lake & those of the Columbia. The road to the summit was through a grove of poplar trees & shrubbery. The trees were small but the grove was the largest we have seen for a long time. The road in the main was good but there were a great many bad places to cross. The descent was better. There were few trees & the grass in some places was a perfect meadow. Large rocks were seen on the sides of the mountains perfectly isolated with grass all around them Mr. Martin came near upsetting uncle G's wagon in crossing a stream. Some of the streams were large & very bad to cross. Springs would gush out of the mountains & large streams would flow from them. We camped on the bottom near a stream. Grass wood & water plenty.

Thursday, July 28—Left Ft Hall[5] about 12[6] miles to the north thereby saving 16 miles & it is said that the road is better.[7] We were in sight of the Three Butes all day. They are three mountain peaks rising high above the chain. We almost suffered with dust & want of water. Near night we came to the Port Neuf river which we had to ford it is large & deep we had to raise our wagon beds. Ft Hall trading post is near.[8] The commander of the Ft. Mr. McArthur[9] is very agreeable. We camped about a mile on near a fine spring. The men from the post came to see us. Chas.[10] Co were near.

Phoebe

Fort Hall now lay before us in the near distance. To this point, located in Eastern Oregon, which we thought lay near the end of our journey, our longing eyes continually turned.

Arriving at Fort Hall,[11] weary and worn with our long journey of more than a thousand miles, after the slow, plodding oxen, our hearts sank with dismay when we learned that eight hundred miles still stretched their toilsome lengths between us and the coveted goal of our ambition. Had we known of the desolation and barrenness of the route that lay before us, I fear we would have been tempted to give up in despair, for its proved by far the roughest and most trying part of our journey.

Looking back over the many conquered obstacles that lay behind us, we were inspired to press forward with renewed courage. We had passed through many rough and dangerous scenes, where the waters were deep, mountains high, and the Indians treacherous, and no serious accident had befallen us, and all were in good health. Surely we had reason to acknowledge Divine protection; and in a hopeful, trustful spirit we pushed forward, up and down, over more rough hills interspersed with springs of water, and soon after made our first encampment on Snake river, a name ominous of treachery and tribulations.[12]

Harvey

We stood on this "rim" [probably somewhere along the Portneuf Range of mountains] at noon of the 27th, and looked across and down and up the great valley of Snake River. Away to the north west the "three buttes" lifted themselves out of the apparent level of the blank plain, and beyond them the snowy pinnacles of the "Teton range" were visible. Away across and down the valley, apparently one or two hundred miles away, sharp, jagged pinnacles lay against the sky. Goose Creek Mountains frowned above many nearer hills. Nowhere before had the scene been so vast; but it was a scene frowning and desolate beyond description. We thought of the story of Hunt and Crook and McLellan as related by Irving in "Astoria," and of "Bonneville"[13] as told by the same fascinating writer, and remembered that we were overlooking the very region of desolation where they suffered so much. What emigrant, worn by his months of travel, with poor and jaded teams, his provisions getting short, and his money shorter, ever looked down this dark valley of Snake River without forebodings of peril? If there have been any we have not met them.

A little down from the summit of the ridge we struck a small creek, and after following it down a few miles encamped in a field of "wild rye," so tall that a man on horseback was almost hidden by it.

One day more and we reached and crossed the Portneuf River, and camped near a trading post of the Hudson Bay Company, auxiliary to Fort Hall and about twelve miles from it, under the direction of Captain Grant,[14] of that service.[15]

As they enter this dry, dusty desert-like terrain, all three chroniclers complain of the heat, dust and mosquitoes, but it's remarkable that Celinda begins her diary entries for five consecutive days with the word, "Pleasant ..." Harvey, citing campfire songs, poetry recitation, amusing stories and theological discussion, also manages to see the bright side, "And so we got our compensations for the discomforts of the days."

Celinda

Friday, July 29—Our road was through sage brush. Before noon it lead along the Port Neuf river sometimes over hills & then along the river bottom. Crossed the Bannoc. Went down into the bottom & camped near the river by a spring. The Ohio Co & the Co where Charles is camped with us. The mosquitoes were very annoying. Heard the Falls.

Saturday, July 30—Pleasant but very dusty. Road lay along by Lewis [Snake] River a good deal of the way. Before noon we came to the American Falls[16] of Lewis river. The falls are not perpendicular but the water dashes & foams down rocks making a grand sight. After noon we crossed Falls creek so named from the many cascades in it. Some very pretty ones are in sight of the road. We traveled in Co. with Charles Co. PM. Towards night we crossed Rock creek. Crossing very bad & rocky. The creek is very rocky. Camped near Lewis river. Some very pretty cedar trees were near. Different from any I had ever seen. Grass was very poor.

Sunday, July 31—Pleasant. Went a few miles & camped not far from the river between some hills. Martha Julia & myself went upon a hill under some trees by ourselves. This is the first day since we came in sight of the Rocky mountains that we have not seen snow & I think the first since we came in sight of Laramie Peak.

Monday, August 1—Pleasant. Camped at noon at Raft River. Went a mile on the bottom in the morning & then went on to the second bottom. Saw no trees except on the mountains & no shrubs but sage only on Raft river. After noon went over a desert of sage. Stopped for tea about 5 o'clock went on until dark but found no water. We had water for ordinary purposes but the cattle had had none since noon & it had been very dusty. Found good grass & camped among the sage not a tree or shrub in sight. Very warm. On Raft river the last California trail leaves the Oregon road.[17]

Tuesday, August 2—Pleasant. By getting some water of Mr Beal[18] got breakfast before starting but could not wash the dishes. Went on through the desert which is 16 miles long. Came to a creek & camped. Remained two or three hours baking—getting dinner &c. Found a wagon there. P M. went on towards night after going I believe about 11 miles came to the river which is here very large. Went on a ways & camped off from the river. No water except from the river & what we had in our casks. Saw snow.

Wednesday, August 3—Pleasant with a very refreshing breeze. It would be very pleasant riding but for the dust. Sage part of the way but in the flat of Goose creek grass willows & rushes. Stopped for noon near Goose creek. Camped for night on the river.

Phoebe

We were immediately beseiged by great clouds of mosquitoes, which annoyed us most unmercifully. By tying down our wagon covers as closely as possible and burning sugar to smoke them out, we managed to get a little sleep; and in the morning left this camp without one regret, like nearly all others from this one to the end of our journey.

Neither time nor space suffices to enter into certain details of each day's experience.

Following down this desolate valley, where scarcely a vestige of vegetable life appeared, we crossed several streams where it was so rough with rocks that it seemed as though our wagons would be broken to pieces.

On reaching Raft creek we filled our water kegs and carried water with us, as our next encampment would be a dry one.

For several days we traveled over a country that was too dismal for description. The whole face of the country was stamped with sterility. Nothing under the brassy heavens presented itself to the eye but the gray sage brush and the hot yellow sand and dust. Our men traveled by the side of their teams, with the burning rays of the sun pouring down upon them—the dust flying in such clouds that often one sitting in the wagon could see neither team nor the men who drove them. Camping at night where water and grass were deficient both in quantity and quality. There seemed but little life in anything but the rattlesnakes and the Snake Indians.[19]

Harvey

July 29. We had camped on the evening of the 28th on the west bank of Portneuf River. Just after starting in the morning we passed a spring remarkable for its size and the clearness of its water. It was not less than fifty feet in diameter, quite deep, and the smallest pebbles were seen as plainly on the bottom in the deepest place as though they had not been covered with some feet of water. A rapid stream eight or ten feet wide flowed out of the fountain. The road then led across a rocky plain, covered with great gray sage for about ten miles, when, descending a sharp hill we encamped on a little bottom on the bank of Snake River. This was a camp to be remembered because it was the first on Snake River, and because it was the most uncomfortable of the journey thus far on account of mosquitoes which filled the air like a cloud, tormenting us beyond endurance by their poisonous bite. We wore gloves and veils, built "smokes," tied up our tents and wagon covers as tightly as possible, but as the night was warm it was a literal purgatory to us without any purgatorial refinings in it. There was but one compensation in it: we had preachers and scientists and philosophers and schoolteachers in our train and so we discussed the question—what are mosquitoes? and of what use are they? quite learnedly and exhaustingly. As in all such discussions we knew just as much when we were through as when we began—and the mosquitoes kept up their torment just the same.

A little below our camp were the "American Falls" of Snake River. The river above the falls is a splendid stream flowing between low banks, on the level of the surrounding plain, but at the falls it begins to plunge down into the deep basaltic gorge through which it flows for some hundreds of miles, or until nearing the eastern line of the Blue Mountains. The road leads down the southern side of the river over a country covered with rocks and often so rough that it seemed a marvel that a wagon came over it unbroken. For three or four days we found only a few tufts of dry bunch grass among the rocks and sage for our cattle, which were growing poor and weak, which compelled us to move with great caution. There was little to vary the hard monotony of comfortless travel in the near surroundings, though the distant scenery was delightful. We crossed what is called Bannack River, and Fall Creek, a very beautiful stream flowing over a bed of vegetable rock composed of the remains of reeds and mosses, and forming tiny cataracts in a few rods. Next was Raft River, the point where the emigrations of the Forties to Oregon and California separated, the California road leading up that stream nearly to its head in the Goose Creek Mountains, and the Oregon continuing down the desolate valley of Snake River. We took our noon halt on the first day of August at the crossing of Raft River and about three o'clock filled our water kegs for use at night and in the morning, and drove forward to a "dry camp" for the night. This was necessary as the grass at the streams was entirely gone, and our animals were our first care, as they were our hope and safety. About sunset we found a fair supply of grass among the sage brush, and in a little hollow halted for the night.

We were several miles from Snake River and could see its black gorge away to the north. On our left and south, only a few miles away, were the "Goose Creek" mountains, dark and precipitous, and our road appeared to be bearing toward their deep defiles. Nothing could give less cheer than the road we had traveled over for a few days past. It was rough and rocky almost beyond description. The dust—a fine alkaline powder—was several inches deep, and covered us until we were almost undistinguishable from each other. From ten o'clock in the morning until six in the evening the hot rays of the sun poured through the rarified atmosphere with a scorching heat, blistering our lips and almost blinding our eyes. The wild sage, with its odor of camphor and turpentine had become odious. Still, when the [line missing] and the splendor of the stars were over us, we forgot some of the weariness of the day, and, around our campfires, our young ladies sung to the moon—as young ladies forever will—as they washed up the tin plates and cups, ready for the morning meal; Mr. M[arti]n quoted poetry, in his pleasant way; O[badiah] H[ines] told some story that set us all in a roar, or the two preachers had some little quiet theological discussion, while the married women put our tents in order for the night. And so we got our compensations for the discomforts of the days.[20]

Celinda

Thursday, August 4—Road rocky some of the way. Warm & very dusty. Camped for noon on Dry branch, for night on Rocky creek. The banks are rocky & look like a great chasm or crevice in the earth. Some packers camped with us one from Hastings Mr. Holcomb.[21]

Friday, August 5—Suffered much with the dust. Camped on Rocky creek for dinner. Crossed the creek here crossing good. Camped on the creek at night. Aunt Lydia was very sick.

Harvey

Our road still bore to the south towards the mountains to avoid the great gorges that cleft the basaltic plain, many of which were utterly impassable for miles, until we were lifted quite on the slope of one of them, and made our next camp at "The Swamp" or "Meadows," where was, as the name indicates, several acres of low, swampy land, with clumps of willows here and there, and a fair supply of grass. Still keeping well under the shadows of the Goose Creek Mountains our road led us across another sage plain a day's drive to Goose Creek, after crossing which we kept up its valley for a day and then across a similar plain a day's drive to Rock Creek, which we reached on the afternoon of the 5th of August. We followed down this stream towards Snake River, encamping on it two nights, finding good water and but little grass. Mornings and evenings the roar of Snake River miles away to the north was distinctly heard, though its flow is imprisoned in a rocky gorge several hundred feet below the level of the plain.

(*Note.* This was the road of the great Shoshone Falls,[22] of the existence of which we had not even heard at this time. It is to avoid the basaltic gorges with perpendicular walls often one or two hundred feet high that the road swings away to the south from the American Falls, and leaves from ten to thirty miles of this rent and riven lava plain between it and the river. The Falls [Shoshone?], if known to anyone but Indians to exist at this time— 1853—were certainly known to very few, and no writer had ever spoken of them. They are among the great curiosities of the continent.)[23]

Idaho State Historical Society

Shoshone Falls

Celinda

Saturday, August 6—Very dusty. Camped for noon on Lewis river. The banks are very steep. Also on the river at night. A great ways to water &

down a very steep bank. Some rapids near.²⁴ Wolves howl.

Sunday, August 7—Pleasant. Remained in camp all day almost impossible to get water on account of the banks of the river being so high & difficult to ascend. The river seems to have worn away the sand & dirt & to have formed a channel far below the surface of the ground. There were some very fine rapids above & below us. Martha Julia & myself went down to the river to cook. Mr Martin went with us. Indians were around almost all day. We bought some very…²⁵ of them. They dry…very bad but we were obliged to remain to rest the cattle.

It was as they approached the vicinity of Salmon Falls that the Hines party, probably at Kanaka Rapids,²⁶ had their introduction to salmon, a welcome fresh supplement to the diet they had long endured. Phoebe, however, also has a downside to relate.

Harvey

Leaving Rock Creek and turning again westward the road is on the high bluff of Snake River, winding around and through the heads of the rocky gorges that cleave the bluff. On the night of the 8ᵗʰ our camp was on the summit of one of these high bluffs, from which we could see the silver thread of the river perhaps a thousand feet below us and two or three miles away. On the opposite of the river a subterraneous stream, apparently forty or fifty feet wide, bursts out of the escarpment perhaps half way below the level of the plain, and flows like a sheet of foam into the river.²⁷ We had scarcely turned our teams out of the yoke when some Indians came into camp with some large Salmon. They were the first the most of us had ever seen, and we did not know what kind of fish they were. G[ustavus] H[ines], however, who had spent five years in Oregon, soon solved our queries, and huge piles of fried Salmon that night, and often subsequently, took the place of bacon which had been almost exclusively our meat for months. Our next camp was on Salmon Creek, and the next day we came to Salmon Falls of Snake River: altogether reminding us we were coming towards the sea.²⁸

Phoebe

On a stretch of more than two hundred miles the country was nothing more than an arid waste; vegetation was so badly parched that our cattle could find but little subsistence. Tom and Jerry, our wheel oxen, became so thin and weak that they began to stagger in the yoke. In my great pity for the suffering creatures, whenever it was possible I walked ahead of the train and gathered into my apron every spear of grass I could find and fed them as we traveled. This, I doubt not, helped to save their lives. When the close of the day's journey brought us good water and grass both, we were rejoiced; and when so fortunate as to find good water, grass and wood, all three, we felt ourselves blessed indeed. No one can fully appreciate these common blessings of life until they have been deprived of them in a hot desert country. The hot sunshine and dust, with the constant disagreeable odor of the ever abundant sage, or greasewood, as nearly resembling each other as horehound and catnip in appearance, took away my appetite, and for a time I became so ill that my life hung in a balance. Mr. Judson managed to keep our poor baby alive on sweetened water. All of the little delicacies we brought with us from home were gone, and we had nothing left but flour, bacon, beans, sugar and tea. And, like the children of Israel, my soul loathed this food and I longed for something fresh. The thought of a baked "kidney" or "pink-eyed" potatoes caused the tears to roll down my face.

The farther we traveled the more meager became our fare. When we reached Salmon Falls, on Snake river, the Indians brought some red-meated salmon to the camp. They were the first ones that I had ever seen. Mr. Judson traded some sugar for a fine, large one and as it was too late to cook it that night, he dressed it and put it into the water keg under our wagon, and then we retired for the night.

Morning seemed a long way off. We were really so delighted with the prospect of salmon for breakfast that we could not sleep. Finally Morpheus stole in upon us unawares, with wandering dreams luring us away home to Lake Erie's beach, where the fishermen were hauling in their nets filled with fish of many varieties; there was the muskelonge, pike, bass, cat, sturgeon and the ever abundant white fish. Not one of them could compare with our red-meated salmon, but, oh, despair! Just on the eve of successfully landing the net broke and let them all back into the lake.

The shock of this disaster effectually dissipated the vision. We awoke to the realities of our wagon home, with the red-meated salmon in anticipation. Mr. Judson sprang out quickly and hastened to build the fire and hang on on the kettle, but, alas! our beautiful fish was missing, and so was Mr. Bryant's dog. As we never saw him again, he evidently indulged in too much salmon for breakfast, and paid the penalty with his life. Consequently there was much lamentaton that morning throughout the camp for the loss of a good breakfast and a good dog.[29]

Celinda

Monday, August 8—Went about five miles to a creek & camped. Good grass about two miles on the bluff. Good water handy to get at. Julia Martha & I went to the creek to wash. There was a warm spring about half a mile up the ravine. Mister Long came to see us. A family camped near us—one wagon. Some fine rapids were near in the river.

Tuesday, August 9—Remained in camp...the men put...the wagon wheel of uncle Harveys wagon which was broken before. Pa found a cow. One of Mr Bryants oxen died. They did not know he was sick. We went about 7 miles & camped on the river. Some part of the road was dangerous. Saw some very fine falls from streams on the north side of the river the first was a perpendicular fall of many feet in height most of the others issued out of the banks of the river & falling several ft. flowed into the river. There were...of them all...interesting...the cattle. Saw some large lizards.

Harvey

From Bear River valley to Salmon Falls [line missing],...hundred miles, we had scarcely a single good camping place. The road was, in most places, rocky, and everywhere the deep dust and sand, heated by the blazing sun, were exceeding offensive. We had been over two weeks amidst the brazen desolation of this desert. The hot sun and dust had shrunk and shriveled the wood work of our wagons so that the wheels were in danger of failing. The wheel of my wagon, which, it will be remembered, I had filled with green ash early in the journey, had given way so much that it was no longer usable, but I had been preparing for this by picking up along the road pieces of broken wagons, generally tough and thoroughly dried hickory, and shaving them into spokes, so that, when we camped here, I had more than enough to refill the wheel. To-day, therefore, I knocked the wheel to pieces, refilled it with first class spokes, set all the tires and long before night had the wagon as strong and good as ever. A few other tires were set at the same time; the "housewives" had a general "clar-in-up time;" and, indeed, everything about the camp was readjusted and rearranged for the remainder of the journey.[30]

At Salmon Falls a fateful decision was made.[31] They could continue along the south side of Snake River, or cross to the north side at this point, thereby committing to a second crossing of the Snake in the vicinity of Fort Boise. After opting for the latter course, it didn't take long for second thoughts to arise.

Harvey

On the 10th we crossed Snake River on a ferry about half a mile above Salmon Falls, and driving over a country covered with great bowlders about five miles encamped on a small creek, in excellent grass, where we designed to rest our teams for a day.

The first days drive after crossing Snake River was across a desert so desolate and rocky that we almost regretted that we had not continued on the south side of that stream. It was about eighteen miles, but as we left our camp quite late it was eight o'clock in the evening before we reached camp at the crossing of the Malad, and then we were obliged to send the stock three miles to find grass. In the morning we found the little river to be a clear, beautiful stream with a rapid, roaring current and very rocky bed. Just below the ford it plunged into a deep crevice in the basaltic rock, perhaps seventy-five feet deep, over which great blocks of rocks formed a natural bridge. Many emigrants called the stream Natural Bridge Creek. The cascade in which the stream makes its plunge into the rocky gorge is very beautiful, but, as often before since crossing the Rocky Mountains, we wondered how such a stream could flow through such a desert, and there not be upon its banks grass nor tree.[32]

Phoebe

We crossed Snake river a little above Salmon Falls, paying the usual exorbitant charge of six dollars per wagon. These ferries were a constant drain on our purses. This route was controlled by the Mormons, who built bridges where they were not needed—most unmercifully fleecing the poor emigrants.

By crossing to the north side of the river we were in hopes of finding a more fertile country. Driving over great boulders, we came to a small stream where we found food for our cattle and concluded to encamp a day, in order to give them a chance to recruit—Captain Hines being very thoughtful for the welfare of our dumb companions

Before leaving this camp, Mr. Judson lightened our load by removing the projection from our wagon. We would not be near so comfortable, but were willing to suffer any inconvenience to save our jaded cattle. And that they should not have an unnecessary pound to draw, I emptied one of our trunks and left it, with my little rocking chair.[33]

Crossing the river did not better our condition and we deeply regretted making this divergence from our course. We were sixteen days sweltering slowly along under the scorching sun, through choking clouds of dust between the two crossings of Snake river. One could hardly conceive a more desolate country. I believe it was Bayard Taylor who said, "If I had any ambition, it was to enjoy as large a share of experience as this earth can furnish."[34]

He should have crossed the plains in the early fifties in an ox wagon, and his ambition would certainly have been gratified.

Many of the experiences of this earth are of a nature that must be endured, instead of enjoyed.

The occasional little oases by which we rested and recruited our cattle were the only "enjoyable experiences" while traveling through this desert country.

Gregory M. Franzwa

The Snake River Canyon near Twin Falls, Idaho, east of Salmon Falls, where the Hines party ferried across.

Celinda

Wednesday, August 10—Went to the ferry a short distance. This family that were with us Mr. Russel[35] lost an ox in the morning. Mr. Beal[36] left our company. Mr Russel had 3 yokes of oxen & one span of horses. Their ladies have walked nearly all of the way. Saw at the ferry a horse which had been bitten by scorpions dying. A short distance below the ferry is Salmon Falls. They are perpendicular…but not very high…very scraggy …very pretty and interesting. Crossed the ferry paying $6.oo per wagon They paid $10.00 to some men for swimming the cattle over on account of the difficulty of doing so for the swiftness of the current and the width of the river & also the weakness of the cattle. Went about 4 miles & camped in a valley by a small stream very beautiful. Good grass sage wood & water. Bad & rocky road.

Celinda's reference to the Russel party is ambiguous at best. Harvey's description is more helpful.

Harvey

As we camped on a small green bottom a little above Salmon Falls, we noticed a wagon standing alone, with two or three dead cattle near, and a couple of living cows near by, and a man and two women moving about as though in great trouble. We found, on inquiring, that the man and his wife and her sister had left the Missouri for Oregon quite early in the spring with a good team of four yoke of oxen and two cows. From time to time the oxen had died until that very morning the last yoke had died leaving them with their wagon, and the little food they had left, and only two small cows eight hundred miles from the end of their journey. It was a sad case. The two cows would not endure to draw the wagon a mile. My brothers and myself had started with 16 yoke of oxen and not an animal had died or been lost. Our loads had grown lighter and lighter, and we now only used three or four yoke to each wagon, and a friend in the train was using one or two yoke as he needed, so we told Mr. R[usse]l and family they were welcome to yoke up four of our oxen and travel with us. The offer was gladly accepted, and they came safely with us, returning the oxen to us in safety on the bank of the Willamette opposite Portland two months afterward.[37]

In his chapter on *Emigrant Interaction,* John Unruh states, "There were numerous...ways in which westbound overlanders cooperated to lessen the demands of the journey, almost always in a cheerful spirit of cooperation without seeking personal gain."[38]

The Hines party's behavior toward the Russels was certainly in keeping with this cooperative spirit, and moreover seems typical of the overall attitude and behavior of the Hines party. Phoebe has more to say about the Russel incident, and about the general character of the party.

Phoebe

One day we came upon a family who had left Missouri in the spring, well fitted out, but who had unfortunately lost all their oxen, the last yoke having just died. Truly, they were in a desperate situation, having only two cows to take the place of their oxen.

I can hardly conceive how they could have made the journey, had not Captain Hines, moved with compassion, offered them the use of a couple of yoke of their loose cattle, which they thankfully accepted and went on their way rejoicing.

It is Emerson who says: "Character is nature in the highest form." Here on the plains each person was comparatively free to act out human nature, and the quality of the character came to the surface. Our little train must have been a model one, for during all the hardships and trying scenes of our long journey I do not remember a harsh word or a murmur.

The oldest couple [They were 48 and 43, respectively!] were good Jedediah Hines (who was called "Diah" for short),[39] and his devoted wife, who was always by his side while he drove the team. When he got into the wagon to rest, she did also, but not before. The influence of these loving spirits was felt as a benediction by all in our little band.

Usually on the Sabbath Captain Hines or his youngest brother, Harvey Hines, preached us a short discourse, of nature to cheer our drooping spirits. The three brothers took turns in leading our daily devotional exercises of the camp. This family altar in the solitude of the wilderness was very impressive.[40]

Celinda

Thursday, August 11—Pleasant. Remained in camp until after noon. Set the…to one wheel of…wagon after…very well. Alta [Bryant] very sick. I stayed with them last night. Julia & I washed for Mrs. B[ryant] & Martha baked for her. Went about 6 miles road hilly went down a very fast hill then up one. Camped on Rock creek. Did not get into camp till after dark. Road— through sage brush.

Friday, August 12—Crossed the two Rocky creeks. The ladies went below where a natural bridge crosses the south creek. The banks of the stream are perpendicular…I should think water comes down in a waterfall just above the bridge and then foams & dashes over under & between huge rocks making a grand sight. The water is nearly 20 ft. deep I should judge. Just below the bridge the other stream comes in. We went a short distance & crossed by the assistance of Mr. Long who was with us. Traveled about 15 miles & camped near a small stream. Grass excellent. I sat up with aunt Elizabeth to cook & slept with…

Harvey

Aug. 12th: The men who went out to sleep with the oxen came in very early with them, and before seven o'clock we forded Malad and continued westward over a country as nearly the picture of desolation as one can imagine.

The sun burned with a horrible fierceness. The dust enveloped us in a whitish cloud, so that frequently the driver could not see more than half his team. The heat wilted the leaves of the sage and filled the atmosphere with its sickening odor. The afternoon, especially, was a test of both patience and piety. The sunshine blazed into our faces and blistered our lips, so that it was with great pleasure that we saw the sun go down behind the west, as we entered the beautiful valley of Clover Creek, and stopped our wagons, and unyoked our oxen on its grassy banks.

The night was as beautiful and refreshing as the days had been oppressive and wearying. A clearer sky had never bent its azure over the earth. It was dark of the moon, and the stars seemed almost within the touch of our fingers. So soft was the atmosphere that we did not pitch our tents. Mr. M[arti]n and myself spread a buffalo skin on the ground quite a distance from the wagons, and, throwing ourselves upon it, studied the stars until sleep closed our vision to their splendor, and then slept on all night. Such a night was a compensation after such a day.[41]

Celinda

Saturday, August 13—Warm & dusty…stream. Good grass & water. Willows for fuel. Mountain wheat higher than my head. Captain Brent[42] & co. from Ft. Vancouver called & made us a visit. Captain took tea with us. He had been to Ft Hall to dispose of some government property. Also to Salt Lake. He brought us a few potatoes.

Harvey

The 13th was Saturday. We drove but about three miles when we came to a beautiful natural meadow the grass from two to six feet high, and plenty of good cool water where we encamped for our Sabbath rest. The meek-eyed oxen almost spoke their gratified surprise when, so soon after starting, we unyoked them, and let them go at their own sweet will among the natural clover tufts and the swaying red-top.

Since our Sabbath camp on Horse Creek among the Sioux we have not had so delightful a Sabbath rest as this. Just as our dinner was spread about three o'clock in the afternoon a company of mounted infantry under Captain Brent, on the way from Vancouver to Salt Lake, encamped only a few rods from us, and the Captain and a couple of Lieutenants, at our invitation, sat down with us and partook of our camp fare. They thought our ladies better cooks than their soldiers.[43]

Celinda

Sunday, August 14—Warm & pleasant. Remained in camp. In the PM. one wagon came & camped near…of the ladies was…Miss Harrison …many seasons in Oswego & its society. Towards eve. a Mr. Rowley[44] & a Mr. Cook from a Ohio train came & made us a visit. Mr. C. has formerly lived in Adams.[45] Gustavus sick.

Monday, August 15—Warm & dusty. I rode on horse back in the AM. for Gustavus who was not much better than yesterday. Several trains traveled near us in one was a lady who was recently married. Her husband had near Pacific springs I hear set her out of the…giving her her…some… Another Co took her in & like her very much. The husband says she was ugly to his children she being his second wife. Went through sage 8 miles Stopped for noon in a bad place on a high hill. Had to go down a steep long hill for water. Went about 4 miles & camped in a valley. Grass good. Also water. Charly came to see us. They have lost 4 yokes of oxen in 3 days. Mr. Bryants…sick yet. Two of our…Rattle snakes in the vicinity. Nelson found…scorpions by his…

Harvey

Monday, Aug. 16. [Should be 15.] The rest of Sunday gave our oxen new vigor, and they moved forward briskly. The travel of this and the following day was over high, sandy, sage plains, but each night brought us to a narrow valley of good grass through which run small streams, rising in the rough range of mountains on our right, and emptying into Snake River some miles to our left. At nine o'clock on the morning of Wednesday we passed a group of hot springs. The morning was cool, and the springs sent up columns of steam. The rocks about the springs were quite hot. At sunset, after stretching over a very rocky, volcanic plain covered with black sage, for about fifteen miles, we came unexpectedly to the verge of a chasm two hundred feet deep in the black basalt, at the bottom of which, meandering through grassy meadows, is another beautiful clear stream called Canyon Creek. The descent to the creek was somewhat steep and difficult. We encamped about forty rods from the upper end of the bottoms. As soon as our oxen were unyoked myself and wife strolled away up the stream a quarter of a mile where we found great quantities of the black haw berries, just ripe, and, to us, delicious. We thought and spoke of the old orchards of our New York home which were just now dropping their early ripeness; for us, alas, only in memory.[46]

Celinda

Tuesday, August 16—Pleasant. Before noon went up some very long hills. Numerous hills were in sight which were very precipitous & flat on the top. The top strata seemed to be of rock which looked as if it was laid up by the hand of man on the sides & on the top & with equal thickness. The hills were very high & seemed as if formed of…Our road was…Camped for night …6 miles before… [As insert: Saw some trees which were a welcome sight to us. They were the black thorn, berries sweet] where the heat was almost intolerable. Several camps were very near. Went about 4 miles. Gustavus was sick. I rode for him. The horse stumbled & threw me off. Camped in the vicinity of numerous pools which I should think proceeded from a stream underground. Sprinkled some in the PM.

Wednesday, August 17—Some part of the day was …& very pleasant. It…some. From all…could get we supposed we had two 15 mile drives before us & we were much surprised at noon on coming to a fine stream. Camped late near a sulphur spring. Other springs were near. It rained in the evening.

Thursday, August 18—In about 4 miles we came to some hot springs. The water was boiling hot. It was with difficulty we succeeded in washing our hands. There were…and streams flowed from them. They were to us a great curiosity. Camped for dinner near a fine stream. A violent shower of rain came on to gladden our hearts. Camped for night near Barrel spring. Valley beautiful. Very high bluffs were on either side. The stream delightful. Black thorn trees a little up the gorge. Grass good. Valley covered with mountain wheat. Have seen…or train for two…some. Road…

Friday, August 19—Road hilly stony in the morning but good the rest of the day. The hills were very peculiar. Huge rocks being on the top of the ground each one seemingly disdaining the acquaintance of his neighbor. Some were I should think nearly 50 ft. in height. The hills all day were of this character. Camped for noon…no water, but…Were in…covered with snow on the south west. Passed through less sage & more grass camped for night near a number of springs. Some were impregnated with iron. Grass up the kenyon eleaven ft. in highth. Mountain wheat hear very high.

Harvey

Aug. 19. Leaving Canyon Creek we found that we had escaped the black, basaltic rock, over which we had been passing, and had entered a region where granite predominated. The granite hills were beautifully rounded, smooth and grassy: here and there great granite blocks, worn by the elements that had beaten on them stood on hill-side and hill-top: and the road wound around and over the smooth pinnacles most enchantingly. The whole country seemed to be made up of granite decayed into a coarse sand. Our road was high up on the shoulders of the range of mountains we had been skirting at a greater distance for a week, giving us a magnificent view of the great Snake River valley for a hundred miles in length, and of the mountains that bounded it on the south, perhaps fifty miles away. We had no pleasanter day than this on our whole journey. We encamped on a small stream tributary of Indian Creek.[47]

Celinda

Saturday, August 20—The road for almost two miles was through kenyon...the road was...willow & rose bushes. Very pleasant. Passed two fine streams before noon. Road hilly. Hills covered with grass. Much prefer a hilly road as it is not so monotonous. We are anxiously looking forward to see where the road goes & what we are coming to next. Camped for noon near some springs. A Co. came & camped near. Glad to have company again. Went...Boise river...did not...(Went about 15 miles) 10 o'clock. Saw a commet[48] very plain in the SW. Found a scorpion near our fire.

Harvey

The sun was not an hour high on the afternoon of the 20th when our wagons stood on the summit of the great hill—mountain in fact—overlooking the long green valley of the *Boise* River. The scene was an absolute enchantment. To our right, towering peak after peak, were the great spikes and pinnacles of the Salmon River Mountains. Before us, and two thousand feet below us, the well wooded valley, green as emerald, the river flashing like silver in its sinuous flow wound away southward for fifty or sixty miles. The deep gorge of Snake River is far to the left, and, beyond that, the Owyhee Mountains touch the cerulean with their lofty summits. It was Saturday evening, and we pushed hard to reach the valley before nightfall, but at last were obliged to encamp on a sandy bench, among great sage brush, and wait for morning to roll to the river. The night was clear and beautiful. A magnificent comet was streaming across the heavens a little to the west of the Great Bear and speculations as to whence it came and whither it was bound made the hour about the great camp fire, built of dry sage brush, a very delightful one. As usual when making a dry camp we chose to guard our cattle rather than go to the river, five or six miles away, to find them in the morning.[49]

Thirty-seven years later, while on his circuit as a Methodist Presiding Elder in the summer of 1890, Harvey returned to southern Idaho and recalls the first time he saw the Boise Valley.

Harvey (reminiscing in 1890)

Wednesday a journey of 45 miles to Canyon creek [from Clover creek], and Thursday another of the same distance to Boise City. This part of my tour was along the old emigrant road. Emigrants of the fifties will remember the Elysian scene that spread out before them as they reached the granite heights that overlook the Boise valley, and saw that beautiful wooded vale sweeping forty miles to the westward. As I halted my carriage on that same summit today, the memory of the 15th [actually, we think August 20] evening of August, 1853, when I first beheld it, and of those with me, then, like myself, full of youth and hope, came over me with a strange and lofty power. With me were ten of my own family relations, making eleven in all. Three only remain. The strong manhood, the splendid womanhood, the alert and aspiring childhood that were there on that beautiful evening are gone to the fadeless land. The last to go was she who stood nearest and walked closest to me for more than thirty-six years after we stood arm in arm, and heart to heart, on that gray summit in that summer eve.[50] Is it strange that thoughts of the departed thrilled my memory, and their presence seemed illuminating the hills about me as I stood alone, now, on that same summit and uncovered my head to the same sky, and the same sun, and the same God, that were over and around me in that sweet evening in the long ago.

Somewhat reluctantly I resumed my seat in my carriage and moved forward down the mountain slope into the fruitful valley, and along the shaded streets of Boise City—the "Damascus of the Plains."[51]

Celinda

Sunday, August 21—Pleasant. Started on before breakfast as we had no water. Crossed over three bottoms before reaching the river. The first is covered with sage. The second with woods. The 3 with grass. The river is skirted most of the way with Balm of Gilead, Poplar &...trees & bushes of...We were truly refreshed by the sight of a grove of trees again. Went about 6 miles before reaching the river. On camping we moved our cooking utensils, victuals &c to an adjacent grove where were plenty of wood & water & withal a delightful shade which none know better how to appreciate than those who have traveled in dust & sage their eyes...by the sight of a tree for weeks...if they chance to see one it is on some adjacent mountain. O we enjoyed this beautiful retreat. Taking grass, wood, water & every thing into consideration I think we have never had a more pleasant camp. From the invitation of a gentleman, uncles went to a neighboring camp to hold meeting in the evening. We went with them...60 persons were ...Had a very pleasant...

Harvey

Sabbath: Aug. 21. Without water for man or beast, we could not remain where we were, so, early in the morning we drove about five miles, and just on the bank of the Boise River under the shade of some cottonwood trees, and in a meadow of luxuriant grass we stopped, before nine o'clock, for our Sabbath bivouac. Here and there, along the crystal stream, other teams were resting after the desert journey along Snake River valley. At evening we received an invitation to hold religious services with a train of United Brethren people who were camped about a half mile from us, and G[ustavus] H[ines] and myself accompanied by our wives and several others from our party went over to the camp for that purpose. G[ustavus] H[ines] preached, and I exhorted, and we had a pleasant hour with our stranger friends.

(Note. This camp was about one mile above[52] where Boise City is now located, and on the opposite, or south side of the river. Boise valley, now so like a garden, was then, and for many years afterwards, only a "natural desert.")[53]

Celinda

Monday, August 22—Went about 10 miles down the river before dinner road good but dusty. PM went about 6 more. Met a Mr Marsh[54] from Michigan, brother in law of L F Devendorf. He & another gentleman Mr Walter have a cart & one span of horses. Camped by the river in a beautiful place grass excellent. Road through grass.

Tuesday, August 23—Pleasant. Mr. Marsh came to see us in the… along all the…bad hill to ascend in the morning. Road went along on the bluffs until noon then struck down on to the river thence on the bluff & down to the river at night. On the bluffs were some sage & some weeds & some grass. Our camp at night was the best we have had on the road. Grass grew luxuriously all about. We were close to the river as pretty a stream… ever saw with a…as clear as crystal. Mr Marsh came & took tea with us & Mr Walter also. The commet[55] shown very brilliantly in the evening. Indians came to the camp at noon we bought some fish of them. Went about 15 miles.

Wednesday, August —Pleasant but uncomfortably warm as it has been since we have been on the Boisse. In the morning a great many indians came to camp with fish which they wished to exchange for clothing. We bought a number. The Salmon …here are…indians (the Diggers) cannot understand the Eng. language. They understand & use the words swap & no swap, which words they make use of in trading. We occasiònally meet one with whom Uncle G & his family can converse in the Chinook dialect & jargon used by the indians of western Oregon. These indians are dressed in any old clothing they can...he emigrants. Some...others are fully clad. They seem most anxious to get shirts & socks. They seem to be better clad than the Sioux but from the fact of not having seen many with clothing of their own manufacture which is a shirt—I should think that aside from what they get of emigrants they wear at least no more than that nation....similar to yesterday...AM. Camped...Went about 9 miles before dinner. Crossed the river after dinner & went down about 6 miles & camped on the north bank (north west) in a very pretty place. It seems so delightful to be among grass & near trees & bushes. Had a fine bath in the river.

Harvey

Down the Boise valley we moved slowly, occupying four days in making a distance we could easily have made in two. This was to recruit our jaded oxen on the rich pasturage, and well did they profit by it. On the 24th we passed over a rocky bluff that abuts against the river on the east side, and crossing the stream, soon after encamped on its west bank.[56]

The river crossing mentioned by Celinda and Harvey on the 24th was very likely at the jog in the Boise River just to the west of present day Caldwell, Idaho, where the river interrupts its generally westward course, turning southward for a mile or so before continuing to the west. Writing in 1890, Harvey says of Caldwell, "It is situated near where the old emigrant road crossed Boise river..."[57]

Celinda

Thursday, August 25—Warm as usual. Much inconvenience from dust. Went about 8 miles before ... Camped on the river ... more after dinner and camped on the river. Had a very fine camp. This is the most beautiful river I have seen. In all the distance we have come down it there has not been a single tributary to it.

Harvey

The evening of the 25th we encamped in a field of native clover on the Boise about two miles from Snake River where we expected to cross that stream in the morning, and nearly opposite the Hudson's Bay post known as Fort Boise. We had come to the place without accident, or sickness, or anything to mar the memory of the journey. And although we were some hundreds of miles from the end of our journey, yet, as our teams were now in excellent condition, and we were all in good health, we were looking forward with most pleasing anticipations to a speedy and happy ending of our pilgrimage.[58]

The Hines party were fortunate that none of their encounters with the Indians along the Snake route were of the dire nature that Phoebe feared at the outset. Nevertheless, as she reminisces about the completion of this segment of their journey, she recounts the experience of another train, one including her in-laws and brother, that traveled this route the following year, in 1854.

Phoebe

Our route lay over high, sandy plains, then down a difficult gorge into Canyon creek, which we crossed, and again over more sandy plains, where we made another dry camp among the sage brush, and soon after reached Boise river.

We traveled slowly through this valley, frequently halting to give our stock the benefit of the pure water and good grass. It was on this river that the massacre of the Ward train[59] (consisting of five families) by the Snake Indians occurred in 1854.

I have been permitted to make a few extracts from the journal of Mrs. Elizabeth Roeder, wife of Captain Roeder, of Whatcom, Washington, who was the dear friend of my childhood, as well as pioneer days.

Thursday, Aug. 22, 1854. This morning we noticed four wagons approaching our encampment, and we waited for them to come up before resuming our journey. This sorrowful company imparted to us the distressing information that "they had been attacked by the Indians, and two of their number killed and another wounded, and five of their horses stolen." They traveled along in our company, and the next night the wounded man died.

Wednesday, the 24th. This afternoon an Indian brought us a message from Capt. Grant, informing us of the horrible massacre of the whole of Capt. Ward's train by the savages. We kept the friendly Indian who brought the message in our camp through the night. Only three miles travel the next morning brought us to the scene of the awful tragedy. Ten men, eight women, and all the children were killed, with the exception of one boy, who, although wounded, made his escape. We sadly assisted in performing the last mournful rites for our murdered fellow beings.[60]

Mr. Judson's father, mother, sister, and my brother William, wife and child, and other friends were in the train with Mrs. Roeder, commanded by Captain Ebey, and witnessed the ghastly scene that she has described.

Captain Ebey was the distinguished Captain Jacob Ebey who served in the war of 1812 under General Harrison. He also commanded a company in the Black Hawk war, in the same battalion with Captain Abraham Lincoln, and was the father of the lamented Isaac N. Ebey, who was murdered at his own home on Whidby island by the Hadiah Indians in the summer of 1857.[61]

---

[1] H. K. Hines, "Emigrant Wagon," January 29, 1885, 2.

[2] Judson, *A Pioneer's Search,* 54, 55.

[3] "We got aboard the steamer Columbia the last day of November and landed in Portland December 5, 1853. The trip was very pleasant and rough only one day. This made us slide back and forth across the cabin on our chairs which made it quite laughable. The steamer landed in Astoria and all the passengers got aboard small river steamers to come to Portland. We were all night going to Portland. A pilot boat brought us in over the Columbia river bar the morning of the 4th of December. The large steamers could not then go up the river. Portland was then a small town with board sidewalks where there were any, and all the streets were very muddy with a few stumps in them here and there. The houses and hotels were just light frame buildings——weather boarded outside, and cloth and paper inside with partitions. It wasn't long till more substantial buildings were put up." Ref. Mrs. Henrietta Pomeroy, *Sketches of my early life as I remember it,* found at http://footprints.org/5-000302.html, submitted by Lorna Borman.

[4] J. W. Hines, *Touching Incidents,* 162.

[5] "The travelers bypassed Fort Hall, [per se, however, see notes below. Ed.], the original site of which is on the Shoshone-Bannock reservation today. While nothing is left of Fort Hall, there is a splendid full-size replica of the old Hudson's Bay post in a Pocatello city park." Personal communication, Gregory M. Franzwa.

[6] Holmes transcribes this as nineteen miles, but a close examination of the original confirms the twelve transcribed in the 1930 Portland paper. Celinda E. Hines, "Diary of a Journey from N.Y. to Oregon in 1853," *Portland Telegram,* March 17-April 18, 1930. Harvey also says "twelve."

[7] Many other 1853 travelers avoided Fort Hall as well, and apparently with good reason. David Dinwiddie, for example, says, "We left Fort Hall to the right eight miles, no travel through on account of the high water washing the road away, the new road is a cut off and saves some fifteen miles." Margaret Booth, Ed., "Overland from Indiana to Oregon, the Dinwiddie Journal," *The Frontier, a Magazine of the Northwest,* March, 1928, 8:115-130, July 19, 1853 entry.

[8] Celinda's description, along with Harvey's later, would place this auxiliary trading post a dozen or more miles south of Fort Hall itself, and somewhere near the Portneuf River, which implies it would be near the present city of Pocatello, Idaho.

[9] Neil McArthur was in charge of Ft. Hall from 1851 to 1854, taking over from Captain Richard Grant, who retired in 1851, after serving there for nine years. Louis S. Grant, "Fort Hall under the Hudson's Bay Company," *Oregon Historical Quarterly,* March, 1940, 34-39.

[10] This is the company that Charles Long joined. It was noted in the previous chapter that Long, after some apparent disagreement with Gustavus, had left the Hines train to join another. As the Hines party approached and began traveling along the Snake, or Lewis River, as Celinda calls it, she makes repeated references (in the form of Chas., Charles, Charley, etc., or simply Mr. Long) to Long and his new company, indicating that they are traveling in close proximity and that there is evidently continued mutual interest.

11 We believe Phoebe is mistaken. According to the others, they actually stopped at an auxiliary post some twelve miles distant from the fort itself. See the several notes immediately preceding this.

[12] Judson, *A Pioneer's Search,* 52, 53.

[13] Here and elsewhere Harvey reveals his fascination with Washington Irving, two of whose well-known works are *Astoria, Or, Anecdotes of an Enterprize Beyond the Rocky Mountains* (1836); and *The Adventures of Captain Bonneville* (1837).

[14] As noted earlier, Captain Richard Grant had retired from the command of Fort Hall in 1851. Given that Grant was retired, it is not clear where Harvey arrives at his characterization of Grant's command of the fort, but he was not alone in this opinion. Rebecca Ketcham, traveling with William Gray and others, and who crossed paths with the Hines party later, mentions that she visited Grant and his family at their home near Soda Springs in early August. She states, "He has charge of Fort Hall, but is up here to trade with the emigrants." Nevertheless, several days later, when she is near Fort Hall, she acknowledges its command by another (Neil McArthur). L. M. Kaiser and Priscilla Knuth, eds., "From Ithaca to Clatsop Plains: Miss Ketcham's Journal of Travel," *Oregon Historical Quarterly,* LXLL, No. 4 (Dec. 1961) 371-375.

[15] H. K. Hines, "Emigrant Wagon," January 29, 1885, 2.

[16] "Most of the American Falls have been drowned by the American Falls Reservoir, but a few dozen yards of rapids remains below the dam, in the town of American Falls." Personal communication, Gregory M. Franzwa.

[17] Celinda's observation is correct—California-bound travelers left the Snake River at the confluence of the Raft, a few miles west of American Falls." Personal communication, Gregory M. Franzwa.

[18] The other transcribers of Celinda's diary (Holmes, Oregon Pioneer Association) read this name as "Beak," but we conclude it is "Beal" from our reading of the original, and this is consistent with Celinda's repetition on August 10. We agree with Holmes that this "Mr. Beal" is likely Tavenor Beale, who is listed in the 1860 U.S. Census for Harrisburgh, Linn County, Oreg., as a cabinet maker, age 44, along with a wife, three sons, and four daughters. Holmes, *Covered Wagon Women,* 107.

[19] Judson, *A Pioneer's Search,* 53, 54.

[20] H. K. Hines, "Emigrant Wagon," February 5, 1885, 2.

[21] The 1850 U.S. Federal census for Hastings lists only an Allen Holcomb and family, and with a neighboring family, a Clinton Holcomb, age 18. 1850 U.S. census, Hastings, Oswego County, New York; image copy at www.ancestry.com; accessed April 14, 2007. While we have no evidence that either of these men is Celinda's "Mr. Holcomb from Hastings," we are mystified by Holmes' conclusion that this is Thomas Holcomb of North Carolina, who with his wife, arrived in Oregon in September. Holmes, *Covered Wagon Women,* 108.

[22] "Even though they were some six miles south of Shoshone Falls, emigrants often related that they could hear the roar of the Snake River falling over the escarpment." Personal communication, Gregory M. Franzwa.

[23] Harvey is not quite accurate here. "Originally identified as Canadian Falls (as distinguished from American Falls farther up Snake River), Shoshone Falls was an impressive natural feature along an old Indian trail that Hudson's Bay Company packers used when they traveled between Fort Boise and Fort Hall. Substantially higher than Niagara Falls (212 feet compared with 182), it occupies a deep lava gorge. When a United States Army company of mounted riflemen came by that way in 1849, they renamed it Shoshone Falls." *Idaho State Historical Society Reference Series, Shoshone Falls,* No. 969, (Boise, Jan. 1993).

[24] These were probably the Kanaka Rapids of the Snake (Lewis).

[25] The page of Celinda's diary is burned off at this point. From the context and the writings of the others, it is likely that Celinda is mentioning here the acquisition of salmon from the Indians.

[26] "Emigrants encountered Indians at Kanaka Rapids (called Fishing Falls by John C. Fremont in 1843). Here they traded with the Indians for fish." Oregon Trail in Idaho, http://www.idahohistory.net/OTkanaka.html; accessed March 17, 2007.

[27] "Harvey is observing Thousand Springs, where water of Lost River tumbles through the valley wall into the Snake. The site, plus Salmon Falls to the west, is east of Glenns Ferry, Idaho." Personal communication, Gregory M. Franzwa.

[28] H. K. Hines, "Emigrant Wagon," February 5, 1885, 2.

[29] Judson, *A Pioneer's Search,* 55-57.

[30] H. K. Hines, "Emigrant Wagon," February 5, 1885, 2.

[31] "The travelers made an unusual decision here. They should have stayed on the south bank to a point west of Glenns Ferry and crossed at the Three Island Crossing, thus avoiding perhaps two dozen extra miles of travel." Personal communication, Gregory M. Franzwa.

[32] H. K. Hines, "Emigrant Wagon," February 5, 1885, 2. H. K. Hines, "Emigrant Wagon," February 12, 1885, 2.

[33] "Almost the entire length of the Oregon Trail was littered with the things emigrants packed that they really didn't need. They had to jettison things that were dear to them, as their draft

animals were wearing down. Discards included such things as stoves, heavy candlesticks, even pianos." Personal communication, Gregory M. Franzwa.

[34] Bayard Taylor (1825-1878) was a prolific, well-traveled writer. Although we have not found Phoebe's quotation, per se, its sense is certainly consistent with Taylor's wide-ranging travels. The Literature Network: Bayard Taylor; http://www.online-literature.com/bayard-taylor/; accessed May 9, 2007.

[35] The Russel family continued to travel with or near the Hines train, and returned the borrowed oxen when they reached the Willamette Valley, as Harvey notes later. The immigration roster maintained by Thomas K. Williams at Umatilla lists just one Russel family (seven members all together) passing in the month of September, and that occurs on September 12, the same day the Hines party are listed, so this is likely the same family. Immigration Roster, the Umatilla Agency, http://linnhistory.peak.org/1853/1853imregis_8.html; accessed April 14, 2007.

[36] By the end of the month, Tavenor Beale and family, along with many others, decided to take the "Elliott Cutoff" at the Malheur River in hopes of reaching the Willamette Valley more quickly and easily, but ultimately had a much longer and far more difficult journey instead. Leah Collins Menefee and Lowell Tiller, "Cutoff Fever, III," *Oregon Historical Quarterly*, June 1977, 129.

[37] H. K. Hines, "Emigrant Wagon," February 5, 1885, 2.

[38] Unruh, *Plains Across*, 141.

[39] As noted earlier (Chapter 5), it may well be that Phoebe always heard Obadiah referred to as "Diah," as that seems to have been his accepted nickname. Thus, when writing her reminiscences, over seventy years after the fact, she may have made the understandable inference that his full name was Jedediah.

[40] Judson, *A Pioneer's Search*, 57-59.

[41] H. K. Hines, "Emigrant Wagon," February 12, 1885, 2.

[42] About a week earlier, on August 7, Rebecca Ketcham tells in her diary of dining near Fort Hall with an American officer from Vancouver, identified by her editors as Capt. Thomas L. Brent, assistant quartermaster, 1852-54. Kaiser and Knuth, "Miss Ketcham's Journal," 375. Holmes "corrects" Celinda's spelling from "Brent" to "Grant," but Harvey independently identifies the officer as "Captain Brent." Holmes, *Covered Wagon Women*, 110. The Grant to whom Holmes refers appears to be the Captain Richard Grant that Harvey described in connection with the outpost of Ft. Hall on or about July 28. Interestingly, stationed with Captain Brent at Ft. Vancouver in 1853 was Ulysses S. Grant, also then a captain. In "... 1853...Brent went overland to take care of some business, transferring his duties to 'Captain Grant' who performed both regiment and post duties." Fort Vancouver National Historic Site, Washington: "An Historical Overview of Vancouver Barracks, 1846-1898," http://www.ccrh.org/center/VNHRHistoryPartOne1846_1898.pdf; accessed May 9, 2007.

[43] H. K. Hines, "Emigrant Wagon," February 12, 1885, 2.

[44] L. H. Rowley, a farmer from Ohio, age 27 in 1860, is listed in the 1860 census. 1860 U.S. census, Briggs, Josephine County, Oreg.; image copy at www.ancestry.com, accessed May 9, 2007.

[45] Celinda most likely refers to Adams, New York, not far north of Hastings where she had lived. The 1850 census for Adams lists a Walter Cook, farmer, age 35, along with a family. 1850 U.S. census, Adams, Jefferson County, New York; image copy at www.ancestry.com; accessed April 15, 2007.

[46] H. K. Hines, "Emigrant Wagon," February 12, 1885, 2.

[47] H. K. Hines, "Emigrant Wagon," February 12, 1885, 2.

[48] This was evidently Comet Klinkerfues (C/1853 L1 by the newer scientific comet designation, or 1853 III by the earlier), which was visible to the naked eye from early August to October, and at its brightest in late August to early September. It was near Ursa Major, or the "Great Bear," as Harvey notes. The New Comet Observation Home Page, http://www.cometobservation.com/bright_comet.html; accessed April 15, 2007.

[49] H. K. Hines, "Emigrant Wagon," February 12, 1885, 2.

[50] Harvey's second wife, Elizabeth Jane Graves, whom he had married in 1852, died January 29, 1890. *Pacific Christian Advocate,* Feb. 12, 1890.

[51] H. K. Hines, "Itinerary—Boise District—No. 2," *Pacific Christian Advocate,* Aug. 13, 1890.

[52] Here, as elsewhere when these writers referred to sites along rivers, "above" means "upstream," not necessarily "northward" as might commonly be supposed.

[53] H. K. Hines, "Emigrant Wagon," February 12, 1885, 2.

[54] This is the first of several references Celinda makes to this Mr. Marsh, who is usually paired with a Mr. Walter. The last such reference comes on October 9 in Oregon, when Celinda says, "Messers Marsh & Walter came to see us." Thus we know they reached Oregon, and we assume they may have settled there. It is possible that Mr. Marsh is the John Marsh listed in the 1860 U.S. census for Forest Grove, who is 25 at that time, and was born in Michigan. 1860 U.S. census, Forest Grove, Washington Co., Oregon; image copy at www.ancestry.com; accessed April 15, 2007.

[55] See note for August 20. By late August Comet Klinkerfues was near its brightest, rivaling the brightest stars.

[56] H. K. Hines, "Emigrant Wagon," February 12, 1885, 2.

[57] H. K. Hines, "Itinerary—Boise District—No. 3," *Pacific Christian Advocate,* Aug. 20, 1890.

[58] H. K. Hines, "Emigrant Wagon," February 12, 1885, 2.

[59] "The Ward Massacre was one of very few such occurrences during trail days. There were far more killings of Indians than of whites." Personal communication, Gregory M. Franzwa.

[60] According to Mattes, there are three more diaries (by Sarah Johnson Handsaker, Winfield Scott Ebey and Phoebe's sister-in-law, Anna Maria Goodell) in addition to the one of Elizabeth Austin Roeder quoted here that describe the 1854 journey of the Ebey train. Mattes, *Platte River Road Narratives,* 436-445.

[61] Judson, *A Pioneer's Search,* 60, 61.

13

August 26, 1853: Tragic Crossing of the Snake River

> *We had spent a week of restful loitering down the*
> *grassy plains of the Boise, and perhaps no morning of all*
> *our journey saw us more joyful or more unsuspicious of*
> *danger. But, suddenly, all through our bright skies, an un-*
> *seen hand threw clouds and darkness and terror.[1]*
> —Harvey K. Hines, January 1881

> *Several times, before coming to the river the last*
> *time, I heard him [Obadiah] remark, that he dreaded Snake*
> *River more than all the rest of the journey.[2]*
> —Gustavus Hines, October 1853

When, on August 10, the Hines party had reached the vicinity of
Salmon Falls on the Snake River, they were confronted with the decision
of whether to continue westward on the south side of the Snake, or to cross
the river here and proceed on the supposedly more favorable north alternate. Choosing the latter course, they had thereby committed themselves to
a second crossing of the Snake when they reached Fort Boise.[3]

Celinda

Friday, August 26—Pleasant. Went about a mile & a half to the ferry.
Crossed the wagons in safety. But in swimming the cattle we soon found our
troubles had but now commenced…with much…they could… swim at all
but at length they were all safely over. Pa who rode a horse, as he had not
done before & assisted in driving them. By some cause or other he went too
far down the river his horse rared with him & saying 'I must take care of
myself' got off. He endeavored to get hold of the horse—as he let go of the
bridle—but being on the lower side the currant took him down & the horse
swam out of his reach. He…to an island but finding…strong turned to
the…dont be scared I am…He soon sank…in heart. Most of the men were
near but none of them dared go in the danger was too great. Uncle G swam in
& got out pa's hat. They had previously hallooed for assistance & some indians
went with a canoe but to no purpose. The men came & informed us of the

242

distressing calamity of which we had heard nothing. I will not attempt to describe our distress & sorrow for our great Bereavement. But I know our loss is his gain that he is yet...& he loves...watch over me & continue to guide me. An indian chief being with us with whom uncle G could talk in the Chinook dialect took several of his men who were expert swimmers & divers & made every exertion to get the body but were unsuccessful. With hearts overflowing with sorrow we were under the necessity of pursuing our journey immediately as there was no grass for the cattle where we were. Messrs Marsh & Walter being with...services were engaged...Marsh drove our team & went about a mile & camped on a river. It seems that Pa had a presentiment that something was to happen as he had often spoken of his dread of crossing at this crossing. Wolves howled.

Michael McKenzie

Snake River, 2002. From the site of Old Fort Boise, looking downstream (north) on the Snake River, from the Idaho side. Note the islands. There are actually three islands visible, and each of these is separated from the other (and/or the bank) by a channel. Is this "the spot?" There is no doubt that the channels and course of the Snake have changed in 150 years, but this view is certainly representative of what the channels would have looked like—except there being less current.—Michael McKenzie

Alta Bryant

Only one death, Uncle Dyer—who was drowned as he was fording the cattle across the Snake River. They stopped half a day to look for the body. Preached funeral sermon. His daughter went on.

Phoebe

When we reached Fort Boise we found that our wagons must be ferried over the Snake river at the exorbitant price of eight dollars per wagon. The families were safely ferried over, and we made hasty preparations to have dinner ready by the time the swimming of the stock should be accomplished. Having replenished our stock of provisions at the fort,, we were enabled to provide a better bill of fare than usual; and as this was the last crossing of this dreaded river we were all in the best of spirits, hoping soon to be out of the Snake river region.

Dinners were ready, and had been waiting for some time, when Mrs. Diah and [Mrs.] Harvey Hines, becoming uneasy at the delay, and fearful that some accident had happened, started to go to the river and were met by a messenger with the shocking intelligence that one of our number was drowned.

From a fearful premonition, or spiritual perception, Mrs. Diah Hines cried, "Oh, it is my husband, I know it is Diah." Yes, her husband was drowned in the treacherous stream. His horse had thrown him, while helping to swim the stock, and he probably was hurt, as he did not come to the surface.

It was with much difficulty that the loving wife who was so suddenly overwhelmed with anguish was kept from throwing herself into the river. As I again recall this pathetic incident of our journey, I find myself again weeping in sympathy with the stricken ones.

Each felt his loss a personal loss, for he was not only a loving husband, affectionate father and brother, but possessed as social and genial a nature as ever animated the human form.

There was no food here for our stock, and, though our sorrowful hearts longed to linger a while near the watery resting place of our beloved friend, we were obliged to proceed on our journey, meditating on the mysteries of death, of which we only see the dark side. Could the veil, or shadow, of material nature be lifted we would witness the transition, and what appears so fearful would then be as glorious to us as to the angels in heaven.

Said John Elliott[4] the apostle to the Indians, "In the morning if we ask, where am I today? our souls must answer, in heaven. In the evening if we ask, where have I been today, our souls may answer, in heaven. If thou art a believer thou art no stranger to heaven while thou livest, and when thou diest heaven will be no strange place to thee. No, thou hast been there a thousand times before."[5]

Harvey wrote of the tragic Snake River crossing on at least three different occasions. We reproduce all three here in order to give the most complete expression of his feelings. That these feelings were indeed deep is attested to by the very fact that he wrote repeatedly of the event.

Harvey (reminiscing in 1877)

In every life there are days and dates consecrated to sadness and sorrow. There are places, too, the associations of which are grief-shadowed. Such a day is the 21st [should be the 26th] day of August, 1853, and such a place the crossing of Snake River at Old Fort Boise.

The summer of 1853 was spent by the writer and his wife, in company with two brothers and their families, in the long journey across "the plains." From early May, when we passed the last settler's cabin on the eastern range of Missouri, we had moved slowly up the plain to the summit of the Rocky Mountains, over and down the western slope, across the lava deserts of Snake River, and made a Sunday camp on Boise river, opposite where Boise City now stands. We moved slowly down that stream for four days, giving our cattle opportunity to recruit on the rich pasturage of the valley, and on the morning of Friday reached Snake River again, and prepared to cross. The families were crossed on the ferryboat, but the stock were to swim a few rods below. The current was rapid and the river deep. All three brothers, with most of the men of the train, mounted horses, designing to trust themselves to the power of the horses to carry them through the deep, angry current. One proceeded. Myself and oldest brother brought up the rear, we had driven the last of the stock in and over; then we rode side by side into the deep current. Strangely enough both our horses refused to bear us. They sank to the bottom, and simultaneously reared backward, plunging us both into the river. Being a good swimmer, and having divested myself of boots and coat before going into the river, I found no difficulty in reaching the shore in safety. Not so with my brother. The current bore him downward with fearful velocity, and in a moment he sank from our sight into the grave of the waters. On the farther bank stood the three families, hearing that one of the brothers was drowned, and, for a moment, not knowing which, it was a dreadful moment. Sad, stricken, mourning, we turned away from the spot of bereavement.

From that day till April 27, 1877, nearly a quarter of a century, I had not looked upon the place. That morn I stood there again. It may well be supposed it was a sad moment. I, alone, of all the three [brothers] am left. My wife, of the three wives, alone is left. Though, strangely enough, all the other members of the three families—with one exception—are living, but so scattered that

> I feel like one who walks alone,
> Some banquet hall deserted:
> Its lights all fled, its guests all dead,
> And all but me departed.[6]

January 1881 found Harvey in his fifth month as editor of the *Pacific Christian Advocate,* and endeavoring to include items of historical interest for his readers. One such item dealt with the Snake River incident, as a means of illustrating, in Harvey's words, "the peculiar dangers and trials under which Oregon was settled…"

Harvey (reminiscing in 1881)

Our historical article this week will be an incident which will bring back to many hearts painful memories of events connected with the overland journey to Oregon from twenty-five to thirty years ago. If it has little that, in its own history, would call for this record, it has much as an incident that illustrates the peculiar dangers and trials under which Oregon was settled, that renders it painfully interesting. To understand it, it is necessary that we make this brief personal note. It records an incident in our own journey to Oregon, in the summer of 1853, in company with two older brothers, the younger of the two Rev. G. Hines, and the elder the subject of this tearful reminiscence; with their families and my own.

On the morning of the twentieth day [should be the 26th] of August 1853 we stood on the north shore of Snake river opposite Fort Boise. Our journey had been unusually prosperous. All of our company had enjoyed excellent health. Our stock was in fine condition, and everything tokened to us all a happy and speedy journey for the remaining five hundred miles. The morning was beautiful. In front of us, fifty miles away, were the Owyhee mountains, away to the right the crests of the Blue mountains, behind us the Salmon river range, around us the wide vallies of Snake and Boise rivers. We had spent a week of restful loitering down the grassy plains of the Boise, and perhaps no morning of all our journey saw us more joyful or more unsuspicious of danger. But, suddenly, all through our bright skies, an unseen hand threw clouds and darkness and terror. Our families, with the wagons and goods had crossed the river on a ferry boat, and my brothers and myself stood conversing on the bank. As the last boat shoved off I desired the older brother, Obadiah, (some twenty-two years my senior) to go over the river on the boat, while the younger men crossed on their horses with the stock. But he declined, and we all three mounted our horses together and entered the river, driving the stock before us. The ford led obliquely downward to the point of an Island, thence perpendicularly across to the southern bank. The Island was reached in safety by us all, although my own horse fell below the ford and into swimming water in a very dangerous position. Eight or ten rods of the river between us and the main land was now very deep and rapid. The men had crossed in safety, and the cattle scattered along the crossing, myself and elder brother slowly bringing up the rear. Coming to the line of deep water we stopped a moment and conversed about the safest crossing. I could see that he was somewhat excited, and I expressed the opinion that there could be no danger if we kept to the left, or up stream. He thought to bear diagonally down stream would be safer. In a few steps more our horses plunged into the channel, and both wearied and weakened with the long journey, refused to swim with us, but reared and plunged backward, leaving us unhorsed in the middle of the boiling river. For myself I had no fear. Being a good swimmer, and having taken the precaution to take off my boots and coat and fasten them to my saddle before going into the water, I felt confident of reaching the shore. But I saw at once for him the terrible hour had come. Encumbered with his boots and coat, and being entirely out of the reach of any assistance I could have rendered him, and swept before a rapid current below the point of the Island, I was as powerless to aid him as though he had been in the middle of the sea. Almost in an instant the waves had closed over him. His wife and daughter and adopted son stood on the bank frantically crying to the waves to give him back; but the waters tore ruthlessly asunder their bleeding heart-strings. It seemed a terrible destiny, fallen so fearfully sudden upon us, that the soul recoiled under its awful blow. For myself I had scarcely known him as a brother until the commencement of our journey. So many years my senior, we never enjoyed together the fellowships of the parental roof, and knew but little of the sweets of brotherly communion. I had become deeply attached to him on the journey. He was magnanimous, forbearing, self-sacrificing. Too ready to bear burdens that we all desired to excuse from his shoulders; that very willingness to do became at last the occasion of his death. This only rendered it the more painful to us. That evening when we gathered around our camp fire we were a sad and stricken group. Our prayers and our praises were solemn, heartfelt, outpourings of stricken souls before our Great Father. O how sadly and wearily we turned away from that valley of sorrows. More than twenty-seven years have passed. My eyes have never rested on that spot but once since that dreadful morning, but it has a fearful, everpresent life in my memory. Whenever I hear or see the name of the river in which he sank, there comes a dirge like murmur of gurgling waters, and a low sad wail of remembered sorrow, through my soul. I wait in hope for the coming of the time when seas and rivers shall give up their dead to greet again the brother whom my heart never yet has willingly surrendered to his grave in these waters.[7]

Harvey (From Chapter 9 of "Emigrant Wagon")

Friday: Aug. 26. The morning came slowly and softly over the eastern plains. In camp one almost sees the dawn, and growing light, and sun setting the Orient in a flame. In these mountain regions the mornings are resplendent. This was one of the most resplendent, and we moved out of camp at an early hour with the spirit of trained conv?ers [?] eager for the goal. In an hour we reached Snake River, put our wagons and families and part of the men on the ferry-boat to be transported to the other shore, the remainder of the men remaining to cross the stock, which was to be done by fording a part of the way, and swimming the remainder. The ford led from the north shore obliquely down the stream to an island, thence slightly up to the opposite bank. Eight or ten rods of the distance between the island and the southern shore was from eight to fifteen feet deep, and the current was strong and boiling. Driving the cattle into two bands G[ustavus] H[ines] and Mr. M[arti]n, each mounted on a horse, drove the first band to the island, and O[badiah] H[ines] the eldest of the three brothers, and myself, followed with the last band. In the same order we entered the other part of the river, the first division of stock passing safely over. We followed, my brother and myself riding side by side for a few rods and then slightly separating, he bearing to the right and down the stream and I to the left and up it. At the same moment our horses struck deep water, evidently plunging off a perpendicular bank. Our horses seemed frightened by the plunge, and both reared backward, throwing us under them in the roaring current. By the time we had risen to the surface we were about fifty feet apart; O[badiah], with his horse's bridle in his hand, and I throwing my arm over the withers of my horse. Both horses sunk again, and again reared backward, leaving us disengaged from them and struggling with the current. O[badiah], buffeted the current an instant, but being encumbered with his boots and a linen coat, and, probably hurt by the struggle of his horse, sank out of our sight almost instantly and never rose to the surface again. I had taken the precaution to remove my boots and coat and tie them to my saddle before entering the water, and, being a good swimmer, was able to reach the shore without difficulty.

This blow fell on our hearts with fearful power. Though my brother, he was so much my senior—twenty-one years—that I had hardly been acquainted with him before we began this journey together. With a clear, philosophical intellect well furnished by general reading, a brilliant and fascinating wit, and a generosity that knew no limit but ability to do, I had become greatly attached to him during the journey. That morning he had led our family devotions before we had left the camp, and as we rode side by side toward the river we were talking of our plans and work when we reached Oregon. It was a withering blow, falling on our hearts all naked to the stroke. Only the faith that in the inscrutable of providence there is yet the infinitely wise and infinitely good, albeit we cannot discover them, could give any light in this dark hour.

As I write these lines more than thirty-two years later, the old sorrow and the old lament comes surging back over my heart. But there comes into the memory of this sad parting the hope of a joyous meeting.

"Over the river:"
"On the evergreen mountains of Life."[8]

Shortly after arriving in the Willamette Valley, and learning of the impending departure of mail,[9] Gustavus wrote to his friend William Hosmer, editor of the *Northern Christian Advocate*, to inform him of their arrival. He mentions, of course, the tragedy at Snake River. Given that this was evidently the first opportunity for mail to the East since the tragedy occurred, this may well have been the means by which relatives and friends in New York first learned of Obadiah's death.

Gustavus

Oregon City, Oct. 13, 1853.

Br. Hosmer:—I am informed that the mail will probably leave to-day for the United States, and I hasten to communicate to you, and through you to the readers of the *Northern*, a few items of information relative to our expedition to this country. We arrived in the lower part of the Wallamette Valley the last of September—having consumed a few days less than five months in our transit across the plains.—Perhaps no emigration has suffered less with sickness, than the one of 1853. There have been very few deaths by disease on the plains, and comparatively little suffering of any kind. A few trains, however, have been called to endure those sufferings which unforeseen casualties often inflict upon the emigrant to the Pacific shores, and which cast a melancholy gloom over the entire enterprise of emigration.—One of these afflictive providences occurred with reference to our train, and, though heart-rending, and almost insupportable, left us no other alternative but submission to the divine decree, and no other consolation (and we needed no other) than that which the hope of the Christian inspires. This providence was the very sudden removal, by death, of an elder brother, Obadiah Hines, who, in company with us, was emigrating to this country with his family. He was assisting us in crossing Snake River with our cattle the second time, and, unfortunately, by taking a different course from those that preceded him, he got his horse into the deep channel of the river, where the current was exceedingly strong, and was borne down by the fierce whirling tide, and found a watery grave. He had conducted himself with great Christian propriety through the whole journey, and for the last few weeks of his life, seemed to live under the influence of a strong presentiment of approaching evil. Several times, before coming to the river the last time, I heard him remark, that he dreaded Snake River more than all the rest of the journey. But he is gone; he sank before our eyes, and we had not the power of rendering him the least assistance.—He was sanguine in the hope of making himself and family a comfortable home in Oregon, but he has gone to that better country, that is, an heavenly.

We were not able to recover his body; the place where it lies will remain a mystery until the seas, and the rivers also, shall give up their dead. I have but a moment more, and will say that in every other respect we have been very fortunate. All the rest of us are through in safety, and in the enjoyment of good health. Our fields of labor have been assigned us, and we have already entered upon our course in this country. You will hear from me occasionally, and be sure and continue to send me the much loved *Northern*.

Gustavus Hines.[10]

George W. Kennedy was a six-year-old boy in 1853 when he emigrated with his family from Illinois to Oregon, along what he called the Old Emigrant Road. As implied in the following excerpt from his 1914 reminiscence, *The Pioneer Campfire*, his party must have been just a few days ahead of the Hines train on the trail, and narrowly averted a tragedy like theirs at the Snake River crossing.

G. W. Kennedy

At Fort Boise, we found a flat boat to ferry us over, though some had been crossing in their wagon boxes.

We had to swim the cattle and horses. The stream there is full of boiling whirlpools. My Father came near being drowned. He was engaged in swimming the cattle. To get some of them off the island where they had lodged, he had to swim over. On the return, he was caught by one of those boiling whirls and was taken down, struggling hard to swim out against that mighty current. An old mountaineer, standing on shore, called out to him to stop his hard strokes—to lie on his back and float below the whirlpool. My Father had often swam the Mississippi—a mile wide—but it had not occurred to him to rest himself. He followed the advice, and soon came to shore, further down the river.

DROWNED.

At the same place, a few days later, Mr. Obadiah Hines (the brother of Revs. Gustavus, H. K. and Joseph Hines, all preachers, en route for Oregon) was drowned. He was swimming over on the back of his horse, which was caught in the whirl, and both were drowned. From this crossing of Snake River on to The Dalles there was much of hardship and suffering, sometimes destitution. Teams gave out—provisions also gave out.[11]

Once they were in Oregon, Kennedy and the Hines brothers were to have many direct encounters. One of these of particular interest will be cited later.

Dillis B. Ward, a teenager in 1853, was traveling with his family and others (including his stepmother's brother, Hilary Cason, mentioned by Harvey in Chapter 11), and crossed the Snake River at Fort Boise probably a few days after the Hines party.

D. B. Ward

Nothing remarkable occurred while traveling down the north side of the Snake river, and in due course of time we reached old Fort Boise, where there was a trader who owned and operated a ferry, charging the moderate sum of eight dollars for each wagon and team and its contents. Horses and cattle were forced to swim the river. It was at this place that Rev. Hines,[12] a brother of Reverends Gustavus and H. K. Hines, prominent pioneer ministers of the Methodist Episcopal Church was drowned while trying to swim the river with his horse. His body, I think, was not recovered. Our company now consisted of my father's family, four wagons, and my step-mother's brother, Hilary Cason, with his family and two wagons.[13]

---

[1] H. K. Hines, "An Incident of 1853," *Pacific Christian Advocate*, Jan. 27, 1881, p. 4.

[2] Gustavus Hines, "Letter from Oregon," *Northern Christian Advocate*, Dec. 7, 1853, p. 1.

[3] "The site of the Hudsons Bay Company's Fort Boise is today beneath the waters of the Snake, west of Caldwell, Idaho." Personal communication, Gregory M. Franzwa.

[4] John Eliot (1604-1690), after graduating from Cambridge and then being attracted to Puritanism, emigrated from England to Massachusetts in 1631, where he ministered to English settlers and Indians for over fifty-eight years. Jesus College, University of Cambridge: John Eliot; http://www.jesus.cam.ac.uk/college/history/eliot.html; accessed May 9, 2007.

[5] Judson, *A Pioneer's Search*, 62, 63.

[6] H. K. Hines, "A Reminiscence of 1853," *The Oregonian*, Tuesday, May 29, 1877, p. 1; the lines of verse are evidently a paraphrase of Thomas Moore's *National Airs; Oft in the Stilly Night*, 1815.

[7] H. K. Hines, "An Incident of 1853," *Pacific Christian Advocate*, Jan. 27, 1881, p. 4.

[8] H. K. Hines, "Emigrant Wagon," February 12, 1885, 2. The last line of the quotation is from a poem by James G. Clark, "The Mountains of Life," that can be found, for example, in Charles W. Sanders, *Sanders' Union Fourth Reader* (New York: Ivison, Blakeman, Taylor, & Co., 1863). (Project Gutenberg, 2005), http://www.gutenberg.org/dirs/etext05/sreadl0h.htm; accessed April 8, 2007. Harvey, too, may have seen the poem here, in that he appears to have quoted unrelated material from the same source elsewhere. (See Chap. 2.)

[9] US Mail service between New York and Oregon, via the Panama route, began in 1848, and within two years was operating on a twice-monthly basis—a marked improvement over the six-month delivery times during Gustavus's original stay in Oregon. John H. Kemble, *The Panama Route, 1848-1869, University of California Publications in History,* (Berkeley: University of California Press, 1943), Vol. XXIX, 43.

[10] Gustavus Hines, "Letter from Oregon," *Northern Christian Advocate*, Dec. 7, 1853, p. 1.

[11] G. W. Kennedy, *The Pioneer Campfire,* (Portland, Oreg.: Clarke-Kundret Printing Co., 1914) 37, 38.

[12] Ward mistakenly "ordains" Obadiah.

[13] D. B. Ward, "Across the Plains in 1853." http://www.yelmhistoryproject.com/
Yelm%20School/1860-1900/; accessed July 15, 2007.

14

August 27—September 8, 1853: On to the Grande Ronde

> *But if our view from the summit of the mountain was so delightful, our descent from the mountain to the plains was sufficiently difficult and dangerous to prove that the law of "compensations" had not forgotten to make the smooth and the rough of life balance each other even here.[1]*
>
> —Harvey K. Hines, September 1853

As the Hines train made its way across eastern Oregon, still deep in mourning from their loss at the Snake River, Harvey outdid himself in describing the succession of scenic views, each of which, if we are to take him at his word, must have surpassed the beauty of its predecessor. On Saturday, September 3, near the Powder River, he says, "A more perfect day never spread its golden sheen over a sweeter and softer landscape than that that lay near us..." A first view of the Grand Ronde two days later inspires the superlative, "But here, locked in its framework of evergreen mountains, we overlooked the most enchanting landscape we had ever beheld." Still later he writes of another scene, "As we rose the slope the whole panorama of the valley unrolled before us. Nowhere had we ever beheld such beauty of landscape."

Celinda

Saturday, August 27—Took water with us & went about 15 miles to Malheur river & camped, road pretty good mostly through sage. Our camp was in a very pretty place but all was sadness to me.

Sunday, August 28—Very pleasant. Remained in camp. The men...nearly all day...The new road... the Willamette valley above Oregon city saving 150 miles distance leaves the old trail near this place. But from all we can learn it is not at present a feasible route except for packers because no wagons have been through. A trading post is near kept by a Mr Turner.[2] He went to Oregon two years ago in the same co. with Mr Judson. They wintered at Salt Lake. The mormons got something against him & he was obliged to

254

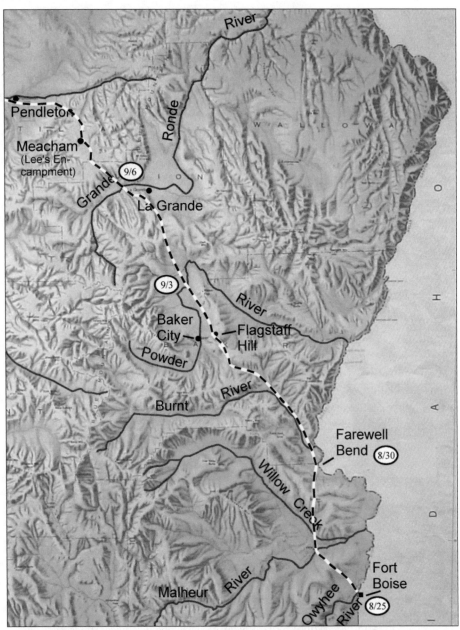

Topographic map of present-day northeast Oregon based on a map from the U.S. Dept. of the Interior, showing the path of the Hines party as estimated from Celinda's diary and Harvey's reminiscent account. Date designations are approximate.

hide himself …mountains. Mr Judson…when no one…but at length two of his associates betrayed him. He was taken back to the city & tried & was acquitted.[3]

Harvey

We turned away from Snake River with a cloud on our hearts, and on the afternoon of Saturday crossed the low ridge that divides between the Owyhee and Malheur, and camped on the latter for Sabbath. Its name: *Malheur*—unfortunate, or unlucky, river—seemed strangely in harmony with our feelings. We found here a large number of wagons whose owners had stopped at the representations of some gentlemen, residing in the upper end of the Willamette Valley, that there was a much better and shorter way into the valley by keeping up the Malheur, and over the Cascade Mountains at the head of the Willamette River, than that by the Dalles of the Columbia and over the Cascade Mountains near Mount Hood. We listened to their speeches, but while many were convinced, and decided to try the new way, we did not believe that the better way had remained undiscovered until now, and so decided to keep the "old paths." Many went with them, however, but found "the new and shorter way" an exceedingly rough and long one, and only succeeded in getting into the valley near the beginning of winter, and with fragments of teams, and themselves nearly famished for food.[4] Still the route actually is shorter from the mouth of the Malheur to Eugene City than by the Columbia River, but it was new, the sage unbroken, the road through the mountains uncleared, the guides got lost, being but little acquainted with the landmarks, and it was criminal in them to persuade emigrants to take an untried way, and foolish and presumptuous for the emigrants to take their advice.[5]

At the "Farewell Bend"[6] of the Snake River the Hines party narrowly averted another tragedy. Celinda's account is unclear because of missing parts of some diary pages, but Harvey and Phoebe relate that Lydia Hines's dress caught fire, and only quick, heroic action by Gustavus saved her from very serious injury. Alta Bryant adds an amusing twist.

Celinda

Monday, August 29—Pleasant. Went about 2 miles & crossed the Malheur river. Took water & went on. Camped for noon under a bluff. Went on until after dark some time no water after crossing the river in the morning made 25 miles. Road rather hilly. Camped by a small stream.

Tuesday, August 30—Warm & dusty. Went over hills to Burnt river…on the river. At…his clothes…& in trying to extinguish the flames uncle G Aunt L & Julia burnt their hands quite bad. Crossed the river twice after noon. After the first crossing the road led through & under a canopy of bushes which would have been delightful had we not been looking out for dangerous places all the time. Went till after dark again. Camped near the river. It was dark & rainy. Lightning played around the mountain tops which rose several hundred feet on all sides of us. The…

Harvey

Aug. 29. Soon after leaving Malheur we crossed Willow Creek, and then over an alkaline desert to a brackish spring on the slope of a sandy hill where we nooned; then drove forward until late at night when we reached another small spring in a shallow ravine, where we encamped for the night, letting our cattle go among the hills.

The next day our road led us winding among barren hills through deep dust for a few miles when we crossed the gravelly bed of a stream coming down from the west, and then five or six miles further to "Farewell Bend" of Snake River, where we made our noon camp.

Here we came near having another tragic incident. In preparing dinner, Mrs. G[ustavus] H[ines], who had on a light lawn dress, passed too near the fire and in an instant her dress was all in a flame. Her husband, who stood near, seized the burning garment, and with one strong jerk disrobed her without ceremony, before fire had communicated to her under garments. His hands were badly burned, but she escaped without injury, other than the entire destruction of the dress. The excitement attending this incident detained us for some time, when we again hitched up our teams and taking a sad farewell look at Snake River, which hereafter was to mean so much of sorrow for us, drove over a large hill to Burnt River, and encamped for the night.[7]

Phoebe

Our next Sabbath encampment was on the Malheur river. I greatly missed my little rocking chair. To sit in the camp, rock my baby, and sing some of the old church songs, made it seem quite "homelike." The hymn beginning:

> "Guide me, O thou great Jehovah,
> Pilgrim through this barren land,
> I am weak, but Thou art mighty,
> Hold me with Thy powerful hand"[8]

seemed especially appropriate while traveling through the barren wilderness.

It was in this region of the country that another one of our company narrowly escaped a terrible death. While preparing for a noon lunch, Mrs. Capt. Hines' dress came in contact with the fire, and before discovered was a mass of flames. The captain, who was fortunately standing near by, saved her life by tearing off her dress, burning both hands severely.[9]

Alta Bryant

Aunt Lydia[10] got afire (Gustavus Hines' wife) was cooking dinner— left me in the wagon. Her husband was standing near—he grabbed her and tore her clothes off then told her to "get to the wagon." She was not burned but he burned his hands.

Celinda

Wednesday, August 31—It was cloudy & cool which was very fortunate on account of hilly bad roads. Stopped for noon on the river. Crossed the river (Burnt) nine times. Our road was the most intricate of any day since we started. Sometimes crossing the river & then recrossing immediately thence through a beautiful grove of poplars & Balm of Gileads then perhaps over a steep high hill & then to the river & then through a thicket of bushes Sumac …cherry so dense that…through them…in the PM. Towards night we left that branch of Burnt river which we had been travelling up nearly all the afternoon & crossed over a very high steep hill & camped on a small stream. Have heard birds sing occasionally since we came on to Boise river.

Thursday, September 1—Not so warm as it has been very pleasant. Road better than yesterday but hilly before noon came on to a flat through which runs Burnt river. Camped on the river at noon. Went up the valley. Road good. Camped at night in the valley…Made about 15 miles…crossing of Snake river we…cattle. Many are…while some are stopped.

Harvey

We were locked in deep embracing hills; mountains, in fact; which seemed to stray away skyward mile after mile. The little river flowed clear and beautiful, in a half circle, on three sides of our camp, with a cooling music after the heat and dust and excitement of the day, and our rest on the little patch of green-sward where our tents were pitched, was calm and sweet.

For two days we traveled up Burnt River, the road leaving it in places where precipices abutted against the stream, and climbing high hills to avoid them. The second night we camped at the foot of a steep hill where the road turned abruptly to the right and left the stream, entering among high, grassy hills, now yellowed by the heat of the summer's sun. A cold west wind swept their summits, whirling the dust in clouds about us, and making our traveling exceedingly unpleasant and tiresome. As the sun went down the wind died away, and an unpleasant day was followed by a delightful evening.

We made our camp—a dry camp—on a little plain a quarter of a mile or so to the south of the road, and just at the foot of a high bald peak,[11] overlooking the Powder River valley. As we were several miles from water it was again necessary to guard our stock so that they might be present for use in the morning.

(This camp was only a few rods from where the Virtue mine[12] is now situated. The high hill at the foot of which we pitched our tents stands just south of the mine.)

Our guard was not very vigilant during the night, and so two of my oxen had stolen away and left me for greener pastures. Knowing, however, that they would scent the water of Powder River four or five miles to the westward, we did not delay in the morning; but yoking up the remainder, drove onward to the river trusting to find them there. Just where we wanted to make our noon halt we found them, lying contentedly on the sward near the water looking the very picture of bucolic innocence.[13]

Phoebe

After leaving Malheur river our road led us over alkaline deserts, up and down high hills, occasionally coming to a stagnant pool whose waters, like those of Marah, "were bitter to the taste."

We were two days traveling up Burnt river, continually enveloped in clouds of suffocating dust.

Making one dry camp, we descended into Powder river valley, and encamped for the Sabbath, where we were made happy by a pure stream of running water. Travelers on the Sahara could not have appreciated it more than these dusty, dirty emigrants, after traveling over high, barren hills, their imaginations haunted by visions of babbling brooks and bubbling springs.

"He sendeth the springs into the valleys, which run among the hills,"[14] making the name of "valley" suggestive of rest and comfort to the toiling emigrant. Traveling high above a beautiful stream, its cool waters in plain view, but utterly beyond our reach, was tantalizing in the extreme, and such was our frequent experience.

There is a living lesson in these scenes. Some souls seem as barren as these deserts, which at that time were too dismal a dwelling place for even bat or owl; but cultivation has made it to bear luscious fruit and to blossom like the rose, where the birds of the air build their nests and sing their songs. There is hope, therefore, for the most degenerate of God's children.[15]

Celinda

Friday, September 2—Pleasant with a cool breeze from the mountains. Went up the valley a short distance which had here become quite narrow. Then taking water struck over the hills the first of which was long & steep to the valley of Powder river. When on the hills we first beheld the Blue mountains proper. Although we had been traveling amid spurs of them for several days. These mountains are mostly covered with timber & appeared as we…them even more grand…than the Rocky…point of greatest…Camped by a little river among the hills for dinner. Ascended soon more hills first saw the mountains & after descending some long ones came on to the valley of Powder river. There we found sage again. Camped in the valley where there was some grass but no water. Went 20 miles.

Saturday, September 3—It rained considerable in the night but it having ceased we started on before breakfast for water. Mountains looked magnificent. Some were nearly enveloped in dense clouds while around others smaller clouds hovered in all a delightful placidity…delightful scenery & but for the casualty which one week ago deprived me of my only earthly parent, how well might I have enjoyed it. Went 5 miles to a slue where we breakfasted. We then went to the river 8 miles & camped for the night. A family with one wagon came & camped near. The man crossed the plains 2 years since & getting out of provisions at the first crossing of Snake river went all the remainder of the way with nothing but fish & such game as they could…In the evening some indians came of whom we bought some peas & potatoes paying $1.00 for 4 qts of peas & the same for one mess of potatoes. Afterwards two others came of whom we purchased salmon. These Kayuse indians seem rather intelligent and often well dressed.

Harvey

Our night camp was at the ford of Powder River. It was a beautiful, grassy place, just a little to the left of the road before crossing the stream. Just after we camped some Indians came to our camp with potatoes and peas to sell. For four months we had been entirely destitute of all kind of vegetables, our main living being bread and meat, with beans and rice as a change. Though our money was not abundant, the sight of fresh vegetables was too great a temptation, and though our Indian had become sufficiently "Bostonized" to ask fifty cents for a dozen potatoes and fifty cents for a quart of peas, we had the luxury of a supper of boiled potatoes and peas, with fried salmon and bacon, and nice warm bread with tea and coffee for those who wished it. Seldom did hungry men and women eat a better meal.

Entering Powder River valley, we seemed to be leaving the gray deserts

"Coming off Flagstaff Hill, the emigrants caught this view of the lovely Baker Valley [Powder River Valley], and the fearsome sight of the Blue Mountains, through which they must pass."[16]

of Snake River behind. From the hills where we had made our last camp before entering the valley, the whole valley lay under our vision, appearing to be twenty or thirty miles long and five or six wide. Down its center the sinuous course of the river was marked by willows and small trees. West of it rose the precipitous and timbered pinnacles of the Blue Mountains; a part of the range reminding us much of many pictures of Alpine mountains. There was over the scene, as the shadows of the mountains crept eastward, a soft dreaminess that soothed the spirit into restful quietude.

Saturday, Sept. 3. We crossed Powder River and, after traveling a few miles, a very clear and beautiful stream coming down from the high mountains, ten or twelve miles, to the west. Soon we crossed another, and, after traveling a few miles over a low ridge, entered one of the most beautiful little valleys we had seen on the entire route. Advancing up this to near where the road left it, and ascending a very rocky hill, we encamped for the Sabbath in a magnificent meadow of native clover and red-top. Just to our left a mountain, wooded with fragrant pine, sloped away to a great height, and along its base were beautiful groves of quivering aspen. A more perfect day never spread its golden sheen over a sweeter and softer landscape than that that lay near us; while the distant scene was an environment of mountain ranges and summits of every outline, gentle and rounded, or steep and pinnacled; here green and tender with soughing pines, and there black and hard with frowning precipices of rock.[17]

Phoebe

Crossing Powder river and several other streams, we ascended a mountain. On reaching the summit, our captain called a halt, that we might more fully view the magnificence of the grand Powder river valley, which lay unrolled beneath us.

The beauty of this enchanting scene filled our souls with delight— surrounded on all sides except the west by blue mountains, covered with evergreen timber.

We rolled down the mountain into this picturesque valley. Crossing to the west side, we encamped near where the city of La Grande is now located.[18]

Gustavus Hines and William Henry Gray (1810-1889), the latter of whom was first mentioned by Celinda on March 19 as "Mr. Grey," were associates at the Methodist Mission and the Oregon Institute in the early 1840s. In his 1850 book, Gustavus mentions attending to mission business along with Gray, and later describes their mutual activities in the establishment of the provisional government of Oregon.[19] Gray in turn mentions Gustavus's name more than 150 times in his own *History of Oregon* in 1870,[20] including many passages quoted directly from the latter's book, as well as Gray's own less-than-flattering characterization of Gustavus's role in the formation of the provisional government.[21] In any case, these two men were clearly acquainted from earlier stays in Oregon, and in 1853 met again on the trail. The meeting of the two trains is mentioned by both Celinda, and Rebecca Ketcham, a young woman traveling in Gray's party.

Celinda

Sunday, September 4—Pleasant. Went 10 miles to water & camped for the day. Road good with some hills. Mr Gray the gentleman from Oregon whom I first saw at St Louis came up & camped with us. He had a drove of sheep. He had a baggage … teams & a light wagon drawn by horses … oxen he was obliged to leave his heavy wagon. He then bought horses & is packing through & takes his carriage for the ladies. His sheep are some ways behind.

Harvey

This was the first Sunday of autumn, and it reminded us that we had spent more than all the summer months moving westward. Near us, on a little elevation, was the grave of "an emigrant," at its head and foot, great rough splinters of basaltic rock standing as fitting memorials of his life and journey and death out here in this wildly beautiful necropolis. A sailor prays that his grave may be the soft depths of the sea, his monument the coral spires that tower in its blue above him, and why not the emigrant wish a burial where great mountains sentinel his resting place, and untainted winds sing holy requiem to soothe his slumbers! But, ah! somebody's heart ached as they turned away from this grave in the wilderness. God love and pity them.

Rebecca Ketcham

Sunday, Sept. 4th Yesterday afternoon started on our way at 5 o'clock. The wind blew very hard and very cold. We had our large shawls on but we suffered very much with cold. One horse nearly gave out and Mr. Gray could only keep them going by constantly whipping them. We went 10 miles and stopped about 8 o'clock. Phil had fallen behind with the mules and horses. We had not seen him for some time...[There follows a long description of their troubles in finding Phil.]...Just before we were ready to start again Mr. Hines' company came up. We had passed them without seeing them. It was so cold this morning we were nearly frozen before we stopped for breakfast. We are now stopping for supper, Mr. Hines very near us. The middle of the day has been quite warm.

Sunday evening, Sept. 4th. We have had supper and concluded to remain here till morning. The valley we now are in is most beautiful. 'Tis perhaps 8 miles wide. On the east side a tiny stream runs from a spring in the mountain. Beyond it the valley gently slopes up to the bluff where the animals belonging to Mr. Hines' company and to us are quietly feeding and resting, and it is really an interesting sight. On the west the hills rise high and they are covered sufficiently with trees to make them look beautiful. We have so many hills and mountains without a tree or shrub, that seeing these really gives me a sort of home feeling. Toward the tops of these hills the forest is dense, down lower the trees are more scattering, forming here and there a grove. They look like some of the spots on the hills about Ithaca. South and southwest we see the Blue Mountains.[22]

Celinda

Monday, September 5—Pleasant. Went about 7 miles to Grande Ronde[23]. This is a fertile valley 8 miles acrost & 20 miles long entirely encompassed by mountains & watered by Grande Ronde river. The road comes in from the south & goes out at the west. Up and down a very bad hill. Camped for...after crossing...valley & near the trading post. We were thronged with indians nearly all on ponies. It reminded me very forcibly of an old fashioned general training. They had plenty of money $50.00 gold pieces & which they probably got by selling horses to emigrants. After dinner we went 8 miles to the other side of the valley. Camped near a pretty mountain stream. Indian lodges near. Thronged with indians during our stay. Some belong to the Kayuses some to the Nez Perces. At our noon camp...Perce chief with whom...some acquaintance He seemed very pleasant & spoke Eng. with such a pleasing awkwardness as to amuse us very much. Others were there who had seen uncle. Before noon we met many mostly women on ponies who said they were travelling to the Shoshone country. They had peas with them for food which they would swap for flour or bread. One proposed to swap her baby for a shirt. These indians here seem more intelligent & happy than any we have seen.

William Henry Jackson produced a fine painting of the emigrants entering the Grand Ronde.[24]

Rebecca Ketcham

The foot of this hill brought us to the Grande Ronde. This is a large, beautiful valley entirely surrounded by mountains. The Grande Ronde River runs through it. Most of the trains spend the whole or part of a day to recruit, there being plenty of water and good grass for their animals. There are some traders and plenty of Indians here, the Nez Perces.

Mr. Gray recognized a good many of them, some of them him. They were all on horses. Bought some potatoes of them, enough for dinner for a fine ____; also some dry peas. Mr. Gray talked to one of the traders about some horses. He had a pair he would let Mr. Gray have for the span he was driving and $100. Of course we went on. Came on 6 miles and stopped for the day. Lots of Indians around all the time.[25]

Harvey

Monday, Sept. 4 [should say Sept. 5]. Out of the beautiful valley of "Clover Creek," we turned up a rocky ravine, in which great boulders filled the road, and down which a little springlet trickled among the rocks, and then over a high ridge, thickly covered with broken blocks of scoria for a few miles further, when we found ourselves on a high summit overlooking *Grande Ronde* valley. It burst upon our vision like an enchantment. The most of our road for four months had been over gray sage plains or among bald mountain peaks, with little except the vastness and grandeur to attract us. But here, locked in its framework of evergreen mountains, we overlooked the most enchanting landscape we had ever beheld. Its contrast with the dry and brazen plains was so marked, its greenness of verdure, even in the autumn noon, so refreshing, its outline so clean and beautiful, that our train, whose chief thought was to get forward, called a halt that we might admire and discuss the beauty of the little mountain-locked Eden before us.

But, if our view from the summit of the mountain was so delightful our descent from the mountain to the plains was sufficiently difficult and dangerous to prove that the law of "compensations" had not forgotten to make the smooth and the rough of life balance each other even here. It was fairly a precipice—the steepest of the journey —that we plunged off to reach the valley. But we reached it, for how could we help it, after once starting downward. Nooning on a creek at the bottom of the precipice, we crossed the southwestern corner of the valley about eight miles and encamped for the night, just at the foot of the Blue Mountains, on its west side, at evening. This camp was just where the city of La Grande is now located, and not a hundred feet from "the old court house."

Our camp on the evening of the 4th [5th]and the forenoon of the 5th [6th] was visited by great numbers of Cayuse and Nez Pecez Indians. Several hundred of them were encamped on Grand Ronde River about two miles away, and they were engaged in trading with the emigrants.

One of the most dignified and finely mounted of them, G[ustavus] H[ines] of our train, who had been at a great council of these tribes at Waiiletpu in 1843, recognized as "Red Wolf," a Nez Percez Chief whose place was on Snake River far to the north. Addressing "Red Wolf" by name, and telling him where he had seen him, Red Wolf shook his head doubtfully. And said "clonas," which is jargon for "I don't know." The Indian then came close up to him, lifted G[ustavus] H[ines]'s hat clear off his head, looked squarely in his face while his hat was off, smiled, and said: "nowitka, mi-ke cumtux,"—meaning, "yes, I know you."[26] In the rough and dusty garb of an emigrant, with his beard covering his face, the Indian could not recall him; but when his hat was lifted and he got a clear view of eyes and forehead he remembered him instantly. They shook hands like old friends.

Up to this point we had lost no oxen out of our teams, but when they were gathered up on the morning of the 5th [6th] two of our finest were missing. One we found dead just where a low hill-point pushed out into the valley about a half mile from our camp, exactly where La Grande Cemetery is now located; and the other we thought unable to proceed further, and gave him to one of Red Wolf's men. We lay in camp until noon, making everything snug in our wagons, preparatory to crossing the Blue Mountains, whose timbered heights were just before us. After dinner we began the ascent, going squarely up the face of the mountain directly west of the end of what is now Main Street in La Grande. As we rose the slope the whole panorama of the valley unrolled before us. Nowhere had we ever beheld such beauty of landscape. The long, green valley, the high mountains beyond towering into the skies, the streams fringed with willows and poplars, winding through the plain made a mystery of beauty that has held its place on the tablet of memory until this day; and we have never yet seen the rival of this landscape.

It was a weary climb: this ascent of the mountain. Just after we had reached the top Red Wolf overtook us and told us that water would be scarce through the mountains, and that the first place we would find water on the road we would find no grass, but that if, when we would cross a certain hollow some distance ahead, we would turn to the right a quarter of a mile we would find a good spring and excellent grass. We followed his directions and found it as he said, and made a camp among the pines.

Through all this journey, which had now lengthened into four months, our camps had not had even the poor shelter of a "juniper tree." Here the great pines spread their umbrage over us, and the gentle mountain zephers were sighing a soft and slumberous monotone among their quivering branches. The sward was green beneath them, and great stretches and slopes and rounded hills of green-grassed lawns spread around us, with the great pines scattered here and there where they seemed most to adorn and beautify the landscape. We had encamped early and spent the two or three hours of the soft autumn afternoon in wandering over the hills. With the coming of the night we put large piles of logs ablaze, and round the "campfire" told our stories, sung our hymns, let our hopes prophesy of the future or our sorrows recite the past until the night had gone far westward before we retired to our slumbers under the lullaby of the pines.[27]

Phoebe

Many Indians were galloping over the prairies, sitting as straight as so many cobs, on the little ponies which run wild over the plains, and must have greatly degenerated since Fernando Cortez first introduced their noble progenitors into Mexico.

Among the Indians Captain Hines recognized "Red Wolf," chief of the Nez Perces tribe, with whom he had become acquainted while living in Oregon.

The next day, while ascending the Blue mountains, "Red Wolf" overtook us for the purpose of letting us know where we would find a spring of water and grass for our stock.

Turning to the right and traveling a short distance we came to the place this friendly Indian had described to us, making our encampment under the fir trees, which rose like stately columns, far above the earth—standing so closely that their boughs interlaced. The ground had a lawn-like appearance, covered with a carpet of grass and free from undergrowth.

This great change from the desert sage plains, where there was no verdure to refresh the soul, or to screen us from the hot rays of the sun, made us feel we had come into a new world and among kind friends, for a tree comes as near being human as any inanimate thing that grows; and no wonder when "planted by the rivers of water" and made to bear good fruit that it is the type of a "good man."

As the smoke curled up among the fir trees, and our young ladies made the air melodious with the sweet strains of the "Silvery Light of the Moon,"[28] we felt nearer the longed for "home" than at any time since the beginning of our journey.

Having been without fuel for so long, except sage wood and willow, and often without even those poor substitutes, we were delighted to do our cooking one more [time] over a good fire. We had tired of living on hard tack and crackers.

Magic yeast and baking powder were an "unknown quantity" in those days, and we did not relish sour dough bread as the "staff of life."

There was only the one kind—the old fashioned "salt rising" that "just filled the bill," as it retained the delicate flavor of the wheat.

As there are many girls and young wives who are not adepts in this simple art of the culinary department, I will give them my experience while journeying on the road over the plains. To one quart of water, one teaspoon of salt, thickened with flour until a stiff batter; I then set the little bucket containing the yeast into the camp kettle (covering it tightly to keep out the dust) and letting it remain in the front part of the wagon where the sun kept it warm. The secret in making it rise was the part the oxen and wagon performed—in keeping it well stirred, or in constant motion. When we came to a halt at noon it was sure to be light and foaming over into the kettle. I then poured it into the bread pan, adding as much more water and thickened flour; when it again became light I kneaded it into a large loaf while the wagon was jogging along; when we reached our camping place at night my bread was ready to put into the "Dutch oven" and bake.

By this method I never failed to bake as light and sweet bread as ever made by modern devices.

Many of the emigrants made their butter by allowing the jolting of the wagon to do the churning.

I did not like to see cows yoked to the wagons and made to haul the load, as was done in some of the trains. I know it was the custom of the Hebrews in the dark ages, when they sacrificed the males of their flocks and herds to atone for their sins, to commit greater ones by working their cows in the yoke. And in some countries even women are seen yoked to the plow and made to do the work of an ox.

When all the inhuman treatment and indignities that have been heaped upon the female sex are done away with, we may look for the millenium, and not before.[29]

Celinda

Tuesday, September 6—Pleasant. Remained in camp till noon. The men…wagon boxes…wagon & ours & lightened loads as much as possible. Uncles bought each of them ["saddle" crossed out] horse with their saddles. One woman wished me to swap a gold ring for an old brass thimble. We went on after noon. The road was very hilly. The hills covered with timber, Firs Pines & a little spruce. The trees are some distance apart. The ground covered with a little grass & rose bushes &c. Went 8 miles & camped in a ravine. Very lonesome. Mr Miner left on foot.

Harvey

Sep. 6. [7] The morning stole slowly and softly through the pine trees, but as its rays touched our eyelids we stepped forth to our day's duty of travel. In about four miles from our camp we passed down a long, gentle slope, lawn-like in beauty, and reached the crossing of Grand Ronde River: a small clear stream flowing over a bed of smoothly washed boulders. On the further side our road led diagonally up the face of a bald mountain, then again stretched away through the open pine forest to "Dry Creek," simply a sharp hollow without water, and then up a steep bench of the mountains covered with sharp fragments of broken volcanic rock, to a long, dry ridge, overlooking many miles of mountain slopes away to the south and east, where, without water we encamped for the night.[30]

Phoebe

We crossed the Grande Ronde river and soon after bid good-bye to the beautiful pine forests and came out upon the summit of a bald mountain that overlooked the great Columbia river valley, and our captain again called a halt, that we might from Pisgah's heights view the promised land in all its magnificent beauty, which was fascinating beyond description.

In the rarified atmosphere of these upper regions this inspiring scene seemed but a short distance away. But we were too weary with our hard day's journey to indulge in any enthusiastic expressions of admiration. The one sentiment animating our souls was to reach Puget Sound as speedily as possible; and we fondly hoped that the remainder of our journey would not be as full of difficulties as that which lay behind.

Oh, vain, delusive hope! For we found the more sublime the scenery the more difficult became our progress. The descent from the mountain was steep and rocky. We made our encampment on the bank of the Umatilla, where we found good grass for our cattle.

This wild, picturesque valley was filled with Indians who were trading with the emigrants. We bought fresh beef from them at twenty-five cents per pound, and potatoes (no larger than walnuts) at one dollar a peck; but they were "potatoes," and we ate our supper and breakfast with more relish than any meal since we left home.[31]

Rebecca Ketcham

Tuesday, Sept. 6th. Left the Grande Ronde about 7 o'clock this morning, Mrs. Dix on horseback, the rest of us on foot. We have come 15 or 16 miles today. We have walked full half of it. The horses have had all they could do to draw the carraige up the hills. Our road has been nearly the whole day through the woods, that is, if beautiful groves of pine trees can be called woods. Stopped for dinner on Grande Ronde River. The grass has been fine all the way except just where there had been a camp. Wherever there were, we found wagons or baggage of some kind left, showing that teams were giving out and people had to get along the best way they could.

Left Mr. Hines' company this morning looking over their loads, preparing to leave a good part. After dinner, when we had ascended the first hill, we looked back upon the country we had passed through; I can almost say I never saw anything more beautiful, the river winding about through the ravines, the forests so different from anything I have seen before. The country all through is burnt over, so often there is not the least underbrush, but the grass grows thick and beautiful. It is now ripe and yellow and in the spaces between the groves (which are large and many) looks like fields of grain ripened, ready for the harvest. We had a very fine view of the Grande Ronde after gaining the top of the high hill which led us out of it. This was beautiful indeed, with the river winding through it, all skirted with trees. We are encamped for the night right among the trees, without water and with the prospect of being without it till late in the day tomorrow. We can do very well tonight, but I expect we shall be hungry and thirsty tomorrow before we get our breakfast.[32]

Celinda

Wednesday, September 7—…Cool breeze every afternoon…very delightful with the exception of being hilly. The road was smooth & nice. The forest beautiful. The ground is covered with grass. The trees are far apart. Often large places entirely devoid of them. Frequently small patch of little trees nearly of a [like?] size looking very beautiful. Our night camp was on an open space covered with little stones & some grass. There was no water but we had come prepared for our noon camp which was in a valley on Gr___ river. In the night…in a…we being alone sounded very lonesome.

Thursday, September 8—Pleasant. Went twelve miles without water. Road bad. Very hilly & in some places stony. Forest more intricate. Sometimes the road was very bad winding around trees &c. Camped at night at Lee's

Encampment. Ritchie's train near.[33] Mr. Bailey one of the men who was with
Mr. Leonard came on says Mr. L & the train Charley is in have gone the new
road. He, Mr. B., is going through on foot as are many others. We have lost 4
oxen in all up to this time.

Harvey

On the following day our road, always among the pines, led us over the
dividing ridge of the mountains, and at about five o'clock in the afternoon we
unyoked our oxen by the side of a pool of water in the bed of a creek, which
evidently was quite a stream early in the season. The place was known as
"Lee's encampment."[34] It was a very pretty spot, though feed was scarce as
all who had preceded us had encamped there, but by driving our cattle a mile
or more to the south we found some open hillsides where was good bunch
grass on which they foraged without guards.

(Note. This camp was on the present "Meacham Creek," about a quarter
of a mile below where "Meacham's" house, for so many years, afforded such
a delightful home to the weary traveler over these mountains. For ten
successive years, 1869 to 1879 this was my own stopping place, "without
money or price" in nearly one hundred crossings of these mountains on my
ministerial work.)[35]

Our drive of the forenoon of the 8th [9th] was still among the pine
openings. The atmosphere was loaded with balm. The long, open slopes looked
like cultivated lawns, and we passed on through them with a wonder that so
near such a desert as we had just crossed, such a very Eden of beauty as these
pine-clad mountains could be found. About noon we came out of the forest
and found ourselves on a high bald mountain summit, overlooking the great
valley of the Columbia, for apparently, a hundred and fifty miles in length
and fifty miles in width. It was a scene never to be forgotten. In all our
journeying we had seen nothing to compare with it. We stopped our teams on
the summit and for a while contemplated the beauty and the grandeur.

We were facing westward. A level vision against the horizon, not less
than a hundred and fifty miles from where we stood, disclosed the dark peaks
of the Cascade range of mountains, and towering high above them the snowy
summits of Mount Hood, Mount Adams, and Mount Reignier[36] sentineling
the range for a length of more than a hundred miles. Dropping the range of
vision a vast stretch of prairie, rounded into hills or lifted into what would be
mountains but for the overshadowing grandeur of the great western and eastern
ranges that bounded them, with here and there long sinuous valleys winding
among them, lay between us and the mountain-limited horizon. Just at our
feet, apparently, though really several miles distant, the Umatilla River stole
out of the mountains at our right, and through its deep bordering of cottonwood
forest swept a circle southward and westward until it seemed lost in the bosom
of the yellow hills. Farther to the right and north we overlooked the valley of

the Walla Walla, and our vision stretched away across the Columbia, we could not tell how far. From where we stood we could see that the road on which we were traveling divided a few miles further on, one branch stretching away to the northwest towards Puget Sound, and one inclining southwest toward the Willamette by the way of the Columbia, and over both of them the long trains were moving, like empire, westward.[37]

In early August while the overland Hines party was still on the trail, many weeks short of their goal, Joseph was already in Portland. There he witnessed scene after scene of heartbreak and destitution as emigrants arrived. It must have been with considerable anxiety that he inquired as to the whereabouts and condition of his relatives.[38]

Joseph

About the first of August, the emigrants began to arrive from the plains, wearied and sometimes sick, and many of them disheartened on account of the loss of teams and wagons during the journey, and the worst of all the death and burial of friends in the desert. Sometimes it was a husband, sometimes a wife, a son or a daughter; sometimes both husband and wife, leaving a number of orphans children to be cared for by strangers, or wander without care, ragged and destitute and forsaken, themselves to perish in the wilderness. No pen has ever been able to adequately describe the terrible sufferings of those early emigrants during the ten years succeeding 1850. Having crossed the Isthmus of Panama, I had a few weeks to spare before the bulk of the emigrants began to arrive, and nothing could exceed the terrible sufferings I witnessed amongst the first arrivals from the plains. Frequently a solitary horseman would arrive bringing news of some special disaster, and the settlers would pack several horses and mules with provisions and clothing and hasten to their relief.

When I arrived at Portland in the Autumn of 1853, I found myself confronted with an unusual number of such scenes, and I soon exhausted all my surplus means, in efforts for their relief, and then began to work for wages in order to be able to accomplish more. As soon as the first emigrants began to arrive in the settlements west of the Cascade Mountains, I began to seek information in regard to my brothers, three of whom had left St. Joseph, Mo.[actually Kansas City, Mo.], in the early Spring. I found they [i.e., emigrants] had begun to arrive quite freely at the Dalles, then the head of navigation on the east of Hood River, where it empties into the Columbia. There were but a few permanent buildings there at that time, but a large number of tents, where traders kept supplies during the emigrant season, and bought up cattle from those just in from the sage brush plains, especially from those whose cattle were run down and were thought to be unable to cross the Cascade Mountains to the grass covered plains of Willamette Valley. It will be remembered that at the Dalles the river branches, one branch leading down the Columbia River, around the Cascades on the west about two miles, then across the tongue of land between the Columbia and the Willamette to the City of Portland.[39]

The Columbia River Gorge, looking east.[40]

---

[1] H. K. Hines, "Emigrant Wagon," February 19, 1885, 2.

[2] "Journals of the early travelers along the Oregon Trail mention the Malheur River crossing and the hot springs where they could rest, take baths and wash their clothes. A temporary trading post, run by a Mr. Turner, was referred to in journals as early as 1853." See *City of Vale, Oregon, "Born and Raised on the Oregon Trail,"* at http://www.ci.vale.or.us/history/index.php; accessed April 15, 2007.

[3] Western historian David Bigler tells the complicated story of G. L. Turner somewhat differently. From letters of Asa Call and Jotham Goodell (Phoebe's father), it appears that Turner stopped work on a construction project for the Mormons when they failed to pay him in a timely fashion. The Mormons then accused him of horse thievery and robbery and set out to capture him. To save their own hides, emigrants wintering with Goodell near the Mormon settlement managed to capture him and turn him over to the Mormon authorities. But, Bigler states, "In the end it all came to nothing. Turner reached an undisclosed accommodation with his main accuser, Brigham Young, who allowed him to go unmolested to California." David L. Bigler, *A Winter with the Mormons: The 1852 Letters of Jotham Goodell,* (Salt Lake City, 2001) 117.

[4] We learn elsewhere that former members of the Hines train, the Joseph Leonard family, and Charles Long, as well as another family they met on the trail, that of Tavenor Beale, all opted for "the new and shorter way," and suffered the consequences described by Harvey. Leah Collins Menefee and Lowell Tiller, "Cutoff Fever, III," *Oregon Historical Quarterly*, June 1977, 129.

[5] H. K. Hines, "Emigrant Wagon," February 19, 1885, 2.

[6] "Farewell Bend is now a state park, located five miles southeast of Huntington, Oregon." Personal communication, Gregory M. Franzwa.

[7] H. K. Hines, "Emigrant Wagon," February 19, 1885, 2.

[8] This is from the first verse of the Welsh hymn, "Guide me, O thou great Jehovah," composed by William Williams in 1745, and translated into English in 1771. The Cyber Hymnal; http://www.cyberhymnal.org/htm/g/u/guideme.htm; accessed May 9, 2007.

[9] Judson, *A Pioneer's Search*, 63, 64.

[10] Alta Bryant and Lydia (Bryant) Hines were distantly related, but we have been unable to determine the precise relationship. Alta may have called her "Aunt Lydia" because others did. (Lydia's niece Celinda regularly referred to her this way—appropriately, of course—and even Joseph, Lydia's brother-in-law, refers to "Aunt Lydie's tea" in Chapter 16.)

[11] Relying on Harvey's subsequent reference to the Virtue Mine location, we can identify this peak as a 4,484-foot hill, five miles east of Baker City, Oreg. Topozone, http://www.topozone.com; accessed March 18, 2007. About three miles further north is a better known, though somewhat shorter peak (3,945 ft), known as "...Flagstaff Hill, atop which is the marvelous BLM's Oregon Trail Interpretive Center, and below that, the intact pristine ruts of the Oregon Trail, leading down to the pastoral Baker Valley." Personal communication, Gregory M. Franzwa.

[12] The mine was named for one of its owners, James William Virtue (1837-1903), an Irish immigrant who served as a lawyer, legislator, real estate agent, banker, and first and foremost, as a miner. "As early as 1871 Virtue's knowledge of mining had been recognized by President Ulysses S. Grant, who appointed him to a commission that would help plan 'an international exhibition of arts, manufactures, and products of the soil and mine' to be held in Philadelphia in 1876 as part of the centennial celebration of American independence." Gary Dielman, editor, "'May Live and Die a Miner': The 1864 Clarksville Diary of James W. Virtue," *Oregon Historical Quarterly*, Spring 2004; http://www.historycooperative.org/journals/ohq/105.1/dielman.html; accessed 2 April 2007.

[13] H. K. Hines, "Emigrant Wagon," February 19, 1885, 2.

[14] Psalms 104: 10 (King James Version).

[15] Judson, *A Pioneer's Search*, 64.

[16] Franzwa, *Oregon Trail Revisited,* 351.

[17] H. K. Hines, "Emigrant Wagon," February 19, 1885, 2.

[18] Judson, *A Pioneer's Search,* 64, 65.

[19] Gustavus Hines, *A voyage round the world,* 138-40, 423-425.

[20] William H. Gray, *A History of Oregon, 1792-1849,* (Portland, 1870).

[21] William Gray, a missionary to the Cayuse, was less-than-flattering to anybody but himself. Personal communication, Gregory M. Franzwa.

[22] L. M. Kaiser and Priscilla Knuth, eds., "From Ithaca to Clatsop Plains: Miss Ketcham's Journal of Travel," *Oregon Historical Quarterly,* LXII, No. 3 (Sept. 1961), 237-87; LXII, No. 4 (Dec. 1961), pp. 337-402. Rebecca's well-written and insightful journal details a trip under the leadership of Gustavus's acquaintance, William H. Gray, that was far less harmonious than that of the Hines train. The editors' introduction provides further background on W. H. Gray, and others.

[23] "The interstate highway enters the Grand Ronde a few miles west of the emigrant road, but the view is no less spectacular. The valley is seventy-five miles southeast of Pendleton, Oregon." Personal communication, Gregory M. Franzwa.

[24] Franzwa, *Oregon Trail Revisited,* 357.

[25] Kaiser and Knuth, "Miss Ketcham's Journal," 397.

[26] Harvey's translation of the Chinook jargon is consistent with the handy jargon dictionary in the appendix to Palmer's little classic, Joel Palmer, *Journal of Travels over the Rocky Mountains...,* (Cincinnati: J. A. & U. P. James, 1847), 148-150. Relevant to the last phrase quoted by Harvey, Palmer has, "Now-it-k: yes, certainly; Mika: you; Kum-tux,: know, or understand."

[27] H. K. Hines, "Emigrant Wagon," February 26, 1885, 2.

[28] A song entitled "By the Bright Silvery Light of the Moon," (or some slight variation thereof) was popular in the mid-nineteenth century, appearing in English broadsides as early as 1847. The Mudcat Café; http://www.mudcat.org/thread.cfm?threadid=51211; accessed June 5, 2007. As early as the sixteenth century, words to popular songs were printed on sheets of varying lengths known as broadsides. Music was not included, the assumption being the songs would be sung to some designated popular tune. Moon River: Featuring folk music and traditional American river songs; http://crossingmoonriver.blogspot.com/; accessed June 5, 2007.

[29] Judson, *A Pioneer's Search,* 65-67.

[30] H. K. Hines, "Emigrant Wagon," February 25, 1885, 2.

[31] Judson, *A Pioneer's Search,* 68.

[32] Kaiser and Knuth, "Miss Ketcham's Journal," 398.

[33] Holmes identifies this as the Matthew and Mary Ritchie family from Iowa. *Covered Wagon Women*, 121. Matthew and Mary are listed in the 1860 census along with their two children from Iowa, and four more born in Oregon. 1860 U.S. census, Springfield, Lane Co., Oregon; image copy at www.ancestry.com, accessed May 10, 2007.

[34] Meacham, Oreg., is at the confluence of several creeks—Two Mile, Beaver, Meacham, and Tod Creek, and lies just off Interstate 84, about halfway between Pendleton and LaGrande. The historical marker at Meacham reads, in part, "Historic Oregon Trail. Meacham. First known as Lee's Encampment, from establishment of a troop camp by Major H. A. G. Lee in 1844. A. B. and Harvey Meacham operated famous "Mountain House" here, which gave the town its present name." http://www.oregonphotos.com/Meacham.html. Also see Harvey's comment in the ensuing text.

[35] H. K. Hines, "Emigrant Wagon," February 26, 1885, 2.

[36] An uncommon misspelling of Mt. Rainier.

[37] H. K. Hines, "Emigrant Wagon," February 26, 1885, 2.

[38] We learn later from Celinda (see Chapter 16) that Joseph encountered the early-arriving William Gray, who would have been able to report on the location and condition of the Hines party in some detail.

[39] J. W. Hines, *Touching Incidents*, 162, 164.

[40] "A Day on the Columbia River;" www.allthepages.org/archives/2006/08/; accessed June 6, 2007.

15

September 9–17, 1853: To the Banks of the Columbia

*...It seemed, then, the fulfillment of a great purpose
when I stood on the bank of the Columbia, laved my feet in
its crystal flow, drank of its pure waters, bathed my face in
its limpid purity...At all events the thrill of conquest was
in my heart as I stood, that Sabbath morning, on the bank
of the great Columbia.[1]*

—Harvey K. Hines, September 1853

Celinda

Friday, September 9—Pleasant. Some part of the way the road was good but hilly but much better than yesterday. Went 17 miles without water. Had no dinner. Before night we came out of timber & were on hills covered with a little grass. Came on to the Umatilla valley & camped on a branch of that river. Several trains were near, also a trading post.

Harvey

The descent from the mountains was, part of the way, steep and rocky, and we found what looked but a few rods to be nearly four miles before we reached the valley and encamped just by a beautiful spring on a knoll that beautifully overlooked the Umatilla valley.

Large bands of Indian horses were feeding on the beautiful plain, and here and there mounted Indians were galloping across the prairies. Soon some Indian "merchant-men" came to our camp with vegetables and fine fresh beef and we were only too glad to part with a few dollars for potatoes at a dollar a peck, and beef at twenty-five cents a pound. Our supper and breakfast were certainly as "savory" as any that ever Sarah cooked for Abraham or Rebekka for Isaac on the plains of Mamre and Zoar. We had no Sarahs nor Rebekkas, but we had Lydias and Elizabeths, and they knew how to cook a "kid" for their household quite as well as their nomad sisters of that earlier age, and possibly, in all other respects were fully their equals.[2]

Celinda

Saturday, September 10—Pleasant went 5 miles to the river then about

277

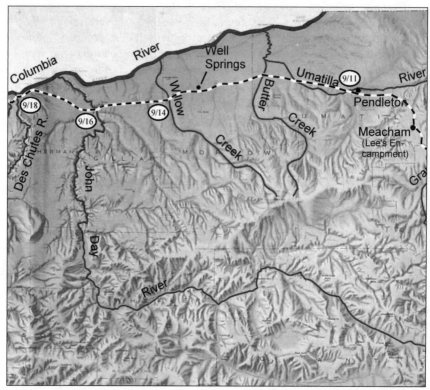

Topographic map of present-day north central Oregon based on a map from the U.S. Dept. of the Interior, showing the path of the Hines party as estimated from Celinda's diary and Harvey's reminiscent account. Date designations are approximate.

2 miles on where we dined. Went down 8 miles. The road was not on the river but the country is a rolling prairie. Camped on the river at night. Timber a species of poplar. Dr Hill's train near.[3]

Sunday, September 11—Crossed the river. On starting Uncle H's wagon upset. No one hurt. Nothing injured except some things…Left the river in about 1½ miles. Up the bottom some and went on to the prairie again. Carried water with us. Dined on the prairie about 4½ miles from the river. Went 9 miles & camped on the river again road good.

Harvey

From this delightful place—the Cayuse Station of so many years since— our road led us down the east side of the Umatilla valley near the foothills for about nine miles, where a point of basalt abutted sharp against the river we forded the stream—my wagon accomplishing the feat of overturning just as it was coming out of the stream, without injury to itself or its occupants—and immediately ascended a long dusty hill to the high prairies north of the river. Just here we met W. C. McKay, now Dr. McKay[4] of Pendleton, Oregon, which town is on the Umatilla about a mile above where we crossed it. Mr. McKay rode by the side of our train for some distance, and here began an acquaintance with him which has continued with increasing pleasure until the present time.

We traveled during the afternoon over a rolling country, covered everywhere with bunch grass, which rippled before the soft September breeze like a vast field of golden grain. At night we again descended a sharp hill to the Umatilla and encamped where there was a great abundance of wild clover, close by the clean pebbly bank of the stream.[5]

Celinda

Monday, September 12—Went about 5 miles, crossed the river, then struck over to a creek ten miles. Road good. Camped for noon 6 miles from starting. Saw at the river a house—The Ind. agency[6]—the first building which looked like civilization since Laramie. Country rolling. A lady came to camp whose husband has died since they started on the plains.

Harvey

Sept. 9. [12][7] Crossed the Umatilla to its south side. The stream was very small, not half as large as where we crossed it about twenty-five miles above, the water having sunk away into the sand. Just after crossing we saw a small house, painted white, about forty rods east of the road, the first house we had seen in four months. On inquiry we found it was the Indian Agency for the Cayuse and Walla Walla tribes. Calling at the house we found Mr. Collins in charge, a gentleman for a quarter of a century afterwards well known in Oregon. He was the father of the gracious lady who presides with such amiable dignity in the Gubernatorial mansion at Salem.[8] We also saw here two Indians celebrated in the annals of Indian life in Oregon. Five Crows and Peupeu-moxmox, the first chief of the Umatillas and the latter of the Walla Wallas.

There was a little flavor of civilization again in the appearance of the painted house, and we started on after dinner with an elevation of feeling that prophesied a speedy end of our journey. Our road during the afternoon, however, did not by any means elevate our hopes. It was barren and sandy, always among sagebrush and thorny cactus, and the hot afternoon sun blazed out of a brassy sky full in our faces. The tired oxen moved forward reluctantly. It was not until after dark that our wheels struck the solider land of a creek bottom, and a few minutes after we stopped our teams by the side of a deep channel in the middle of the bottom, in which were a few little pools of water. It was called "Butter Creek." It was late before our "house-work" was completed and we were again ready to stretch our wearied limbs on our ground-bed for rest; but when it came it *was* rest.[9]

Celinda

Tuesday, September 13—Went 18 miles over a rolling country without water except what we carried for culinary purposes. Road good. Scenery pretty. Camped for night by a spring. I have drank more unhealthy water but never muddier…camps near. Wind blew very hard all the PM. Dust very oppressive. Sand blew into the tent during supper so as to cover the dishes. Rained at night.

Harvey

Sept. 10.[13] Our drive today was eighteen miles, up long, sloping hills, through sharp ravines, across high, bunch grass prairies, sometimes toiling though blistering sands, then rolling over solid and beautiful roads, and not a drop of water in the entire distance. In the afternoon the wind began to blow from the west with great violence and grew stronger as the day declined until when we reached our intended camp at "Well Springs"[10] it was sweeping through the sandy valley where they were with fearful velocity. It was very cold. Overcoats and blankets were necessary to keep us at all comfortable. We could build no fire, and cook no supper, and after locking our wagon wheels to keep the wagons from sailing away before the wind, went into them, tied down the curtains as closely as possible and tried to sleep, but the whistling and moaning of the wind through all the night gave us little slumber. Our eyes watched for the morning, and we were glad when the dawn appeared.[11]

Phoebe

After crossing the Umatilla river our road led us over a desperate country—up and down steep hills and through rocky canyons, in which grew nothing but sage brush and thorny cactus, many times traveling all day under a scorching sun, without water, our eyes, ears, nose and mouth filled with dust. One night in particular, I shall never forget. We were obliged to make a day camp—the wind was blowing a hurricane so that we were unable to build even a sage brush fire. Locking the wheels of the wagons to keep the wind from running them down a chasm, we went thirsty, hungry and dusty to bed.

Strange to relate, while the wind was buffeting the wagons with such force that they seemed in imminent danger every moment of turning bottom side up, I fell asleep and dreamed we were living in our "ideal home" on Puget Sound, except that the ideal was lacking, for it was located on the wrong side of the river, and I was not at all pleased with the home of my vision. Glad was I to wake and find it only a dream.

These experiences of the old pioneers while crossing the plains in an emigrant wagon in the early days, to California and Oregon, for the purpose of digging gold and carving out homes for themselves on donation and pre-emption claims, will never be forgotten; and I doubt if a tract of land equal to that given to Fernando de Soto in Florida (which was ninety miles long and forty wide) would tempt them to again pass through those terrible experiences.[12]

Celinda

Wednesday, September 14—Road very much as yesterday if any thing more hilly. Not so windy as yesterday. No water. Made 18 miles. Camped on a creek. A trading post was near kept by a gentleman from Oswego County. 18 graves near. Several camps around. Have passed trading posts nearly every day since we left Grand Ronde.

Harvey

Sept. 11.[14] When morning came the wind abated, and we were only too happy to be able to build a fire out of the sage brush and cook supper for last night and breakfast for this morning at once.

Our road was still on the bunch grass plains, broken by sandy canyons. The canyons were all filled with sage brush, but the plains were a great meadow of ripened grass. There was no water for twelve miles when we came to another channel through a narrow bottom in which were pools of water. This channel was called Willow Creek. We reached it about noon, got our dinner and remained about two hours, then drove forward into the dry, grassy hills about ten miles and camped without wood or even sage brush, but with abundance of excellent grass for our stock.[13]

Celinda

Thursday, September 15—Several horses & cattle were missing & we remained in camp till after dinner when all were found. Went about 10 miles. Very hilly. Road good. Cold & windy. Scenery pretty when on the hills. Made a...

Harvey

On the 12th [15th], after a few miles our road struck the head of a dry hollow, apparently the bed of some ancient stream, which with an almost even width of sixty or eighty rods wound among the yellow hills toward the west. We followed it for several hours and came at last to a small spring bubbling out of a sandy hillside near which stood a juniper tree; hence the place was called "Juniper Springs." It was a very desolate dreary place, and our camp was anything but a pleasant one. We had been traveling for a week directly towards Mount Hood. It looked, a week ago, so near that it seemed we could reach it in a day, but day after day we had stretched through the weary hours toward it, in the heat and dust, anxious to drink from its snowy fountains, but it seemed no nearer now than when we first saw it the day we stood on the summit of the Blue Mountains. In recalling the impressions of those days we are reminded of the journal of the emigrant over the plains of Colorado many years later. He had not yet learned the clearness of the atmosphere of the inter-mountain regions and so he wrote: "July 10, Pike's Peak in plain view. Shall reach it by dinner." Next day he wrote: "July 11, Pike's Peak in plainer view, hope to get there by supper." Next day he wrote: "Pike's Peak in still plainer view. The Lord only knows when we will get there." So it seemed to us as day after day we traveled directly toward the hoary pinnacle up there against that blue western sky.[14]

Celinda

Friday, September 16—Went about a mile & over hills & then came into a valley went up it 9 miles to a spring then struck over the hills to John Days river.[15] The descent to the river is steep & rocky in some places but smooth most of the way. Dined by the river then crossed & ascended a very bad hill. Very long & rocky much more so than any we had passed before. The river is about 3…from the spring. Went two miles from the river & made a dry camp. After ascending the hill we came to two roads one leading to the upper & the other to the lower ferry of the DeShoots river. We took the lower road because the river is sometimes fordable at the lower ferry.[16]

Harvey

Sept. 12th[16th] In the morning we ascended quite a hill out of the long hollow in which we had been traveling, and, in a few miles, found ourselves on a bald summit almost overhanging a gorge cleft through the basaltic rock apparently to the depth of two or three thousand feet. In the bottom of the gorge was a small strip of green bottom land, and in the middle of this the silver ribbon of a stream called "John Day's River" glittered in the sunlight.

The road dropped over the face of the escarpment at a point where the attrition of ages of frost and snow and wind and rain had worn and ground the perpendicular basaltic rock away so as to permit us to go down without absolutely falling over a precipice. We reached the "river" in a little over an hour and halting on its banks made a cup of coffee, took our noon lunch, and then filling our water kegs from its clear current, drove up to the opposite heights, along a very rocky canyon, and after reaching the beautiful grassy plain on their summit, made our camp for the night. Mount Hood was "in plain sight." There seemed absolutely nothing between us and it, and had we not understood the illusion of vision so usual on the plains we would have been sure we could ride to its snow in an hour.[17]

Phoebe

At John Day's river we stopped only long enough to fill our water kegs and then drove on up the canyon to a grassy plain and encamped for the night.

Indians often swarmed around the wagon while in camp, begging for food. One more hideous than I had yet seen came to our wagon while Mr. Judson was away with the stock, and begged for bread. As I had none to give him, I continued singing to my baby. He sat down on the wagon tongue and mocked me. It makes me smile now, when I think of the ugly faces he made, but when he began mocking my baby, it filled me with indignation. I paid no attention, though much afraid, and he soon tired of the performance.[18]

Celinda

Saturday, September 17—Rather cold. Road hilly but good. Went 15 miles without water. Camped near…of very impure water. A trading post near by flour 25 a pound. First came in sight of Mount Rainier.

Harvey

Sept. 13th[17th] Our road was over high prairies, covered with most luxuriant bunch grass all day. Just toward evening it descended a sharp hill and entered a little valley down which we traveled a mile or so and came to a spring which afforded a scant supply of water. Just below the spring the hollow dropped off into a rocky gorge with walls of columnar basalt, which were broken and ground into splinters and blocks, and lay in sublime confusion down the gorge. Looking down the gorge to the north the great river flow of the Columbia[19] was before us, though two or three miles away. It was our first view of the mighty river toward which we had been looking and journeying so long. We stood and gazed upon it, and felt the thrill of the successful explorer in our hearts as when the goal of hopes attained rises to the vision.

While we were conversing myself and wife noticed an emigrant wagon standing entirely apart from any company, and by it stood a woman who was engaged in trading off some garments to an Indian for a salmon. It occurred to one or both of us that she would not be doing that if they were not reduced to destitution: as the garments were such as they could not afford to spare. We walked slowly down to where she stood bargaining with the Indian for the purpose of ascertaining if she was in absolute want. We found a very pleasant-faced woman of middle age, and, on inquiring about her trip, soon, by that amazing necromancy that reveals kindred hearts to each other, ascertained, without her telling us, that she was a Methodist. There was a tone of trust and a presence of piety in what she said that showed that she had brought some of her faith with her all across the plains: and had not, as too many did, boxed up her religion and sent it around by water while they came overland without it. After a few moments conversation I returned to our own camp and left the two women alone. I knew that one would not be long in finding out all that she ought to know about the other. In a little time Mrs. H[ines] returned. She had found out that the family of this emigrant woman had been entirely out of food and money for quite a number of days, and had been trading away necessary clothing with the Indians for salmon which had constituted almost their entire living. But still the noble, trusting woman had said: "We shall get through. God has not brought us so nearly through the wilderness to let us die just on the borders of the promised land. We have kept our faith and He will keep His promise." Of course some bread and meat and tea and sugar and such other things as our scant stores afforded went down, "in a woman's apron," from our wagon to theirs—for what woman would let a sister suffer while she herself had bread?

It was a calm and beautiful night this. The air was soft and still and seldom had we passed a more refreshing and delightful night on the entire journey.

Sept. 14 [18] It was Sunday morning, but water was so scarce for our cattle that it seemed a necessity for us to move to a more eligible camp. Before going, however, we went again to see our friends of yesternight, and offer them aid in reaching the Willamette valley, if they would travel with us. Their faith in providence had, however, been justified in another way. A gentleman from the valley had proffered to furnish them abundance of food and pay all other expenses, for one yoke of their oxen, and they had accepted his offer, and would soon start "over the mountains." We bade them "good-bye." They arrived safely in the valley, and though entirely destitute of money or food found friends and Christian sympathy, and in a very few years had a good home and were in comfortable temporal circumstances. "God careth for his own."

A few miles from our camp brought us to where the road descended the Columbia bluff, just below what is now known as Spanish Hollow, and we stopped for a few moments on the sandy shore of the mighty river. At last on its banks! River of the hopes, desires, and imagination of my boyhood! With Olney's Atlas[20] before me I had sat for hours, day after day, when I was from seven to fifteen years of age and studied the long flow of the grand river from its fountains in the mountains to its burial place in the sea. I had said in my heart, I shall one day stand on its banks. I had traced the line and limits of the "Great American Desert" and, with the stories of Captain Riley and others on the great African Sahara stimulating imagination, had pictured myself traversing this great desert on a camel, almost a wild Bedouin myself. The great "unexplored regions" that stretched from far east of the Rockies to the Pacific, and from about the 35 to the 45 degrees of north latitude had a strange charm to my eyes, and my soul sung its prophesy of adventure in these unknown wilds. It seemed, then, the fulfillment of a great purpose when I stood on the bank of the Columbia, laved my feet in its crystal flow, drank of its pure waters, bathed my face in its limpid purity. True, I had come in a way and for a purpose I did not forecast in my boyhood's dreams, but I had come. The camels with which, in my early thoughts, I would sail the desert sea were changed to oxen: the fleets of the caravan were transformed into "prairie schooners:" the wild huntsman's garb and prowess were changed into a commission of the gospel of peace: but I had come: and who shall say these dreams of my boyhood were not God's way to prepare my heart for the purpose and work of my life? At all events the thrill of conquest was in my heart as I stood, that Sabbath morning, on the bank of the great Columbia.[21]

Phoebe

Mt. Hood had been in view for several days, the transparent atmosphere, annihilating space, made it appear but a short distance away. We traveled towards it slowly and patiently, day after day, never seeming to diminish the distance between us, when finally, one Sunday morning, while searching for a good resting place for our stock, we suddenly came onto the banks of the great Columbia. At last, at last, at long last, we were surely near the end of our journey.[22]

As the overlanders continued their westward trek, Joseph had left Portland and was making his way eastward to meet them.

Joseph

As it was uncertain which route my folks would take, I was advised to go up to the Dalles and await their coming there. So I took the advice, and, traveling the usual route[23] in about twelve hours, arrived at the place of destination. I put up with a friend with whom I had become acquainted in Portland, and sought his advice in regard to my future movements: About midnight, we were aroused by a voice at the door of our tent with the inquiry, "Is there any one in the place that can perform the marriage ceremony?" He was answered in the affirmative by my friend and told that inside the tent there was a Methodist preacher who could attend to such matters when desirable. A few words explained the situation. There stood a neat and gentlemanly appearing young man, and at his side a blushing damsel of about 18 years of age. The young man said they were all from Missouri,[24] were all members of the Methodist Church, and were camped miles out near the crossing of the Des Chutes River, and would be in town as soon as possible in the morning. They desired to be married without delay so as return to the camp before they were missed. I told them that I would require a clear, truthful statement of the exact situation before I would consent to perform the ceremony. They told me that the mother of the girl was willing and anxious for them to be married before their leaving home, but the father, who was of a miserly turn, was unwilling because the young man was poor. To avoid the marriage of his daughter to this poor young man, he had sold his property and crossed the plains with his entire family. Such was the attachment of the young people to each other that the young man had taken the next train and had followed the girl across the plains. Last night he had made himself known to the mother and daughter, and had come in together to the business that they had so ardently desired. I then performed the ceremony making them man and wife. I then told them to return immediately, acquaint the mother of all that had happened, and I would be out early and have a talk with the father. They promised strict compliance with my request, and shaking them by the hand, while a glistening teardrop trembled over the fair, sweet face of the happy bride, I invoked the blessing of God upon them in all their future life.

Early in the morning, having procured a good riding horse of my friend, I rode out to the camp, and, speeding over the rolling prairie, soon drew rein at the door of the tent and asked to see the proprietor of the same. The father of the bride came to the door, and, with a quiet, yet somewhat abrupt, tone, asked what I desired. I asked him if his wife was in the tent, and being answered in the affirmative, inquired if it would be agreeable to them to hold a few moments' interview with me alone. He gave his consent, but intimated that they were in a great hurry, and wished the interview to be as brief as possible. I then related the events of the past night, and told him that if he would remain a few days at the Dalles, I had a friend there who would be able to give them some information of especial value to the whole family. I told him that I was out on the plains to meet brothers who had crossed the plains in present year, and I presumed would soon be in the Dalles. He said he intended to stop there for several days and he would wait there for my return. I told him that as we had all come a long distance, to build up homes in a new and strange land, we should strive to help each other as much as possible. Evidently the old man felt a little sore over the course things had taken, but I gained my point in getting him to wait my return.

They soon moved on into the Dalles and pitched their tent for a few days' rest, and to await my return, while I rode down the hill towards the Des Chutes River to meet my brothers, whom I knew could not be many miles away.[25]

Epilogue: The Young Couple

From a published history of Wasco Co, Oregon,[26] we learn that the young couple married by Joseph in September of 1853 were George Snipes and Martha Imbler. The story of their courtship and marriage became part of the folklore of early Wasco County. Below we quote directly from William

H. McNeal's *History of Wasco County, Oregon,* retaining, as elsewhere, the spelling and punctuation in the original. Only three of the seven purported versions of this tale are specifically noted by McNeal. We will quote excerpts from each of these three versions. The general story line is the same in each version, but many details differ. For example, in the three different references to the preacher involved, one (mis)identifies him as "Rev. Gustavus Hines,"[27] one as "Rev. Hines," and only the last one as "Joseph Hines."

The George Snipes Love Story

This is the No. 1 pioneer love story in the history of Wasco county. We have read 7 different versions of this story by that many writers. While the thread of the different stories were the same there were some bits of meat in one that was mission in another. Some facts mentioned herein may be new to the reader who has not read all 7 versions.

A cussing father, a haughty youth, a pretty maid, those were the factors of a True Pioneer Romance of The Dalles; so said the *Portland Oregonian* in 1920.

George Snipes was born (1832) near Raleigh, N.C. At age 5 he went to Tenn. with his parents and in 1850 they went to Iowa.

Martha Imbler, a daughter of Pater Imbler was born (1836) at Louisville, Ky. And her family went to Iowa in 1850.

Emigrants for Oregon were notified in 1852 to meet at Keokuk and it was there that George Snipes and Wm. Luce met. George hired to Luce as an ox driver to Oregon for next March. On the Old Oregon Trail, headed west, one day George's team came to a creek where Pater Imbler's oxen stalled and no amount of gouging could get them started. When George had made the opposite bank, Imbler called to him for help to get the Imbler team out of the mire. Snipes replied that he had troubles of his own and had no time to devote to the draying business.

This angered Imbler and he spoke unprintable words to Snipes, who replied in like kind; about this time a pretty girl put her beautiful head out of the wagon canvass and laughed. George Snipes smiled back. That was their introduction and the beginning of the greatest pioneer love story in the recorded history of Wasco county![28]

According to George Snipes himself, the above version already diverges from fact. Snipes indicates that he knew Martha Imbler well before they started on the trail. The following excerpts are from George's own account.

The reason I came to Oregon when I did, leaving my family, was because of my girl. She was leaving Iowa for Oregon with the spring emigration with the Imbler family. I took the next ox-train that left 2 weeks later. We did not overtake the Imbler train until we reached Salmon Falls, Idaho. Then we traveled a day behind or a day ahead until we reached The Dalles on the 16th of September when I was a day ahead of their train. I was 21 years old the day we entered South Pass. I came with the Luces, 2 brothers...

... As we were hitching up to start [from Fairfield, on 10 Mile Creek], intending to take the Barlow Pass road into the Valley, I saw a card on the ground and picking it up I saw the name of Dr. C.W. Shaug of The Dalles on it. I had known him in Iowa where he was our family physician. I asked one of the boys to drive to 15 Mile (Dufur) while I went to town to see Dr. Shaug and would meet them later at 15 Mile. The doctor was out to his ranch, the place I now have. He thought I ought to stop at The Dalles and offered to help pick out a place here for me.

I told him that was what I wanted but that I had to go on as I was going to get married when I got to the valley; that the old man wouldn't give me his girl and that I would have to steal her as soon as I got there. He wanted to know if the girl was willing to be stolen and I told him she said, "yes".

"Well why not steal her and stay here?" he asked, "I'll get some fellows to go with you and I'll furnish the horses and I know where I can get a side saddle for the girl; and you can steal her now. Let's go back to town and talk it over with my wife."

We went back to town and Mrs. Shaug was delighted with the plan and I concluded to try it. They told me to go into the tent and write a letter to Martha telling her just what to do. In the meantime the doctor got Jim Thompson and Jim Griffin to go with me and he furnished the cayuses for the three of us and one with a side-saddle for the girl. When we got to 15 Mile (Dufur) we found my train but the Imblers had gone. We went on to the Brookhouse place and found the Imblers had made a dry camp.

Griffin and myself waited at a safe distance while Thompson rode to camp. He tied his horse to a wagon and went to where they were eating supper. He asked for Mr. Imbler and told a yarn about expecting to meet a brother with that train. He was asked to eat supper but replied that he had just had supper but would be sociable and drink a cup of coffee with them. On waiting until Miss Imbler went to the wagon, he made an excuse to tend to his horse and managed to give her the note. He returned to the campfire and told so many yarns that when he finally took leave the old man became suspicious and called the men together and told them he believed that a gang was coming to steal their stock. They all got excited, rounded up the stock and stood guard over them.

When Miss Imbler got the letter, she called her sister who brought a candle and they read it together. By the time she was ready to start the cattle had been rounded up and her two brothers were standing guard over them directly opposite her wagon. There was nothing to do but wait with patience for an opportunity to escape. While the boys were talking with their backs to the wagon she slipped away and walked down the road to where we three were waiting for her. Upon joining us we quickly mounted and started for The Dalles where we arrived at 2:30 A.M. at Dr. Shaug's tent.

We told him everything was all right and he said, "I have good news for you. I have a preacher here. Rev. Hines came up on the boat[29] to meet a brother."

We had expected to have to go to Portland to be married. The doctor called in several witnesses and we were married within an hour after our arrival.[30]

We are tempted to conclude the Snipes' story with, "...and they lived happily ever after." In fact, George and Martha prospered at farming, and raised a family of fourteen children. And in the 1870s George reconciled with his father-in-law.

In 1877 Mr. Imbler came to Mr. Snipes and acknowledged his mistake in opposing the marriage of George Snipes, a penniless young man, to his daughter Martha. He had not reckoned with the determination of Mr. Snipes, who left home a penniless boy to work his way across the U.S. as an ox-team driver, 2000 miles to Oregon, so as to be near as possible to his sweetheart and be able to marry her at the first opportunity! His father-in-law needed a loan of money and Mr. Snipes made the loan to Mr. Imbler which indicated all was forgiven and no permanent hard feelings existed between the two. If more young men of today (1952) had to work their way across the U.S. to get their sweethearts, marriages would be more secure and permanent.[31]

---

[1] H. K. Hines, "Emigrant Wagon," March 5, 1885, 2.

[2] H. K. Hines, "Emigrant Wagon," February 26, 1885, 2.

[3] See note for Celinda's Sept. 12 diary entry.

[4] William Cameron McKay and his two brothers, John T., and Alexander, accompanied Jason Lee in 1838 on a trip east. W. C. McKay was enrolled in a medical school in Fairfield, New York, later returning to Oregon where he became a prominent physician in Pendleton. Brosnan, *Jason Lee*, 99, 103. The three McKay brothers maintained a trading post near present-day Pendleton, according to Kaiser and Knuth, *Miss Ketcham's Journal*, 399. This is likely the trading post referred to by Celinda in her Sept. 9 diary entry.

[5] H. K. Hines, "Emigrant Wagon," February 26, 1885, 2.

[6] On Sept. 12, 1853, the roster of immigrants recorded at the Umatilla Indian Agency included: G. Hinds w 1d [presumably Gustavus, with wife and daughter]; Mrs. Hines 1s 1d [must be Obadiah's family]; H. Hudson w 1s 1d [probably Holden Judson and family]; C. Bryant w 1s 1d [Charles Bryant family]; some Martins that may have included Mr. Martin in Hines company; and H Hines w [Harvey and wife]; *The Oregonian*, Portland, Oregon, October 22, 1853, 1. Also on the roster are Hill, Dr. R. C., w, 6s, 3d, affirming Celinda's Sept. 11 comment, "Dr Hill's train near."

[7] For several days in mid-September, Harvey's dating of entries in his reminiscent account are in accord with neither the calendar, nor with Celinda's diary entries for matching events. Given that Celinda's diary is contemporaneous with the events, and that it consistently matches the calendar (For example, September 9, 1853, was indeed a Friday, as her diary states), we accept her date designations in favor of Harvey's.

[8] Harvey's implication here seems to be that the wife of the governor of Oregon at the time of writing, i.e., 1885, was the daughter of this Mr. Collins. But in 1885, the governor of Oregon was Z. F. Moody, and according to his biography, he married Mary Stephenson in 1863; no other spouse is mentioned. Early Public Lands Surveyors in the Northwest, Zena Ferry Moody, http://www.plso.org/readingroom/moody.htm; accessed April 16, 2007.

[9] H. K. Hines, "Emigrant Wagon," March 5, 1885, 2.

[10] "Well Spring is near the southern border of the Boardman Bombing Range, and although it is no longer used for that purpose, permission is still required to enter the site." Personal communication, Gregory M. Franzwa.

[11] H. K. Hines, "Emigrant Wagon," March 5, 1885, 2.

[12] Judson, *A Pioneer's Search*, 68, 69.

[13] H. K. Hines, "Emigrant Wagon," March 5, 1885, 2.

[14] H. K. Hines, "Emigrant Wagon," March 5, 1885, 2.

[15] "Today at times the John Day is only ankle deep and visitors can wade across it. It was

easy to ford the Deschutes at the mouth, as a great delta has been formed there. These travelers evidently forded north of there." Personal communication, Gregory M. Franzwa.

[16] As will be seen in the next chapter, a surprise awaited them at the lower ferry. Might they have missed this if they had chosen the upper ferry?

[17] H. K. Hines, "Emigrant Wagon," March 5, 1885, 2.

[18] Judson, *A Pioneer's Search,* 69, 70.

[19] "The first view of the Columbia today is reached at Biggs, Oregon." Personal communication, Gregory M. Franzwa.

[20] "Jesse Olney, 1798-1872, American geographer and teacher. His *Practical System of Modern Geography* (1828), a standard work for decades, revolutionized the teaching of geography." Infoplease online encyclopedia, http://www.infoplease.com/ce6/people/A0836595.html; accessed March 22, 2007.

[21] H. K. Hines, "Emigrant Wagon," March 5, 1885, 2.

[22] Judson, *A Pioneer's Search,* 70.

[23] That is, Joseph went up the Columbia River, with a portage around the Cascades. See later notes.

[24] Joseph was either misinformed or he had a memory slip when writing this reminiscence later. The young couple were actually from Iowa. (See following epilogue to this chapter.)

[25] J. W. Hines, *Touching Incidents,* 164, 166.

[26] William H. McNeal, *History of Wasco County, Oregon* (The Dalles, Oreg., 1953) 87-90.

[27] In a curious twist, it was this erroneous reference to Gustavus that led us to this story. It was while involved in a separate project that we were searching for references to Gustavus and came across this item. At first we were surprised to find Gustavus involved in this strange episode, but as we read on, we recognized some familiar features of the story told by Joseph. More recently we encountered another departure from accuracy. The obituary writer for Martha Imbler Snipes claims, "...the young couple were united in marriage by Rev. H. K. Hines." 'MARTHA SNIPES DEAD FROM TYPHOID PNEUMONIA,' *The Dalles Chronicle*, October 25, 1901.

[28] McNeal, *History of Wasco County,* 87.

[29] Note that this clarifies Joseph's route from Portland to The Dalles. He came up the Columbia River, rather than the alternate route over the Cascade Mountains.

[30] McNeal, *History of Wasco County,* 87, 88.

[31] McNeal, *History of Wasco County,* 90.

16

September 18–27, 1853: Surprise at Deschutes River

> *...Before crossing we very unexpectedly met Uncle
> Joseph Hines who was sent out as a missionary after we
> left NY...We were almost overjoyed at so unexpected a
> meeting.*
>
> —Celinda Hines, September 18, 1853

The Hines family reunion at the Deschutes River on September
18, 1853, must have been a joyous occasion for all. To the overlanders, still
grieving for the loss of Obadiah less than a month earlier, Joseph's surprise
appearance may well have seemed like the return of another departed brother,
for they had said good-bye in New York with the expectation they might
never see each other again in this life. And though the reunion was no
surprise to Joseph, who had planned it, he was surely pleased to be reunited
with family he had not seen for nearly seven months.[1] Moreover, we can
almost see the pride on Joseph's face as he demonstrates his economical
means for crossing the Deschutes, and goes on to describe how he single-
handedly "destroyed the Des Chutes Ferry." But "Pride goeth before a fall,"
or in the form more familiar to the Hineses, "Pride goeth before destruction,
and an haughty spirit before a fall."[2] We will leave it for Harvey to relate,
with undisguised amusement, his older brother's faltering follow-through
in the days after their reunion.

Joseph

...I rode down the hill towards the Des Chutes River to meet
my brothers, whom I knew could not be many miles away. When I
arrived at the ferry landing, I found the boat had just crossed to the
opposite side of the river, where alone there was a chance to rest
before starting on the last 15 miles to the Dalles. On the opposite
side, from a small elevation, one could see the road for nearly four
miles away, and I was anxious to see if there were any trains of
emigrants now at hand. So I called to the ferryman to come and take
me over, and offered him the dollar which the law required. He refused

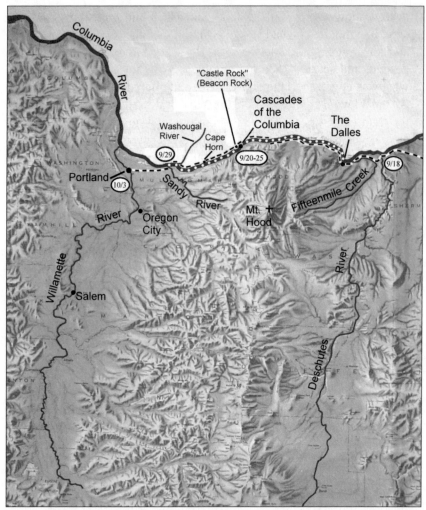

Topographic map of present-day northwest Oregon based on a map from the U.S. Dept. of the Interior, showing the path of the Hines party as estimated from Celinda's diary and Harvey's reminiscent account. Date designations are approximate.

to come, and told me to wait unto the next train came up and then he would come. I informed him that I had come all the way from Portland to meet some friends, and the next train, which was then about one mile away, might be the train, and I desired to meet them on the other side. He turned abruptly away, saying he could do nothing for me. "Very well," I replied, "then I will help myself." I rode up to an Indian nearby, showed him a silver dollar and asked him to lead my horse over. In a moment he had tossed his lariat over the head of my horse and was dragging me into the river. He seemed to understand what I desired, and seemed to know exactly to do. They soon discovered what was going on at the ferry above, and offered to come over and get me if I would go back. I told them that I guessed I would wait until the train came up, then we would all go back together. We passed safely over, the water in no place being higher than the horse's knees. The stream having divided about 300 yards below the ferry, it was easily fordable on horseback. Strangers, of course, knew nothing about this, and the ferry people, by exaggeration and deception, had kept it a secret a great length of time.

As soon as I was over, I at once rode up to a little elevation, and there, right before my eyes, was the train I had come nearly 200 miles to meet. I knew them at a glance, but I was entirely unrecognized by them, although six months before they had left my house in the State of New York. So I turned back, and, riding down near the river, awaited their arrival. In a few moments, my elder brother, leading by the hand his little adopted daughter, the only child of Rev. Jason Lee, the founder of the Oregon Missions. They were walking leisurely along, searching for a suitable place to stop their wagons. I was sitting upon my horse not 100 feet away when they went by, barely giving me a casual glance. After selecting a suitable place, they started to inform the incoming team. This led them a little nearer to me. All at once, the little girl paused, looked up towards my face, her great blue eyes dilating with wonder and awe; she lifted up her little hand and cried out, "Papa! papa! come here! Come here!" all the time staring wildly at my face. Brother, no less excited than the little girl, cried out, "Merciful Heavens, Joseph, is that you, or is it your ghost?" I guess the Des Chutes River never saw a more surprised and excited crowd than stood on its banks at that hour.

We were soon refreshed and brought to our senses by a cup of Aunt Lydie's tea, and we mutually agreed that no explanation should be required of the ghost who had a few moments before entered camp; as it had acted towards Aunt Lydie's tea just as the original did way back in the State of New York, until a more convenient season arrived. The entire company was called together for consultation, as a crisis evidently was near at hand. I had provided myself with about $20.00 to pay my expenses on the trip, not thinking that an emergency might arise like the present. In talking the matter over, I incidentally alluded to my adventure with the Indian in getting over the river, and gave it as my opinion that we had no use for a ferryboat. I told them that if they were willing to take the risk, I would guide them over the stream the same way I had come. I mounted my horse, rode over, showing them the marks I had made on the shore, and on my return all concluded to make the venture. My youngest brother, who, by the way, was celebrated as an expert driver, and had a well trained team, was selected to take the lead the rest were to follow close behind. All were instructed that, in case of the upsetting of a wagon, by the swift running waters, to be sure to seize hold of some secure part of cover and not be separated from it, to roll up the curtains of the cover so as not to be caught under them. I put my lariat around the off ox which was the fartherest down stream. All being ready, the word was given and the long lash whirled over the backs of the oxen, the riders driving the loose stock pressed close behind and in just about 15 minutes after the wheels of the first wagon had touched the run of the river, the last of our three teams had reached the opposite shore. Other teams came rolling up behind us, and others behind them, leaving a well beaten track, which revealed the deception of the Des Chutes ferry and numbered it with the things that were. A ferry has not been run there from that day to this, and in all probability never will be again, as a railroad bridge has been built a short distance above, and a well known ford is all that is needed for local travel, except in very high water. And that is the way I destroyed the Des Chutes Ferry. So perish all liars and deceivers, who seize on the gifts of God to man and strive to deceive and rob the people.[3]

Celinda

Sunday, September 18—Pleasant. Went 5 miles to the Columbia down it about 2 then we forded the DeShoots near its mouth. It is a large river & very rapid. Before crossing we very unexpectedly met Uncle Joseph Hines who was sent out as a missionary after we left NY. He left NY May 20th [should be June] with his family who are now near Portland all well. He ascertained from Mr Grey who had arrived at P[ortland] our whereabouts & came out to meet us. We were almost overjoyed at so unexpected a meeting. Uncle J piloted us across the river (An indian had just done the same for him). The current was so strong that it was almost impossible to guide the oxen & prevent them from going down stream. We came very near upsetting in the river in very deep water & the current was so strong. We went out 4 miles & camped near a stream. Our road was very hilly. Mr Marsh left us this morning but is still in the train.

Harvey

When the road reached the Columbia, there was nothing but the great river to interest us, except the utter sterility and desolation of the spot. It was a wilderness of sand dunes, without a blade of grass, or a tree or shrub to cast a cooling shade over us. One side of us was the wide flow of the river, and on the other tall basaltic cliffs only a few hundred feet from the water's edge. Though it was Sunday it was impossible for us to camp in this desolation, and so, after a half hour's rest just at the river's brink, we drove on down the stream hoping to find, ere long, a place to spend at least part of the sacred day in quietude. About five miles below where we descended the bluff, we came to Des Chutes River; a bold, strong stream, cleaving the giant hills to their foundations, and rushing over a rent and chasmed bed of basalt into the Columbia in several foaming rapids—hence its name.

As we approached the latter stream, G[ustavus] H[ines]' team was in the advance and mine in the rear of the train, and about thirty or forty rods apart. Noticing that he had stopped, and was conversing with a gentleman not belonging to our train, dressed in black clothes and wearing a "plug hat,"[4] —a very "unprofessional garb" for an emigrant—I stopped my own team and walked down toward them. The gentleman in black stood his back towards me, not less than twenty rods distant, but I had scarcely stepped out of the dust of the wagon, until I recognized him as our brother, J. W. Hines, whom I had bidden "good-bye" on the morning of the seventh day of March in the old parsonage of Warsaw, N.Y., of which station he was then pastor. We had not the slightest intimation or suspicion that he was nearer us than that place until he met us here. About the first of June the Bishop having charge of the Oregon work had proffered him a transfer, which he accepted, and coming by the way of Panama, had already been six weeks in Oregon, and had come thus far eastward to meet us. It was, as all will imagine, a wonderful surprise, and our greetings were full of thankfulness.

After stopping but a few minutes for conversation, as there was not a blade of grass for our stock near where we were, we forded the Des Chutes in the midst of its foaming rapids, and then ascended the great hill to its westward, and almost immediately descended one just as great to a beautiful little valley where was excellent grass, through which meandered a clear rivulet known as "Fifteen Mile Creek," where we encamped.

Soon after we had pitched our tents there came to our wagons a medium sized young man, with raven black hair and deep black eyes, who then became known to us as a young local preacher, and who, like ourself, was on the way to "Oregon." Then began an acquaintance with this man, that circumstances afterward made very intimate and that was continued with uninterrupted confidence and pleasure for thirty-two years. A year or two after he entered the Oregon Conference as a traveling preacher, and yet remains in the body, a careful, prudent, true-hearted man and minister. He and the excellent family with which God has blessed him can be found now in the parsonage at Hillsboro, Oregon and his name[5] is Nelson Clark.[6]

Phoebe

How our drooping spirits revived under the magical inspiration of the very name of "Columbia river." This name had long been associated with all that was desirable in the new country. And now we stood upon the bank of its mighty rushing waters. There was nothing attractive in the scene, not a tree, spear of grass, or vegetation of any kind to be seen, so we drove on down the river for a few miles and came to the Des Chutes river. Its bed was filled with great boulders, against which the rapid waters dashed and foamed as it sped on its way into the Columbia, making a hazardous fording place.

Here we met another of the Hines brothers, who was waiting to meet his out-coming relatives. We were obliged to continue our journey to find food for our stock, and after climbing several high hills came to a beautiful grassy valley, through which meandered a clear rippling stream called Fifteen Mile creek, and thankfully made our encampment for the night.[7]

When they reach The Dalles, the Hines party make a change in plans. As Harvey put it, they "…had determined, instead of attempting to cross [the Cascade Mountain Range] by the wagon road, to pass it by the way of the Columbia River." Celinda indicates that this decision was based on the advice of Joseph.[8] Whatever the reason, this choice of route committed the travelers to a zigzag path alternating between the river itself and then on one or another of its banks. The following summary will help readers find their own way through the sometimes confusing narrative.

Departing The Dalles, Gustavus, Harvey, some of the other men, and all the women and children board a small, makeshift steamboat to go by river to the Cascade rapids, while Joseph and the rest of the men start driving the cattle down the south bank of the river. The plan is for the men and cattle to cross via ferry to the north bank about three quarters of the way along, and meet up with the others at the Upper Cascades, where all will make a north-bank portage around the rapids. Part of the men and cattle arrive at the rendezvous, but Joseph and the rest fail to appear, so Harvey and Gustavus start out on foot along the north bank to search for them. After first missing the ferry crossing, they backtrack, cross to the south bank, and ultimately find Joseph bedridden with the "ague." Harvey then takes Joseph by canoe downstream to the Upper Cascades, and Gustavus helps the other men with the cattle to complete their route.

When the portage has been completed, most of the party, including

William Cullen Bryant, *Picturesque America* (New York, 1872)

View of The Dalles on the Columbia

the still ailing Joseph, board another steamer and take the Columbia farther downstream to the mouth of the Sandy River, about a dozen miles east of Portland, where they await Harvey and several of the men who drive the cattle along the north bank of the Columbia, finally crossing by ferry to the south bank at the Sandy.

Celinda

Monday, September 19—Pleasant. Went about 7 miles over hills & then down the river 3 to the Dalls. It had been our intention to cross the cascades but uncle J advised us to go by the Dalls…our wagons & go ourselves down the river and send the cattle & horses down the pack trail which goes along near the river. In the eve. we went to a store & found a Mr Newell[9] with whom Uncle G was acquainted in Oregon. Dr N was the first man who crossed the plains with wagons. He said he often wished his wagons would break so that he might have an excuse for leaving them but they did not & he came with them, a thing which we have often spoken of as being impossible. The Dr treated us very kindly & gave us some apples.

Harvey

Sept. 15 [19]. We are again involved among the great hills that margin the Columbia on either side and shut it into a vast canyon. We can hear the deep roar of the torrent of the river away to the right as though it chafed in anger at the mighty rocks that hem it in and stay and turn its flow. Our road continued among hills for a few miles and then descended again to the sandy bank of the Columbia, and then continued down its southern bank for a few miles to a sand bar at the mouth of a small stream that came in from the southwest, where we encamped. At this point the city of "The Dalles" is now located. Two or three small buildings, and several traders' tents, with a much larger number of emigrant tents, made the city at that time. However it was considered, as it really was, the advanced outpost of eastward settlement in Oregon. A few "claims" had been taken a couple of miles down the river. The old mission station of Lee and Perkins[10] had stood about a half mile back of where we camped, and some of us made a visit to the place where it had stood. The stone foundations of the buildings were there yet, but the buildings themselves had been destroyed in the Indian war of 1848, following the massacre of Dr. Whitman and wife[11] at Waiiletpu.[12]

Celinda

Tuesday, September 20—Very warm. The men had engaged a barge to take us to the Cascades & we put our things on board & went on ourselves but it began to leak & we were obliged to get off also to remove our baggage. Dr Newell told us if we would leave the baggage until the next day & go down on the steam boat he would be responsible for their safe arrival in a day or two....Martin, Judson, Marsh & Walter with them...& Uncle Joseph went with the cattle. Accordingly we took what provision & clothing was necessary & repaired on board the steam boat Allan which was already crowded with passengers. It is a poor apology for a boat very small having no cabin & we were obliged to seat ourselves as best we could on the floor or whatever we could find to sit upon. This is the only steam boat which plies between the Dalls & the Cascades. It was brought here last spring from the Sacramento being the first steam boat which ever run on that river. Were about 7 hours running down (50 miles). The scenery was very romantic indeed. The banks of the river are mostly perpendicular rocks from one to a hundred feet in height. This river is not so wide as the Ohio but much deeper and unlike that river the waters of the Columbia are clear & pure. We landed on a stony beach after dark but succeeded in finding a sandy place & made our camp. We had brought our beds but had no tents so we made our beds under the star-spangled arch of heaven & thought no one could wish a more magnificent canopy. The bluffs along the river are covered with fir trees, some dense and some very scattered.

Harvey

We had now reached a point in our journey that required a complete change of plan and mode of travel. The Cascade Mountain range was just before us. We had determined, instead of attempting to cross that range by the wagon road, to pass it by the way of the Columbia River. However, there was no road, and our alternative was to transport our wagons and camp impediamenta in the river in such flotilla as we could procure, and drive our cattle down the sinuous and rocky trail, over the rocky mountain points and through the dense underwood of the bottoms. We found Dr. Robert Newell at The Dalles, who owned, or had charge of a Hudson's Bay bateau that lay at the mouth of the creek. This we hired, and loaded all our wagons and camp material into it, but had scarcely pushed it into the stream before it began to sink, the water pouring through every seam in torrents. To unload everything, dry our drenched baggage and provisions, and then find some other vessel to convey us was very necessary though not a very pleasant duty. Our cattle, meanwhile, had been started down the trail, under charge of our brother, J. W. H[ines], who volunteered this service to relieve us, who had, as he thought, become wearied with our long journey, from the great fatigue of the work.

While we were anxiously debating the question of "ways and means" a little strange looking craft called the "Mary" [Celinda says "Allan"] came up the river and landed near us. It was a steamer: at least it was called so: but consisted only of a hull in which was incased a small engine, which propelled it through the water at perhaps five or six miles an hour. We engaged our passage on this craft, and after a voyage of eight or ten hours were landed at the Upper Cascades and pitched our camp on the river bank, just under where the old Block House[13] now stands, on the evening of Sep. ___ [20, according to Celinda] expecting our cattle and horses to arrive by the trail on the following day.[14]

William Cullen Bryant, *Picturesque America* (New York, 1872)

The Cascades of the Columbia

Phoebe

The next day our road led over high hills that bordered the Columbia, and, after descending its banks, we came to a little trading post called The Dalles, which at that time was composed of a few zinc cabins and tents occupied by Frenchmen, who lived with Indian women and trafficked with the emigrants and Indians.

We had decided, before reaching this place, instead of attempting to cross the Cascade mountains by the wagon road, to pass it by the way of the Columbia river.

Our captain hired an old Hudson Bay bateau, on which we loaded all our wagons and camping outfit. Just as we got it completely loaded, it seemed as though every seam opened, and the water rushed in and the old thing began to sink. Nothing remained for us to do but to wearily unload and go through the oft repeated process of drying our goods. We were in a great dilmena; how to proceed on our journey was an unsolved problem.

Our goods were dried, but still no signs of relief. But on the second day a nondescript craft made its appearance on the river. Its enterprising proprietor had placed a small engine in a discarded hull.

Thankfully we boarded this unique relief boat and were off on a ten-hour voyage to the Upper Cascades, where we made our encampment on the gravelly beach.

Celinda

Wednesday, September 21—In the morning we found we were very fortunate in the selection of a camp ground as it is the only place near the landing which is level & uncovered by stones. Many were less fortunate. A boat came in before noon laden with emigrants who camped around us. There are several barges that pass between The Dalls & this place. Few boats except those of the Hudson's Bay Co. run over the Cascades. This Co. run over the Cascades losing it is said about one boat in ten. Our baggage not come.

Thursday, September 22—Pleasant. Walked out to see the scenery which is very romantic We are entirely hemmed in by the Cascade Mountains some of the immediate peaks of which some of our party judge to be 1000 ft in heighth. There is a mountain on the north side of the river some distance from it. The side next to the river of which is perpendicular & clearly shows the action of water & I should think that this perpendicularity was caused by the Columbia's first bursting through the mountains & that the channel of the river was once near its base All the mountains here are covered with fir trees some very densely, others more sparingly. The Cascades here are…rapids nothing in comparison to the rapids at Niagara. The indians say—some of the eldest—that they can remember a time when there were no cascades here & they ran their canoes through the mountains, that they were caused by land-slides from the mountains. There are three stores here a bakery & boarding house & there is a wooden rail road between here & the lower landing 5 miles. At night the steam boat came in towing the barge on which were our wagons & luggage. All were safe. It sprinkled some in the evening.

Friday, September 23—Messrs Judson, Marsh & Walter came with some of the cattle. The others were behind—they thought that they would not be here in a day or two as there is so much danger of losing the trail as there are so many diverging from the right one. They had taken provision for but two days the length of time we were informed it would take to come down but we have ascertained it usually takes five but provision is to be obtained at the ferry.

Harvey

Our wagons had been all taken apart for shipment, and G[ustavus] H[ines] and myself busied ourselves in putting them together and loading our baggage into them so as to be ready to make the portage of the Cascades, about six miles, as soon as the men should come with the oxen. Night came, however, and neither oxen nor men, and we began to be uneasy, as they ought to have been there, if all was right, by noon. As the hours of the next day wore onward our uneasiness increased, and towards night G[ustavus] H[ines] and myself walked two or three miles up the trail, but were compelled to return at dark without tidings of them. We determined to make an early start on the next morning, and not return until we had ascertained what had caused such delay.[15]

Celinda

Saturday, September 24—It rained in the night & the temporary tent which uncle H had put up leaked & we became very wet not many of our things were wet but the bedding. Called at one of the stores & the merchant gave us some peaches which were truly a rarity as we have been deprived of fruit all summer. Some of the emigrants left to day. They make the portage of 5 miles & then take a boat again. Uncles G & H started this morning to meet those with the cattle. The[y] would [have] went yesterday but were obliged to put the wagon together which had been taken apart at The Dalls.

Harvey

It was scarcely light before we had put up a little budget of food and started; telling our families not to look for us until we returned. We were on foot, the trail was very rough and difficult passing over the rocky mountain points that came down to the river's edge. On our way up the trail we met several droves of oxen, but their drivers, some of whom had left The Dalles nearly two days after ours, had seen nothing of our men or oxen. We kept on up the trail until noon, when at the foot of "Wind Mountain"[16] we lost all signs of it. We passed on however around the foot of the mountain, when we came to a mountain torrent crossing down from the north, clear as crystal and almost as cold as ice. It was about fifty feet in width and two feet or more in depth. We forded it, taking off our shoes and stockings, and finding it so literally full of salmon that we had to push our way through them. Just above this stream a perpendicular basaltic bluff[17] projected into the river, and as we could find no way round it nor over it, we decided we must have passed the place where the trail crossed the Columbia, and so turned back again and after retracing our steps a few miles night came on, and building a fire in a forest of cottonwood trees on a sandy bar we prepared to spend a frosty night in the most comfortable way we could, without blankets. After we had sat about our fire for an hour or two a hallowing from the south side of the river called us to the bank, and we found that we had built our fire directly opposite the landing of the flat boat used for ferrying stock. We asked the ferryman to come over with a canoe for us, which he did, and about ten o'clock we reached the south bank of the river, opposite Wind Mountain. The ferryman loaned us a couple of blankets, and we spread one on the ground and the other over us, and, under a yew tree slept soundly until morning.

Our ferryman invited us to share his bread and bacon and coffee, which we did with thanksgiving. He had not seen or heard of our men or stock: and even looked a little incredulous when we told him our errand. We judged that he thought it likely we were trying to find somebody else's cattle.

Traveling up the trail five or six miles over some precipitous mountain points, we came at last to a tent in the door of which stood a pleasant faced woman of whom we inquired for our lost man. She hesitated to answer, but then drew aside the door of her tent and invited us to come in. Entering, we found stretched upon a pallet our lost brother, J. W. H[ines], the same who, fresh from the rest of six weeks in the Willamette valley had so generously volunteered to help us out on this part of our journey. He had gotten this far, when the ague fiend had seized him, and for two or three days had held him with so tight a grip that he had been unable to leave the tent. Our coming, however, proved a tonic as good as quinine, and in a very short time his dolorous countenance was in a broad grin as we rallied him about the help he had so kindly given us poor, wayworn and weak emigrants. G[ustavus] H[ines] remained to aid in bringing down the cattle, while

I took the sick man in a canoe, with a man to return it, and spreading a blanket on a pole for a sail we soon passed the fifteen miles of river that took us to our camp at the Cascades. I had put on a pair of new shoes when I left the camp three days before, and when I returned from this expedition they were so worn and rent by the sharp rock that I could wear them no more. If Sister Coston[18] of Walla Walla should read this chapter—as she will—she will remember the time when we first looked into each other's faces in the door of this tent in the dark forest of the Cascade Mountains.[19]

Celinda

Sunday, September 25—Warm & pleasant. I was sick all day. Our party received several calls from gentlemen stopping here & I am informed that the land in this vicinity is nearly all taken.

Monday, September 26—Another barge came in loaded with emigrants. Dr. Hill & Mr Richie among the rest. Messrs Bryant & Judson with their families left this morning. About noon Uncle H. & J. came uncle J has the ague & fever so they came down the river. They think the cattle will be here to day. It seems that they were induced to cross at the upper ferry & the road was so bad that it delayed them two days. They came before dark & a tired Co. they were.

Tuesday, September 27—Very warm. Uncle J had the ague & fever which detained us here to day. Had an invitation to attend a party at the boarding house.

Phoebe

Our men drove the stock over a trail. The trip should have consumed one day, but they unfortunately missed their way among the many Indian trails, and it was three days before they rejoined us.

Although so near the settlements, I doubt that we spent three more uncomfortable nights during our long journey than these, passed on pebly couches, under cold, foggy skies. We greatly missed the comfort and protection of our wagons, as it had been necessary to take them apart for shipment.[20]

---

[1] This surprise meeting piqued the interest of others as well. The Rev. Thomas Fletcher Royal mentions it in his diary entry of March 15, 1854, wherein he is describing events at the second annual Oregon Conference of the Methodists at the Belknap Settlement. "We all

went to meeting together and heard a good discourse from Br. J. W. Hynes who was transferred from Troy Co. and came by water this last season and was here in time to meet his two brothers Gustavus and H. K. very unexpectedly directly after they got in across the plains—they did not know he was coming. They said they were behind us on the plains and heard of us often, and tried to get with us. Br. Hynes text tonight was—'Go ye into all the world and preach the gospel to every creature.'" *Diaries of Thomas Fletcher Royal,* Manuscript #161, Book #3, 1854, 279, The Southern Oregon Historical Society, Medford, Oreg. Harvey himself also describes the 1854 Conference in Chapter 18 of the present work.

[2] Proverbs 16:18 (King James Version).

[3] J. W. Hines, *Touching Incidents,* 166-169.

[4] "Plug hat—a hat that is round and black and hard with a narrow brim; worn by some British businessmen" The Free Dictionary by Farlex; http://www.thefreedictionary.com/plug+hat; accessed May 11, 2007.

[5] Nelson Clark served as a pastor in the Oregon Conference from 1855 through 1916, according to Yarnes, *History of Oregon Methodism,* 313.

[6] H. K. Hines, "Emigrant Wagon," March 12, 1885.

[7] Judson, *A Pioneer's Search,* 70, 71.

[8] Recalling from Joseph's earlier narrative of traveling from Portland to The Dalles, he followed "…the usual route in about twelve hours…" This must have sounded attractive to the mountain-weary Hines party. Nevertheless, as Franzwa points out, the so-called "water route" was not without its own disadvantages. "The travelers rejected the idea of the 1846 Barlow Road (a toll road), opting instead for the much more dangerous Columbia River route and its long portage." Personal communication, Gregory M. Franzwa. See also the note in the epilogue to Chapter 15, where Dr. Shaug confirms that Joseph indeed "came up on the boat" from Portland to The Dalles.

[9] Robert Newell (1807-1869), pioneer and trapper, besides driving the first wagons across the plains to the Columbia in 1840 and on into the Willamette Valley, as Celinda notes, was active politically in the Oregon Territory, and worked closely with the Indians, including acting as Indian agent by appointment of President Johnson in 1868. Ref. Howard McKinley Coming, ed., *Dictionary of Oregon History,* (Portland, Binfords & Mort, 1956), p. 175.

[10] Rev. Daniel Lee (1806-1895) and Rev. H. K. W. Perkins jointly founded and served at the Wascopam Mission at The Dalles from 1838 to 1843. Lee first arrived in Oregon with his uncle, Rev. Jason Lee, in 1834 and helped establish the mission on the Willamette; Perkins came as part of a reinforcement for the Methodist missionary efforts in 1838. Daniel Lee and Joseph H. Frost, *Ten Years in Oregon,* (New York: J. Collard, 1844).

[11] The story of the widely celebrated Marcus and Narcissa Whitman is recounted, for example, by Harvey in H. K. Hines, *Missionary History of the Pacific Northwest* (Portland, 1899), 447ff.

[12] H. K. Hines, "Emigrant Wagon," March 12, 1885.

[13] Harvey's phrase "…now stands…" suggests that this block house was constructed some-time subsequent to this brief visit in 1853. Most likely, this was Fort Lugenbeel, which was built in 1856 to provide some measure of protection of settlers from hostile Indians. "The Upper Cascades was only a village during the March 26, 1856, battle [against attacking natives]. Civilians defended themselves from nearby Bradford Store until Colonel George Wright caused the Indian withdrawal on the 28th. He ordered immediate construction of Fort Lugenbeel." *The Columbia River, A Photographic Journey,* http://english riverwebsite.com/LewisClarkColumbiaRiver/Regions/Places/fort_lugenbeel.html.

[14] H. K. Hines, "Emigrant Wagon," March 12, 1885.

[15] H. K. Hines, "Emigrant Wagon," March 12, 1885.

[16] "The 1,903-foot-high Wind Mountain is located on the Washington bank of the Columbia River, at River Mile (RM) 156.5, just upstream of where the Wind River meets the Colum-bia. The Collins Point Landslide is immediately upstream. Wind Mountain and Shellrock Mountain, which lies directly across the Columbia, are nicely visible from the parking lot at Starvation Creek State Park, Oregon. Wind Mountain can also be seen from the mouth of the Wind River, and looming above Home Valley, Washington." *The Columbia River, A Photographic Journey,* http://englishriverwebsite.com/LewisClarkColumbia River/Regions/Places/wind_mountain.html; accessed March 28, 2007. Gustavus and Harvey, after cross-ing to the south side of the Columbia by aid of the ferryman's canoe, spent the night near what is today Lang Forest State Park Wayside on Interstate 84.

[17] This was probably what is today known as Dog Mountain. "Dog Mountain contains the thickest (over 4,000 feet) section of Grande Ronde Basalt in western Washington. It lies on the Washington side of the Columbia River at River Mile (RM) 160, thirteen miles up-stream of Stevenson, WA. Downstream from Dog Mountain is Wind River and Wind Moun-tain." *The Columbia River, A Photographic Journey,* http://englishriverwebsite.com/LewisClarkColumbiaRiver/Regions/Places/dog_mountain.html; accessed March 28, 2007.

[18] This must be Eveline Coston, listed with her husband Zara Coston in the 1880 Federal Census for Walla Walla, Wash., at age 46, making her a young woman of 19 when Harvey met her in 1853.

[19] H. K. Hines, "Emigrant Wagon," March 12, 1885.

[20] Judson, *A Pioneer's Search,* 71, 72.

17

September 28—October 3, 1853: Portland at Last

We were fairly in Oregon, but these gigantic forests, filled with the densest undergrowth of hazel and dogwood and vine-maple dashed many of our visions and images of the land to pieces: but we were judging prematurely.[1]

—Harvey K. Hines, October 3, 1853

Celinda

Wednesday, September 28—Very warm. We started for the lower Cascades early. There is a wooden rail road[2] 2½ miles down. The highway is very bad. We were obliged on that account to go all the way on foot. We arrived there without any accident. The walk down was delightful. Were it not for our anxiety about the teams it would have been truly enchanting. The scenery is exceedingly wild. Mountains towered 100's of feet above us & the river now rolling in terrific madness now as placid as a sleeping infant's brow. Camped at the Lower Cascade for the night. A gentleman presented us a water melon. There is one public house here, a two story frame one. Steam boat Multnomah came up. Four sail boats were in.

Thursday, September 29—After dinner went on board the steam boat Peytona on which we had previously conveyed our things & went down 30 miles to Sandy. The trip was delightful. Rocky islands rear their craggy peaks far above the surface of the water. There is a high rocky precipice called Cape Horn. The scenery is very beautiful here. When some more than halfway down we were startled by the intelligence that the boiler was empty. The fire was immediately put out & the boiler refilled. Had this not been discovered when it was we should probably been the victims of an explosion. When nearly down we were somewhat frightened by the captains rushing up to the pilot in great agitation who seemed also to be much excited the cause of which we knew not, but it seemed the boat struck a snag & was in danger. Camped at the Sandy. Found a Mr. Crosby[3] there who invited us all to his house.

309

Phoebe

Gladly we hailed the appearance of our cattle. Preparations were quickly completed, and we were off for the lower Cascades.

And oh, such a road! It was simply no road at all. Along the banks of the river we drove, bounding and bumping over large and small boulders. Fortunately for us, it was only a half's day travel, but the roughest of all our rough journey.

From this point a flatboat propelled by steam carried us to the mouth of the Candy [Sandy]. Again we were obliged to wait two days while our cattle were being driven around the trail. How my heart chafed at the delay, for only five miles separated me from my twin sister, Mary.

"It's a long lane that has no turning," but these long, seemingly endless days at last dragged to a close.

Here we parted from the little band with whom we had shared the pleasures and trials of our long journey. There had been no falling out by the way to mar the friendship that time has not broken, and will soon be renewed and perpetuated in the spiritual realms above.

Our captain had watched over us with a fatherly care. When our oxen became weak, he offered us the use of a yoke or two, just as we needed, and by observing the divine plan of resting one day out of seven our cattle were saved. Out of the fifty head belonging to the train, only two were left behind.[4]

Alta Bryant

Got to the Cascades and camped there til the rest of the things came—loaded them in wagons and went to the Sandy river—a day's journey to East Portland. Stayed at Sandy river for a while and rested. Mrs. Judson had a sister there and stayed there[5]—rest went on and camped at East Portland—looked across the river and counted every house in Portland—ferried across and drove to Humphreys[6] 3 miles west of Portland. Father went to work.

Pa knew his folks (the Humphreys) stayed there a week while Pa looked around over the country to look for a home—Pa was sick—got 320 acres with a cabin on it. A man was in it when they got there had just taken advantage of its being empty. Father had to pay him to leave.

Harvey

Early on the following day our teams arrived, and soon after were hitched to the wagons and we were moving down towards the lower Cascades. The road was—well, there was no road.[7] It was simply now driving our wagons on the great rocks and boulders that lay on the river's bank, or then out among the yew and fir and hemlock that covered the mountain points. Of all the rough places of which we had seen wheels roll this was the roughest. We drove through an Indian burying ground where grinning skulls and bleaching bones lay here and there upon the ground; relics of a departed era, and a rapidly dying people. After four or five hours bouncing and bounding over the rock or trailing among the trees we reached a point not far from the present steamboat landing on the north side of the river where lay a steam flatboat called the Peytona on which we embarked our people, wagons and all our camp equipage for a ride to the mouth of Sandy River, while the cattle and horses were to be taken down the trail over the Cape Horn Mountains. Having tried fresh help from the Willamette on one such trip, we thought it wise to send *him* down by steamboat in the care of the women and children this time. It was nearly night when all were embarked, and then, with two men, I drove the cattle down to the base of Castle Rock[8] and encamped for the night.[9]

Sept. 24 [28]. The light of our camp fire near the base of Castle Rock seemed to lift the body of the great basaltic pillar out of the darkness, but left its pine-crested top lost in the shadows of the sky. It looked a very wonder of weird beauty. Springing out of a sandy plain, separated by a distance of near a mile from any mountain, it shoots almost a perpendicular shaft of columnar basalt, about forty rods in diameter, to a height of several hundred feet. On its summit are tall fir trees, and a few evergreens, finding root in the cleft rock, tasselate its sides. The night was delightful. The stars shone in the blue autumn sky like points of fire. The air was cool but balmy, and though our bed was only a blanket on the ground and another one over us, yet we slept soundly after the wearying day. Before daylight the following morning our breakfast was cooked and eaten, and as early as we could well discover the "trail" our cattle were driven forward through the heavy fir forest towards the bold bluff known as "Cape Horn" which jutted into the wide Columbia a few miles below. With me were M[arti]n and two other men of the train, while all the rest had gone down the river to the mouth of Sandy on the "Peytona." The trail down the shore until we came to Cape Horn was exceedingly rough, full of fallen trees and broken rocks, and margined by such a dense growth of timber and underbrush that we could not stop a moment after we started until about the middle of the afternoon. Though we had horses it was impossible to ride them through the forest, and so, turning them loose with the cattle, we were all on foot. What with running through the woods to bring back cattle that were refractory, and the continued yelling and shouting necessary to keep the cattle moving along the trail this was one of the most wearisome days of our entire journey.

About the middle of the afternoon we had reached the plateau on the summit of Cape Horn mountain, and coming to an opening in the fir forest of twenty or thirty acres we called a halt to ascertain if we had lost any of our cattle on the way, and to get our dinner.

After counting, we found all were there, and we sat down on a great fir log and rested for an hour; our cattle as glad as we to have the opportunity for repose.

While resting, a tall young man came walking up the trail and turning aside to where we were sitting, said: "Is there a gentleman by the name of H[ine]s in this company?" I replied: "That is my name." He looked a little surprised, as I was the youngest and smallest and looked like the "boy" of the company. He said, however, "About a mile down the trail you will come to a house. There is a woman there who wants to see you."

Dinner over, we drove on down the trail through the great fir openings, among tall fern and hazel, until we came to a log house on the right of our path. The door stood ajar in the warm September afternoon. Before the door and around the house was a small enclosure in which were a few vegetables growing, and some late summer flowers were in bloom in some beds near the door. As I walked down the path towards the house "a woman" came to the door, and stood within it as I came near. I introduced myself, and without giving her name or answering my words, she said: "And do my eyes again look upon a Methodist preacher?" Her lip quivered and her eyes moistened when I told her that I was one, and had come to Oregon to engage in the work of a Methodist preacher. She related in a few words her history, told me she had been a Methodist from girlhood, had crossed the plains the year before and settled with her family in this lonely spot, and had not seen a preacher of her church since. The day before some passer-by had told her that I was on the trail, and she had sent her son up the trail about the time she expected my coming on purpose to intercept me. We spent a few moments in conversation, kneeled in prayer together, shook hands, and I went forward after the men and cattle.

Four years later I was stationed at the city of Vancouver. Reaching the place late Saturday night, Sunday morning I entered a crowded congregation that I thought were all strangers to me. While preaching my eye continually wandered towards the face of a woman past middle age that seemed to have a strangely familiar look, and whose eye had the light of recognition in it. At the close of the service she came forward and as she spoke I recognized her as the woman who stood in that cabin door, and welcomed me to my work in Oregon. She sleeps now in the cemetery near that beautiful city, and the tall young man who met me with her message that September afternoon also sleeps there. Any who remember "Mother Tooley" and "George" may know of whom I write.[10]

I had taken a riding horse out of the band when I stopped so that I could the better overtake the men who had gone forward. My musings, as I rode rapidly down the trail, were delightful. This was the first house of an actual settler I had entered or seen. To be greeted with such a welcome sent a prophetic light down my path; and after the lifetime of a generation has gone, the light of that woman's eye in that low and lonely cabin door shines over my memory as it then shone over my hopes.

I overtook the men with the cattle just after they had descended from Cape Horn mountain and were going out of the forest upon the grassy river bottom that stretched a few miles above the Washougel Creek. It was sunset, and we hastened forward desiring to reach the ferry on the Columbia before we halted. After dark we forded the arm of the stream to Goodwin's Island,[11] and letting our cattle stray at their own sweet will upon it, built our camp fire under a great oak that stood near Mr. Goodwin's house. We had made our drive from the Cascades quicker than any company had done before us.[12]

Celinda

Friday, September 30—Mr. C came with oxen to take our wagons & everything up there. Here we sat in a chair for the second time since leaving Missions. Slept in our wagons. One of Uncle Gustavus appointments is here.[13]

Saturday, October 1—Very pleasant. We were camped near Mr. Crosby's. Country very fine. Every kind of vegitable grows large. Melons plenty. Cattle came this morning all well. Concluded to remain over Sabbath.

Harvey

On the 16th [30th] which was Friday we ferried our stock once more over the great Columbia. We could recognize our wagons and people encamped on the sandy beach across the river. They were greatly surprised when we landed our first head of cattle, as they did not expect us until Saturday. By the middle of the afternoon all were over the river, our oxen again hitched to our wagons, and driving out through the river timber about a mile we encamped on a beautiful knoll covered with great oak and fir trees, and overlooking a wide reach of bottom land, where we intended to rest over the Sabbath—a rest greatly needed. We could see from our camp quite a number of log houses along the edge of the open river bottom, and one, the residence of Dr. Crosby, was near our camp. The quaint old gentleman gave us the freedom of his garden without money or price, besides furnishing us with some nice fresh beef, butter, and milk. We laid aside our bacon and hard bread that had journeyed with us all the way from St. Louis without regrets, and luxuriated for two days in food fit to set before a king.

Worn and wearied, we needed and took a few days at this point to rest, and prepare ourselves for appearance again in the homes and society of civilization.[14]

Celinda

Sunday, October 2—Held meeting. Mother not well. Mr. Martin left for Portland. Went to see Mr. Russels people who were camped near. Mrs. C has taken Benny Eliza's horse.

Monday, October 3—Started for Portland with two wagons & two yokes of oxen on each. Road not very good on account of the close proximity of the trees. The land is all taken on the road. We took the things out of the wagons. Went to the parsonage with our baggage. Uncle G had left his at Sandy. There we met Rev C S Kingsley[15] who invited us to his house where we went & were very pleasantly entertained. Mr. S[16] is principal of the academy here. Mr. & Mrs. Dryer called.[17]

Alta Bryant

When [we] reached the Sandy River camped two or three days when the wagons and oxen got there then drove to East Portland. Camped over next day, ferried across the river and drove to Homer Humphreys and stayed in their house. Arrived in October. Pa went to hunt a place to live. Someone had built a cabin and abandoned it; he went over to Mr. Lavery's and got him to stay and work, he did not stay at work and another man took the house and Pa had to pay $100.00 for it. Had to camp a day or two before everything came.

Harvey

Oct. 3. Again, and for the last time, I took my ox yokes one after another on my shoulder, and brought under the yoke "Jim and Joe," "Nig and Black," and "Ben and Bolt," and letting the other two yokes remain among the loose cattle, as the wagon was almost empty, hitched them to the wagon and moved on towards Portland, only twelve miles away. Our road led us through a forest of gigantic firs, with here and there a small opening that some hardy pioneers had hewn out of the mighty forest.

We were fairly in Oregon, but these gigantic forests, filled with the densest undergrowth of hazel and dogwood and vine-maple dashed many of our visions and images of the land to pieces: but we were judging prematurely.

Soon after noon we came out of the forest again on the banks of the Willamette opposite a small village of low buildings among high trees, that we were told was "Portland." I took the yokes off the necks of the oxen and put them and the chains in the wagon, just on the east bank of the river about two rods above the present landing of Stark Street Ferry. After a little time a heavy, leaky old flat boat rowed by two men with long, sweeping oars, and steered by another, took us and our baggage over the river, where we were greeted by a medium sized, solid built man with black hair and eyes who introduced himself as "C. S. Kingsley." He threw open his doors and welcomed us to the hospitality of his home—which stood quite back in the forest then, though now in the heart of the city. He soon said to me "You will be glad to learn that your goods were unloaded from the ship yesterday." We had boxed them up at Niagara Falls in December, 1852, and sent them round Cape Horn by sailer, and it really seemed a providence that they should make their voyage while we crossed the continent and thus meet us here.[18]

Harvey (Reminiscing in 1890)

July 30 A ride of 35 miles up the mountain slopes, and among the piny pinnacles, took me before six o'clock, p.m. to Idaho City, and my usual welcome to the home of Calvin S. Kingsley. That name and this home stirs memories of the long ago. Under the always generous and hospitable roof of Brother Kingsley I slept my first night in the City of Portland, then a rude hamlet, on the 3rd of October, 1853. Then we were both young. Now we are both —, but why write it![19]

Harvey

Having, at the Conference preceding my arrival, been stationed in Portland, on the next day we set up house-keeping again in the parsonage of the present Taylor Street Church, and our life "In an Emigrant Wagon" was ended.

One chapter more and my story of it is done.

Oregon Historical Society, Neg. # OrHi 949

Front street in the heart of "downtown" Portland, 1852, just one year prior to the arrival of the Hines party. The buildings housed such businesses as "a Chinese laundry, a hotel, a foundry, a bakery and confectionery, a newspaper, a stove and tin store, and a pharmacy."[20]

---

[1] H. K. Hines, "Emigrant Wagon," March 19, 1885.

[2] This was a precursor to modern railroads along the Columbia. "In 1851, Hardin (or Justin) Chenowith built a railroad consisting of one wagon on wood rails pulled by a single mule. Chenowith charged 75 cents for every hundred pounds of freight. He added more mules and cars (the first railroad in the future Washington state) and sold it to the Bradford family, which expanded it further and built a hotel. By 1854, Upper Cascades included a store, a hotel, a blacksmith forge, and corrals for stock." *The Online Encyclopedia of Washington State History,* http://www.historylink.org/essays/output.cfm?file_id=7811; accessed March 31, 2007.

[3] Accounts of both the Dunbar (http://www.historicgresham.com/pioneers_dunbar.htm) and Powell (http://www.historicgresham.com/pioneers_powell.htm) families, who were pioneers to this area in 1850 and 1852, respectively, mention a Dr. Crosby. It is also noted that "the village…was called Sandy, then Cleone, and, finally, Fairview, as it is today." Thus the village visited by Celinda and the others should not be confused with the present-day town of Sandy, which is located upstream from Fairview on the Sandy River.

[4] Judson, *A Pioneer's Search*, 72.

[5] By "stayed there," Alta evidently means that the Bryants as well as the Judsons stayed with Phoebe's sister, Mary (Goodell) Meloy, for elsewhere in the notes which we have from Alta's daughters it is stated, "…transferred and stayed at Mrs. Judson's sister's on the Sandy River (12 miles out from Portland) and waited for our things."

[6] Listed among 1852 immigrants to Oregon were Homan(?) and Lydia C. Humphrey from Wyoming County, New York, from which county the Bryants hailed. And in the 1860 U.S. census for Multnomah County, Oreg., there is a listing for the H. M. Humphrey family. Evidently the Bryants and Humphreys had been acquainted in New York. A list of 1852 immigrants is posted at: http://linnhistory.peak.org/1852/1852hi.html; accessed April 19, 2007.

[7] As we compare Harvey's phraseology here with that of Phoebe, noting the striking similarity, it is well to keep in mind that Harvey was writing in 1885, and Phoebe in 1925, probably with Harvey's account before her, as we have noted previously.

[8] This is now known as "Beacon Rock," and is located in Beacon Rock State Park in Washington. At *The Columbia River, A Photographic Journey*, we find "Beacon Rock was called 'Castle Rock' for many years…Confusion arose however with another Castle Rock, located along the Cowlitz River. In 1916 the United States Board of Geographic Names made official 'Beacon Rock'." http://englishriverwebsite.com/LewisClarkColumbiaRiver/Regions/Places/beacon_rock.html.

[9] H. K. Hines, "Emigrant Wagon," March 12, 1885.

[10] "Mother Tooley" was evidently Margaret Sloan (Brown) Tooley (1808-1867) who married John Tooley (1806-1875) January 15, 1829, in Columbus, Indiana (Bartholomew County); died September 12, 1867, in Vancouver, Wash. She was born April 19, 1808, in N.C. One of their sons was George J. Tooley (1831-1883), who died September 15, 1883; born August 18, 1831, in Bartholomew County, Ind. Personal correspondence with Dr. Nancy Todd, descendant of John Tooley/Tuley and Margaret Sloan, http://www.geocities.com/drnancytodd/tooley/tooleytuley.html; accessed April 19, 2007.

[11] This is evidently what is now known as Lady Island. Posted on the Web we find "An 1857 cadastral survey (tax survey) for T1N R3E shows a 'Goodwin' house on the east tip of Lady Island. The island is not named. The 1863 survey has 'Goodwin' written in pencil (?) in the middle of the island. Again, the island is not named." *The Columbia River, A Photographic Journey*, http:iinet.com/~englishriver/LewisClarkColumbiaRiver/Regions/Places/lady_island.html; accessed April 2, 2007.

[12] H. K. Hines, "Emigrant Wagon," March 19, 1885.

[13] Gustavus was appointed to Vancouver, Cascades, and The Dalles (which evidently included a number of smaller stations) in the Willamette District for the 1853-54 year by the Oregon Annual Conference. *The Oregon Statesman,* March 26, 1853.

[14] H. K. Hines, "Emigrant Wagon," March 19, 1885.

[15] Both Calvin S. Kingsley and Harvey were assigned to Portland and Portland Academy in the Willamette District for the 1853-54 year by the Oregon Annual Conference. *The Oregon Statesman,* March 26, 1853.

[16] This was Adam Randolph Shipley (1826-1893), then principal of the Methodist Academy and Female Seminary, who, a little less than a year later, on Sept. 30, 1854, was to become the husband of Celinda, with her Uncle Harvey officiating.

[17] T. J. Dryer was the founder and editor of the Portland *Oregonian* newspaper. In the issue of October 8, 1853, he wrote, "An old Oregonian Returned.—Rev. Gustavus Hines, formerly a resident of Oregon, has lately returned by the overland route with his family, to make Oregon his future home. Mr. Hines some two years ago, published a book on this country which we regard as the most impartial history we have seen. We learn that it has met with a large sale in the Atlantic States, and is now passing though a second edition. Mr. Hines was accompanied by a brother and family, who was stationed here by the late conference of the M. E. church. The party all arrived in good health."

[18] H. K. Hines, "Emigrant Wagon," March 19, 1885.

[19] H. K. Hines, D.D., "Itinerary—Boise District—No. 3," *Pacific Christian Advocate,* Aug. 20, 1890, 36:33.

[20] Dodds, Linda, and Carolyn Buan, *Portland Then and Now,* (San Diego, 2001), 10.

18

October 1853: Getting Settled

Is this the land of my early dreams? How changed.
Not the smooth, variegated, beautiful land; but rough,
rugged, and rocky. I lifted up my eyes and looked upon it.
I sat me down and wept. But I had not seen it all.[1]
—Harvey K. Hines, March 1855

October 1853 found the various members of the Hines family settling into their new environment. Celinda, an experienced teacher, secured employment immediately, as well as an opportunity for singing lessons. Gustavus, Joseph, and Harvey all had their assigned ministerial stations to serve. For Gustavus the territory and routines were familiar from his earlier stay in Oregon, as he relates in correspondence with former colleagues in New York. We are offered a view of Joseph's early efforts through the eyes of a young boy, G. W. Kennedy, who was later to become a Methodist preacher himself. Harvey's reflections on his own beginnings in Oregon, "Two Years from Home," are predictably poignant, and provide the fitting final expression of the mixture of emotions attending this family's move from New York to Oregon.

Celinda

Tuesday, October 4—Remained at Mr. Kingsleys. This is a very pleasant location overlooking the city. Mount Hood rears its snow capped summit in the distance. I engaged to teach for Mr Kingsley at…a week & board. Went down to the parsonage which is a very fine house. The ship on which our boxes were shipped has arrived and is discharging her cargo. Uncle H's boxes are out now. Mr. Miner came.

Wednesday, October 5—Aunt Lydia, Julia & Lucy Anna started for Oregon city intending to stop at Mr. Durhams[2] where aunt Elizabeth is. I went into school. Liked it very much. The girls are in my department and the boys in Mr. K's. Went to singing school.

Thursday, October 6—Pleasant. Like school as well as yesterday.

319

Uncle H's people went to house keeping. I went to prayer meeting in the evening. Uncle Joseph & family are at uncle Harveys. Gustavus earned $2.00.

Friday, October 7—Every thing pleasant in school. Mother is sick and has been since she has been here. Took calomel to day. Aunt Elizabeth has the ague. Gustavus earned $2.00 chopping.[3] I went to uncle Harvey's. Saw uncle G's family for the first time. Uncle G thinks I can do better teaching at Oswego. Attended singing school in the evening. Mr. Shipley teacher. Pleasant. Received a line from Julia. Uncle G returned to Sandy.

Saturday, October 8—No school to day. I went to uncle Harvey's & opened our boxes which have been out a day or two. Every thing comes out right. Nothing damaged. Went down town for the first time. Was surprised at the business aspect of the place...returned to Oswego.

Sunday, October 9—Attended church AM. Much pleased with the looks of the congregation. Did not attend in the evening on account of rain. Mother a little better. Messers Marsh & Walter came to see us.

Monday, October 10—Uncle H's people went to Oswego. Rather rainy this morning. Gustavus splitting wood here.

Tuesday, October 11—Commenced raining a little before noon.

On Thursday, October 13, 1853, the ill-fated *Robert Campbell* steamboat, which had run afoul of a snag while the Hines families were aboard on their way to Kansas City, "caught fire and burned to its waterline at a St. Louis wharf."[4]

Harvey

There was both sadness and joy when we finally unloaded our "Emigrant Wagon." Six families had started together from near Kansas. One, as related early in our story, left our train on the morning of the first Sabbath after starting because he "could not afford to lose one day in seven on this journey." He had a fine outfit of oxen and horses, and was himself a frontiersman, accustomed to life in the camp, and, it might have been well supposed, ought to have known what was best on such a trip. He was a good man, a steadfast Methodist, and we have never doubted acted according to his best judgment, but erred in putting a false notion of expediency before a divine ordination. The result was that our train in six days a week traveled more miles than he did in seven. Our teams came through in fine condition, we losing only two cattle out of fifty head, and reaching the valley in good time: he losing nearly all of his, and getting into the valley about six weeks later than we.[5] From not resting one day in seven for many weeks at the beginning of the journey his teams became exhausted and he was compelled to lay by days at a time, and then nearly all his cattle died. This Brother settled in Linn Co. and died a good, honest man and member of the Church.

The other five families continued together until we reached the Willamette valley, making the entire journey not only without a word of difficulty, with a friendship that has remained unbroken, only as death has broken the band, until the present time. G[ustavus] H[ines] and his wife sleep at Salem—"City of Peace"—type of the Peace of the Eternal City on which they have entered. How oft we sang together about the camp fires of the plains:

Have you heard: have you heard of that sun-bright clime:
Unstained by sorrow, unhurt by time:
Where age hath no power o'er the fadeless frame,
When the eye is fire and the heart is flame,
Have you heard of that sun-bright clime.

Brother, sister, mine: ye have not only "heard of that sun-bright clime," but your eyes have looked upon it.

Mrs. O[badiah] H[ines], patient and true hearted amid all the vicissitudes of a troubled life rests quietly under the spreading branches of an oak in Linn County.

Miss G[rave]s, afterwards Mrs. W[alt]s of Portland, after a life of consecration to home and family scarcely exceeded, was laid to her repose in "Lone Fir Cemetery."

And then there was a young girl [Lucy Anna Lee, daughter of Jason Lee, raised by Gustavus Hines and his wife]: tall, deep eyed, *spirituelle*, with the insight of age in the heart of a child: her sensitiveness to wrong and cruelty of any form a perpetual pain to her, who bore a name more honored than any in the records of Oregon life. Reaching Oregon, she became a student at Willamette University, graduated with distinguished honor, took her legitimate place there as its "Preceptress" and won there a queenly renown: and then, in other places, vindicated that renown by the purity of her life and the brilliancy of her intellect. She, too, "rests" in "Lee Mission Cemetery."

Where could the daughter of Jason Lee rest so sweetly and so well as there?

These are all of the adults of the train whose story has been told in "An Emigrant Wagon" who have passed "over the river." We could not bid farewell to our company without this parting word—this heart tribute—to the companions of one of the most trying, difficult, weird, dream-like voyages that Argonauts ever took. Over the brows of the living are now clustering the silver threads where auburn and gold then floated. I can fancy the deep blue eyes, that could then read by moonlight, now peering through spectacles to read this story of one of the great chapters of their own life: as I look through them to write it. Are we growing old? Yes, but all of our company, we joyfully trust, are living in preparation for that life

Where age hath no power o'er the fadeless frame.

A generation has gone. The ox-cart has given place to the palace car. The five month's journey is reduced to less than five days. The midnight guard-mount has given place to luxurious rest on the soft berth of a Pullman. The watch, rifle in hand, against the treacherous savage or the beast of prey is ended forever. And with them is ended much of that discipline of body and mind that made the Oregon pioneers, the emigrants of '44 to '60: the most self-reliant, brave-hearted, broad-minded men and women who ever founded a commonwealth. Oregon will forever have occasion of gratitude that her founders were of the loftiest manhood and purest womanhood: men and women who packed in their bundles of treasures the Bible and the Spelling Book, and built Churches and Schools and Homes at once.

And now to the remains of our company we send the greetings of a pleasant memory out of the olden years and of a warm loving heart out of the living present. Shall we ever meet again? It *would* be pleasant to kindle once more the camp fire in memory of 1853.

And appending, not as a personal reference, but as a token of our estimate of the noble Pioneers of Methodism, who, whether coming by the long, weary march of the Plains, or the not less weary sail half way round the world, the following song; and our story is ended.

THE PIONEER PREACHER[6]

I.

Towards the low, setting sun goes the old Pioneer.
By his side is his brave loving wife:
And they enter the twilight with faith's vision clear,
They have fought well the good fight of life.
Full of wonderful tales of the years that are past,
Full of memories of deeds that are brave.
Crowned with honor the victors have come near at last
To a sweet, peaceful rest in the Grave.

Chorus
Let us honor the hero, the old Pioneer;
On his brow let a chaplet be laid,
For the Master will soon give the victor's reward,
E'en the Crown that will never more fade.

II.

It is near fifty years since there rang through his soul
The command of his Lord, Preach the Word;
And he went on his mission of mercy to all
With a warm glowing zeal for his Lord.
Though the store of his learning was meager at best
He'd a wit that was keen as a blade;
And in strife theologie, it must be confessed,
He was never at loss nor afraid.

(Chorus)

III.

He'd a heart that was tender, an arm that was strong;
He was cheery and joyous as youth,
He was strong and unyielding in battling a wrong,
He was loyal and firm for the truth.
He was brave 'mid the dangers of forest and streams,
He endured amid hunger and cold;
But the dark, lonely hours of the night brought him dreams
Of a city radiant with gold.

(Chorus)

IV.
Like his Lord he was homeless, a wanderer here,
Not a spot called his own for his head;
But he kept in his bosom a claim ever clear
To a mansion of joy overhead.
Many times in the church, or 'mid cool forest aisles,
When the voice of the preacher rang out,
There were scenes that enwreathed e'en the angles with smiles
And awakened the earth with a shout.

(Chorus)[7]

By January 1854 Gustavus was able to take time to write letters to two of his minister friends in New York. They in turn evidently shared the letters with the editor of the *Northern Christian Advocate*, where they were subsequently published.

Gustavus

For the Northern Christian Advocate

OREGON

The following, which we are permitted to copy, is perhaps, the latest intelligence from Br. Hines. We have another letter about the same date, which we shall give next week.—Ed.

Oregon City, Jan. 10, 1854.

Rev. Israel Chamberlayne:[8] *My Dear Brother:*—I have not forgotten the promise I made to write to you, when we had our last interview at Lyndonville. I will not detain you by apologies for not writing sooner, but will come directly to those matters concerning which, I am sure, few men will feel a deeper interest than yourself.

We arrived in the lower part of the Wallamette Valley, the very last day of Sept.—having consumed 147 days in our journey from Westport, Missouri. We were overtaken on our journey by a providence which overwhelmed us with sorrow, and cast a melancholy gloom over the whole enterprise of immigration. A beloved brother, whom we had induced to accompany us, in crossing the Snake river at Fort Boise, was carried down by the deceptive current, and sunk before our eyes. With this exception, we were exceedingly fortunate. We arrived in the country with three wagons, twenty-eight oxen, ten cows, and three horses. Two horses and one cow have died since we arrived. The rest of the animals are doing well. Cattle are worth, in this country, at the present time, from $100 to $200 a yoke, according to the quality. But so many cattle are lost on the plains, that it does not become much of an object to attempt to drive them from the States. If I were to cross the plains again, my team should consist of mules and light wagons. My place of departure would be Council Bluffs, and I would take the road on the north side of the Platt, and the south side of the Snake river. I would start from the Missouri river as early as the 20th of April, and then should expect to reach this valley by the middle of August. But I will not be particular concerning the journey across the plains: you will obtain from other sources, all the information necessary.

You will doubtless be anxious to know what the present state of the country is; and I am aware that it will be somewhat difficult to satisfy you on this point. To say that the country is rapidly improving, would not be sufficient, as it would leave the matter exceedingly indefinite in your mind. Then fancy that you have been travelling in a wild, romantic region, far away from the abodes [of] civilization, where nothing but the appendages of savage life appeared around you; and upon the banks of some beautiful river, overshadowed by majestic forests, you had reposed in weariness, and had fallen asleep; and during your slumbers you had dreamt of the wilderness passing away as by a miracle, of cities rising around you as by magic, the signs of savage life giving place, as in a moment, to the appurtenances of civilization, and the dreary solitude around you at once converted into a scene of gaiety and the hum of business; and awaking, you find yourself actually surrounded by the very circumstances, the outlines of which had passed before your imagination; and you will have some idea of the wonderful changes that are taking place in this western world. Cities and towns are growing up in every direction. Commerce whitens our rivers. Our valleys are filled with quite a dense population, and everywhere the signs of permanent prosperity appear. The land is principally taken up west of the Cascade Mountains. There are, however, large portions of timbered land, yet to be taken, as good as any land in the country.

As soon as the people in the valley get their titles perfected, they will begin to sell portions of their claims, and the population will become more dense. This is a very desirable change. There are large portions of fertile country east of the Cascade Mountains, as delightful as ever the sun shone upon, that must yet be covered with a civilized population. The climate of this part of the country is most delightful, having the advantage even of the Wallamette Valley. There is an abundance of room, however, west of the Cascades, for the next year's emigration, however large it may be.

The prices of things in the country will be to you an interesting item. The common departments of labor command from $30 to $75 per month. Mechanical labor from $3 to $6 per day. Flour is $8 per hundred; Pork, from 20 to 30 cents per pound; Beef, from 12 to 15; Butter, 65; and other things in proportion, except vegetables—they are quite low. Potatoes sell for 75 cents per bushel; onions $2 50. These prices are much lower than they were last year at this time. This renders it much easier for the recent emigrants to obtain a living than it was for those of last year. Indeed, the general report is, that last year there was a great amount of suffering for the want of the necessaries of life, whereas, the present year, there is not only an abundance of all kinds of provisions, but a large surplus will be on hand when another harvest shall arrive. While on the subject of supplies, I would say, that the soil of Oregon retains its former character, with respect to the generosity and magnificence of its gifts. Its wheat, its potatoes, its onions, its turnips, its cabbage, and its all other kinds of vegetables, are superior in quantity and quality to those of any other country of which I have any knowledge. Only think of potatoes weighing from four to six pounds, onions measuring from four to eight inches in diameter, cabbages weighing from fifty to eighty-five pounds, and other things in proportion. As incredible as these things may appear, they are so common among us that they cease to be marvelous.

The emigration into Oregon, the past year, across the plains, amounted to about 10,000 souls. Some 300 of these crossed the Cascade Mountains on the north side of the Columbia River, into Washington Territory; about 7,000 came into this valley by the way of Mt. Hood, the usual route; 1,500 took a new road, into the southern part of the valley, and the remainder took the route of the Humboldt, and crossed into Rogue River valley, near the California line. The party that took the new route and crossed the Cascades into the upper part of the Wallamette valley, suffered considerably before they got through. Their provisions failed, and they were obliged to live for six weeks on poor emigrant beef. They lost many of their cattle and horses, and were obliged to leave most of their wagons in the mountains. They arrived at length in the valley, with the loss of one or two persons, in very destitute circumstances; but finding themselves in the midst of abundance, they soon forgot the fatigues and losses of the plains and mountains, and by availing themselves of the facilities for gaining a livelihood everywhere presented, they generally succeed in raising themselves above suffering and want, and, in most cases, in securing the comfort arising from plenty.

Perhaps the emigration of the past year, was a more stable and reliable accession to the country than any that it had previously received. I was generally well pleased with the appearance of the emigrants along the road. They were mostly of the better class of citizens—forehanded, intelligent, enterprising, go-ahead class of men—just such men as will make their mark in the world, wherever they may go. It is a grand mistake that the ignorant, the low-live, and the semi-savage are the people that come to Oregon. True, there are some of these classes, but in the general, in point of real intelligence, and expanded views of men and things, and that independence of character resulting as well from extensive observation as from a superiority of intellectual endowments, the people of Oregon will suffer nothing in comparison with any other community in any part of the world.

We have a remarkably pleasant and mild winter, which, from the temperature of its atmosphere, is perfectly astonishing to all New Yorkers. I did not escape taking a severe cold early in the fall, during several of the last years that I remained in New York, and then coughing, sneezing and shivering the remainder of the year; but here I have escaped entirely, and I do not think I have seen a person with a bad cold during the whole fall and winter to the present. For two days during the last week, the mercury fell in Fahrenheit, to seventeen above zero; with this exception, it has scarcely fallen below freezing point. The temperature has been exceedingly uniform, and, as a natural result, cases of serious illness in the country are exceedingly rare. This is one of the last countries that a doctor should emigrate to, with the expectation of getting rich by his practice, especially if he had in his possession that valuable commodity called conscience. However, doctors do get rich in this country, but it is by charging to the tune of five dollars for a village call, and twenty-five and upwards for a call in the country.

Now, Br. Chamberlayne, may we not look for you next fall? This is precisely the climate for yourself and family, and the journey across the plains is no very serious matter. It may be made rather a pastime, and with good luck, profitable withal.

Gustavus Hines.[9]

For the Northern Christian Advocate

CORRESPONDENCE

Oregon City, Jan. 12, 1854.

Rev. D.F. Parsons[10]—*My Dear Brother:*— The emigrant road leading into this country, divides several times east of the Cascade Mountains, and the different forks cross the Mountains at different points, the main road crosses a little south of Mount Hood, and about 30 miles south of the Columbia River. Another, which has been made the past year, yet very new and difficult, crosses over on to the head waters of the Wallamette, near the Three Sisters, and about 150 miles from the old road. A third, takes down the Humboldt, and crosses some 150 miles south of the second mentioned, on to the head waters of Rogue River. A fourth, crosses the Columbia River northward, and scales the Cascade Range in the direction of Pugets Sound. A fifth route into the Pacific country, is by the way of the Columbia River. The emigrant designing to take this route, comes to the Dalls of the Columbia with his teams. Here he ships his wagons on board a boat (a steam-boat or a flat boat, as he may choose) and sends them down to the Cascades, the distance of about 50 miles. He drives his cattle down the river, on what is called the "Pack Trail." On reaching the Cascades he receives his wagons, puts them together, and makes a portage of four miles across the Cascades, to the boat-landing below. Here, he again ships his wagons and surplus passengers, and sends them down to the mouth of "Sandy," a stream that rises in the mountains, and empties into the Columbia about 35 miles below the Cascades. The cattle are again driven down a "Pack Trail," from the Cascades to the mouth of Sandy, where the cattle and wagons are again united, and the emigrant is ready to go into whatever part of the

Wallamette valley he may prefer. I have been more particular on this route, because it is the route which we took to get into this valley. On arriving at the mouth of "Sandy," which is about 20 miles above the mouth of the Wallamette River, I found myself at about the center of the field of labor which had been assigned me by Bishop Ames, in anticipation of my arrival. I therefore made up my mind to proceed no further, at present, but to go directly at my work. My circuit extends from Vancouver to the Dalls, the distance of about one hundred miles on both sides of the Columbia River, and contains eleven appointments. To get to these appointments, I have to resort to all the methods of travelling that have ever been known in this country. Sometimes I am on horseback, sometimes on steamboats, sometimes in small skiffs, or canoes, but mostly on foot. I have traveled on foot from the Cascades down the "Pack Trail," over what is called Cape Horn Mountains, and through carrion so deep that I doubt whether the sun ever shone to the bottom of it, wading through mud and water half-leg deep; and after two days of excessive exertion, have succeeded in reaching a little log cabin on the Columbia Bottom, where three anxious ones have been long waiting my return. I tell you, Br. Parsons, this traveling an Oregon circuit, is altogether a different business from that of a Methodist preacher in Western New York. But it does not take me on surprise. I understood the whole matter before I returned to this country. I was fully prepared even for the very worst. And, thank God, I do not recoil at the nature of the work. I am *glad* I am here, because I believe I am where God would have me be. Perhaps you will consider me presumptuous in daring to entertain this opinion, so much in opposition to that of a few wise heads in Genesee Conference, and also to the views of Bishop Ames. But so it is, and I dare to breathe it at least in the ears of my friends, that I consider Oregon as my appropriate field. As I have never done or said aught in relation to Oregon, or of its missionary operations, of which I am ashamed, or that I now think to have been erroneous in any essential part, I have no acknowledgments, no concessions, no apologies to make. I have such a consciousness of integrity in my course, that I regard all opposing remarks and influences as the idle wind, come from whatever source they may. I stand upon a glorious independence, and am ready for peace or war, but in any event, I am bound to contend for the right.

My observations in the country have not been very extensive since my return, but judging from what I have seen, I should think that some prosperity was being experienced in the different departments of our work. Portland, which is now a city numbering about 3000 inhabitants, and is rapidly advancing, stands at the head of ship navigation, on the Wallamette River, and is blessed with a flourishing Academy under our control, and a good Methodist Church. My Br. Henry[11] officiates as the minister. It has fallen to the lot of Joseph to organize a circuit between Portland and Oregon City, a little place eight miles above Portland, called Oswego, being the headquarters. This is a promising charge.

Oregon City, four miles above Oswego, and at the falls of the Wallamette, is a thriving place, about half the size of Portland, but destined to a more continued, and permanent advancement, on account of its unparalleled hydraulic facilities. Here, we have a fine little church, which was commenced during my first residence in this country, but which I have had the privilege of dedicating since my recent return.—Here is an efficient and wealthy society, that pays their minister to the tune of 1000 dollars per annum. The people here have cause for gratitude that they are favored with the faithful and zealous labors of Br. Buchanan, formerly of the Michigan Conference. Salem, you are aware, situated on a delightful prairie, about 45 miles above Oregon City, is the established seat of government for the territory. It is about the size of Oregon City, and improving. The Oregon Institute, which is now a chartered University, is located within the corporation, and under the efficient management of Br. Hoyt. This institution is the leading star of literature in Oregon, and though surrounded with embarrassments, yet we entertain the hope that it will finally come forth, relieved from all its entanglements, and become indeed, if it be not already, the most important literary institution in the country. At Salem, we have the best house of worship there is of Oregon. It would be no dishonor to any place in the Genesee Conference. Brother Roberts, assisted by Br. Leslie and Br. Hoyt, officiates as the minister. Religion is in a low state at this point at the present; but the people are looking for better days, and it is hoped that these days will soon come.

I cannot write particularly with regard to any other localities, as my observations, since my arrival, have extended only to those already alluded to. I shall conclude my letter, therefore, in general remarks. We have in this country an extensive and important field for ministerial enterprise. The population of Washington territory, north of the Columbia, and of Rogue, and Umpqua river valleys in Southern Oregon, is rapidly increasing, and the time will be upon us in a very few years, when the Oregon conference will be divided, and subdivided.— The country at the present time demands a great increase of the right stamp of ministerial help.—But let no one indulge the idea that *any* thing will do for Oregon.

No man will be likely to succeed in this country as a minister, who has not the ability to succeed in the Genesee Conference. The congregations in Oregon are as intelligent as can be found in any country, and no milk and water ministry is going to answer their purpose. This view of the matter should influence our Bishops in the transfer of men to this country. I write this with deference, but Bishops are men, like ourselves, and liable to err. Sometimes they send men that they ought to keep at home, and at other times they keep at home, that they ought to send abroad. We hope, however, in part, that the future necessities of the country will be met, by a ministry raised up in Oregon. I learn that there are a few young men to be recommended to our Conference, in March next, who promise much for the future welfare of the Church. We are expecting Bishop Simpson, at our coming Conference, but have not yet heard of his leaving the States. And now, Br. Parsons, I wish to say, that, as a family, we are quite satisfied with being in Oregon. In all our feelings, and interests, we have adopted this country as our own. It will constitute our home the small fragment of time which may be allotted us here, and when we shall remove to our home on high, its soil will doubtless cover our remains.

We shall remember the many pleasant interviews we have enjoyed in your family, so long as we live, and should be exceedingly happy to be permitted to resume them in the most delightful valley of the Wallamette. Come, Br. and sister Parsons, to this healthy, romantic, and delightful country, and spend the evening of your days in health and peace, and finally go down to the grave with old age. Mrs. Hines and the girls join me in expressions of changeless love for yourself and your dear family.

Gustavus Hines.[12]

In Chapter 13 we saw G. W. Kennedy's description of the Snake River incident. Later in his book, Kennedy tells of his family's first religious service in their new home in the wilderness, and the part played by Joseph Hines.

G. W. Kennedy

Scarcely were our first log cabins built, when the "circuit rider," the Methodist preacher, came around. The body of our cabin was up, and Father was in the woods riving clap boards to cover it with. Over the hill, down the trail, came riding a gentleman on horseback. He had a large and beautiful horse; good saddle; something swinging across the saddle behind and buckled underneath to the cinche—sort of a leather carry-all, or a pair of them. The man was well dressed. I noticed he wore a "starched collar and a white necktie." Having seen all this, I ran into the tent and said to mother: "A man just rode up on the finest horse I ever saw, and he is surely some great man; maybe he's the Governor." (We had been told marvelous tales about "Jo Lane," Governor and Indian fighter). "Won't he have to come around and see all us new comers, and settle us on good claims?"

By this time the stranger had dismounted, tied his horse to a tree, and was approaching the door. Tipped his hat and saluted Mother, and said: "Hope you are getting well settled. Heard you had come in—thought I'd come around and get acquainted, for I hear you are of our people. My name is Hines; the church has appointed me to the Upper Willamette Valley for a circuit, and bidden me look up the 'lost sheep of the house of Israel'—they call me the flock tender, hereabouts. I preach in some school houses, but mostly in the log cabins of the people. Can I leave an appointment, and come and preach in your house?" My mother welcomed him, most heartily, promised him the use of our cabin upon a certain Sunday in the coming month. Gave him Father's and her own name; and told father in the evening that "we had a church organized." Rev. Joseph Hines was our first pastor, and this the first visit of a preacher to our home in Oregon.

Not long after this, a good old neighbor lady called—we had not yet moved into our cabin. We had heard of "Old Lady Mason." She came early one morning, and began to talk before she got within 50 yards of the tent door. "Wal' howdy do? jest thout I'd come over and git acquainted with ye; I'm yer neighbor over across the stream thar. Been in the kintry since '47 and seen hard times, cartin. Won't be that away with youons. Our first sack of flour cost us $20, but my husband paid for it at one day's haulin' with the yoke of steers. But I'm not gittin' to my irrend. I wanted to tell you that our preacher has promised to come and hold meetin's 'mong us next fall, and preach in our cabin. Jest had a few preachin's in the whole region of the kintry since our comin'. We are meetin' people, and hope youons are. We b'l'eve in the kind of religion Peter Cartwright used to preach in Missoury. When a man gets it he'll know it, an' will make a different person uv yer; the kind ye kin sing and shout and praise God with!" O, how it cheered Mother's heart to meet that good old Christian neighbor. "Old Lady Mason" was always a welcome visitor in our home. She looked so much like our Grandmother, left in Illinois. Mother told her of the appointment of Brother Hines, for preaching in our cabin home next month, and they rejoiced together over the prospect. She agreed to work with Father and Mother in the neighborhood for a congregation and a church.

The first Sunday in June came and the preacher came. The people also, from far and near. Not a family in five miles but that was at that meeting. Our cabin could not hold the half of the people. Some seats on logs, were provided close about the door, and many sat on the ground. Our seats within the house were of the rudest kind, made of split logs, laid on blocks of wood. Joseph Hines was a good preacher, at times great. That day he announced that old communion hymn:

And are we yet alive
And see each other's face?
Thanks and praise to Him belong,
For His redeeming grace.
Preserved by power divine,
To full salvation here,
Again in Jesus' praise we join,
And in his sight appear.[13]

The preacher had a splendid voice for song. The people, how they did sing—memories of the days, and of the worship far away. The hollowed hush of God's presence at this first meeting here in the wilderness—the glory that shone all around, all was inspiring. Tears overflowed, and rolled down many a cheek. Brother Hines took the text, Gen. 12-7, "Unto thy seed will I give this land. And there builded he an altar unto the Lord, who appeared unto him." The application of the subject was most practical. The obligation upon us all to build altars unto the Lord in this fair land of promise, the direct gift of God to us, His pilgrim people. Religious home life for Oregon. This day was soul reviving, vital every way. Church life was begun with us, in the wild west.[14]

Harvey

TWO YEARS FROM HOME

Sadly, two years ago this day, in company with a small band of uncompelled exiles, I seated myself in the car which was so rapidly to roll me away from the land of my youth. Thoughtfully I gazed, with tearful eye, upon the minarets of the city of Buffalo, until they were lost in the receding distance. Shall I see them again? and when? were the questions I asked, but could not answer. Desire pointed down the future, and whispered in my heart, you may; but a dark uncertainty stayed my vision and I could not see the when. On, on, unceasingly on, the steaming car bore me cruelly away. Away from what? I will not open the sanctuary of my soul or the eyes of my curiosity and say from what. The rattling car, the deep breathing steamer on the broad Ohio, the boiling Mississippi, the yellow and turbid Missouri, had soon conveyed me, unwillingly willing, seventeen hundred miles from the spot where I gamboled in glee and glory when my life was young. And then the restless neighing steed, or the slow and obstinate ox, or my own trusty powers of locomotion, conveyed me up the long green way to the verge of the dreary and dusty desert, the great hot heart of North America, ungenerous and relentless heart, unmoved at famine, disease and death—can hear without a sigh the widow's groan, and see the orphan's tear.—But it was no bar to progress. Still on, over its burning sand, the weary way was lengthened, until, having forded, ferried, or swam more than twenty miles of river's breadths, and traveled forty hundred, we issued from the evergreen wilderness upon the eastern bank of the Wallamette, west of the dark, rocky peaks of the Cascade mountains, and their snow-white domes. Dreary deserts, broad rivers, wide ranges of high mountains are passed, and we have reached the land beyond them from the rising sun. Here

"Flows the Oregon, and hears no sound
Save its own dashings"[15]

Is this the land of my early dreams? How changed. Not the smooth, variegated, beautiful land; but rough, rugged, and rocky. I lifted up my eyes and looked upon it. I sat me down and wept. But I had not seen it all.

Portland is the commercial metropolis of Oregon. Here, in a

city of two or three thousand inhabitants, my destiny for some months had been fixed by those who had rule over me.[16] Doffing, therefore, the wild garb of the plain and the chase, I donned, what I had been longer accustomed to wear, that of a Methodist preacher. But the contrast. For months all the preaching I had done had been to rough bearded men, dusty with travel, myself patriarchal with beard; and now, in again entering a church and standing in a pulpit, with an audience of silks, satins and broadcloths, stiff with forms and mannerisms, I *did* find it difficult to lay entirely aside the free and true of unconventionalized life, and assume the hollow and artificial of a manufactured society. Poor, stupid thing, made for a purpose and spoiled in the making; I pity it. Months came and went. Sabbaths rose and set. Audiences gathered and dispersed; "but the work of God was not bound." And as a demonstration of its freedom, it brought a score of souls to the foot of the Cross, to the door of the Church. And now the time has come when the "Oregon Annual Conference" is to convene, one hundred miles away. The manner of reaching it was, twelve miles by steamboat, then a portage of a mile around the falls of the Wallamette, at Oregon City, then again by steamboat to Corvallis, seventy miles above, and thence on foot or horse as one might chance, twenty miles further, to a log school house in Benton Co., where a band of men, commanding most of the moral and educational interests of Oregon, assembled March 16th, 1854. Bishop Simpson not having arrived, it fell to the lot of Rev. T. H. Pearne, then the only Presiding Elder, to preside.—The venerable Leslie, who had seen seventeen years of service in Oregon; the tall, iron Waller, next in years of service; the chaste, gentlemanly Roberts; and the cheerful, fatherly Wilbur, with others of not less years, though fewer of service in Oregon, gave our young Conference a sage and venerable air.[17] In the usual routine of Conference business, and religious services and anniversaries, the few days of the session passed pleasantly away; and in a marvelous style we were trooping over the hills toward Corvallis and *home.*

My move was a short one and easily accomplished, Oregon City being but twelve miles from Portland and connected by steamboat. The plan of my new work was, preaching twice at the City each Sabbath, and every four weeks a series of appointments, five in number, from six to twenty miles from town. The field was large and responsible, with all the interests of a station and a large circuit to care for, and I feared its effect upon my constitution, never, perhaps the strongest. Three hundred times during the last twelve months I have preached, traveled on foot or horseback from fifteen hundred to two thousand miles, held a camp-meeting without any ministerial help, at which I preached, in four days, fourteen times; and as immediate results, have received fifty souls into the Church. Yet the main fruit of labor here is remote, and will be gathered after many days. Yet it will finally be gathered, and those who have sowed in tears will reap again in joy.

Whether a person is pleased with Oregon life and labor, will depend very much upon the strength of his devotion to God; unless he is all for God, not simply in passive love, but in being all for men, they will not please him. Yet it is strange to us that an unwillingness to leave the richly clustering fruits of other men's labors, and plant instead of reaping, is so general that our Bishops have to communicate to us the information "that the work is so hard, and fare so poor in Oregon," our brethren at *home* choose to remain there. So be it, and if that is an expression of the heart, we choose they should. Though there are but few men for the work, yet altars are being erected and fires kindled thereon, and though we cannot see who shall minister at them in the time of the morning and evening sacrifice, as Abraham upon Moriah, we name them all Jehovah Jireh.[18]

H. K. Hines.

Oregon City, O.T., March 8, 1855.[19]

In his letter above, Harvey describes the Oregon Annual Conference of a year earlier, held in Benton Co., far to the south. But in 1855, the Conference session was in Oregon City, right where he was stationed. A daguerreotype was made of all the preachers present (*next page)*, which included all three of the Hines brothers, Gustavus, Joseph and Harvey.

Bishop Baker, who presided at the conference, described the scene in the following caption that accompanied an engraving made from the original daguerreotype.

FIRST M. E. CHURCH ERECTED WEST OF THE ROCKY MOUNTAINS.
    The above engraving is a correct representation of the first frame church erected west of the Rocky Mountains. The daguerreotype, from which the engraving was executed, was taken during the session of the Oregon Conference in 1855, and the preachers are represented standing in front of it. The house is situated at Oregon City, which place was known in the early days of the Oregon mission as Willamette Falls. The scenery about the falls is quite romantic. As you ascend the Willamette River and bend around a projecting rocky point opposite the Clackamus River, you enter a narrow

defile, having the Willamette Falls directly in front of you, and Oregon City at your left. The city is built on a narrow bluff, from twenty to forty feet above the river, just wide enough to admit of a street with houses and gardens on each side, and then another precipitous bluff rises some seventy or eighty feet above the main street. The church is built directly in front of the second bluff. A few shrubs, vines, and flowers grow in the fissures of the trap rock of which the bluff is composed, and renders the scenery, though somewhat wild, yet really beautiful. —Bishop Baker.[20]

FIRST M. E. CHURCH ERECTED WEST OF THE ROCKY MOUNTAINS.

Oregon Historical Society, Neg. # OrHi 638-A

Daguerreotype of the Methodist Episcopal Church in Oregon City, where Harvey Hines was stationed in 1855. It was also the site of the 1855 Annual Conference session. Pictured in front of the church are the preachers of the conference, including Harvey and his older brothers, Gustavus and Joseph. Each of the brothers was short in stature, standing only five and one-half feet or less. We can only speculate as to which of the shorter than average preachers in the picture must have been these brothers. According to Harvey in a separate letter, a copy of the picture was sent to Bishop Baker as a gift following the conference.

[1] H. K. Hines, "Two Years from Home," *Northern Christian Advocate,* May 23, 1855.

[2] This may be Mr. L. A. Durham, whose household in nearby Washington County represents the only Durhams in Oregon in 1850. 1850 U.S. Census, Washington County, Oregon; image copy at www.ancestry.com; accessed May 12, 2007.

[3] Holmes transcribed this as "Gustavus *spent* $2.00 *shopping.*" Holmes, *Covered Wagon Women,* 130. A close examination of the original diary supports the present transcription, and imparts less of an "easy come; easy go" character to young Gustavus than does Holmes' version.

[4] William R. Nester, *From Mountain Man to Millionaire,* (Columbia: University of Missouri Press, 1999), 187.

[5] Part of Joseph Leonard's greatly extended travel time was due to an additional unfortunate decision: along with an estimated thousand or more others, he opted to take the "Elliott Cutoff" at the Malheur River, the same cutoff that the Hines party rejected in favor of staying with the "tried and true" main Oregon Trail. Leah Collins Menefee and Lowell Tiller, "Cutoff Fever, III," *Oregon Historical Quarterly,* June 1977, 129.

[6] We surmise that this poem is Harvey's original work.

[7] H. K. Hines, "Emigrant Wagon," March 26, 1885.

[8] Israel Chamberlayne (1795-1875) served as a Methodist Episcopal minister in New York's Genesee Conference from 1813 until his superannuation in 1848, and remained as a widely respected member of the Conference until his death in 1875. F. W. Conable, *Genesee Annual Conference,* 70, 567, 733.

[9] Gustavus Hines, "Oregon," *Northern Christian Advocate,* April 19, 1854.

[10] De Forest Parsons (1805-?) entered into the Methodist ministry in the Genesee Conference in 1830, just three years prior to Gustavus, and served for thirty-five years. F. W. Conable, *Genesee Annual Conference,* 313, 734.

[11] This is undoubtedly a careless typesetter's substitution of "Henry" for "Harvey."

[12] Gustavus Hines, "Correspondence," *Northern Christian Advocate,* April 26, 1854.

[13] This is the Charles Wesley hymn, "And are we yet alive?"

[14] Kennedy, *Pioneer Campfire,* 151-155.

[15] Here Harvey paraphrases (substituting "flows" for "rolls") William Cullen Bryant's oft-quoted "Thanatopsis," which can be found in full on-line at http://www.msu.edu/~cloudsar/thanatop.htm; accessed June 16, 2007. As noted in the Prologue of the present work, the Columbia River was discovered and named by Capt. Robert Gray in 1792, but the rumored "River of the West" had been called "Oregon" earlier and this latter name persisted

as late as 1817, the year of publication of "Thanatopsis." Carey, *General History of Oregon*, 1-15.

[16] At the first Oregon Annual Conference, in March 17-19, 1853, while Harvey was en route to Oregon, Bishop Ames had assigned him to Portland.

[17] Bishop Matthew Simpson, D.D., an advisor to President Lincoln who gave his funeral oration, was praised elsewhere by Harvey for his inspirational leadership and address on this occasion. The full names of the pioneer ministers mentioned were Thomas H. Pearne, David Leslie, Alvan F. Waller, William Roberts, and James H. Wilbur. H. K. Hines, "My First Conference in Oregon," *Pacific Christian Advocate*, November 5, 1890.

[18] The allusion is to Genesis 22:14 and the sparing of Isaac on the altar his father, Abraham, has built. Abraham names the site Jehovah Jireh, which has frequently been translated as "The LORD will provide."

[19] H. K. Hines, "Two Years from Home," *Northern Christian Advocate*, May 23, 1855.

[20] The *Methodist Almanac* (1858), 47.

19

After 1853

A great deal of biographical material is available for the three Hines brothers, Gustavus, Joseph, and Harvey. In what follows, we quote liberally from that material to trace their activities after their migration to Oregon, as well as some of their prior work. Phoebe Judson, in her autobiographical book, also provides an extensive picture of the Judson family's life on the West Coast.

Gustavus

Historian Robert M. Gatke, in his comprehensive history of Willamette University,[1] has provided a summary of Gustavus's life that expands upon some of the background we have sketched in Chapter 1, but also covers his activities after 1853. We repeat Gatke's biography here.

The outstanding events we always sketch in telling of a man's life are briefly told in the case of Gustavus Hines. He was born in New York State September 16, 1809, of parents who came from well-established New England families of prominent connections. In 1830 he married Lydia Bryant and moved shortly afterwards to Western New York where they took up their residence in a small log cabin on the frontier. It was from this locality that he entered the Methodist itinerant ministry in 1832 and traveled the pioneer circuits of western New York. His effective preaching and pastoral work, ably supplemented by the devoted help of his wife, brought him constantly more important appointments. In 1839 he accepted the call to become a member of the Oregon Mission under Jason Lee and came to Oregon as a member of the "great reinforcement."

Hines, like other leaders of the mission group, not only interested himself in the religious, moral, and educational problems of Oregon, but also in its civic concerns. We find him one of the leaders in the movement to establish the Provisional government. Of a portion of these meetings, he served as secretary and exercised considerable influence upon their actions.

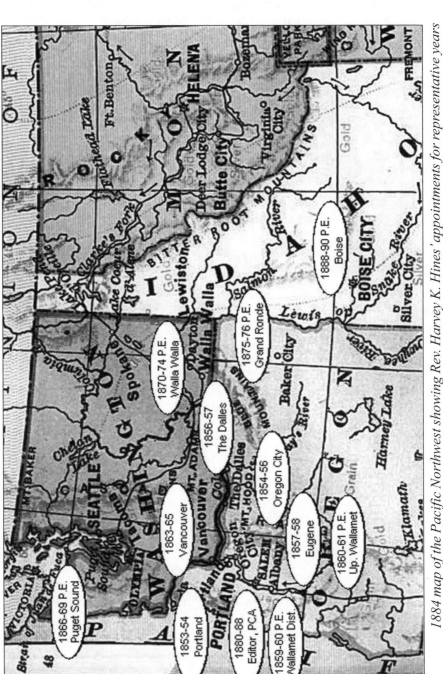

1884 map of the Pacific Northwest showing Rev. Harvey K. Hines' appointments for representative years after 1853. (P. E.: Presiding Elder) Adapted from an original map at the USGenWeb United States Digital Map Library hosted by RootsWeb at http://www.rootsweb.com/~usgenweb/maps/usa/

His first work in connection with the mission was with the Indians, and he was given charge of the Mission Manual Labor School. Later he worked among the whites being pastor at many of the principal settlements. He held important positions, including that of presiding elder and represented his conference at the General Conference in 1868. As we learned earlier, his name has become associated with Jason Lee's by the fact that Lee entrusted his motherless daughter to the care of Lydia and Gustavus Hines when he was forced to make his last trip East; and as death claimed him while there, the little girl, who was destined to become one of the great teachers of early Willamette, was reared by them as their own. The story of Hines in Oregon is so briefly and effectively told in one of the older standard histories of the Pacific Northwest that it is desirable to quote a portion of this narrative:

In the autumn of 1843 occurred an incident that illustrated the determined and fearless character of this pioneer. A fine saddle horse of his had been stolen during the spring: and he had given it up for lost. In the autumn a band of two hundred Mollala and Klamath Indians, painted and insolent, camped in the Clackamas bottom about two miles from the Falls: and a friendly Clackamas Indian informed Mr. Hines that his stolen horse was among theirs. At mid-day, when the Indians were all in their camp, he mounted another horse, and taking a lariat in his hand rode alone into the midst of the grim and painted warriors, and throwing the lariat over the neck of the stolen horse led him out of the camp, not an Indian daring to interfere with him.

While residing at Oregon City, the then only Indian agent west of the Rocky Mountains, Dr. Elijah White, solicited Mr. Hines to accompany him on a tour to the interior to assist in appeasing an intense excitement then agitating the Cayuses and Nez Perces on the Walla Walla, Umatilla and Clearwater rivers. Several were engaged to accompany them; but, when the time of departure came, all refused to go; and Doctor White and Mr. Hines, against the protest and advice of Doctor McLoughlin, and all of the gentlemen of the Hudson's Bay Company, were left to go alone or leave the mission stations of Doctor Whitman at Waiilatpu and Mr. Spaulding at Lapwai without an effort to save them from threatened extermination, and all the scattered settlements of the Willamette valley from most imminent peril. By canoe to The Dalles and then on horseback, they went among these fierce tribes, met and treated with their chiefs such as Yellow Serpent, the Peu-peu-mox-mox of the Indian war of 1855-56, Five Crows, Red Wolf, Ellis Lanitan, and thus averted for some years the tragedy of Waiilatpu and the long Indian war which followed it.

In 1845 Mr. Hines returned to New York by the way of the Sandwich Islands, China and South Africa, and resumed his labors in the Genesee conference, where he remained until the winter of 1852, when he was again transferred to Oregon, and crossed the plains in the summer of 1853, reaching Portland early in October of that year. His work in Oregon subsequently had a very wide range, and was of a very diversified character. He was stationed at Salem, Albany, Lebanon and The Dalles, and was also presiding elder of districts that embraced all of the country on the Columbia river and southward to California west of the Cascade Mountains. He pursued his work with indefatigable industry and the most conscientious faithfulness; and few indeed are the men of any denomination of Christians on this coast who had more seals to their ministry, or have left a sweeter memory behind them than he.

Mr. Hines was naturally and essentially a pioneer, with a magnificent physique, great physical strength, indomitable will, a voice of great compass and force, and an intellect of more than ordinary power. He was splendidly equipped by nature for the part he was called on to fill in laying the foundations of civilization and Christianity on the shores of the Pacific. He died in Salem, Oregon in 1873 [December 9], leaving an enduring mark on the history of his state and church.

His last few years were years of decreased activity, forced upon him by a long lingering illness from which he did not recover. At the meeting of the Willamette board on June 25, 1873, according to the minutes, "Rev. G. Hines addressed the Board relating to his connection with the University at an early day, that his failing health warned him that this would more than likely be the last annual meeting he would have the pleasure of attending."

It was true that before the next annual meeting of the Board this good man who had given so many years of faithful service had passed to his reward. He belongs with Leslie, Waller, Parrish, Wilbur, and Roberts in that inner group of valiant workers for the pioneer university, without whose work and sacrifice the school could never have survived and served the successive generations until now it enters its second century of service.[2]

Lydia Bryant Hines

The best biographical information we have found for Lydia Hines is her obituary, written by Gustavus' first cousin, Rev. Nelson Rounds, which we include verbatim here. It sheds further light on the circumstances of the Hines family life during both stays in Oregon.

Outlines of the life of Mrs. Lydia Hines

She was born in Winfield, Herkimer Co., N.Y., March 27th, 1811. She was the daughter of Royal Bryant, Esq., and connected with the large family of Bryants in Massachusetts. Her father and mother were both praying people, and noted in community for their ardent and uniform piety. These traits of character led them to commence the moral and religious training of their children in early infancy, and continue it so long as they remained under the paternal roof. As a result they had the satisfaction of seeing all their children walking in the ways of religion.

Though often concerned for her spiritual welfare, the subject of this memoir did not receive permanent religious impressions until she arrived to maturity. She was fully awakened to a sense of her spiritual destitution in 1828 under the labors of Rev. Ephraim Hall, of precious memory; and after passing through a most severe struggle in breaking away from the gay world, at the shrine of whose pleasures she had been an ardent devotee, in September of that year, she bowed before the family altar at which her father and mother were knelt, and besought them to pray for her.

The prayer of faith at once ascended to the throne, and while in the fullness of her agonizing heart she was repeating the words of Dr. Watts:

"Here, Lord, I give myself away, 'Tis all that I can do," the precious answer came, and peace and joy filled her soul. From this it will be seen that her conversion was remarkably clear, and knowing from this bright experience that Christ hath power on earth to forgive sins, she at once became an ardent laborer in the Lord's vineyard. She immediately united with the M.E. Church, to the communion of which she was soon followed by her parents, who for many years had been devoted members of the Baptist Church; and also by all her brothers and sisters who had arrived to adult years. She was married in the church at West Winfield, Oct. 17th, 1830, by Rev.

Calvin Hawley, to Gustavus Hines, then a private member of the church. In the following winter, by sleigh, through accumulating snows, they removed westward to the distance of 250 miles, and settled in the woods of Cattaraugus Co., Ellicottsville township. Here her surroundings for two years were indeed of a very humble though honorable character. The log cabin, rough on the exterior, but ornamented within by love and industry, in connection with the furniture of the shoe-bench,[3] and pressboard of the tailoress—a small clearing in the forest, where beech, maple, linn, oak and hickory stumps gave evidence that the axman had commenced the process of opening a farm; these and such like characteristics of a wilderness country just beginning to yield to an advancing civilization, marked the scenery in the midst of which she and her youthful companion found themselves in the summer of 1832. In October of this year her husband received his first license to preach the gospel, and was appointed by his presiding elder to travel the circuit on which they were living; and by this strange providence she very unexpectedly found cast upon her the responsibilities incident to the life of a Methodist itinerant preacher's companion. In all her calculations for the future, she had made no reckoning for this; and for a while it was a source of the severest trial. Itinerating as a Methodist minister's wife, was to her synonymous not only with crushing responsibilities, but with want, destitution, mendicancy. The prospect appalled her, and she recoiled in its contemplation. By a few months, however, of mingling with people, during which she contributed largely to the promotion of an extensive revival, she became convinced that the call of the Church was indeed the call of God: and accordingly yielded the controversy and prepared herself as best she could to become a co-laborer in the gospel field.

In this capacity, the following are the outlines of her travels. Beginning with the Franklinville circuit, Genesee Conference, in Western New York, the next field of labor was the old Ridgeway circuit, 100 miles northward; the next Pekin, Erie Co., embracing Niagara Falls; from thence to Otto, Cattaraugus Co.; and then in the following year to Lodi, and the next to Pike village in Wyoming Co. On each of these fields of labor there were extensive revivals, in each of which she took an active and very efficient part. During her seven years residence on these fields of labor she witnessed the conversion of about 600 souls, and in counsel, exhortation, and altar work, was perhaps the most successful laborer employed. Besides this, possessing the rare faculty of adapting herself to circumstances, she was remarkably popular with all classes of people among whom she was called to move. Early in the spring of 1839 she was called upon to endure perhaps the most severe trial of her life; the severing of all ties that bound her to the land of her nativity, the committal of herself to the treacherous storms of ocean, and in connection with others, to seek, as a missionary, a far distant home on the then almost unknown shores of the great Pacific.

A few months were employed in visiting her friends and bidding them what she then supposed her last adieu. This accomplished, with her husband, she then repaired to New York city, and the evening of Oct. 9th, 1839 found her for the first time on the deck of a ship. Nearly eight months of ocean life, during which she was permitted to look in upon Brazil, Chili, and the Sandwich Islands, acquainted her with the lights and shadows of a sea voyage in a crowded vessel, of 2,200 [must have been more—perhaps 22,000?] miles. June 1st, 1840 found her at Vancouver, and exchanging the ship *Lausanne* for a Chinook canoe, by which craft the waters of Oregon were then navigated, she arrived on the 15th of the same month at the old Mission stand, situated ten miles below the present city of Salem. Early in the spring of 1841 it was her lot to occupy a small shanty located near what is called the "old parsonage" in said city, and thus she had the honor of being the first white woman that lived in the original precincts of the present Capital of the State of Oregon. Thrown as she was into the midst of savages, and often witnessing evidences of their hostile dispositions, and hearing of their murderous designs, she entertained at times great fear that she and her family would yet fall victims to savage fury— and the more so as she now had under her protection a young and helpless sister. One day, at the dusk of evening, in the fall of the year, while the neighborhood was agitated by rumors of Indian outbreaks, there appeared immediately in front of the parsonage 12 mounted savages of the Molalla tribe, painted and accoutred in the most hideous and frightful manner, and rushing up into the very dooryard, all dismounted, giving evidence at the same time that their visit was not friendly. Mr. H. went out to meet them, and approaching the one who appeared to be their leader, offered him his hand in token of friendship. He refused the proffered signal, and immediately the whole band set up a horrid laugh. This demonstration of hostility so alarmed Mrs. Hines that she resolved to take her little sister, and if possible, effect her escape to a house on the north side of Mill Creek, now North Salem, occupied by the families of Messrs. L. H. Judson and James

Olley, the only house within many miles. She took a circuitous route for a distance down the little stream running in the rear of the parsonage, so as to keep from the sight of the Indians as long as possible. Sometimes leading little Julia by the hand and at others lifting her in her arms, she struck across the prairie northward, struggling through the tall grass with her precious burden, while expecting every moment to be pursued and feel the violent hand of a savage laid upon her. On reaching the creek, not daring to extend her flight to a foot bridge a short distance below, she dashed straight through the current, bearing her sister in her arms. Not being pursued, she gained the house in safety, and collecting all the adult persons belonging to the families, she returned with them through the darkness to look after the fate of her husband. The savages had in the meantime encamped in [the] rear of the parsonage, where they remained quietly for a few hours, and then before daylight decamped, bearing with them as booty some provisions and a valuable horse, the property of Mr. H. Here was the scene of Mrs. Hines' cares and labors to Dec. 1843. In the spring of 1842, by the death of Mrs. Jason Lee, their infant daughter, but three weeks old, was taken by Mrs. Hines from the bed where its mother, just deceased, still reposed, and conveyed to her own home. This was the providence which resulted subsequently, when Mr. Lee was on his dying bed, in his full commitment of this beloved daughter to her sole guardianship and training during the period of her minority.

For reasons which need not be inserted in this sketch, Mr. Lee, Mr. and Mrs. Hines and family, left Oregon in Feb. 1844, intending to proceed to the Eastern States. But on arriving at Honolulu it was found that there was no vessel which would sail for any of the Atlantic ports for several months. It was however ascertained that a small Hawaiian schooner about to sail for San Blas, on the coast of Mexico, would take one person on board. And Mr. Lee being exceedingly anxious to proceed, took passage in hope of being able in some way to get from Mexico to New York: while Mr. Hines and family, including Mr. Lee's daughter, decided to return to Oregon. It was here, on the Island of Oahu, in the midst of the solitudes of the great Pacific, and after the little company had spent a whole night in prayerful solicitude, without any prospect of ever meeting again this side of Heaven, that Mrs. Hines received more fully the important charge committed to her by Mr. Lee. It was on the 28th of Feb., 1844, that with flowing tears and words of tenderest sympathy and love Mrs. Hines received the daughter from the arms of the weeping father, and made a solemn pledge before

Heaven, that all a mother could do for a daughter she would do, God being her helper, for the motherless child that then in her heart of hearts she adopted as her own. Mr. Lee never saw his child again, and she was never separated from that second mother until a few days since, when that mother took her flight to Heaven.

According to arrangement Mrs. Hines with her family returned again to Oregon, and arrived at Oregon City the last of April. Residing there for the best part of two years, she was remarkably active in Church interests, but especially in searching out the destitute among the emigrants who crossed the plains, and in affording the needed relief. During the years 1844-5, in company with her husband, she visited every portion of Oregon then occupied by whites, for Missionary purposes, traveling on horseback and in canoes.

In September 1845, for reasons that need not be here appended, it became the duty of Mrs. Hines to leave Oregon again and return to the States. Accordingly, she with Mr. H. and their two adopted daughters bade a second adieu to the wooded mountains of Oregon, and on the Brig *Chenamus* performed another voyage to the Sandwich Islands, where they arrived on the 15th of October. This was her third visit to these Islands, where in all she spent upwards of three months. Providence so ordered that from the Islands, she had the opportunity of crossing the Pacific Ocean to the coast of China and of spending upwards of two months among the Celestials at Hong Kong, Macao, and Canton. From thence, in the good ship *Leeland*, the Chinese and Java Seas were traversed, the Straits of Sunday penetrated, the Indian Ocean crossed, the Cape of Good Hope doubled, the Atlantic Ocean again traced, and on the 5th of May the missionary family arrived in safety at New York city.

The following September found the subject of this memoir a resident in the town of Victor, Ontario Co., to which her husband had been appointed, who during all these years had retained his connection with the Genesee Conference. Her travels for the next eight years may be summed up in few words. They were removed from Victor to the village of Pike, thence to Covington, thence to Lancaster, and last to Spencer's Basin [later known as Spencerport]. Her uniform character during these years was that of a faithful, devoted, useful, Methodist preacher's wife. While residing in the latter place, in 1853 [should be 1852—Gustavus' transfer was published in the paper in Dec. 1852], very unexpectedly to her husband she informed him that she would be glad to return again to the Pacific Coast, and there spend the remainder of her days. Sympathizing in this feeling, Mr. Hines asked of Bishop Waugh and obtained a transfer to the Oregon Conference, with the privilege of returning to the country by way of the Plains. The journey across the Plains, which was performed the same year [actually the next year, 1853], was one of great interest to Mrs. Hines though attended with great toil and exposure. It was also marked by many thrilling incidents, all but one of which must here be passed over. The company to which she belonged were nooning on Burnt River where the grass and herbage were exceedingly dry. While she was engaged in preparing dinner, the sun shining brightly on the earth, she did not observe that the fire was running under her feet. Her dress, which was of cotton, took fire and she almost instantly became enveloped in flames. Some one exclaimed "Mrs. Hines will burn up." Mr. Hines hearing this and looking up saw that not an instant was to be lost; and, springing at once to the rescue, seized the burning dress with both hands, and with one effort tore the entire garment from her person, and casting it upon the ground, in one moment it was reduced to ashes. She has always believed that she was thus saved from the terrible fate of being burned to death. Their first place of residence after reaching Oregon in October, 1853 was on the Vancouver circuit; and in the spring of 1854 by virtue of the appointment of Mr. H. to Salem she became a resident of that city. On this year she received a third orphan [this was Marie Smith] into her family and into her heart: and in her education and training she ever manifested the care, solicitude and affection of a most devoted mother. Here, for fourteen years she has had a settled home, though from time to time she has extended her travels to various parts of the State and Washington Territory. Wherever she has been she has not failed to leave the impression of her many excellencies upon all who understood her character. In this home she closed her highly useful and eventful life in great peace, March 14th, 1870. Though her last sufferings were great, and protracted, her patience, her faith, her hope were strong and unwavering. Her joy in the Lord at times was triumphant. "All is peace;" "All is bright;" "Praise the Lord" were some of her last expressions. The dying hour of the Christian! 'Tis the most solemn, yet it is the most sublime, the most glorious hour of their lives.[4]

After Lydia's death, March 14, 1870, Gustavus married Ann Johnson on February 21, 1871, and she in turn died March 19, 1875, leaving behind their orphaned daughter, Gussie, who survived only until May 29, 1880.

As to children of Gustavus and Lydia, it is reported, "...after losing their only child, a daughter, raised Jason Lee's daughter, Lucy."[5]

Lucy Anna Maria Lee

Lucy Lee, like her adoptive parents Gustavus and Lydia Hines, as well as her own father Jason Lee, was closely associated with Willamette University. For her story we turn again to Willamette's able historian, R. M. Gatke.[6]

Lucy Anna Maria Lee was born February 26, 1842, at Chemeketa, the principal station of the Methodist Episcopal Missions on the Pacific Coast, of which her father, Rev. Jason Lee, was Superintendent. Her mother was Lucy Thompson, of Barre, Vermont, a cultured lady whose valedictory address at Newbury Seminary attracted the attention of Jason Lee, then on a tour of the States in the interest of his Missions.

On the death of her mother, and the departure of her father for the East, in 1844, she became the ward of Rev. Gustavus Hines, with whom, on the closing of the Missions, she made the voyage to New York via China and the Cape of Good Hope, to learn on arriving that her father had, more than six months previously, closed his earthly career.

Rev. Gustavus Hines, with his family, returned to Oregon, crossing the plains in 1853, and made his home at Old Chemeketa, Salem, the capital of Oregon, where "Lucy Anna" grew to womanhood.

Her education was at the Oregon Institute and Willamette. She graduated in 1863 and, as we have already learned, taught some before graduation and continued in regular faculty relation after graduation. She taught English literature and French and in 1866 became the first preceptress of Willamette, which position she held until 1869. She was married to Francis H. Grubbs a year after their graduation. The two taught together at Willamette and, afterwards, elsewhere until ill-health forced her to give up the teaching she loved so much. At The Dalles, on April 25, 1881, death claimed her at the early age of thirty-nine.

According to Gatke, "As though they had agreed together, all the many classmates and students of Lucy Anna Lee Grubbs insist upon speaking of her in terms that glow with eulogistic praise...this teacher of old Willamette was made of a superior clay to that from which the ordinary run of human beings are made." He goes on to quote from several students' tributes, one example of which we include here.

Ellen J. Chamberlin, a pupil of Lucy Anna Lee, and herself long a beloved teacher at Willamette, University of Washington, and Oregon State College, wrote:

> She was a woman of such high ideals and lofty purposes, of so much quiet dignity and poise of character that the inspirations caught from her example and words of encouragement were sweet and lasting ...
>
> It would be hard to tell what methods of instruction Mrs. Grubbs followed in her classwork to obtain good results—for they seemed to be purely original—a part of her very self. Her own enthusiasm to drink deep from the wells of learning incited everyone to highest and best efforts. Girl-nature she thoroughly understood, and though full of love and sympathy for all, she would tolerate only earnest, conscientious work.[7]

Marie Elizabeth Smith

Lucy Anna Lee was not the first child adopted by Gustavus and Lydia Hines—Lydia's younger sister, Julia Bryant was first—nor was she the last. In 1855 a third daughter, Marie Smith, joined the family. Reminiscing for journalist Fred Lockley many years later in 1925, Marie adds some insight into the character of the Hines family, and tells a captivating story of her own. We have space for only a few relevant excerpts here.

Mrs. Marie Smith Marsh is the owner of the Marsh Printing company in Portland. Waif Grubbe [should be "Grubbs"], granddaughter of Jason Lee, is manager of the company.

"My mother, Mrs. Cornelius Smith, married J. C. Geer of Butteville, June 24, 1849," said Mrs. Marsh. "He had 10 children, she had eight, and within the next few years they had three more children. Mother died in the spring of 1855. Prior to her death she sent me up to Salem, to my sister Ella, who was working for Mrs. Joseph Holman, with instructions to Ella to find some good woman who would adopt me. Ella took me to the home of Mrs. Gustavus Hines, who said I could stay there till Ella found a home for me. Mrs. Holman, with whom my sister Ella stayed, didn't like Mrs. Hines. At a class meeting Mrs. Hines refused to testify how she was growing in grace all the time. She said that was a matter between herself and the

Lord. Mrs. Holman had come to Oregon as a missionary. She was very religious, never missed a class meeting, always testified and told how she was crucifying the flesh and growing in grace. Mrs. Holman thought Mrs. Hines was too good-natured and indulgent to children, and too pleasant and easy-going, so she did not like Ella to go to see me at the home of Mrs. Hines. I went to Mrs. Hines' home to stay until my sister could find someone who could adopt me, but after I had been there a short time Mrs. Hines told my sister she had already adopted two children and one more would make very little difference, so she would adopt me.

"I shall never forget how astonished I was when I first went to the home of Mrs. Hines. I had been accustomed to seeing people with blue or gray eyes. Mrs. Hines had black eyes, abundant hair, black as ink, and heavy black eyebrows, with long, black eyelashes. Her husband had two brothers, Harvey and Joseph. When these men got together it was as good as a circus. They were all fond of laughing, joking, and telling stories, and you couldn't help liking them. When I first went to their home I was afraid of Mrs. Hines, on account of her dark hair and dark eyes. Mrs. Hines introduced me to her youngest sister, Julia Bryant, who lived with her, and to Lucy Ann [should be "Anna"], daughter of Jason Lee. They had adopted Lucy Ann when her father, Jason Lee, died. Lucy Ann was wearing a blue-checked silk dress, and when Mrs. Hines said, 'Lucy, here is a little girl who is going to be your sister,' I could see that Lucy didn't like me at all. She was jealous. My sister Ella had brought me to the home of Mrs. Hines and left me there. I can remember yet how the big tears rolled down my cheeks as I tried to stifle my sobs when she left. I wasn't afraid of Mr. Hines, because he had blue eyes and brown hair, but I was very much afraid of his dark-haired, dark-eyed wife. Julia Bryant, Mrs. Hines' sister, was a teacher. She took me up on her lap and tried to comfort me. Later, Julia married Judge C. N. Terry, one of the well-known officials of Oregon Territory in the early days. After supper, Mrs. Hines told me I could sleep with Lucy so I wouldn't be lonesome. I saw that Lucy didn't like me, so I rolled over to the extreme edge of the bed and lay against the side of the wall. The next morning I slipped out of the house and went to the oak grove nearby so I could cry where no one would see me.

"Late that afternoon Lucy relented and told me I could go with her to Professor Hoyt's pasture to get our cow. She let me hold her hand. When we got to the pasture she said, 'You can go in and drive the cow out and I will stand here at the gate to keep the other cows from coming out, or I will go in and get the cow and you can stand here to keep the other cows from coming out.' I was only 7 years old, I was very small, and these cows looked very fierce to me, I told her I would stand at the gate. If you think children never have any trials and don't have to exercise courage, you are mistaken, for I can still remember the terror with which I saw the other cows coming toward the gate to get out. I thought they would run over me and hook me and step on me, but I shooed them back, and they didn't come out.

"Lucy Ann Lee, whose daughter, Waif Grubbe, now manages my printing plant, and I became firm friends. Mr. and Mrs. Hines had been in China. While there they had got a lot of silk at a low price. My own mother could have been no better to me than was Mrs. Hines. She made dresses for her sister Julia and for Lucy Ann Lee from this silk. She ripped up some of their old silk dresses and made them into dresses for me. It seems, as I look back now, that Mrs. Hines was always at work. In those days people were constantly dropping in to eat dinner or to stay overnight, so that between her dressmaking and sewing and regular housework Mrs. Hines had a busy job caring for the extra guests. Mr. Hines traveled between Salem and Jacksonville, preaching. He had two bay horses and a light buggy. He took his cooking utensils and provisions along, and camped where night overtook him. Before he started on one of these trips Mrs. Hines would be busy for a day or two ironing a supply of shirts and collars for him and baking a lot of bread and meat.

"I attended Willamette university and graduated there. Miss Lizzie Boise taught a private school. The children always called her Miss Massachusetts because she talked so much about what a wonderful state Massachusetts was. She decided to make a trip back to Massachusetts, so she had me take charge of her school. I taught her school a year or more. Among the pupils were Nez Bush and Althea and Bertha Moores.

"One thing I shall never forget was Mrs. Hines' calling me into her room one day and saying, 'Marie, I have not told you before, but I am going to die soon, and I want you to have the Irish poplin that father got for me. I want you also to take that roll of black silk that N. P. Willis gave me.' N. P. Willis had boarded at our home, and we all liked him very much. I couldn't keep from crying when Mother Hines told me she was going to die, and I told her maybe she was mistaken. But she knew what she was talking about, for she died a few months later.

"Mr. Hines married a young woman, and they had a child, a little girl. They had decided to name the child, which they thought was going to be a boy, Gustavus, so they compromised on Gustena, but they always called her Gussie. Mr. Hines' first wife, my foster mother, died of tuberculosis. His second wife did not live long. She died of the same disease. Before dying she wrote to Lucy Ann Lee, who had married Francis Grubbe, asking her to adopt her little daughter, Gussie. Lucy's father, Jason Lee, had died of tuberculosis, and Lucy herself was not very strong, so she thought it would be unwise to adopt Gussie. A family near Columbus, now called Maryville [probably "Maryhill"], adopted Gussie. She died of diphtheria when she was 10 years old."[8]

Julia Bryant

Lydia (Bryant) Hines' younger sister Julia accompanied Lydia and Gustavus on the 1839 sea-going trip to Oregon as a four-year-old. A young woman when she returned in 1853, she married Chester N. Terry, an attorney, who served for eighteen years on the Board of Trustees for Willamette University—still another link between that school and Gustavus' extended family.[9] The 1860 U.S. Census for Salem lists in the C. N. Terry household C. N. Terry, 36; J. M. Terry, 25; E. C. Terry (male), 3; G. Hines, 48; L. Hines, 40; L. A. Lee, 18; and M. E. Smith (female), 13. It seems that Julia, who lived with her sister and husband for so long, now had returned the favor and provided residence for them, as well as for their adopted daughters, Lucy Anna Lee and Marie Elizabeth Smith. In the 1870 census E. C. Terry and M. E. Smith remain in the household, but Lydia had died earlier that year, Gustavus had moved to The Dalles where he was now assigned as pastor and Lucy Anna Lee and husband Francis Grubbs were in their own home with their daughter, Ethel Waif Grubbs.

Joseph

Joseph's stay in Oregon lasted only until 1859 when he was transferred to California. The 1860 U.S. census for Fairfield, Solano County, California, lists the family as Joseph, Elizabeth, Melissa A., George E., John M., and Ida A. Joseph continued in the ministry at various locations in California through the mid-1870s and afterward remained active in religious and civic affairs until his death in Santa Clara in 1913. In 1911 he published his autobiographical *Touching Incidents*,[10] the first chapter of which was a sketch of his origins and career. This chapter appears to have been written for earlier publication in a history of California; we judge the sketch to have been written by J. M. Guinn with aid from Joseph.[11] The entire sketch is reproduced here.

REV. JOSEPH WILKINSON HINES, the subject of this biographical sketch, is at the present writing (1904) the president of the Santa Clara County Society of California Pioneers, a member of the board of trustees of the University of the Pacific and also actively identified with several other local associations designed to promote the various material, social and intellectual interests of the State for whose expansion and up-building he has, in various relations, spent the prime and strength of his manhood. From the time his feet first pressed the soil of California, nearly half a century ago, until now, when his brow wears the silver crown of nearly four score years, his hand has never wearied and his heart has never faltered in honorable and intelligent effort to make his adopted state what it confessedly is at the present time—one of the grandest and most promising commonwealths in the great American Union. Independent but not obtrusive, zealous but not impulsive, possessed of a wonderful versatility, his mental habitudes were well adapted to the varied and pressing demands of a new and rapidly growing community, where ideals for future guidance were to be created, and various uplifting and progressive agencies were to be employed and fitted to the demands and exigencies of a rapidly shifting and varying scene. A mind thus endowed could scarcely be expected to remain indifferent to any phase of society that might, in the process of social development, present itself for consideration by the people.

Mr. Hines, therefore, in common with many others at that early day in our history, lost no time in fearlessly grappling with all questions of interest as they successively presented themselves. His genius for planning and pushing forward all enterprises calculated to improve the conditions and prospects of society in all its essential needs was truly wonderful. No community that ever enjoyed the benefits of this counsel and labor but could show in many directions substantial evidences of his public-spirited efforts in its behalf. His consciousness of personal honesty and integrity would never allow him to apologize for appearing in the foremost ranks of progress and reform, or to participate in efforts to compromise with wrongdoing in order to gain some personal advantage by the sacrifice of the public good. His mind was never groping in the dark alleys of agnostic uncertainty or striving to feel its dubious way in the twilight uncertainties of questionable expediency. With a positiveness sometimes bordering upon obstinacy he always stood

"Firm as an iron pillar strong,
And steadfast as a wall of brass."

Like all men of advanced views, with positive and aggressive feelings and purposes, he was compelled at times to wait with patience for the day of vindication; but that day was sure to come, responsive to the demands of a faith that would never falter and a spiritual instinct that cheerfully allied itself with the omnipotent energies of eternal truth.

Mr. Hines, in common with a host of others of similar traits of character, was privileged to live during one of the most trying eras in the history of the Pacific coast. And we are assured that to their wise and determined efforts the people of the present day are greatly indebted for the prosperous and enviable condition of its material, social and religious interests. But very few of those heroic men who faced the fearful crisis of 1860-1865 and saved human freedom for ourselves and for the world are with us today. Nearly all are now dwelling in that "city not made with hands, eternal in the heavens."

The subject of this sketch took a prominent part in organizing the Republican party, which at that time was the only reliable force that could be depended upon to turn back the rapidly rising tide of secession in California. He was a delegate to the first general convention of that party in the State, served on the committee on platform, of which he was the chief author, and labored with unflagging industry and devotion in carrying the state for Lincoln and Stanford.[12] This political victory saved the Pacific Coast from becoming plunged into the dark, yawning gulf of rebellion, and drew the eyes of the nation to her unrivaled importance as a member of the American Union.

When our national authorities wisely decided not to call for recruits for the Union army from California he took an active part in raising the seventeen thousand volunteers who so bravely and effectually guarded our extended frontier, which then reached from

Puget Sound to the borders of Texas. It was those noble men who headed off the expedition from the South who were expected to form a junction with a band of conspirators from California and together sweep the whole coast into the Southern confederacy. Then Maximilian would have had an empire on the Pacific, and Jeff Davis another on the Atlantic, and the sun of religious and civil liberty would have set forever. Men of today, will you remember the men who trod the burning sands of the desert and scaled the rocky summits of the mountains that you and your children might have a country to love and defend, and a brightening hope to cheer the generations yet unborn?

At the opening of our Civil War Mr. Hines received commissions from the proper authorities in the east to act as agent of both the sanitary and Christian associations on the Pacific Coast. He at once entered upon his work with his accustomed zeal and devotion. His entire time, together with all his surplus income, were freely given to the cause of the country; and his success in raising money and other supplies for the army was such as to call forth an autograph letter from General Grant, which he now has in his possession and which is kept as an heirloom valued beyond all price. The special incident which called forth this letter from the general may be stated in the following words: The ladies of Humboldt county, where Mr. Hines and family then resided, and where Grant, when but a captain in the United States army, had once been stationed, conceived the idea of sending a unique memorial present to Mrs. Grant. In order to do this, and at the same time raise funds for the Christian commission, they made a quilt composed of thirty-six separate and distinct Union flags, with the coat of arms of the United States wrought on a field of blue as a centerpiece, and the coat of arms of each state on a blue field for each separate banner. These thirty-six flags represented the number of states then in the Union, while eight silver spangles on the border stood for the number of the territories then existing. The material of which this quilt was composed was beautiful colored silk, and the stars, numbering about six hundred, and the coat of arms, both of the United States, and of each separate state, were of floss silk, and all wrought by hand, nearly all by Mrs. Hines, she being especially skillful in the use of the needle. When this unique gift was completed (but very few people having been left into the secret) almost the entire population for miles around came together to witness the unveiling. It was given out that each banner would be sold separately and only those coming from the state the banner represented could vote upon it. The central field, representing the United States, was to be bid for promiscuously, without regard to state lines or nationality. The interest in the affair was most intense and at the close it was found that the sum of $2,400 had been raised for the cause of the Union. The quilt was then sent to Mrs. Grant, and in response the general returned the short but beautiful autograph letter now in the possession of Mr. Hines. When General Grant and his wife made the circuit of the world they visited San Jose and she stated to Mrs. Hines that she cherished that beautiful quilt, made by the ladies of Humboldt, as one of her most valued treasures.[13]

Space will not permit of an extended recital of the thrilling adventures and hairbreadth escapes through which Mr. Hines passed in his travels over the coast during its pioneer history. They would fill a volume, and if told in his graphic and earnest style would be deeply interesting and instructive to future generations. His travels in the earlier days frequently took him among the Indians tribes of Oregon and northern California, and into association with the rough element of our frontier settlements; but such was his tact and quiet, fearless demeanor that he never failed to command, and never lost the confidence and respect of both the good and the bad with whom he came in contact. He never carried about his person any deadly weapons and never displayed any doubts or fears; and even the wildest Indians seemed so attracted and pleased by his cordial, unsuspicious conduct that they were at once disarmed of all feeling of hostility.

When the Civil war closed with the signal triumph of the Union cause Mr. Hines, with the same broad patriotic feeling that had characterized his conduct during its continuance, bent all his energies to bringing about those feelings of mutual sympathy and respect between the north and the south, without which he felt that no permanent union or prosperity could be expected for the country. He fully endorsed the sentiment expressed by General Grant at the surrender of Lee, "Let us have peace," and he labored to that end with constant and intelligent devotion.

Having been elected as superintendent of public instruction for one of our most populous counties, Mr. Hines found himself associated with many of the leading educators of the state in revising our common school system and bringing it more in harmony with the advanced ideas of the eastern states. This work was accomplished in such a thorough and satisfactory manner that California stands today without a superior in all the states of the Union for the perfection and practical operation of its common school system. He served also for about two years as agent of the University of the Pacific. His success in that position was so signal and timely that the board of trustees passed a vote of thanks, in which they ascribed the success of its financial affairs largely due to his devoted and determined effort. In more than one pressing emergency he bravely met the demands of the crisis and caused the somber clouds of doubt and uncertainty to give place to the sunlight of hope and assurance.

Mr. Hines possesses a decided literary taste, and has always managed, notwithstanding the pressing duties incident to a new and growing state, to keep in touch with the literary and scientific progress of the age. As editor of the first labor paper published on the Pacific Coast[14] his editorial writings attracted the attention of the secular press throughout the country, and were universally regarded as masterly expositions of social and economic science. His contributions to other periodicals, both religious and secular, were numerous and able, and read by the people in general with decided interest and profit. As a ready entertaining speaker he was everywhere listened to with decided appreciation. He possessed in a wonderful degree the power of concentration, one very competent judge having once declared that "he could say more in five minutes than any other man he ever heard." As an after-dinner speaker he had but few superiors.

By referring to the ancestry of Joseph Wilkinson Hines, we find that he was the tenth child of James and Betsey (Round) Hines, the latter a daughter of Bertram and Alice (Wilkinson) Round. Bertram Round was the son of James and Susannah (Seamen) Round, and was born in Rehoboth, Mass., December 11, 1741. James Round was born in Rehoboth, Mass., July 19, 1722, and was the son of George and Susanna Round. George Round was the son of John and Elizabeth Round. John Round's will is recorded in the town records as made October 16, 1716. This John Round was the boy saved from the Indian massacre of Swansea in 1675. It is probable his parents were then killed. James Round and his son Bertram, who was grandfather to Mr. Hines, emigrated from Swansea to Rhode Island, and thence to Richfield, N. Y., in 1793, where he died October 1, 1835, leaving two hundred and thirty-six descendants; one of whom, Stephen Hopkins of Rhode Island, was a signer of the Declaration of Independence. The Round family was of pure English descent. Alice Wilkinson, wife of Bertram Round and grandmother of Mr. Hines, was the daughter of Joseph and Martha (Bray) Wilkinson, great-granddaughter of Samuel and Plain (Wickenden) Wilkinson and great-great-granddaughter of Lawrence and Susanna (Smith) Wilkinson.

Lawrence Wilkinson came to Providence, R. I., in 1645. His ancestry is given in a book entitled "Americans of Royal Descent," page 287-289, and shows him to have been the fifteenth from King Edward I of England, and also that he was descended from the royal house of both France and Spain.[15] The Wilkinson genealogy is given fully in a volume published in 1869, by Rev. Israel Wilkinson of Illinois.

Mr. Hines was married August 30, 1847, to Miss Elizabeth Meridith, of Steuben, Oneida county, N. Y. Her parents were both natives of Wales, but were brought to this country when children, and were reared in full sympathy with American life and institutions. Eight children, four sons and four daughters, were born to Mr. and Mrs. Hines. Three of these, one son and two daughters, died in early life, while three sons and two daughters now live within easy access of the paternal home.

We have here attempted to give a few incidents in the long, eventful career of one who was ambitious only to live a true, manly life, devoted to the best good of universal humanity. His ideals of life were always found to harmonize with man's highest needs and his purest and most earnest aspirations. Such men, though not always understood and appreciated while living, generally have an influence that will unfold itself in the flowering beauties and ripening harvests of future generations. To lose such lives from the records of time is to obstruct in a positive degree the march of civilization and to foster the sinister impulses that will tend to gradual but fatal retrogression. So let us give the world the light that we now have, and when the summons comes drop into the swelling current of the stream of time those noble influences that will make it a broader, deeper and a swifter river. Through these and their work, as the prophet has said, "Instead of the thorn shall come up the fir tree, and instead of the brier shall come up the myrtle tree, and it shall be to the Lord for a name, for an everlasting sign that shall not be cut off."[16]

Elizabeth (Meredith) Hines

MRS. J. W. HINES IS DEAD AT COLLEGE PARK HOME[17]
Was One of Those Who Made Possible Founding of College of Pacific.

Mrs. Elizabeth Hines, widow of the late Rev. J. W. Hines, died yesterday morning at her home at 555 Stockton Avenue, at the age of 86. The funeral will be held Tuesday afternoon at 2 o'clock from the mortuary chapel of the W. L. Woodrow Undertaking company.

The decedent, with her late husband, J. W. Hines, was among those who made possible the founding of the College of Pacific in Santa Clara. It was later moved to College Park, and was given the name of the College of the Pacific.

The decedent was born in Steuben, Oneida County, New York state. She was married on August 30, 1847. She and her husband came across the Isthmus of Panama on the backs of burros in the early 50's. They first settled in Oregon, near Salem. There Mr. Hines took up his work as a Methodist missionary.

At that time Oregon was a very wild and unsettled country. While Mr. Hines would be off on the long trips necessitated by the nature of his calling, his wife would often join with her neighbors in resisting the attacks of Indians on the little settlement. She often would sit up all night making bullets to be used by the settlers in the defense of their homes.

Leaving Oregon, Mr. and Mrs. Hines went to Humboldt county, Cal. They were there at the time of the outbreak of the civil war. Mr. and Mrs. Hines were given a commission by religious organizations in the east to carry on the work of these organizations during the war. They won special mention for the manner in which they raised money and other supplies for the army of the Union, and General Grant sent a letter of thanks to them.

From Humboldt county they moved to Vallejo. There Mr. Hines was superintendent of education. Coming to Santa Clara county, the devout and capable missionaries took an active part in the founding of the University of the Pacific. Mr. Hines was one of the first trustees of the institution. Mrs. Hines throughout her lifetime made substantial contributions to the college.

For many years Mr. and Mrs. Hines had owned a ranch on the Brokaw road, and had resided at 555 Stockton Avenue, in College

Park. Mr. Hines died February 22, 1913.

Mrs. Hines was the mother of Mrs. O. D. Conterno, Mrs. Annie Sprinkle of Oakland, John M. Hines and the late George E. Hines, grandmother of George C., Lloyd, and Will M. Hines, Walter and Eddie Burns, and George M. Sprinkle. She was the aunt of Miss Jennie Phillips of Vernon, N.Y., and Miss Lina Rogers of Westernville, N.Y.

The Hines talent for writing has continued through Joseph's line. His grandson, William Meredith Hines, was a journalist and newspaper executive of national reputation.[18] His son in turn, William Meredith Hines II, was also a highly respected journalist whose career spanned nearly fifty years and included award-winning coverage of the U.S. space program from its infancy in the Eisenhower administration through Hines's retirement as Washington Bureau Chief of the *Chicago Sun-Times* in 1986.[19]

Harvey

Harvey's *Illustrated History of the State of Oregon*[20] includes a biography of unstated authorship. If Harvey himself wrote it, we would certainly not accuse him of modesty.

H. K. Hines, D.D.,[21] the youngest of twelve children of James and Betsy (Round) Hines, was born in Herkimer county, New York, in 1828. His ancestral line, on his mother's side, is clearly traced back to Edward I of England through Lawrence Wilkinson,[22] from whom Mr. Hines is the fourth in descent. His own grandfather, Bartram Round, was an Ensign and Lieutenant in the Revolutionary war. On his father's side he is a descendant of the Hopkins of Rhode Island, and of the Churches of Massachusetts, who came from England in Governor Northrup's[23] fleet in 1630 and landed at Plymouth. It will thus be seen that he inherits pioneer blood.

His early life was spent in Oswego county, New York, to which his family emigrated when he was three years of age. Then almost literally a wilderness, that region afforded him very limited scholastic advantages. In his fourteenth year he was converted, and before he was sixteen he was licensed to exhort by Rev. William Peck, an older brother of Bishop Peck. Early in his nineteenth year he was licensed to preach, and soon after, removing to Western New York, he was employed as a supply on Eden circuit in the Genesee Conference to take the place of Gilbert De la Matyr, whose health had failed. When just twenty he was admitted into the Genessee Conference on trial. In that conference he served such appointments as Wyoming, Pearl Street, Buffalo, and Niagara Falls.

In December, 1852, he was transferred by Bishop Waugh to the Oregon Conference, and the following summer crossed the plains with an ox team, reaching Portland October 3, 1853, to which charge he had been appointed by Bishop Ames at the first session of the Oregon Annual Conference. His time of actual service on this coast has been thirty-nine years; eleven years on stations, sixteen as Presiding Elder, one as College Agent, eight as editor of the Pacific Christian Advocate, and three as Theological Professor.

As Presiding Elder he has had charge of all the State of Washington, nearly all of Oregon and Idaho, and his travels over them have made him more widely known, personally, without doubt, than any other minister of the Pacific Northwest.

He represented the Thirteenth General Conference District in the General Missionary and Church Extension Committees of the Methodist Episcopal Church, from 1876 to 1880, and on the resignation of J. H. Wilbur from the same committees in 1886 he was elected by the Board of Bishops to succeed him, thus making six years' service therein.

He was elected by the General Conference Commission on Ecumenical Conference one of the seven representatives of the Fourteenth General Conference District in that body, and attended its sessions in Washington, D.C., from its opening to its close.

Dr. Hines estimates his travels in the service of the church on this coast to have been by rail and steamboat 75,000 miles, by stage 5,000 miles and by his own private conveyance not less than 100,000, making an aggregate of 180,000 miles. He has preached about 6,000 sermons, held 900 quarterly meetings, dedicated 54 churches, and been called to deliver many memorial addresses of pioneers, both preachers and people.

He has also been quite active in political life. During the days of secession he was one of the staunch supporters of the Union, and delivered the first political speech coming from any minister on the coast. He was president of the Territorial Council of Washington, and a member of the Legislature during the sessions of 1864 and 1866. In 1876 he was a Republican delegate to the National Convention at Cincinnati, which nominated R. B. Hayes for president.

Dr. Hines was married at Wyoming, New York, in 1852, to Miss

Elizabeth J. Graves, a lady endowed with the true Christian spirit and great strength of character. She was an able helper in all missionary work, and by her personal effort and enthusiasm was organized the Woman's Christian Temperance Union of Oregon, of which she was the first president. She was well and favorably known throughout the State for her many deeds of kindness and charity. She was called to her last rest in January, 1889, leaving a bereaved husband and two children, James A. and Lua A. The latter is now the wife of C. K. Cranston. The Doctor lives with his daughter at the corner of East Washington and Seventeenth streets, Portland, where he built a handsome residence in 1884.

As trustee he has had a close connection with the Willamette University since he came to the State, and during 1890 and 1891 was Professor of Theology in that institution. In May, 1892, he was a delegate from the Idaho Conference to the General Conference of the Methodist Episcopal Church at Omaha. He is a member of the Sons of the American Revolution, and is Past High Priest of the Chapter of Royal Arch Masons.

Dr. Hines is now one of the honored professors of the theological department of the Portland University. His forty-four years of faithful work have been of great service and have been marked by ability, industry, constancy, and efficiency. His capacity for hard work in both study and field has supplemented his ability in the pulpit and the promise of his early years has been fulfilled. The wide field covered by his labors and the variety of the work to which he has been called, has enabled him to an extent given to but few, to impress himself for good on the civil and ecclesiastical affairs of the Empire of the Northwest.

He is still vigorous in body and mind and promises to do work equal to his very best for a number of years to come.

Not mentioned in the above is Harvey's first marriage, to Angeline Seymor, on Nov. 1, 1846.[24] No children of that marriage are recorded. The 1850 U.S. census lists just Harvey Hinds [sic], age 22, Angeline, age 21, and Lucy A. Nichols, 19.[25] After Angeline's death on June 19, 1851,[26] Harvey married Elizabeth Jane Graves June 26, 1852. According to an obituary, Harvey and Elizabeth had six children, but only two, James and Lua listed above, survived to adulthood. The 1860 U.S. census for Linn County, Oregon, lists three children: James, Edward, and Udora.[27] Following Elizabeth's death in 1889, Harvey was married a third time, to Celinda

Minerva Gillette Judkins, on January 2, 1892.

According to two obituaries, when Harvey died January 19, 1902, he was working on his nearly completed memoirs, but we have been unable to locate either this manuscript, or any of the extensive collection of personal papers upon which it was reportedly based. Even without these materials, though, his literary legacy includes five published books, three serials, eight years worth of editorial writing in the *Pacific Christian Advocate*,[28] and numerous articles written for that newspaper and for other publications.

Elizabeth Jane (Graves) Hines

We feel compelled to include a separate account of the activities of Harvey's wife, Elizabeth, because of the breadth of those activities. A tribute written after her death by longtime family friend, Rev. A. J. Joslyn,[29] follows.

Elisabeth Jane Graves Hines was born in the town of Covington, Livingston county, New York, on the 30th day of June, 1828, and departed this life at her home in East Portland, Oregon, at midnight of the 29th day of January, 1890, aged sixty one years and seven months.

Her parents were from Salem, Massachusetts, and were of the sturdy stock of the Pilgrims. They were of the earliest settlers of Western New York, west of the Genesee river, and began their life in true pioneer form and spirit, in an almost unbroken wilderness.

Her early education was obtained in Wyoming Academy, in the beautiful village of that name, which became her home through the years of her young womanhood. Later she entered the Genesee Wesleyan Seminary, at Lima, New York, one of the most popular and successful of Methodism, which became her *alma mater* about 1851.

On the 26th day of June 1852, she was united in marriage with Rev. H. K. Hines, who had been her pastor at Wyoming during the ecclesiastical years of 1850-51, but was then pastor of Pearl street church in the city of Buffalo. Her acceptance of whatever duty or deprivation the relation of pastor's wife might bring her, was intelligent and complete from the first, and she never faltered in the one, nor drew back from the other, to the end.

In September, 1852, they were appointed to the Niagara Falls station and entered upon their work in that popular field with great success. In December, however, they were transferred to the Oregon conference, by Bishop Waugh, and immediately closed their work in the Genesee conference, preparatory to assuming that which was, in their own intention, as well as the providence of God, to be their life work in the great Pacific Northwest.

They came to their chosen home, not in a palace car, with the luxury and comfort of modern traveling, but from Kansas City, Missouri, then a village of 250 inhabitants, all the way to Portland, Oregon, in an emigrant wagon, drawn by patient, but heedless oxen. From the 9th (should be 5th) day of May, 1853 to the 3rd day of October, they spent in the toilsome, tedious, heart-wearing journey, reaching Portland, then a small town in an almost unbroken wilderness, on that day.

Mr. Hines had been appointed by Bishop Ames to Portland station, at the preceding conference, and the following Sunday took up his work in the old Taylor street pulpit and she took up hers in the Sunday school and in any line that Providence opened up for her.

It is not possible here to follow the events that marked and distinguished her long life of devotion to the work of the church on this coast. That work was so blended with that of her husband and was so essential a part of his, that the two cannot be separated in fact or statement. Of the thirty-six years thus spent, eleven were spent in the pastorate; sixteen in the presiding eldership, one as a college agent, and eight as editor of the Pacific Christian Advocate. In all these high and holy places and fields to which the church has called them, and where they have honored the church, she was ever by her husband's side; his willing, able and efficient helper and counselor in every field of his toil.

She was the first state president of the Woman's Christian Temperance Union of Oregon, and as such traveled nearly all over the state, delivering addresses, organizing unions and laying deep and well the foundations of the present prosperity of that great moral force in the state. When, after several years' devoted service, increasing feebleness compelled her to resign her place, she received the most flattering testimonials of the love and confidence of her devoted sisterhood all over the state. None mourn her more sincerely than they.

Some of her peculiar personal qualities, these things that gave her that peculiar roundness and symmetry of moral and spiritual life that always distinguished her, ought to be noticed.

The intellectual and spiritual were the all-controlling forces of her being. Physically she was always feeble and for the last ten years of her life a great sufferer; yet her intellectual and spiritual force held her feeble and suffering physical being under almost supreme command and compelled it to do their bidding. So she wrought where others would have rested; she lived where others would have died.

She had, naturally, a self-poised and self-controlled spirit. Everything was faced with calmness; burdens were borne without repining; wrongs were suffered without resentment. She personally suffered in her own home some of the sorest bereavements of life, culminating in the loss of three out of four children in the short space of eight days, and one of them in the absence of her husband on the work of the church, but her spirit walked the awful valley fearing no evil and she came out of it serene, uplifted, glorified. So was it ever.

Her religious experience and life were in full harmony with these natural qualities and tendencies. They were equal and harmonious; yet full of purpose and consecration.

She began her public Christian life at ten years of age. Her family were Baptists, but her heart chose the Methodist church and alone she entered its pale at that early age. Her attachment and devotion to it never faltered to the end. But she made no sounding professions and made no boasts of what she enjoyed or did in the religious life. Still her life was pure as it is given to mortals to live and her work had in it a strange power of intellectual and moral uplift. But a few months ago an eminent lawyer, long an intimate friend of herself and family, though himself more a scientific rationalist than a Christian believer said of her: "Whatever Mrs. Hines touches she uplifts, sanctifies, glorifies. To have known her is forever to be a better man."

The acquisition and impartation of knowledge was with her a passion. She easily gained knowledge. She loved the truth and sought it everywhere with keen intellectual avidity and moral relish. She read but little of what is called light literature, and that always the very best; but she read and studied the standards of science and history, of philosophy and theology with absorbing interest. During the last two months of her life she read and studied with great care Haygood's "Man of Galilee," Roche's "Life of J.P. Durbin," Townshend's "The Bible and the Nineteenth Century," and Bishop Foster's new and wonderful volumes. Her desire to use what she gained for the good of humanity led her early to the work of teaching. At fourteen she had charge of the "village school" and she continued to teach except when attending school, until she exchanged the school room for the manse. In her work on this Coast she was preceptress of some of our church schools at different times and places for eight years or more. Her work there was always a success intellectually and morally as the hundreds of her pupils, now grown to manhood and womanhood, scattered all up and down this coast would gladly testify could they be here to be heard. Among them was the wife and companion of the present writer, whose life as a school girl was materially fashioned for future faith and work by the teaching and example of our just glorified sister.

The death of Mrs. Hines was like her life—calm, serene, peaceful. She had been absent with her husband on his district at Boise City, but felt a desire to be at home with all her family about her once again. Her husband accompanied her on the journey and after a tedious blockade of a week on the railroad, they reached home Tuesday night, January 21. For two days she was comfortable and radiantly happy: "so glad to be at home with all the dear ones." She was then taken down and despite the best of medical aid and the tenderest nursing grew constantly weaker until midnight January 29, when she went to sleep on the bosom of her God, as calmly and peacefully as ever an infant dropped to slumber on the bosom of its mother; beloved and revered in her family, and the memory of her disinterested and self-sacrificing goodness cherished by thousands all over the land. Really in the light of her example it seems a noble thing to live; a glorious thing to die.

Martha Graves

In the introduction to his chapter on Celinda's diary, Kenneth L. Holmes states that "Martha was married in January 1854 to a well-known carpenter-builder of Portland, Abram Walts."[30] Like so many surnames in the nineteenth century, this one was rendered with various spellings in the census and other documents. The 1860 U.S. census has the spelling "Waltz," but in the 1880 U.S. census it appears as "Watts." This spelling is repeated in later real estate transfer documents.[31] The 1880 census shows the family with four children, Nellie, 21; Alvin, 17; Eva, 14; and Rowland, 8. Census entries for Alvin and Rowland in later years use the "Waltz" spelling which seems to be the settled spelling. See also the Alta Bryant note concerning builder Abram Waltz on a later page.

Celinda

In her diary entry of October 7, 1853, Celinda mentions a Mr. Shipley, "Attended singing school in the evening. Mr. Shipley teacher. Pleasant." Celinda and Adam Randolph Shipley were married a little less than a year later, on September 30, 1854, with her Uncle Harvey officiating.[32] In the 1880 U.S. census for Oswego, Clackamas County, Oregon, there are six children listed: Milton, 22; Cora, 21; Lester, 18; Celinda, 15; Alfonso, 13; and Randolf, 8. A. R. Shipley's occupation in this census is listed as "farmer," and he evidently was a very successful one, raising mainly grapes,[33] though certainly not exclusively.[34] He was also active in several institutions and organizations, including the Portland Academy and Female Seminary,[35] the State Horticultural Society,[36] and the Board of Regents of the State Agricultural College at Corvallis,[37] as well as his church choir. In 1854 he was named U.S. postmaster of Portland.[38]

From a newspaper clipping appearing in 1875, we find that A.R. Shipley and family were held in high regard:

> ...Half an hour's walk brought us to the residence of Mr. A. R. Shipley, a well-to-do and widely-known gentleman. His farm is one of the finest in Clackamas County, is under good cultivation, well-equipped with barns and outhouses, and excellently adapted to all the purposes of an agricultural life. Mr. S. is famous for the superiority of his vineyard and its products, and never fails to carry off the first premium upon his grapes at the Oregon State Fair. He is the happy possessor of an amiable wife (nee Celinda E. Hines, niece of the late Rev. Gustavus Hines) and an intelligent and interesting family.[39]

Eliza Hines

Eliza, the widow of Obadiah, and stepmother of Celinda, married Fielding Lewis August 18, 1857, but died less than a year and a half later, on January 26, 1859.[40] The 1860 U.S. census for Brownsville, Linn County, Oregon, lists Lewis as a "tavern keeper(!)," along with C. Nancy Lewis, 43 (presumably his new wife), and three children. Young Gustavus Hines, Celinda's only sibling on the 1853 trip, is not listed in the household, nor do we find any record of him elsewhere.

Holden and Phoebe Judson

The excerpts we have included in earlier chapters from Phoebe

Judson's *A Pioneer's Search for an Ideal Home*[41] comprise about one third of that work; the remaining two thirds are devoted to their continuation into Washington Territory and eventual settlement near the Canadian border. The following account of the Judsons' post-1853 activities is based on Phoebe's description, except as specifically noted.

When Phoebe, her husband Holden, and their two small children, Annie and Charles La Bonta departed from the Hines party near Sandy, Oregon, in late September, she notes that "...only five miles separated me from my twin sister, Mary." Mary, together with six siblings and their parents, Jotham and Anna Goodell, had left Ohio in the late spring of 1850,[42] and after wintering with the Mormons in what is present-day Utah, arrived in the Willamette Valley in 1851. Following a brief but joyful reunion with her twin, Phoebe and family traveled further northward into Washington Territory, where they met up first with her brother Melancthon, and then the rest of the family at Grand Mound, W. T., where the elder Goodells had staked out a land claim after leaving the Willamette Valley.

The gravelly soil of the Grand Mound area did not prove to be suitable for their "ideal home," so after about six years Phoebe and Holden moved to Olympia, and then finally to the far north wilderness of the Nooksack River. Their settlement there eventually grew to become the town of Lynden, Washington, first incorporated in 1891, just two years after Washington became a state, with Holden Judson as its first mayor. This was not Holden's first elected office; he served two terms in the territorial legislature in the late 1850s and early 1860s, and later was a county commissioner for Whatcom County, and postmaster for Lynden. He was also a highly successful businessman.[43]

Like virtually all the women in our story, Phoebe, though certainly supportive of her husband in his many pursuits, was an active player in the events of her time as well. This is well illustrated by her description of Washington Territory's brief flirtation with women's suffrage.

> For four years, from 1883 to 1887, the territory of Washington enjoyed impartial suffrage. I took my turn on petit and grand jury, served on election boards, walked in perfect harmony to the polls by the side of my staunch Democratic husband, and voted the Republican ticket—not feeling any more out of my sphere than when assisting my husband to develop the resources of our country.[44]

According to the website for modern Lynden, "The Judsons were primarily responsible for the burgeoning trade in early Lynden, and credited for "civilizing" the children—both Native American and white—in the area. The Judsons held the first public school at their home."[45] Phoebe, who had shown fear and sometimes revulsion for Indians while on the trail in 1853, came to befriend many of them. The 1880 U.S. census for Lynden, Whatcom County, Washington Territory, includes in the Judson household: Holden, Phoebe, her mother, Anna Goodell, two Judson sons, and six other children (two Pattersons and four McClanahans) whom Phoebe identifies in her book as offspring of Indian mothers and white fathers—children who had been given to her care because of her demonstrated compassion for them.[46]

Although far removed from the Willamette Valley of Oregon, where most of the their co-travelers settled and lived out their lives after 1853, the Judsons did not completely lose touch, thanks in part to Harvey's wide-ranging activities. As mentioned earlier, much of his church work was in Washington Territory, and while he was in Portland, Oregon, as editor of the *Pacific Christian Advocate,* he had frequent communication with acquaintances far and wide. We repeat here an excerpt from the *Advocate* in 1882 that was quoted earlier in a note for Chapter 6.

Brother J.A. Tennant, from Ferndale, W. T.[Washington Territory], under date of June 6th, adds the following P.S. to a communication:

"Our camp meeting commences at Ferndale July 11th, and continues one week. A steamboat will come direct from Seattle, leaving there on Sunday evening, the 9th. Come over and *rest,* and we will give you such a rousing welcome and show you what wonders God has wrought among the poor Indians that you will be astonished. Bring no *preacher in charge* to take *charge of* you; well, you can have a good time. Sister Judson will most likely have a tent on the ground, and we will allow her to take charge of you. Why not get a few good workers and come? Will be a good vacation, and do you good and benefit us and help on the cause. Just put a line in the glorious old P.C. Advocate and say yes, and make us glad. Pray for us, that the Great Shepherd will be present in power. I think Sister Hines might do some good temperance work here."

Most reluctantly do we say to Bro. Tennant that it is impossible for us to go. "Sister Judson" and Bro. Judson were members of our company in the long, trying journey of five months, with ox teams from Westport, Mo., to Portland, Oregon, in 1853. Our memory sweeps the years, as we write this line, and rests on the events of that weary way with unspeakable thrill. How delightful it would be to sit down in the "tent" again and talk over, in the old familiar way, the pains and perils past. But work, not inclination, keeps us from it now.[47]

Ferndale is situated not far removed downriver from Lynden on the Nooksack, and J. A. Tennant was a close friend of the Judsons, of whom Phoebe writes, "Mr. Tennant was an able minister and filled many appointments throughout the surrounding country."[48]

Charles and Mary Bryant

According to Charles and Mary's daughter Alta, her baby brother, Lee, who had been ill on the trip, died soon after they arrived: "We had only been in Oregon about three weeks when Lee died, November (21 months old)." So in late 1853, the Bryants were a family of three. Alta further notes,

> After getting to Homer Humphreys sent cattle to Mrs. Judson's sister's to be wintered, three head, all we had left out of five yoke of oxen and the cow, old Red.
> Pa helped build a grist mill at Salem.
> Pa worked at Oregon City—helped build Judge Waite's home, he and Abram Waltz.[49]

By 1860, according to the U.S. census for Linn Precinct, Clackamas County, Oregon, the Bryants had four children: Alta, 10; Hale, 5; Vesper, 3; and Ellen, 1. In 1870, Alta married Asbury Anderson, but the 1880 census shows Alta Anderson living in the Charles Bryant household again, along with several siblings: Charles, 16; Myra, 13; and Cordelia, 11. We could find no record of Asbury Anderson in the 1880 census; it appears he may have been deceased by then. There also is no 1880 census record of Asbury and Alta's daughters, who, according to the web posting of Craig E. Bryant,[50] were Bertha, born in 1871, and Mary, born in 1873. Bertha married A. Holmes, and Mary married Eugene D. Funk. Each of these daughters recorded their mother's reminiscences of the 1853 trip west, and their typescripts are the basis for the brief accounts from Alta that we have been able to include in the present work.[51]

Misters Long, Martin, Miner and Nelson

The information we have for the several young men who accompanied the Hines train is very limited. Robert Nelson, the young Swede who assisted the Judsons, may very well be the Robt. Nelson, age 36, who appears in the 1860 U.S. census for Portland, Multnomah County,

Oregon. This is the only man of that name listed in either the Oregon or Washington census for that year,[52] and he is indicated to be of Swedish origin. His occupation in 1860 is listed as merchant.

There are far too many Martins on the West Coast in 1860 to be able to identify one with the Mr. Martin who is referred to a dozen times by one or another of the Hines party. His name is frequently paired with Mr. Miner, and for the latter we can make an informed guess that this is the James Miner, carpenter, 26, appearing in the U.S. census for Rock Creek Precinct, Clackamas County, Oregon, along with Ann, 17, and a two-month-old daughter. No other entries for Miner appear in either the Oregon or Washington censuses for 1860.[53]

The first we hear of Charles Long is in Celinda's diary entries of April 28 and 29, in which she notes, "Mr. Long came" and, on the 29th, "Mr. Charles Long, who had previously engaged to go to Oregon with us, being left here to take care of the oxen. He appears to be very handy." Later, when Harvey's wagon wheel needs repairing, she records, "Mr Long who was a wagon maker went to work at the wheel the others assisting as much as they could." This latter note tempts us to identify our Charles Long with the one, age 23, in the 1850 U.S. census for Jackson County, Missouri, who is listed as a wagon maker. However, the 1860 Jackson County census again lists Charles Long, albeit as a confectioner!, and in both censuses a Catharine Long is paired with him. So we have no firm indication of our Charles Long's origins. On the other end, the last mention of him by our chroniclers is Celinda's entry of September 8, while they are at Lee's encampment, "Mr. Bailey one of the men who was with Mr. Leonard came on says Mr. L & the train Charley is in have gone the new road."[54] But if he settled in Oregon, we have not been able to confirm it.[55]

James Round Hines

One final post-1853 item deserves mention here. Another Hines brother, James Round Hines,[56] followed the others west in 1884, leaving only Adolphus, the oldest of the six brothers, back in New York. It is interesting that, although James was not an ordained minister as were three of his brothers, he nevertheless was called upon "practically every Sunday to preach" in some locale, according to family lore.[57]

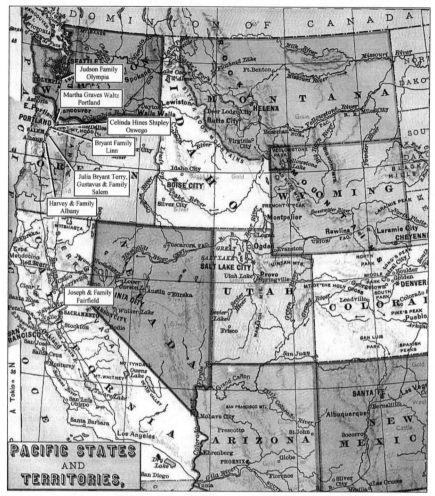

Map labels:
- Judson Family, Olympia
- Martha Graves Waltz, Portland
- Celinda Hines Shipley, Oswego
- Bryant Family, Linn
- Julia Bryant Terry, Gustavus & Family, Salem
- Harvey & Family, Albany
- Joseph & Family, Fairfield
- PACIFIC STATES AND TERRITORIES,

1884 map of the western states, showing homes of the Hines party members in 1860. Adapted from original map at the USGenWeb United States Digital Map Library hosted by RootsWeb at http://www.rootsweb.com/~usgenweb/maps/usa/

---

[1] Robert Moulton Gatke, *Chronicles of Willamette: The Pioneer University of the West,* (Portland: Binford & Morts, 1943) 151, 152.

[2] Gatke, *Chronicles of Willamette,* 151, 152.

[3] In Chapter 2 of the present work, we quoted Gustavus's own characterization of himself as a young, "journeyman in a shoemaker's shop." Gustavus Hines, "Notes of Travel," *Northern Christian Advocate,* August 1, 1849.

[4] N. Rounds, "Outlines of the Life of Mrs. Lydia Hines," *Pacific Christian Advocate,* April 2, 1870, Vol. XVI, No. 14.

[5] Howard M. Coming, *Dictionary of Oregon History* (Portland, 1956), 114.

[6] Gatke, *Chronicles of Willamette,* 246-248.

[7] Gatke, *Chronicles of Willamette,* 247.

[8] Fred Lockley, "Impressions and Observations of the Journal Man," *Oregon Journal,* August 3-7, 1925.

[9] Gatke has high praise for Terry: "That [1856] was the year that Chester N. Terry became a trustee and established an exceptional record of service during the next eighteen years. Few were the meetings he missed, and committee jobs both little and big had a way of falling on him as they are likely to do upon any able man who gives of his time cheerfully. Terry was a lawyer highly regarded in his profession. He was the clerk of the Oregon Constitutional Convention; in fact the *Oregonian* editorially once credited him with bringing to Oregon a copy of the new Indiana Constitution, which according to this editorial 'was made the basis——indeed, almost the sole source—of the Constitution of Oregon.' Legal practice gave time for him to serve as clerk of a legislative assembly, to be an aid on the Governor's staff, and county Judge of Marion County, and to follow other civic and political interests. A Democrat in politics, he was a leader in the loyal faction of his party which opposed what was considered the disloyal actions and attitude of Governor Whitaker, especially his appointment of Benjamin Stark to succeed Baker as Senator. He took an active part in seeking union action of the two political parties in support of the war." Gatke, *Chronicles of Willamette,* 328.

[10] J. W. Hines, *Touching Incidents.*

[11] J. M. Guinn, *History of the State of California and Biographical Record of Coast Counties, California,* (Chicago: Chapman Publishing, 1904).

[12] Hines' political affiliation was much more complicated than suggested here. The first Republican state convention in California was held in 1856, three years before Hines arrived from Oregon, so he could hardly have been much involved in the party's founding. There is evidence that he was involved in writing a party platform, but it was for the Peoples' Party, not the Republicans. Indeed, there is good evidence that after his Civil War era affiliation with the Republican party, he became aligned with several, more leftward-leaning political parties over the course of his career, including the Democrats, the Knights of Labor, the Prohibitionists, the Greenback Party, the Nationalists, and the Farmers Alliance. H. J. Peters, *Who was J. W. Hines?* (Santa Clara, 2006), 26.

[13] The quilt eventually found its way back to Humboldt County and now resides in the Clarke Memorial Museum in Eureka, Calif., where it is brought out for display on the Fourth of July. Kaaren Beaver Buffington, "A Quilt for General Grant," unpublished paper held by the Archives in Special Collections, Library at Humboldt State University, Arcata, Calif.

[14] There is documentation for Hines having founded two newspapers, *The Humboldt Bay Journal* in 1865, and *The Pacific Union* in 1889. Both papers dealt with labor issues, but neither could be fairly characterized as "the first labor paper published on the Pacific Coast." Peters, *Who was J. W. Hines?*, 26, 33, 34.

[15] Charles Browning cites at least two pedigrees starting with Edward I of England that include a Lawrence Wilkinson, purported son of Mary (Conyers) and William Wilkinson. However, the author notes in his "corrigenda" that this parentage, and even the marriage of Mary and William "cannot be substantiated by any evidence." Charles Browning, *Americans of royal descent; collection of genealogies showing the lineal descent from kings of some American families* (Baltimore: Genealogical Pub. Co., 1969).

[16] Isaiah 55:13 (King James Version).

[17] *San Jose Mercury Herald,* January 4, 1915.

[18] A 1937 magazine article telling of his efforts to revive struggling newspapers in two cities, the *Boston Transcript*, and the *Brooklyn Daily Eagle* and *Time Union* also hailed his earlier rescues. "His first case was *The San Francisco Bulletin*. When he came on as managing editor, it was tottering toward bankruptcy; when he quit as publisher, it was striding prosperously in the other direction. A two-year stretch as assistant business manager of *The Philadelphia Record* acquainted him with more front-office mysteries. After that he put in two years as assistant managing editor of *The New York Evening Post*, another J. David Stem paper. Hines doesn't claim to have put either of these dailies on its feet. His twin sojourns, however, coincide with remarkable increases in circulation and advertising revenue." "DOCTOR: Newspaper Patients in Two Cities Keep Hines Busy," *News-week,* May 8, 1937.

[19] Debra Pickett, "William M. Hines, 88, former *Sun-Times* bureau chief," *Chicago Sun-Times,* March 8, 2005.

[20] H. K. Hines, *An Illustrated History of the State of Oregon,* (Chicago: Lewis Publishing Co., 1893), 634.

[21] Harvey, though lacking any formal education beyond the primary level, was awarded the honorary Doctor of Divinity degree during the June 1882 commencement exercises at Willamette University. *Pacific Christian Advocate,* June 22, 1882. Remarkably, the same year he received an honorary D.D. degree from the University of the Pacific in San Jose, California. *Catalogue of the University of the Pacific, 1885-1886*, p. 65.

[22] The purported linkage to Edward I, cited both here and in Joseph's biography, is of doubtful validity. See the earlier note with Joseph's biography, about Lawrence Wilkinson's genealogy.

[23] The "Governor" referred to here must have been John Winthrop, who in 1630 led a company of about 900 people on a voyage from Yarmouth, England, to New England, and was governor of the Massachusetts Bay Colony for many years. *Encyclopedia Americana,* 1944 Ed., Vol. XXIX, 405. To date we have not been able to determine which, if any, of Harvey's forebears were aboard for that trip.

[24] "Married," *Northern Christian Advocate,* November 11, 1846.

[25] 1850 U.S. census, Wales, Erie County, New York; image copy at www.ancestry.com; accessed April 27, 2007.

[26] *Northern Christian Advocate* (Auburn), July 30, 1851.

[27] The ages given for the three children are 10, 8, and 6, respectively, but these surely are in error, as no children of Harvey and Elizabeth are listed by any of the chroniclers of the 1853 trip. The census entry includes the notation, "Absent and information could not be ascertained," implying that the census taker, in the absence of the residents, somehow estimated the ages of the children. 1860 U.S. census, Albany, Linn County, Oregon; image copy at www.ancestry.com; accessed March 17, 2007. Later census data suggests James was born in the latter half of 1854 or early 1855. 1880 U.S. census, Dalles City, Wasco County, Oregon; image copy at www.ancestry.com; accessed March 10, 2007. An 1875 article indicates that three children, Edward O., Harvey L., and Dora A., died in 1863. *Pacific Christian Advocate,* August 12, 1875.

[28] In the last column he was to write as editor of the *Advocate,* Harvey claims, "During the eight years that we have been its editor we have put into the paper original matter of our own enough to make twelve large volumes of five hundred pages each." "Eight Years Retrospect," *Pacific Christian Advocate,* August 30, 1888, 1.

[29] A. J. Joslyn, "Mrs. H. K. Hines," *Pacific Christian Advocate,* February 12, 1890.

[30] Holmes, *Covered Wagon Women,* 79.

[31] In 1856, for example, Elizabeth, Martha and their husbands transferred property to one Joseph Clark: "HARVEY K. HINES & ELIZABETH J. (GRAVES) HINES his wife and ABRAM WATTS & MARTHA M. (GRAVES) WATTS his wife to JOSEPH CLARK This Indenture,…". (Harvey, Elizabeth, et al., carried this out in absentia, as they were all residing in Oregon at that time.) Wyoming County, New York Deed Book 24, Page 486 Dated 8 July 1856, Recorded 6 April 1858.

[32] Private communication from C. M. Sisk, great-granddaughter of Celinda and A. R. Shipley.

[33] Holmes, *Covered Wagon Women,* 80, 81.

[34] For example, the following note appeared in a newspaper in 1870: "Mr. A. R. Shipley, of Oswego, raised 18 or 20 bushels of Early Rose potatoes last season from one peck of seed. He speaks highly of these qualities for table use." *Pacific Christian Advocate,* January 1, 1870.

[35] In 1859, for example, he was listed as secretary of the board. *Pacific Christian Advocate,* February 19, 1859.

[36] For a time secretary of the society. *Pacific Christian Advocate,* January 7, 1875.

[37] In November, 1889, it was reported, "The governor has recently appointed the Hon. A. R.

Shipley, of Oswego, regent of the Agricultural College. Brother Shipley is a man of good native ability, fine education, much force and sound judgment. He will 'fill the bill.'" *Pacific Christian Advocate,* November 13, 1889.

[38] Holmes, *Covered Wagon Women,* 80.

[39] *Pacific Christian Advocate,* March 25, 1875.

[40] Holmes, *Covered Wagon Women,* 79.

[41] Judson, *A Pioneer's Search.*

[42] "In 1850 Jotham, now forty-one, and Annie Goodell gathered seven of their ten living children—Mary Weeks, a twin, eighteen; Melancthon Zwingle, fourteen; Emeline Davis, twelve; Nathan Edward, ten; Henry Martin, seven; Charlotte Elizabeth, four; and Jotham, Jr., barely one—and headed for Oregon. They were accompanied by Holden A. Judson, husband of their other twin daughter, Phoebe Newton, who remained in Ohio, as did their oldest son, William Bird." David L. Bigler, Editor, *A Winter with the Mormons: The 1852 Letters of Jotham Goodell,* (Salt Lake City, 2001).

[43] "We think it was in'84 that Mr. H. A. Judson started his store which was run in a small log building which was first constructed for a cooper shop. The postoffice was also in the same building. He soon found, however that his quarters were not the thing, and so built him a nice large store building and hall, as well as the fine residence in which he now resides. Mr. Judson has just completed at a cost of $8,000 one of the finest public halls in Washington, the auditorium of which, with the gallery, will seat 800 people, and having a fine large stage, fitted up with all necessary ante-rooms, scenery, etc. The whole building is an imposing structure, and has two of the best store rooms, in the lower story, to be found anywhere. The hall occupies the upper floor and is 40x80 feet in size. Mr. Judson's store occupies the largest room below, which is 25x80 in size, with beautiful fixtures, telephone room etc. The postoffice occupies the other room, which affords it comfortable quarters." *The Blaine Journal,* October 31, 1889. Lynden, The Queen of the Nooksack Valley, http://www.rootsweb.com/~wawhatco/townhistories/lynden.htm; accessed October 15, 2003.

[44] Judson, *A Pioneer's Search,* 277.

[45] Lynden Chamber of Commerce: Pioneer History, http://www.lynden.org/visiting/history.php; accessed April 28, 2007.

[46] Judson, *A Pioneer's Search,* 210-214, 231-233.

[47] *Pacific Christian Advocate,* June 22, 1882, 4.

[48] Judson, *A Pioneer's Search,* 253.

[49] It seems likely that this "Abram Waltz" is the same Abram/Abraham Walts/Watts who married Martha Graves.

[50] RootsWeb.com: New England Bryant Genealogy Site, http://wc.rootsweb.com/cgi-bin/

igm.cgi?op=GET&db=bryantweb&id=I14701; accessed April 28, 2007.

[51] Mary's descendant, Mr. Duncan Funk, of Bloomington, Ind., has kindly provided copies of the typescripts.

[52] There is one Robert Nelson listed in the 1860 California census, but he is not listed as being from Sweden, and at age 45, he seems older than we would expect for the "young man" that accompanied the Judsons. He also appears to be married, with a wife, 40, and a son, 18, and all indications are that the Judsons' Nelson was single. 1860 U.S. Census, Camptonville State Range, Yuba, California; image copy at www.ancestry.com; accessed April 28, 2007.

[53] California, a seemingly less likely destination, cannot be conclusively ruled out. Forty-seven male miners are listed in the 1860 federal census for California. www.ancestry.com; accessed April 28, 2007.

[54] That Long took the new road (the "Elliott Cutoff") is confirmed by Menefee, et al., where it is stated that "...Charles O. Long, who had earlier traveled with Leonard[,]" and seven other men formed an advance party to push ahead for the Willamette Valley, where they hoped to find help to take back to their now desparate fellow travelers on that ill-fated road. However, it is also stated in a note that, "Nothing is known about the later careers of Long and McFarland." Leah Colllins Menefee and Lowell Tiller, "Cutoff Fever, IV," *Oregon Historical Quarterly*, September 1977, 213.

[55] The name Charles Long appears four times in the 1860 U.S. census for Oregon, and not once for Washington. Of the four in Oregon, three are 12 years old or younger. The fourth, in the Lower Mollala Precinct of Clackamas County, is listed as 26, making him only 19 in 1853, which still seems a bit young for the rather experienced Charles Long described by Celinda. 1860 U.S. census, Molalla, Clackamas County, Oregon, image copy at www.ancestry.com; accessed April 28, 2007.

[56] From his obituary we learn, "He was born in Herkimer county New York, in 1822. When quite young he moved with his parents to Oswego Co. N.Y. He was married in 1846, in the town of Hastings. In the same year he moved to Brockport, Monroe Co., N.Y. Here he resided for ten years, moving to Michigan in 1856, making his home in Delta, Eaton Co... In 1875 he moved with his family to Grand Ledge. In 1884, he went to Portland Oregon, and later, to Manning Washington Co. Or. where he has a Son and Daughter residing. Here he died Dec. 18, 1892. A widow, who is a member of the Methodist church, and five children, Gustavus W. Hines, Mrs. Martha J. Whitney, Mrs. Harriet M. Kent, Mrs. Angeline C. Stoner, and Mrs. Rose L. Whitney survive him. He also leaves two brothers, Rev. Joseph Hines of California, and Rev. H. K. Hines, of Portland Oregon, and a sister Mrs. Malissa Robinson, who resides in Grand Ledge Michigan."

[57] Personal communication, Mrs. Margaret Ann (Whitney) Fender, second great-granddaughter of James Round Hines.

20

Views of the Trip through Other Lenses

Through good fortune we have been left with three different comprehensive accounts of one party's participation in the great westward migration of the mid-nineteenth century. Thus we have had the benefit of viewing this particular journey through the differently ground lenses of a man and two women. From Celinda we have the crystalline clarity of her daily diary entries; from Harvey and Phoebe more philosophical views, as refined through many years of reflection, thirty years in the first instance, more than seventy in the second.

Further perspective can be gained from still other lenses; we have selected four to consider here. The first is inspired by John Unruh's sweeping work *The Plains Across;*[1] the second derives from John Mack Faragher's *Women & Men on the Overland Trail;*[2] the third is based on Clyde Milner's *The Shared Memories of Montana's Pioneers,*[3] and the fourth is the very personal lens of the editor of this volume.

John D. Unruh

In his comprehensive review of historical treatments of the nineteenth century western migration, Unruh points out the almost universally narrow focus of all the efforts, be it their concentration on a single year or two, an isolated route, or a single emigrating group. While proposing a broader approach of his own, he nonetheless credits the narrower efforts for the contribution they make. The present volume, concentrating as it does on the journey of one small party clearly belongs to the narrow variety. Generalizing from many such more focused works, together with an enormous array of other primary sources, Unruh has produced a big picture of the migrations over the twenty-year period, 1840-1860, emphasizing the change over time, and the cooperation among emigrants and between emigrants and both Indians and Americans already resident in the West. We now turn this around and look at our single journey against the background of his large canvas.

Two chapters of Unruh are devoted to the influence of public opinion on the emigration, largely through the press.[4] Gustavus Hines cited the newspaper appeal for missionaries in his letter to the bishop requesting assignment to Oregon in 1839.[5] And it is likely he was made susceptible to the appeal by numerous accounts of Jason Lee's addresses that preceded it in the same paper. Upon returning from Oregon Gustavus published his book that among other things extolled the virtues of Oregon and evidently had its own influence on emigration, particularly among protestant congregations, as witnessed by Phoebe Judson's comment, "On hearing the name of Gustavus Hines we surmised at once that he was the author of a history of Oregon in which we were much interested before leaving home, …"[6] Harvey, under the guise of "Mr. Cathard," cites a letter in the newspaper as the triggering event for his 1852 decision to seek transfer to Oregon.[7] Having no direct evidence, we can only speculate that Gustavus, Harvey, and the others found written accounts of the rigors attending the overland journey to be sufficiently favorable, or at least not so unfavorable as to deter them. For Joseph, the length of the overland trip was well-enough publicized that he was aware his mid-June transfer left insufficient time for him to make that trip ahead of winter weather in the mountains, thus dictating his alternate route.

In his "Motivations and Beginnings" chapter,[8] Unruh credits economic factors, "farms, fish or gold," as being the prime motivators for the emigrants. This seems likely for the Judsons (recall Phoebe's …Search for an Ideal Home) and the Bryants, and perhaps in part for Obadiah Hines, but for Gustavus and Harvey, there can be little doubt that they were going for the purpose of spreading the Gospel, just one of many characteristics that placed them in a decided minority. As for Unruh's "Beginnings," the Hines group chose Kansas City/Westport as their jumping-off place, where they completed their outfitting for the trail, and then waited for the vegetation on the trail to mature to a point sufficient for feeding their livestock. Although this northwest Missouri area had traditionally been a most popular starting point, by 1853 the Council Bluffs region was seeing more emigrant departures according to Unruh,[9] and given its more northern location, it is surprising that the Hines party, leaving as they did from New York State, did not choose Council Bluffs. In fact, as Gustavus writes back to his friends in New York, after completing the trip, "If I were to cross the plains again, my team should consist of mules and light wagons. My place of departure would be Council Bluffs, and I would take the road on the north side of the Platt…"[10] Having selected Kansas City/Westport as their point of departure, they next chose to start on a route that was, in Harvey's words, "a little aside from the usual one for the first hundred miles, being a little more to the east and north."[11] Indeed, this route was so unusual that it appears on only one of the many trail maps we have examined.[12]

In 1853, according to Unruh, over 20,000 overlanders were on the trails west, with 6,000 of these headed to Oregon, leading to remarks from the emigrants about "no lack of company," and other such references to the density of the emigration.[13] Our chroniclers make frequent mention of other emigrants, citing no fewer than fifty by name. Celinda notes at the crossing of the Big Blue River that, "I should think there were a hundred wagons in sight during the day,"[14] and at the Laramie Fork she notes, "…we could not ferry as there were 150 wagons ahead of us in waiting." And just to emphasize the rarity of being alone, she says on July 21, "I do not remember where we have camped before when other camps were not in sight."[15] The concentration of people with common goals made for frequent interaction, much of it positive, according to Unruh,[16] as is borne out by the Hines experience. We noted earlier their sharing of oxen with the struggling Russel family.[17] On another occasion, they joined with other emigrants for a shared religious service.[18] From time to time, other families traveled together with their small train, providing mutual support.

One of the most common ways in which emigrants found advantage from their fellow travelers, according to Unruh, was in the reuse of items discarded by their predecessors along the trail. An instance of this is reported by Harvey in early August,

> The wheel of my wagon, which, it will be remembered, I had filled with green ash early in the journey, had given way so much that it was no longer usable, but I had been preparing for this by picking up along the road pieces of broken wagons, generally tough and thoroughly dried hickory, and shaving them into spokes, so that, when we camped here, I had more than enough to refill the wheel. To-day, therefore, I knocked the wheel to pieces, refilled it with first class spokes, set all the tires and long before night had the wagon as strong and good as ever.[19]

However much the Hines train profited from interaction with other emigrants, they seem to have frequently found it to their advantage to avoid the main body of emigrants. At the very start of their overland journey, they crossed the Kansas River and then proceeded along the north side of the river while the great majority of emigrants were on the south side. And weeks later, when they were near the Kansas-Nebraska border, Phoebe made the observation, "We kept aloof from the great body of emigrants, that we might have the advantage of the little patches of grass and pools of water that lay along our way—which enabled us to advance more rapidly than in a larger company."[20]

Interactions with Indians came early and often to the Hines Train. They had barely begun their overland journey, just having crossed the Kansas River at the Delaware Ferry, and, as Harvey reports,

> ...when the morning came our two mules were missing, and a part of the company were compelled to remain in the same place for another day and night, when a Christian Wyandotte Indian— "Gray Eyes"—whom we had met on the Sabbath spent with these people of which mention has been made, brought them to our camp, having tracked them twelve miles before overtaking them.[21]

At this point the little train was poised to continue northward toward Ft. Leavenworth, but Celinda notes that another Indian suggested otherwise, "A very intelligent Delaware chief...advised us to take the divide route instead of the government road by Ft Leavenworth as it is nearer & they say a better road."[22] Much later, in eastern Oregon in early September, as they were entering the Blue Mountains near present-day La Grande, an Indian named Red Wolf, who was acquainted with Gustavus from his earlier trip in the mid-1840s, made a special effort to direct their train to an off-the-trail campsite with "a good spring and excellent grass."[23] Were all interactions with Indians so benevolent? Unruh argues that far more often than not, they were.[24] Certainly that was the case for the Hines train. Beyond the incidents noted above, there were nearly two dozen other encounters with Indians mentioned by one or more of our chroniclers, involving such benefits as trading for fresh produce and fish, or assistance in crossing rivers, and only two encounters bordered on being hostile.[25] One of the latter occurred when a band of Indians sent a chill through the Hines group while in pursuit of two white men who had killed one of their number in an earlier dispute, and the other involved an Indian-instigated stampede of the train's livestock. In no instance was there a Hollywood-style attack by Indians upon their train, disappointing as that may have been to adventuresome young Harvey.

The federal government's impact on the overland journey was present from the 1840s onward, but according to Unruh this began increasing significantly in the mid-1850s.[26] Most of this buildup, in the form of increased troop presence, improved roads and better mail service, came too late to be of much benefit to the Hines train. They did indeed take advantage of the service and supply offerings at several government forts along the way, but there is no acknowledgement of any increased feeling of security brought about by military buildup. Most comments about road conditions were negative, and the only mail service they appeared to have had between the frontier in Missouri and the Willamette Valley in Oregon was at a single site: Ft. Laramie.

Unruh's characterization of emigrant experiences with private entrepreneurs along the trail focuses on high prices, legal squabbles and rowdy, drunken behavior.[27] In light of the latter, and given the Hines' adherence to their religious principles and practices, it is striking that discussion of such behavior does not appear in their accounts. There is talk of prices, however, and the discussion is mixed. On the one hand, Celinda, shopping at the Delaware Trading Post, says, "I purchased a pair of shoes as cheap as I could in New York." While at the Green River, Phoebe complains, "The Mormons owned the ferry, and we were again compelled to pay six dollars per wagon for crossing." But the most notable encounter with entrepreneurs was Joseph's dispute with the ferry operators at the Deschutes River. Finding a fording opportunity as an alternative to the expensive ferry whose operators evidently tried to discourage any hope of fording, Joseph provides significant savings for himself, his relatives, and all later emigrants crossing the Deschutes. He concludes his account with "And that is the way I destroyed the Des Chutes Ferry. So perish all liars and deceivers, who seize on the gifts of God to man and strive to deceive and rob the people."[28]

Joseph also provides the most prominent instance of what Unruh terms "West Coast Assistance."[29] Many a travel-weary party managed to finish the trip only through the assistance of those already on the West Coast who had preceded them, and were able to bring them fresh provisions or draft animals. In the case of the Hines party, Joseph arrived in Portland well ahead of his brothers and their families and therefore went eastward to meet them and help them complete their long journey. As they together started down along the Columbia, younger brother Harvey's records, "Our cattle, meanwhile, had been started down the trail, under charge of our brother, J. W. H[ines], who volunteered this service to relieve us, who had, as he thought, become wearied with our long journey, from the great fatigue of the work." The "relief man" took ill on the trail, however, and had to be rescued by his brothers. On the next leg of their journey, Harvey drove the cattle himself. He says, "Having tried fresh help from the Willamette on one such trip, we thought it wise to send him down by steamboat in the care of the women and children this time. It was nearly night when all were embarked, and then, with two men, I drove the cattle…" So much for "west coast assistance."

In his concluding chapter, examining "The Overlanders in Historical Perspective," Unruh reiterates his central theme of how the emigration experience changed with time over the 1840-1860 twenty-year period. Gustavus Hines, along with his wife Lydia and her younger sister Julia, provide a case in point. In 1839 the overland route was so forbidding that they and their missionary companions took the eight-month long sea route around Cape Horn at the tip of South America instead. Others continued to use the Cape Horn route on into the 1850s, but during this time exploration and use of the overland route rapidly increased. Fourteen years after their first trip, Gustavus, Lydia, and Julia together with their extended family joined thousands of others and followed the footsteps of tens of thousands more along a now well-beaten path on a journey that, while still no "walk-in-the-park," could be negotiated with a calm confidence in its outcome. As Gustavus himself summarized in the aftermath of the trip, "...the journey across the plains is no very serious matter. It may be made rather a pastime, and with good luck, profitable withal."[30] Those pioneers who did travel overland in the early 1840s dared not embark without a seasoned guide and a carefully assembled outfit. By 1853 many were venturing forth sans even the guidebooks that had replaced the guides, although the Hines party prudently carried guidebook(s) and planned their outfits with care.

By the early 1850s a third alternative to the Cape Horn and overland routes had come into widespread use: the Panama Route. Unruh reports that travel times for this route were as short as three to four weeks from New York to San Francisco (with an additional few days to go on to Portland), and through competition the price dropped to as low as $100 per person. In comparison, the travel time along the overland trail, for just the Missouri to Oregon trip, averaged nearly 130 days.[31] For the Hines family, Joseph's trip on the Panama route took from June 20 to about the first of August—little more than six weeks, including a week's layover in San Francisco. On the other hand, his relatives on the overland trail took 154 days—from May 4 to October 3—nearly five months, and this did not even include their trip from New York to their jumping off place, nor their long wait at the latter spot. Unruh points out that the geographic location of emigrants' homes was a big determinant in their choice of route, with eastern seaboard residents most frequently selecting seagoing routes and more western residents usually opting to go overland. So from the standpoint of travel time and geography, the natural choice for the Hines party would have been the Panama route.

From the above it would appear that the most likely reason that they nevertheless chose to go overland was comparative cost. Gustavus himself, in responding to a question from prospective co-travelers, cites $500 as a likely figure for outfitting a family of five with wagon, draft animals and provisions, on top of the cost of getting to the Missouri frontier.[32] We do not know what cost estimates were actually available to them for the Panama alternative. Perhaps the estimates were significantly higher and this then dictated their route selection. We do know, however, that after both their journey and brother Joseph's journey via Panama were completed, and hard comparative figures must have been available to Gustavus, that he was still discussing emigration with his former colleagues in New York solely in the context of overland travel.[33] From comparative cost figures described by Unruh, it is difficult to imagine that the expenses per person for Joseph's family would have been significantly greater than for the other Hines families. This leads us to conclude that, after all other factors have been considered, the overriding issue for Gustavus and Lydia may have been their seagoing experience of 1839-40. Perhaps they felt that the trials and dangers of any sea journey outweighed the touted advantages in travel time.

What did the travelers expect to see at the completion of their journey? The Hines family in 1839 contemplated a destination that was raw wilderness with nebulous attachments to any civilized nation and an American population numbering fewer than 100. In 1853, while not all wilderness had been tamed, nor all natives subdued, Oregon's settler population exceeded 20,000,[34] and statehood was being discussed. On his first trip, in 1839, Gustavus arrived to join a handful of other Methodist missionaries endeavoring to reach the Indians. In contrast, he and brothers Harvey and Joseph in 1853 were to become part of the newly formed Oregon Annual Conference, comprising some twenty ministers and thirty-five local preachers serving a church membership of nearly 1000, almost all non-native.[35]

John Mack Faragher

For the greater part of the western migration—1840 to 1860— emigrants from what were then considered the "western" states of the U.S. (Missouri, Iowa, Wisconsin, Illinois, Michigan, Indiana, Ohio), what is generally known today as the Midwest, dominated the numbers on the trail. John Mack Faragher focuses on these Midwesterners and their farm origins as he discusses the circumstances and experiences of *Women & Men on the Overland Trail*.[36] Among the members of the Hines party, Holden and Phoebe Judson, being from a farm in northern Ohio, fit Faragher's profile, if not all of his generalizations. Similar comments apply to the Bryants, farmers from western New York. The Hineses per se, however, were of a different stripe.[37] Nevertheless, it is illuminating to examine them as well through Faragher's lens.

In his discussion of "masculine men and feminine women," Faragher asserts, "Nowhere was this divergence between men and women more clearly evidenced than in the dispute over the Sabbath."[38] We can say in parallel that nowhere is the divergence between the Hines character and that of Faragher's generalized emigrants more clearly evidenced than in their observance of the Sabbath. This of course arises from the circumstance that two of the three Hines brothers were ministers (and the third equally devout) in contrast to the typical emigrant. While the male leaders of most trains pressed forward seven days a week, setting aside the wishes of the women and bowing to the perceived necessity of squandering no travel time, the Hines men just assumed that their train would of course rest on the Sabbath in keeping with their strongly held religious beliefs. Moreover, according to Phoebe Judson, Gustavus, Harvey and Obadiah took turns leading daily devotions though the week.

The religious element in the Hines character evidenced itself in numerous ways. By Faragher's analysis, the common ingredients in men's social gatherings were whiskey, gambling, and rowdy behavior. In contrast, consider Harvey's description of an evening in the Hines camp.

> ...we forgot some of the weariness of the day, and, around our campfires, our young ladies sung to the moon—as young ladies forever will—as they washed up the tin plates and cups, ready for the morning meal; Mr. M[arti]n quoted poetry, in his pleasant way; O[badiah] H[ines] told some story that set us all in a roar, or the two preachers had some little quiet theological discussion, while the married women put our tents in order for the night.

To be sure, there is evidence here of the clear division of labor between the sexes—a prominent theme of Faragher—but the activities of the males are 180 degrees out of phase with his generalization.

Religious beliefs were also no doubt the basis for the general decorum that appears to have characterized the Hines party. Faragher quotes liberally from women's diaries attesting to the swearing that men so often resorted to as they encountered frustrations. In contrast, there is not a single reference to swearing in all the pages of Celinda's diary, Phoebe's reminiscence, nor for that matter, Harvey's own account.

Faragher's male emigrant was unemotional. "To be the master of your feelings—this was a definitional male assignment." And later, "Crying, an emotional display absolutely foreign to the notion of masculinity, defined the outer limits of accepted masculine behavior."[39] Harvey, again, counters this image. In the midst of New York farewells, he recalls, "Mrs. Hines, her sister, Miss M. M. Graves, and myself took our tearful leave of the parental home of Mrs. H." Later, on the train out of Buffalo, "Thoughtfully I gazed, with tearful eye, upon the minarets of the city of Buffalo, until they were lost in the receding distance. Shall I see them again?... When?" Aside from tears as such, Harvey's acknowledgement of his own emotions occurs openly and often throughout his reminiscence, as even the most casual reading will confirm.

Harvey's behavior and language repeatedly belie Faragher's generalizations. This is not to deny the validity of the generalizations, but rather to underscore the exceptional character of Harvey, and by extension, other members of the party as well. Faragher writes, "Men's writing was usually plain, unadorned, and terse." Women's writing was generally highly elaborative. In light of this observation, it is interesting to compare the different manner in which our three chroniclers, Harvey, Celinda, and Phoebe, recount one particular event, the crossing of Big Blue River on May 24. Celinda records in her diary, "...almost impossible to swim cattle but we had no difficulty with ours we all crossed in safety & camped on the other side." We won't repeat here Harvey's 199 words to describe the same event. Phoebe's description is equally elaborate, but in this instance so closely mirrors Harvey's that we have to conclude she relied heavily on the latter.[40] On other occasions Celinda's descriptions are extensive while the others' may be much briefer, or even absent. Overall, each of the three often wrote at length to describe events and experiences, while at other times more briefly. We see fewer of the briefer notes from Harvey and Phoebe because we have only their reminiscences, from which they have omitted material they considered less interesting (however much *we* would have liked to have seen it all!).

Another distinction Faragher finds between the writing of men and women is that "most men wrote about objects and things, most women about people."[41] While we have not performed a quantitative analysis in the manner of Faragher to test the present material on this issue, it is doubtful that a clear distinction of this type would be found. Harvey, Gustavus, and Joseph all wrote extensively about people, and both Celinda and Phoebe frequently wrote about objects and such.

In the division of labor on the trail, Faragher notes that women were the purveyors of health care, and this was particularly true with regard to pregnancy, "when men were absolutely incapacitated and women in fine fettle."[42] The Hines train experience seems completely in keeping with this. When Phoebe Judson is about to give birth to a child, most of the company are led off on a day-long diversion. In Harvey's words, "...some of our ladies—good, Christian women they were, too—after a little mysterious conversation together, proposed that nearly all the gentlemen and ladies of the train take a long walk..." They return at dusk to find a "new emigrant" has arrived—quite without the assistance of any man.

Not all expectant mothers on the trail were so well attended by female companions according to Faragher.[43] And more generally many women on the trail found themselves longing for feminine companionship, or for that matter, companionship of *any* variety. The women of the Hines train were fortunate to have a number of female co-travelers—sisters, sisters-in-law, others of a similar age. Several times Celinda tells of how the women grouped themselves in pairs to tend to different domestic tasks, and she repeatedly describes side excursions that a group of them took, often joined by one or more of the men.

The very decision to go west in the first place was another matter that divided the sexes. "In their diaries and recollections...not one wife initiated the idea, it was always the husband...most of them accepted it as a husband-made decision in which they could only acquiesce."[44] What can we ascertain about emigration decisions among members of the Hines party? We know from his musings (see Chapter 2) that Gustavus had long envisioned a return to Oregon, but we also know from Lydia's obituary that she appears to have initiated the actual decision.[45] For younger brother Harvey, to the extent that we can accept "Mr. and Mrs. Cathard" as faithful facsimiles of him and his wife Elizabeth, the decision appears to have been jointly made, although Harvey (in the person of Mr. Cathard) was indeed the one to initiate the idea. Phoebe Judson starts her discussion of the decision with the phrase, "The motive that induced *us*..."[46] [emphasis ours] and consistently uses "us," "we" and "our" as she continues telling of their hopes and dreams of a new home. So the implication is that theirs, too, was a joint decision. For the others in the party, we simply have no evidence regarding the emigration decision. We can say, however, that in Celinda's diary she makes no comment, directly or indirectly, that would suggest either she or her stepmother were against emigrating, whether or not they may have participated in the decision.

All in all, then the men and women of the Hines train displayed some of the characteristics described by Faragher, but more frequently departed from his generalizations. The most notable departures were in the decorous behavior of the men, and the absence of loneliness and despair among the women.

Clyde A. Milner II

It seems particularly appropriate to examine the Hines party's journey through the lens of Clyde Milner,[47] who compares the content of diaries and reminiscences to illustrate how the passage of time and the shared experience of others can shape and distort the historical record. Among other materials, Milner had access to a rare combination: a diary and later reminiscent memoir written by the same person (a woman who pioneered in Montana in 1863), along with other accounts of the same trip. While we share part of Milner's good fortune, being in the possession of a diary, letters, and reminiscent accounts of an 1853 journey, the diary and other accounts are by different people. Nonetheless, we can use Milner's insights to make some pertinent observations about our writers and the events they chronicled.

Montana memoirs, Milner points out, exaggerate the Indian threat to emigrants, in comparison to diary accounts of the same journeys. In these reminiscences, more Indians are encountered and they are more threatening than how they are depicted in diaries. We find no evidence of this sort of exaggeration in the present case. Based on an approximate tally, there are more references to Indian encounters in Celinda's diary than there are in either Harvey's or Phoebe's reminiscent accounts. And in the matter of the most threatening encounter, occurring on June 18 and for several days thereafter, the three accounts are quite similar. Phoebe's description is the most vivid, but neither her nor Harvey's reminiscence paints a significantly different picture than Celinda's diary.

As the basis for part of his discussion of memoirs, Milner quotes David Lowenthal, "…we need other people's memories both to confirm our own and to give them endurance…In the process of knitting our own discontinuous recollections into narratives, we revise personal components to fit the collectively remembered past, and gradually cease to distinguish between them."[48] This may explain Harvey's depiction of his wagon wheel repair. Perhaps sensing his audience's expectation of tales of pioneer self-reliance, he transformed the incident which Celinda in her diary portrays as engineered by Charles Long, the wagon maker, and Mr. Jones, the blacksmith, with incidental help from others, into one in which he, Harvey, took the lead role, employing tools he had wisely brought along and which he had learned to use in his youth.

In going from diary or journal to a memoir, pioneer writers often tried to see their own journey against the backdrop of a broader historical perspective, to see themselves as players in the grand march of history.

Milner observes that

> Montanans' memoirs are indicative of a broadly American process of creating historical identity through an insistence on new beginnings. The American Revolution, the creation of a new nation, and the near cult of the Founding Fathers have been the greatest expressions of this process. In her memoir, Harriet Sanders [Milner's featured memoirist] compared the 1863 arrival of her overland party at Bannack to the 1620 landing of the Pilgrims at Plymouth. Her comparison implied that her group of pioneers had, for Montana, a similar historical significance, but she did not claim the Pilgrims as ancestors of her own "little band."

Among our chroniclers, Harvey is the one who not only draws historic comparisons in the manner of Harriet Sanders, but moreover abandons her reticence about pilgrim ancestry. He strongly hints of his pioneer self-image in the introduction to his *Emigrant Wagon* serial incorporated in our Prologue, but in a later address to a gathering of Oregon pioneers, he says it in a way that leaves no doubt.

> ...I care but to identify those who became the pioneers of this coast as the lineal and logical descendants of those who were the pioneers of the Atlantic shore. The instinct of emigration was the inspiration of their birth. The stories and fame of their fathers fanned that instinct into a genius. The very names that glorified the roster of the Mayflower, honored the founders of New York and Ohio, of Pennsylvania and Illinois. Jamestown and Savannah reproduced their nomenclatures in Kentucky and Tennessee. In turn, they all gave up their patronymics, proud as they were, and standing for as much of history and freedom as they did, to the pioneer missionaries and the pioneer immigrants who followed so quickly on their trail up the Rocky mountains and down to the sea...The Puritan and the pilgrim, the Cavalier and the Huguenot have brought alike their passion and their chivalry, their iron hardihood and their stubborn faith, and poured them all together into one, common human mold, in the very heart of Oregon, to make and sanctify the "crowning race of human-kind."[49]

H. J. Peters

My own earliest recalled introduction to the Hines family occurred when I was about 13 and my mother came home with a copy of the minor classic, *Doctor in Buckskin*,[50] the historical fiction account of Marcus and Narcissa Whitman, including their tragic end in Oregon. My mother mentioned that some of "Grandma Flansburg's relatives"[51] had gone to

Oregon at about the same time and were acquainted with the Whitmans. At the time this information struck me as mildly curious, but serious interest in the Hines branch of my ancestry did not emerge until many years later, in 1998, during the visit of one of my mother's sisters, then terminally ill with cancer, when I talked at length with her about her children and grandchildren, close relatives of mine, but some of whom I had not even met. These conversations led to a family reunion and in the preparation for that, I began working on family genealogy. With the aid of the Internet I was within a few months able to go beyond "brick walls" that my mother had encountered after many years of "on the ground" research. But as any beginning genealogist quickly learns, the number of family lines that are candidates for exploration grows exponentially as the researcher proceeds backward in time, generation by generation. My own response to this richness of opportunity was to focus on lines for which the most documentation was readily available. Five and a half years later, I am still working my way through the mass of material pertaining to the Hines branch of my family tree.[52]

In a parallel way, my acquaintance with the Oregon Trail began in my teenage years when I wrote a book report on Francis Parkman's classic.[53] The level of my interest in the topic at that time can be inferred from the brevity of my report (one page, handwritten) and the fact that I had only *skimmed*, not *read*, the book. Real interest only came about as I was learning the details of the Hines's 1853 trip.

I cite all the above to indicate that a) I am a very recent student of the Hines family; and b) my study of the Oregon Trail is even newer. Moreover, I have come to these topics with no formal background as a historian. Rather, my observations and opinions are those of an amateur genealogist who has taken the trouble to track down many leads to learn as much as possible about the long trip taken by some relatives 150 years ago. My comments that follow are from that perspective.

The first printed reference I saw to the Hines journey was in Joseph's book,[54] in which he refers to his *two* brothers, both ministers, traveling overland toward Oregon. It was quite some time before I deduced that he was referring to Gustavus and Harvey, and that any reference to Obadiah was evidently deemed irrelevant since he didn't make it all the way.

My real introduction to the journey came with the purchase of Volume 6 of *Covered Wagon Women*[55] and the reading of Holmes's transcription of the last half of Celinda's diary. At that time I didn't know there was more to the diary. The first big question arose: how did they get to Kansas City from New York? This was answered when I obtained a copy of the newspaper serial publication of the full diary.[56] It wasn't until just recently that I was able to fill in more details by reading 1853 newspapers from St. Louis, St. Joseph, and Liberty in Missouri, as well as from Buffalo, New York. But each new piece of information leads to further questions.

How did the Hineses pay for their trip? Gustavus, Joseph, and Harvey were poorly paid preachers, after all. Did the Genesee Conference of the M. E. Church cover their trip expenses? What about Obadiah? Surely his employment as a "gatekeeper"[57] did not allow the accumulation of much in the way of savings. Did any of the wives have some independent wealth?[58]

In my first naïve imaginings of my relatives on the trail, I saw them as a solitary small train making their way across uncharted wilderness. It was eye-opening to learn of their thousands of fellow emigrants, all traveling on established roads. More questions. How did they know the names of the roads[59] and the many rivers and streams? Did this knowledge come from maps and/or guidebooks? If so, which ones, and do any copies still exist?[60]

A related question pertains to mileage traveled each day. My first speculation was that this, too, probably came from a guidebook. But examination of Celinda's mileage notes (see Appendix) suggests otherwise. It is unlikely that any guidebook would have provided the mileage details that Celinda reports. More likely, although we find no specific mention by any of our chroniclers, is that one or more of their wagons was equipped with an odometer. Odometer expert Norman Wright,[61] in fact, suggests that an inquisitive student of trail lore might speculate that there are four ways in which emigrants came up with mileage figures: 1) They *estimated* the distances; 2) They *measured* the distances; 3) They *extracted* distances from trail guides and maps; or 4) They recorded distances *supplied by others*. As we have done, he concludes that measurement was the means, and he goes on to describe odometers in use on the trails in the mid-nineteenth century in some detail. In a relatively short list of emigrants known to have used odometers in the period 1847 to 1876, he includes five who traveled overland to Oregon in 1853. So it is not at all improbable that the savvy Hines party would have equipped themselves with such a device.

Another road-related matter came up in Gustavus's musings about home while he was resting by the Columbia River during his first stay in Oregon. He daydreams about "smiling villages and towns, with their splendid turnpikes and McAdamized roads."[62] This was a big surprise to me; I had no idea that paved roads had been in use at such an early date.

Peoples' names mentioned by Celinda in her diary have been a continuing fascination. Of significant interest to the budding genealogist early on was the March 7 reference to "...cousins Lydia and Sylvester

Flansburg." This was the very first reference in any of the printed Hines material to any of my own family line, indicating the direct connection.[63] One of the remaining gaps in the Hines genealogy that we have been helping fill in is the mystery of four unidentified sisters of Gustavus. From various sources we know that there were six sisters in all,[64] but we know the names of just two: Malissa Hines Robinson (1813-1900) and Catharine Hines Carley (1817-1848). So when we come across a source of many names, such as Celinda's diary, we consider each one carefully for family clues. In the March 3 entry, "Cousin M L Higgins" is mentioned, and to date we have not been able to determine the relationship with Celinda. Another Higgins, "Cousin Licotta," is mentioned by Celinda on June 19. Her February 16 entry includes "Stayed all night at Cuddebeck's." which raises the possibility that these may have been relatives, but that, too, remains unresolved.[65]

The names of people other than relatives also arouse curiosity. Of those fellow travelers in the Hines party, we wonder where Charles Long and the other helpers came from, and where did they settle in the West? Did any of them ever write letters telling of their experiences on the trail, and if so, do any of these survive yet today? And what about the other travelers met on the trail—similar questions apply to them. For some of these people we have a few facts or educated guesses, as indicated in earlier chapters, but for most of them, we have only a name.

How did the travelers receive or send mail en route? This question occurred to me the first time I saw a reference to mail in Celinda's diary, and recurred when I read similar references by Harvey. Their family and friends knew that they would be in Kansas City for several weeks, so it is reasonable to assume that they were able to pick up mail addressed to them at a post office. But what about on the trail? If everything on the trail was traveling by beast of burden, how did any mail ever catch up with them? To start with, it appears that the only place they could send or receive mail on the trail was at Fort Laramie. And an article in a Leavenworth, Kansas, newspaper of 1854 sheds some light on the speed of travel for the mail: "The mail party traveled from Laramie to this place in nine and a half days. The fastest time out."[66] This compares with the fifty days it took the Hines party to travel a comparable distance, from Grinter Place on the Kansas River to Ft. Laramie. So even before the advent of the Pony Express, the mail carriers, presumably unencumbered by wagons, could evidently have easily outpaced the overlanders and delivered mail to Ft. Laramie that had arrived in some city on the Missouri River long after the overlanders had departed.[67] And indeed, just as they were approaching Ft. Laramie, Harvey noted, "A few hours before an enterprising express-man carrying a mail had passed us, and when we reached the fort we found letters from "home" awaiting us; the first we had received since leaving the Missouri river, and the last we received until we reached Oregon."[68] We should note also, however, that Barry repeatedly refers to the "mail stage," implying that stagecoach was the principal means of mail transport.[69]

Numerous aspects of the everyday language (and more formal language for that matter) of 150 years ago catch the interest of anyone who enjoys spotting variation in usage. A minor instance that caught my eye was Harvey's quotation from Byron's "Childe Harold's Pilgrimage," canto IV in Chapter 10. Byron had: "There is society where none intrude," while Harvey substitutes "companionship" for "society." I find that curious because I had become accustomed to these folks saying society when they meant companionship (as when Betsey said at Gustavus' first leave-taking, "…We not only expected to have enjoyed your society from time to time…") —and here Harvey has turned it around.

It seems clear from their accomplished writing style, as well as their numerous literary citations that most of the Hines family members— and Phoebe Judson, for that matter—were avid readers. Primarily self-educated, their wide ranging knowledge has impressed me repeatedly and has prompted questions as to what their personal libraries must have contained. To cite one instance, Harvey's use of the Latin phrase, *nolens volens*, in describing the birth on the trail of Phoebe Judson's son set me to wondering, where did he see this phrase used? (Despite my own dozen and a half years of formal education, it was new to me.) Was its meaning implicit in the context? Did he own a dictionary? What might it have been? All trivial questions, perhaps, but they illustrate how I probe at getting to know these people. And I find the challenge entertaining. In the case of *nolens volens*, I found 171 "hits" in the 10,000 books and 50,000 journal articles from the nineteenth century included at the Making of America website.[70] Notable among these hits were eight from the time period 1845 to 1852 in the *Ladies Repository,* a Methodist journal devoted to literature and religion. Might Harvey have seen the Latin phrase in such a place? He certainly must have read this publication; he himself published at least three articles in its pages.[71] Did he resort to a dictionary for clarification of the meaning? If so, a likely candidate would have been the 1846 edition of Noah Webster's work, whose definition, in part, reads, "Unwilling or willing."[72]

Among the many things I have learned about my Hines relatives, one of the most surprising to me was how short in stature the men were. The best I've been able to determine is that Gustavus, Joseph, and Harvey were each on the order of five feet, six inches or less in height. In Harvey's case, at least, he made up for any deficiencies in height with an over-abundance of spunk. Phoebe noted this in several instances in earlier chapters, but my own favorite commentary on the matter comes from an 1875 article describing a church dedication over which Harvey, as Presiding Elder of the district, officiated.

> Dedication at Baker City
> Editor Advocate:
>   The new M. E. Church in this city was dedicated to the worship of Almighty God on Sunday, January 17, Rev. H. K. Hines officiating...
>   All honor is due our presiding elder for brooking danger and exposure of one our most severe storms ever known in our country; but failure is never in his bill of fare, he arrived in good time for the dedication service. H. K. is a little man, but in the classical language of the Red man of the forest, he has a "skook um tum-tum..."[73]

The most moving chapter of the entire story, of course, especially for us relatives, is the tragedy at the Snake River on August 26, 1853. My mother has told me that when she listened as a child to her mother retelling the story of the drowning, she resolved that she never wanted to see that terrible place, and the very mention of the river's name always precipitated a sense of foreboding. Perhaps through some unknown means Harvey has shared his sentiment with her (she had not seen any of his accounts until I uncovered them recently): "Whenever I hear or see the name of the river in which he sank, there comes a dirge like murmur of gurgling waters, and a low sad wail of remembered sorrow, through my soul."[74] For myself there is the lingering mystery of what must have been in Obadiah's mind as they approached the crossing. Did he experience some kind of premonition? Quoting Celinda, "It seems that Pa had a presentiment that something was to happen as he had often spoken of his dread of crossing at this crossing." Gustavus had a similar observation, "...for the last few weeks of his life, [he] seemed to live under the influence of a strong presentiment of approaching evil. Several times, before coming to the river the last time, I heard him remark, that he dreaded Snake River more than all the rest of the journey." Perhaps Obadiah had shared his fears with his wife, for Phoebe had this to say, "From a fearful premonition, or spiritual perception, Mrs. Diah Hines cried, 'Oh, it is my husband, I know it is Diah.'" But if crossing this river was such a fearful prospect for him, why then did Obadiah, according to Harvey, insist on helping drive the cattle rather than riding in the boat? I wonder if he said to himself, "I must conquer this fear, and I can only do it by facing it forthrightly and with courage." So he spurned the boat ride and, in Celinda's words, "…rode a horse, as he had not done before & assisted in driving [the cattle]." This last from Celinda is a remarkable statement. The most straightforward interpretation is that Obadiah had never ridden a horse before (although he had most certainly driven them as they pulled a carriage or other conveyance). My friend Prof. Michael McKenzie has argued strongly against this interpretation, saying that *of course* any man of that era from rural New York State would have had experience riding horses. I am not so sure, and in any case I think we would have to interpret Celinda's statement as *at least* implying that Obadiah had not, on horseback, ever driven cattle across a river before. By whichever interpretation, it seems clear to me that Obadiah went to great lengths to avoid surrendering to his fears, and in so doing may have assured their realization.

Having met Obadiah only posthumously, and only through the words of his immediate relatives and friends, I have nevertheless come to feel very close to him, and despite my personal skepticism regarding an afterlife, I can empathize with Harvey's, "I wait in hope for the coming of the time when seas and rivers shall give up their dead to greet again the brother whom my heart never yet has willingly surrendered to his grave in these waters."

To shift to a lighter vein, a trait I have especially appreciated in these Hines brothers is their sense of humor. Two samples may suffice. The first comes from a marriage announcement submitted by Gustavus in 1848.[75]

Married.
In the town of Eagle, on the 15th of February, 1848, by Rev. Gustavus Hines, Mr. Otis Partridge to Miss Miriam M. Lyon, both of Eagle.

Truly an age of wonder this,
When strange affinities do spring,
A *Partridge* weds a *Lyon*-ess—
Whoever heard of such a thing?

But still more strange than all the rest,
The Partridge and his Lyon bride,
Took quarters in an *Eagle's* nest,
Where peacefully they now abide.   G.H.

A second illustration of Hines humor comes in the form of an incident recalled by their fellow Methodist minister, Rev. G. W. Kennedy, who we have quoted before.

> Dr. H. K. Hines, presiding elder, came over soon, to hold my first quarterly meeting. There was just one school house in all that country, and we held meeting in that. Out from those log cabin homes came the people, and that school house could not seat the half of them, but they stood around, looked through the windows, and so got to hear the Gospel preached. A very amusing circumstance occurred on Saturday when the congregation was not so large. Brother Hines was preaching—a dog from one of the homes had followed in, and lay down near the stand. But while we were hoping for good behavior on the part of the canine, lo, a cat appeared. True to his instincts, the dog made a dash for the cat, and the cat jumped on the desk, and next leaped through the window, smashing the glass to smithers. The dog turned toward the door and went yelping out to chase the poor cat away into the brush. Referring to it afterwards, Dr. Hines said that that was the most "dogmatical" and "categorical" discourse that he had ever preached in his life.[76]

Not all of the Hines humor was so low-key. In the experience of young Marie Smith, "When these men [i.e., Gustavus, Joseph, and Harvey] got together it was as good as a circus. They were all fond of laughing, joking, and telling stories, and you couldn't help liking them."[77]

This description rings true for me. It would be a fitting description for my own maternal grandmother, Catherine Caszatt Dowling, granddaughter of Lydia Carley Flansburg, and great-grandniece of that jovial trio.

In closing this look at the long Hines journey from my personal perspective, I want to say that my enchantment[78] with this 150-year-old saga will not abate before I have personally retraced much of my relatives' itinerary in person, camera in hand, in an attempt to recapture some of the scenes so grandly portrayed by the chroniclers in this volume.

---

[1] John D. Unruh, Jr., *The Plains Across*, (Urbana: University of Illinois Press, 1979)

[2] John Mack Faragher, *Women & Men on the Overland Trail*, (New Haven, 2001), 2nd Ed.

[3] Clyde A. Milner II, "The Shared Memory of Montana Pioneers," *Montana: the magazine of western history*, Vol. 37, No. 1, 1987, 2-13.

[4] Unruh, *Plains Across*, Chapters 1, 2.

[5] See Chapter 1.

[6] See Chapter 5.

[7] See Chapter 2.

[8] Unruh, *Plains Across,* Chapter 3.

[9] Unruh, *Plains Across,* 97, 98.

[10] Gustavus Hines, "Oregon," *Northern Christian Advocate,* April 19, 1854.

[11] H. K. Hines, "Emigrant Wagon," December 18, 1884, 2.

[12] Barry shows this as part of the route departing Parkville, Missouri, which is a little east of the Delaware Ferry, where the Hines party joined the route. Barry, *Beginning of the West,* 1076, 1183, inside back cover.

[13] Unruh, *Plains Across,* 120.

[14] See Chapter 7.

[15] See Chapter 11.

[16] Unruh, *Plains Across,* Chapter 4.

[17] See Chapter 12.

[18] See Chapter 12.

[19] See Chapter 12.

[20] See Chapter 8.

[21] See Chapter 6.

[22] See Chapter 6.

[23] See Chapter 14.

[24] Unruh, *Plains Across,* Chapter 5.

[25] In Alta Bryant's notes there is this interesting view of the Indians from the perspective of a three-year-old girl: "I, Alta Bryant, sat in the front of the wagon and they let me use the cattle whip to keep away the Indians (friendly but curious). They liked to tease me—run up and jump back. A quiet train—gave Indians pretty colored things for their babies, beads, etc. gave some baby clothes."

[26] Unruh, *Plains Across,* Chapter 6.

[27] Unruh, *Plains Across,* Chapter 8.

[28] J. W. Hines, *Touching Incidents,* 169.

[29] Unruh, *Plains Across,* Chapter 10.

[30] See Chapter 18.

[31] Unruh, *Plains Across,* 402-3.

[32] See Chapter 2. In fact, Gustavus reports later that the three Hines families together spent over $1300 for stock alone, with no indication of what provisions may have cost, nor what their expenses were in getting to Kansas City. A further cost that may not have occurred to them beforehand was cash needed for paying for ferries at river crossings en route, and other incidental expenses along the way.

[33] See Chapter 18.

[34] The 1850 U.S. census reports 12,093 as the Oregon population, and the combined 1851 and 1852 emigration added 13,600 more (although a small fraction of the latter trickled into Washington Territory). Unruh, *Plains Across,* 120.

[35] Yarnes, *History of Oregon Methodism,* 95, 303.

[36] Faragher, *Women & Men on the Overland Trail,* Chapters 1, 2.

[37] Though they may well have engaged in some farming, Harvey and Gustavus were primarily preachers. As to their rural vs. urban affiliation, it is illuminating to consider Celinda's March 31 diary entry as they were unboxing some of their gear: "When the bystanders saw the wagons as they were taken from the boxes they remarked that none but Yankees would have thought of boxing them up, or especially sawing the tungs into. They said they had counted we were city folks & did not know how to take care of ourselves, but they were now convinced we would arrive safely in Oregon & if they were going they would wish to go with us." See Chapter 5.

[38] Faragher, *Women & Men on the Overland Trail,* 95.

[39] Faragher, *Women & Men on the Overland Trail,* 91.

[40] See Chapter 7.

[41] Faragher, *Women & Men on the Overland Trail,* 130.

[42] Faragher, *Women & Men on the Overland Trail,* 139.

[43] Faragher, *Women & Men on the Overland Trail,* 139, 140.

[44] Faragher, *Women & Men on the Overland Trail,* 163.

[45] We repeat the note of Chapter 2, quoting from Lydia's obituary, "While residing in the latter place [Spencerport, New York]…, very unexpectedly to her husband she informed him that she would be glad to return again to the Pacific Coast, and there spend the remainder of her days. Sympathizing in this feeling, Mr. Hines asked of Bishop Waugh and ob-

tained a transfer to the Oregon Conference, with the privilege of returning to the country by way of the Plains." N. Rounds, "Outlines of the Life of Mrs. Lydia Hines," *Pacific Christian Advocate,* April 2, 1870, Vol. XVI, No. 14.

[46] See Chapter 2.

[47] Milner, "Shared Memories," 2-11.

[48] David Lowenthal, *The Past is a Foreign Country* (Cambridge: Cambridge University Press, 1985), 196.

[49] "Rev. H. K. Hines Address to Pioneers," *The Sunday Oregonian,* (Portland) June 19, 1898.

[50] T. D. Allen, *Doctor in Buckskin* (New York: Harper, 1951).

[51] Lydia Carley Flansburg, my mother's maternal great-grandmother, was a daughter of Catharine Hines Carley, and therefore a niece of Gustavus and his brothers.

[52] This statement from 2003 remains valid in 2007, but the time has expanded by four years, and the piles of source material continue to grow.

[53] Francis Parkman, *The Oregon Trail: Sketches of Prairie and Rocky Mountain Life,* (Boston, 1883).

[54] J. W. Hines, *Touching Incidents,* 160.

[55] Holmes, *Covered Wagon Women,* 77-134.

[56] Cousin Cecil Mary Sisk, great-granddaughter of Celinda, kindly supplied the copy of this. Celinda E. Hines, "Diary of a Journey from N.Y. to Oregon in 1853," *Portland Telegram,* March 17-April 18, 1930.

[57] The 1850 census lists Obadiah's occupation as gatekeeper. 1850 U.S. census, Hastings, Oswego, New York; image copy at www.ancestry.com; accessed April 16, 2003.

[58] These questions from 2003 remain for the most part unanswered in 2007.

[59] See, for example, Celinda's reference to the "divide route" and the "government road" in her diary entry of May 7, in Chapter 6.

[60] As can be seen from a comparison of the diary narrative with our maps, the best we've been able to locate for the early to mid 1850s, there are significant discrepancies between the maps and the diary. They surely must have had different maps than we have yet located.

[61] Norman Wright, "Odometers: Distance Measurement on Western Emigrant Trails," *Overland Journal,* Vol. 13, No. 3, 1995, 14-24.

[62] Biography.com: John Loudon McAdam Biography "Inventor of macadamized roads, born

in Ayr, South Ayrshire, SW Scotland, UK. He went to New York City in 1770, where he made a fortune in his uncle's countinghouse. On his return in 1783 he bought an estate and started experimenting with new methods of road construction. In 1816 he was appointed surveyor to the Bristol Turnpike Trust, re-made the roads there with crushed stone bound with gravel, and raised the carriageway to improve drainage. In 1827 he was made surveyor-general of metropolitan roads in Great Britain, and his *macadam surfaces* were adopted in many other countries." http://www.biography.com/search/article.do?id=9390190; accessed April 29, 2007.

[63] A later significant event was my May 2001 discovery of the obituary of Lydia's mother, Catharine Hines Carley, which listed her parents as James and Betsey Hines of Brockport, New York, i.e. the parents of Gustavus and brothers. *Northern Christian Advocate,* May 3, 1848.

[64] For example, Harvey, in describing a visit to his sister Malissa in 1891, mentions, "Here resides my only living sister, the last of six..." *Pacific Christian Advocate,* October 21, 1891.

[65] While these questions cited in 2003 remain unresolved in 2007, another related question has been answered without having been clearly posed in the first place. The entry, "M. E. Smith, female, age 13" in the household of Julia Bryant Terry in the 1860 Salem census aroused only mild curiosity at the time we cited it in 2003. Two years later we were astounded to find an obituary for Marie Elizabeth Smith Marsh that identified her as having been adopted by Gustavus and Lydia Hines. This led to our including her fascinating and informative story in Chapter 19 of the present edition.

[66] *Kansas Weekly Herald,* Leavenworth, Kansas, October 13, 1854, 2.

[67] Note that emigrants would have had to advise their correspondents with something like, "To ensure its getting to 'Fort Laramie,' nothing more is necessary than to direct it 'Fort Laramie, via Independence, Mo.'" *Liberty Weekly Tribune,* March 18, 1853.

[68] See Chapter 9.

[69] See, for example, Barry, *Beginning of the West,* 1142.

[70] http://quod.lib.umich.edu/m/moagrp/; accessed June 20, 2007.

[71] Titles include, "Ascent of Mount Hood," "Overland in Winter," and "Waiiletpu." All can be found at the MoA website. http://quod.lib.umich.edu/m/moagrp; accessed June 20, 2007.

[72] Noah Webster, *An American Dictionary of the English Language,* (New York: Harper & Brothers, 1846) s.v. "nolens volens."

[73] *Pacific Christian Advocate,* February 4, 1875. According to 1845 trail traveler Joel Palmer, this Chinook jargon phrase is best translated as "strong heart." Palmer, *Journal of Travels,* 151.

[74] See Chapter 13 for all the quotations in this section regarding the Snake River tragedy.

[75] Gustavus Hines, "Married." *Northern Christian Advocate,* February, 1848.

[76] Kennedy, *Pioneer Campfire,* 190-91.

[77] See Chapter 19.

[78] 1 have seen it stated that one has not mastered a foreign language until one dreams in that language. Analogously, perhaps the depth to which the Hines 1853 trip has penetrated my psyche is indicated by the fact that it has entered my dreams. In early August 2003, a time when I was working on parts of this chapter, I had a vivid dream one night which involved my relatives on the trail. I heard them conversing with one another in voices which reminded me of British dramas I had seen on TV. But the most bizarre aspect of this conversation was the topic: they were discussing the wisdom of the purchase just made by one of their party (was it Celinda?) of a Kirby *vacuum cleaner!* I awoke in the midst of this dream, quite convinced of its reality. "I must check to see how early Kirby vacuum cleaners were sold ..." I said to myself at 1:30 A. M.

Appendix
Mileages and other notes from Celinda's diary

Interspersed seemingly at random through the photocopy of Celinda's diary obtained from the Yale University Library are pages of notes that list places passed along the trail, together with mileages between those points. In many cases the pages have been damaged and the mileage figures and other information are illegible or completely missing. Nevertheless, the notes in general provide some useful data for ascertaining details of the Hines party's itinerary.[1]

The following appears as an insert after the Sept. 7 entry in our copy:

To the river again	3
To a rocky pass	8
Fall creek	6
Down the river	7
Raft River	6
Up the river crossing & recrossing in the distance	14
... the Bend	8
To big marsh	15
To river	11
Goose Creek	4
... river(?)	9
... Branch	12
... creek(?) crossing	8
... leaves the	

The rest of the notes follow the last dated diary entry—Oct. 11:

bluffs(?) of creek

Salmon Falls creek	20
Salmon Falls	6
Lewis River	23(?)
Boisse River	70
Down the river to Fort	46

There seems to be but a few permanent residents at the Falls. But there are about 20 families ["near" crossed out] about there. I should think from appearances that there were several people trading there who would remove at the close of emigration although they have here...trade with the...

(New page begins here.)

The settlement is situated on the south side of the Columbia on a small plain almost entirely surrounded by hills. The scenery is very pretty.

(New page begins here.)

Mr. Marsh informs us that he found the dead body of the indian whom Mr. Babb(?) shot the next morning after the affray & has his wife now in his possession. He & his brother saw at night this Indian lying on his back with his horse grazing beside him. But as they were near a trading post they supposed he was drunk & did not molest him. But seeing him there in the morning they went to him & found he was dead. He... discouraged his wife...

(New page begins here.)

To Platte ferry	5
Mineral Springs & Lake:	12

Poisonous; Water clear & has no bad
taste until disturbed; it then turns
bra…(?)

To Avenue Road; Rocks	8

form a gateway through which the
road passes

Alkali Swamp. Several springs	?
Clear Spring Creek:	4
Willow Spring	3
Prospect Hill(?)	1
Grease Wood Creek	6
…eratus Lake	6
Rock Independence	

A curiosity on account of… magnitude. Entire(?)
on the top of the ground in a[n]
open (?) space. On the north side
&…the south east corner it may
be easily ascended. Lat. 42°…

Crossing of Sweet Water	?
To Devil's Gate Rocks	
400 ft high	?
Alkali lake…river	11(?)
Leave the river…Bluff	8
Bitter Wood creek	7
Fd. No 2 of Sweet Water	6
Fds. No 3 & 4	2
No. 5	8
Ice Springs & alkali also	6
Fd. No 6	10
…Rat creek	4
…	?
…Creek	7
Quaking Aspen Creek	1
[can't transcribe]	3
Willow Creek Water ??? & ???	

Fd. No. 9	5
South Pass altitude 7,400 ft	10

Ascent & descent so gradual that
it is difficult to ascertain the precise summit; but it is supposed to
be between two small hills about
60 ft high about Lat: 42° 18' 58'
Long. 108°   40'

Pacific Springs	5
Dry Sandy	9
Junction Salt Lake & ??? roads	
Little Sandy	
Big Sandy	
To Green river by the old road 50	
miles ???	5
Little Bear River	6
To Lost River	8
Cedar Springs	??
Red Sand Branch	??
O'Hara's Creek	4
Quaking Aspen Hill	8
Ham's Fork	3
Foot of the mountain	2
Summit/A fine spring	2/2
To fir tree grove	9
Stony creek	6
Summit spring	1
Bear river bottoms	8?
…ine spring	3
… Fork	5
…	11
Thomas' Fork	4?
Pleasant spring	1
Brooks…creek	3
Summit of mountains	2
To Bear river	6
…Rom…Branch	8
Swift Water	1
Indian creek	7
White sand Hill	3

Black Mud Creek 8
Soda Springs 9
These springs are scattered over perhaps 40 acres of ground. The continual boiling of them creates a store of a peculiar(?) ??? arriving...a uniform height(?)... has ceased to run from some of them & bursted out in some other place.
To Steam-Boat spring 1?
Junction of Ft. Hall & California??
To Basin Spring 2?
Lady's creek 15?
Crossing of Shoshone creek 7
Summit of the dividing ridge between the Bear river & Columbia
To a fine ??? 4?
We did not go by Ft. Hall but 15 miles nearer(?)
From Ft. Neuf [Portneuf?] river to the Bannock 3 miles
...10 ft. wide 5
...river 11
... 2

(Next page in my copy of the diary clearly skips back to an earlier part of the trip.)

From Catholic mission to Big Vermilion 11 miles. Camping good.
To Little Vermilion 12 miles.
To Salt Creek [half line above: 60 ft wide]
wood & water every few miles. 20
Middle Fork of Blue river 5
Bottoms heavily timbered
To Big Blue 70 yds wide 7
To junction of Ft. Jo road 13

One mile beyond this is good camping
Branch of Otter Creek [half line above: between] No wood or water 17
To Otter Creek Camps good 14
To Little Blue. In this distance cross three small 25
Streams Sa...
Up the river. Grease Wood & water ??
Leaves the river passes over a high rooling [rolling?] plain
Up the river. The road h...
Leaves the river & ...the plain to(?)
...

(New page begins here.)

To Platte Road good camps ??
To Ft Kearney 8
To South Platte ford 1 mile wide???
Up South Platte 8
To North Platte over sand hills 2?
Up the river bottom 10
Leave the river no grass or water 15
Up the river some springs 16
To steep hill here the road leaves the river 8?
To Ash Hollow, occupies 20 acres 8?
Down it to Platte 1?
To Castle Bluffs up the river 10
To a creek 20 ft wide good camp 8?
To Court House Rock 4
To Chimney Rock 250 ft high 11?
Scotts Bluff (here leave the river)??
...to a spring 9
... 10

(New page begins here.)		Deer(?) Creek	??

To Platte just to… ???	6
To river again	5
Up Laramie river to Ft	15
To Platte	2
Up the river, Forks of road here	8
To Bitter Wood creek & lake	
to the right is said to be poison	
Up the creek	6
To Horse-Shoe Creek	14
To Reed(?) hill one mile to	
summit	2
To La Bonta	16
To a Fine Branch	3
To La Prele 3 ft wide	14
To Forche Bois	??
To Platte	??
To Muddy Stream	??

(New page begins here.)

    Ft. Laramie is in Lat. 42° 19' 09" Lon 104° 11' 51". From the Ft there are two roads. The one to the left passes immediately over the Black Hills & is very rough & uneaven but is some shorter than the other.

    At Ft Hall trading post a ??? told us that last winter ('52) he went out one day hunting and saw during the day the skeletons of 200 indians who had died that fall & winter from smallpox which they…from wearing the…clothing(?) of emigrants.

---

[1] For example, consider the following comparison of diary narrative and mileage notes.

Date	Event (from diary narrative)	Mileage note
May 16	Passed the Catholic Mission	
May 17	Crossed the Vermilion	Catholic mission to Big Vermilion 11 miles
May 18	Crossed the Little Vermilion	To Little Vermilion 12 miles
May 19	Crossed Salt Creek	To Salt Creek 20
	Middle Fork of the Blue	Middle Fork of the Blue 5
May 21	Go north about 7 mi. to ferry	To Big Blue 7
May 24	Crossed Blue	
		To junction of Ft. Jo road 13
		Branch of Otter Creek 17
May 27	Crossed Otter Creek	To Otter Creek 14
May 30	Arrived at…"Republican Fork"	To Little Blue…cross three small streams 25

It can be seen that the notes thus supplement the diary narrative as a means for working out the itinerary.

Family Tree
and
Photo Album

James and Betsey Hines Family Tree[*]

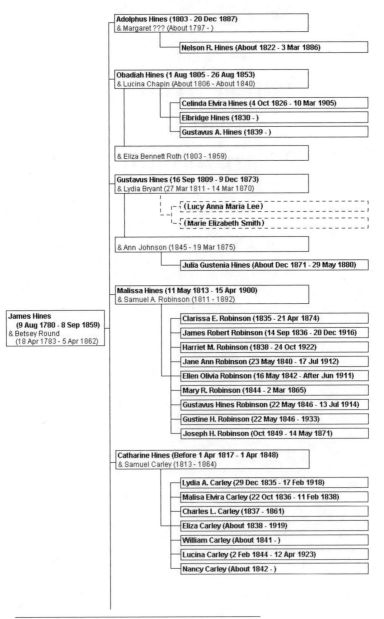

Adolphus Hines (1803 - 20 Dec 1887)
& Margaret ??? (About 1797 -)

Nelson R. Hines (About 1822 - 3 Mar 1886)

Obadiah Hines (1 Aug 1805 - 26 Aug 1853)
& Lucina Chapin (About 1806 - About 1840)

Celinda Elvira Hines (4 Oct 1826 - 10 Mar 1905)

Elbridge Hines (1830 -)

Gustavus A. Hines (1839 -)

& Eliza Bennett Roth (1803 - 1859)

Gustavus Hines (16 Sep 1809 - 9 Dec 1873)
& Lydia Bryant (27 Mar 1811 - 14 Mar 1870)

(Lucy Anna Maria Lee)

(Marie Elizabeth Smith)

& Ann Johnson (1845 - 19 Mar 1875)

Julia Gustenia Hines (About Dec 1871 - 29 May 1880)

Malissa Hines (11 May 1813 - 15 Apr 1900)
& Samuel A. Robinson (1811 - 1892)

Clarissa E. Robinson (1835 - 21 Apr 1874)

James Robert Robinson (14 Sep 1836 - 20 Dec 1916)

Harriet M. Robinson (1838 - 24 Oct 1922)

Jane Ann Robinson (23 May 1840 - 17 Jul 1912)

Ellen Olivia Robinson (16 May 1842 - After Jun 1911)

Mary R. Robinson (1844 - 2 Mar 1865)

Gustavus Hines Robinson (22 May 1846 - 13 Jul 1914)

Gustine H. Robinson (22 May 1846 - 1933)

Joseph H. Robinson (Oct 1849 - 14 May 1871)

Catharine Hines (Before 1 Apr 1817 - 1 Apr 1848)
& Samuel Carley (1813 - 1864)

Lydia A. Carley (29 Dec 1835 - 17 Feb 1918)

Malisa Elvira Carley (22 Oct 1836 - 11 Feb 1838)

Charles L. Carley (1837 - 1861)

Eliza Carley (About 1838 - 1919)

William Carley (About 1841 -)

Lucina Carley (2 Feb 1844 - 12 Apr 1923)

Nancy Carley (About 1842 -)

James Hines
(9 Aug 1780 - 8 Sep 1859)
& Betsey Round
(18 Apr 1783 - 5 Apr 1862)

*James and Betsey had twelve children: six boys and six girls. As of November 2007 we have identified only the eight shown on these two pages.

410

James Hines
(9 Aug 1780 - 8 Sep 1859)
& Betsey Round
(18 Apr 1783 - 5 Apr 1862)

James Round Hines (4 Feb 1822 - 18 Dec 1892)
& Harriet Clark Weidman (22 Aug 1829 - 10 Jun 1905)

Lewis L. Hamlin Hines (12 Feb 1848 - 15 Dec 1871)

Gustavus Weidman Hines (21 Aug 1850 - 26 Apr 1924)

Martha Josephine Hines (30 Oct 1852 - 23 Sep 1937)

Harriet M. Hines (1855 -)

Celinda E. Hines (Jul 1856 -)

Angeline C. Hines (About 1862 -)

Rose L. Hines (28 Sep 1867 -)

Joseph Wilkinson Hines (7 Jan 1824 - 21 Feb 1913)
& Elizabeth Meredith

Melissa Elizabeth Hines (1851 - 6 Jan 1932)

George Emory Hines (23 Jun 1850 - 31 Jul 1905)

John Meredith Hines (20 Jun 1856 - 26 Apr 1938)

Idletta Amelia Hines (1858 -)

Edwin U. Hines (1864 - 18 Feb 1909)

Annis Amelia Hines (25 Oct 1867 - 12 Feb 1959)

Willie Austin Hines (1869 - 22 Jul 1878)

Lillian Eva Hines (1873 - 19 Nov 1887)

Harvey Kimball Hines (21 Jul 1828 - 19 Jan 1902)
& Angeline Seymor (22 Oct 1828 - 19 Jun 1851)

& Elizabeth Jane Graves (30 Jun 1828 - 29 Jan 1890)

James A. Hines (About 1854 - Before 1 Oct 1903)

Edward O. Hines (1856 - 1863)

Dora A. Hines (1858 - 1863)

Harvey L. Hines (1860 - 1863)

Lua Aurora Hines (3 Oct 1864 - 4 May 1901)

& Celinda Minerva Gillette (1838 - 6 Aug 1921)

Obadiah Hines (1805-1853)

Gustavus Hines (1809-1873)

Malissa Hines Robinson (1813-1900)

James Round Hines (1822-1892)

Joseph Wilkinson Hines (1824-1913)

Harvey Kimball Hines (1828-1902)

Six of the Twelve Hines Siblings

Sources

Obadiah Hines—Private collection, courtesy of Cecil Mary Sisk

Gustavus Hines—H. K. Hines, *Missionary History of the Pacific Northwest,* (Portland, 1899), p. 363

James Round Hines—Oregon Historical Society, Neg. # CN 007901

Malissa Hines Robinson—Private collection, courtesy of T. R. Gray

Joseph Wilkinson Hines—J. W. Hines, *Touching incidents in the life and labors of a pioneer on the Pacific Coast since 1853,* (San Jose, 1911), frontispiece

Harvey Kimball Hines—Private collection, courtesy of Mildred Clark

Gustavus Hines, c. 1850

Harvey K. Hines, 1868

Celinda E. Hines Shipley, 1857

Lucy Anna Lee Grubbs, c. 1865

Holden and Phoebe Judson, 1899

Six of the 1853 Emigrants *(in other years)*

Sources

Gustavus Hines—Gustavus Hines, *A voyage around the world: with a history of the Oregon mission...*(Buffalo, 1850), frontispiece

Harvey K. Hines—William Wallace Youngson, *Swinging Portals...*,(Portland, 1948)

Celinda E. Hines Shipley—Oregon Historical Society, Neg. # 5197 (cropped)

Lucy Anna Lee Grubbs—H. K. Hines, *Missionary History in the Pacific Northwest* (Portland, 1899), p. 319

Holden and Phoebe Judson—Courtesy of Lynden Pioneer Museum, Lynden, Wash.

Collection of Mildred Clark

Celinda's cousins, Sylvester and Lydia (Carley) Flansburg, and family, ca. 1890
Back row: Lucy, Catherine, Gazella, Charles
Middle row: Zelina, Andrew, Nettie
Front row: Emma, Sylvester, Lydia, James

On March 6, 1853, as she is saying her good-byes to family and friends, Celinda mentions, "Receive a visit from cousins Lydia and Sylvester Flansburg." Lydia's mother was Catharine Hines Carley, sister of Obadiah (Celinda's father), Gustavus, Joseph, and Harvey. At the time of that visit, the Flansburgs had two baby daughters, Catherine and Emma.

Ellen Robinson Lazell (1842-1911)
Harriet Robinson Lamson Foreman (1838-1922)
Gustine Robinson Krupp Wiseman (1846-1933)
Jane Robinson Holmes (1840-1912)   James R. Robinson (1836-1916)

Collection of Tom Gray

Five of the nine children of Samuel and Malissa (Hines) Robinson, all first cousins of Celinda and members of "Uncle Robinson's family," mentioned by her on March 3, 1853. The photograph was taken in the early 1900s.

Lynden Pioneer Museum, Lynden, Wash.

Phoebe and Holden Judson's "Ideal Home," the first house in Lynden, Washington Territory.

Lynden Pioneer Museum, Lynden, Wash.

The combination store and public hall built by Holden Judson in Lynden, Washington.

Bailey, Margaret Jewett. *The Grains or Passages in the Life of Ruth Rover, with Occasional Pictures of Oregon, Natural and Moral.* Edited by Robert Frank and Evelyn Leasher. Corvallis: Oregon State University Press, 1986.

Barry, Louise. *The Beginning of the West.- Annals of the Kansas Gateway to the American West* 1540-1854. Topeka: Kansas State Historical Society, 1972.

Bigler, David L., ed. *A Winter with the Mormons—The 1852 Letters of Jotham Goodell.* Salt Lake City, 2001.

Brosnan, Cornelius J. *Jason Lee—Prophet of the New Oregon.* New York: Macmillan, 1932.

Conable, F. W. *History of the Genesee Annual Conference of the Methodist Episcopal Church.* 2d ed. New York: Phillips & Hunt, 1885.

Corning, Howard M., ed. *Dictionary of Oregon History.* Portland: Binford and Morts, 1956.

Dana, Charles A. *The United States Illustrated in Views of City and Country.* New York: Herrmann J. Meyer, 1853.

Daughters of the American Revolution (Kansas City Chapter). *Vital Historical records of Jackson County, Missouri* 1826-1876. Kansas City, Missouri: DAR, 1933-1934.

Faragher, John Mack. *Women & Men on the Overland Trail.* 2d. ed. New Haven: Yale University Press, 2000.

Federal Writers' Project of the Works Progress Administration. *The Oregon Trail— The Missouri River to the Pacific Ocean.* New York: Hastings House, 1939.

Franzwa, Gregory M. *The Oregon Trail Revisited* Silver Anniversary ed. Tucson: The Patrice Press, 1997.

_____. *Maps of the Oregon Trail.* St. Louis: The Patrice Press, 1990.

Gatke, Robert Moulton. *Chronicles of Willamette—The Pioneer University of the West.* Portland: Binford and Morts, 1943.

Hines, Celinda E. "Diary of Celinda E. Hines." *Transactions of the Oregon Pioneer Association* (1918): 69-125.

Hines, Gustavus. *A Voyage Round the World—With a History of the Oregon Mis-

sion. Buffalo: G. H. Derby, 1850.

Hines, Gustavus. *Oregon & Its Institutions—Comprising a Full History* of *the Willamette University.* New York: Carlton & Porter, 1868.

Hines, H. K. "On the Frontier: Or Notes of Field, Camp and Trail in the Farthest West." *Pacific Christian Advocate,* 5 January 1882 through 3 August 1882.

_____. "In an Emigrant Wagon." *Pacific Christian Advocate,* 4 December 1884 through 26 March 1885.

_____. *An Illustrated History of the State of Oregon.* Chicago: Lewis Publishing Co., 1893.

_____. *Missionary History of the Pacific Northwest Containing the Wonderful History of Jason Lee.* Portland: H. K. Hines, 1899.

Hines, Joseph W. *Touching Incidents in the Life and labors of a Pioneer on the Pacific Coast since 1853.* San Jose: Eaton & Co., Printers, 1911.

Holmes, Kenneth L. *Covered Wagon Women: Diaries & Letters from the Western Trails, 1853-1854.* Vol. 6. Lincoln: University of Nebraska Press, 1986.

Howell, Erle. *Methodism in the Northwest.* Edited by Chapin D. Foster. Seattle: Pacific Northwest Conference Historical Society, 1966.

Judson, Phoebe Goodell. *A Pioneer's Search for an Ideal Home.* Bellingham: United Printing, Binding and Stationery Co., 1925.

Kemble, John Haskell. "The Panama Route: 1848-1869." *University of California Publications in History.* 29 (1943).

Kennedy, G.W. *The Pioneer Campfire.* Portland: Clarke-Kundret Printing Co., 1914.

Ketcham, Rebecca. "From Ithaca to Clatsop Plains: Miss Ketcham's Journal of Travel, Part I," Leo M. Kaiser and Priscilla Knuth, eds. *Oregon Historical Quarterly,* 62 (September, 1961), 249-287.

Lockley, Fred. "Impressions and Observations of the Journal Man," *Oregon Journal,* August 3-7, 1925.

Loewenberg, Robert J. *Equality on the Oregon Frontier: Jason Lee and the Methodist Mission 1834-43.* Seattle: University of Washington Press, 1976.

Mattes, Merrill J. *The Great Platte River Road: The Covered Wagon Mainline via Fort Kearny to Fort Laramie,* vol. 25 of Nebraska State Historical Society *Publications.* Lincoln, 1969.

_____. *Platte River Road Narratives: A Descriptive Bibliography of Travel over the Great Central Route to Oregon, California, Utah, Colorado, Montana, and Other Western States and Territories, 1812-1866.* Urbana: University of Illinois Press, 1988.

Milner, Clyde A. II. "The Shared Memory of Montana Pioneers," *Montana: The Magazine of Western History,* 37:1 (1987).

Palmer, Joel. *Journal of Travels over the Rocky Mountains to the Mouth of the Columbia River.* Cincinnati: J. A. & U. P. James, 1847.

Parkman, Francis Jr. *The Oregon Trail.* Penguin Classics Edition. New York: Viking Penguin, 1982.

Peters, Harold J. *Who was J. W. Hines?* Pioneer papers (California Pioneers of Santa Clara County), Dr. Martin Luther King, Jr. Library, San Jose, Calif., 2006.

Schlissel, Lillian. *Women's Diaries of the Westward Journey.* New York: Schocken Books, 1992.

Unruh, John D., Jr. *The Plains Across: The Overland Emigrants and the Trans Mississippi West, 1840-1860.* Urbana: University of Illinois Press, 1979.

Wright, Norman. "Odometers: Distance Measurement on Western Emigrant Trails," *Overland Journal,* 13:3 (1995).

Yarnes, Thomas D. A *History of Oregon Methodism.* Edited by Harvey E. Tobie. Portland[?]: Oregon Methodist Conference Historical Society, 1958[?].

Index

About the editor

After completing his B.S. and M.S. in physics at Case Institute of Technology, H. J. Peters taught college physics for several years and then resumed his schooling at Michigan State University (Ph.D., Biophysics in 1969). Since that time his professional activities have been devoted to computer-based instruction, first at Bell Telephone Laboratories, then at Hewlett Packard Co., the University of Iowa, and, since 1986, as a free-lance author and consultant. His published software includes Models for Electric Current (coauthored with Professors Eric T. Lane and Vincent N. Lunetta), English Basic-Mechanics, Verbal Calisthenics, Medical Terminology, Body Language (human anatomy), and ChemSkill Builder (coauthored with Professor James D. Spain.)

Research for *Seven Months to Oregon* began as a part-time activity in late 1998; and was nearly a full-time job for the first half of 2007. Additional books on the editor's remarkable third-great-granduncles, Gustavus, Joseph and Harvey Hines, are in the planning stages.

In August 2004, Peters and his wife Elinore moved from their long-time home in Iowa City, Iowa, to Santa Clara, Calif., where they are near their four adult children and one grandson, and within walking distance of the home of Joseph W. Hines, more than a century ago.

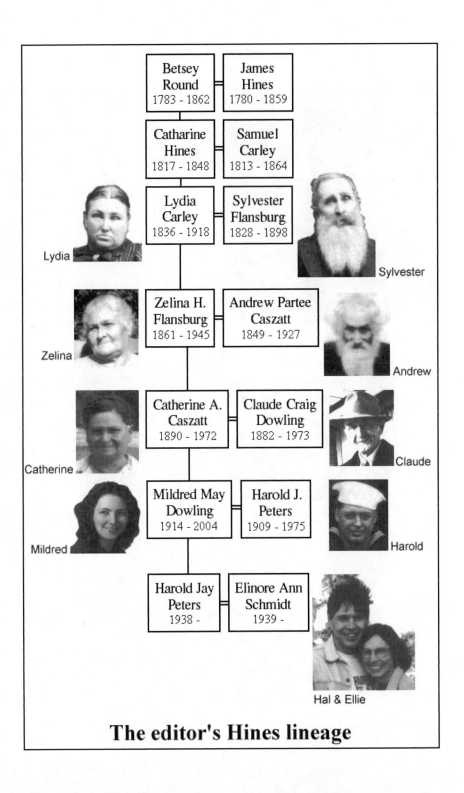

Betsey Round 1783 - 1862	James Hines 1780 - 1859	

Catharine Hines 1817 - 1848	Samuel Carley 1813 - 1864	

Lydia

Lydia Carley 1836 - 1918	Sylvester Flansburg 1828 - 1898	

Sylvester

Zelina

Zelina H. Flansburg 1861 - 1945	Andrew Partee Caszatt 1849 - 1927	

Andrew

Catherine

Catherine A. Caszatt 1890 - 1972	Claude Craig Dowling 1882 - 1973	

Claude

Mildred

Mildred May Dowling 1914 - 2004	Harold J. Peters 1909 - 1975	

Harold

Harold Jay Peters 1938 -	Elinore Ann Schmidt 1939 -	

Hal & Ellie

The editor's Hines lineage